ECONOMIC INEQUALITY

Ralahine Utopian Studies

Volume 32

PETER LANG
Oxford - Berlin - Bruxelles - Chennai - Lausanne - New York

Donald Morris

ECONOMIC INEQUALITY

UTOPIAN EXPLORATIONS

PETER LANG
Oxford - Berlin - Bruxelles - Chennai - Lausanne - New York

Bibliographic information published by the Deutsche Nationalbibliothek.
The German National Library lists this publication in the German National Bibliography; detailed bibliographic data is available on the Internet at http://dnb.d-nb.de.

A catalogue record for this book is available from the British Library.

Library of Congress Cataloging-in-Publication Data

Names: Morris, Donald, 1945- author.
Title: Economic inequality: Utopian explorations / Donald Morris.
Description: Oxford; New York: Peter Lang, 2024. | Series: Ralahine Utopian studies, 1661-5875; volume 32 | Includes bibliographical references and index.
Identifiers: LCCN 2023056297 (print) | LCCN 2023056298 (ebook) | ISBN 9781803741765 (paperback) | ISBN 9781803741772 (ebook) | ISBN 9781803741789 (epub)
Subjects: LCSH: Utopias in literature. | Income distribution in literature. | Social problems in literature.
Classification: LCC PN56.U8 M68 2024 (print) | LCC PN56.U8 (ebook) | DDC 809.93372–dc23/eng/20240129
LC record available at https://lccn.loc.gov/2023056297
LC ebook record available at https://lccn.loc.gov/2023056298

Cover image: Slums, Public domain photo from Rawpixel <https://www.rawpixel.com/search/slums?page=1&sort=curated&tags=%24publicdomain%2C%24photos&topic_group=%24publicdomain>.
Cover design by Peter Lang Group AG

ISSN 1661-5875
ISBN 978-1-80374-176-5 (print)
ISBN 978-1-80374-177-2 (ePDF)
ISBN 978-1-80374-178-9 (ePub)
DOI 10.3726/b20831

Published by Peter Lang Ltd, Oxford, United Kingdom
info@peterlang.com - www.peterlang.com

This publication has been peer reviewed.

To my grandfathers,
John Edward Lautner (1865–1943) and Ernest James Morris (1889–1982)
and my loyal COVID casualty, Gato.

“Where is the fulcrum to uplift our world and roll it forward?”

—W. E. B. Du Bois, *Dark Princess* (1928)

Contents

Acknowledgments

In this work's early going Lyman Tower Sargent was instrumental is guiding me toward a number of utopias that treat of the redistribution of income or wealth using progressive taxation. Sargent's database of "Utopian Literature in English: An Annotated Bibliography from 1516 to the Present" (<https://openpublishing.psu.edu/utopia/>) proved an invaluable tool as did the wealth of scholarship published in *Utopian Studies* and presented at The Society for Utopian Studies conferences. The nascent version of this book was read by my friend Dana Plank. His editorial suggestions were always valuable and timely. James Bockmier edited the finished work contributing greatly to its overall readability. His expansive background and meticulous eye were an invaluable resource. The support of Anthony Mason, Peter Lang Senior Commissioning Editor, Ireland and the UK, as well as the anonymous reviewers is greatly appreciated. An earlier discussion of some of the issues this work explores appeared in the journal *Utopian Studies*, "Three Moderate Solutions to Income Inequality in Utopia: Hertzka, Herzl, and Wells." All pictures are licensed from Mary Evans Picture Library, London.

Introduction

This work explores what utopian writers have said about economic inequality. Its transdisciplinary focus is literary utopias—some familiar and some long forgotten—works that E. F. Bleiler calls novels of social theory.[1] It is not an economic analysis but a study in utopian social philosophy; as such, its aim is to challenge assumptions about economic inequality by prodding the moral imagination. I have not selected the authors I discuss in this book for their popularity or notoriety—though some are among the most widely read—but for their utopian focus on economic inequality. "Very few utopias stand out as great works of literature," notes Krishan Kumar, as their "didactic purpose overwhelms any literary aspiration."[2] In such works, observes Yevgeny Zamyatin, "the writer first concerns himself with an abstract idea and then embodies it in images, events, characters." The resulting plots, Zamyatin concedes, "seldom achieve faultless literary form."[3] Utopian treatments of economic inequality are no exception.

While our current age struggles with the prospect of a handful of people owning half the world's wealth, it may be useful to reflect on the nature of this problem (if it is a problem) in its broadest contours including utopian precedents warning us of its coming and directing us to possible solutions. In *Inequality*, philosopher Harry Frankfurt discusses the extent to which economic inequality is a problem. Frankfurt argues that if economic inequality is morally undesirable, "it is on account of its almost irresistible tendency to

1 E. F. Bleiler, "Introduction," in *Three Prophetic Novels of H. G. Wells* (New York: Dover Publications, 1960), ix. "Utopian social theory" is one of three forms Sargent identifies. Lyman Tower Sargent, "The Three Faces of Utopianism Revisited," *Utopian Studies* 5, no. 1 (1994): 1–37, 4.

2 Krishan Kumar, *Utopia and Anti-Utopia in Modern Times* (Oxford, UK: Basil Blackwell, 1987), 25.

3 Yevgeny Zamyatin, *A Soviet Heretic: Essays by Yevgeny Zamaytin*, ed. and trans. Mirra Ginsburg (Chicago: The University of Chicago Press, 1970), 166–167.

generate unacceptable inequalities of other kinds."[4] As utopian writers envision a future taming or at least tempering the extremes of both poverty and wealth, it is instructive to explore the instruments they employ; by what measures have they defeated poverty or diminished the threats boundless fortunes pose, thereby revitalizing society?

Plato's ideal society in the *Laws* stipulates that no one should be more than four times wealthier than their less fortunate neighbors.[5] Regarding people's intuitions about income inequality psychologist Pascal Boyer reports, "Humans do not generally believe that any individual's contribution could possibly be hundreds or thousands of times greater than anyone else's."[6] This has led some utopians, like Thomas More and Edward Bellamy, to level everyone's income (discussed in Chapter 6). But many utopians see benefits from unequal but controlled economic outcomes. George Orwell, for example, believed that while rigid limitations on income are not possible, "there is no reason why ten to one should not be the maximum normal variation," since "within those limits some sense of equality is possible."[7]

Chapters 2–4 describe numerous remediating devices—whether economic, social, or political—utopians have proposed to reduce the extremes of economic inequality. These measures include (among others) alternative allocations of surplus labor, equalizing opportunity, expunging racism, free universal compulsory education, gender equality in the workplace, motherhood as a paying job, public housing, redistribution of income or wealth through progressive taxation, reimagining marriage and divorce, transparency—economic and political, universal basic income, and (in Chapter 5) violence and revolution. Chapter 7 explores utopias (or dystopias) that picture our future if economic inequality is left to flourish unchecked; its discussion includes the works of H. G. Wells, Kurt Vonnegut Jr, Kim Stanley Robinson, Octavia Butler, and Cory Doctorow.

4 Harry G. Frankfurt, *Inequality* (Princeton, NJ: Princeton University Press, 2015), x.

5 Plato. *Laws*, trans. A. E. Taylor in *Plato: The Collected Dialogues*, ed. Edith Hamilton and Huntington Cairns (New York: Pantheon Books, 1961), bk. 5, 744.

6 Pascal Boyer, *Minds Make Societies* (New Haven, CT: Yale University Press, 2018), 198.

7 George Orwell, "The Lion and the Unicorn: Socialism and the English Genius," in *Essays* (New York: Everyman's Library, 1998; Alfred A. Knopf, 1968), 336.

In *An Economics of Utopia* (1993) Simon Zadec notes, "there has been no systematic review of the economic content of utopias."[8] This work addresses only one aspect of the economic content of utopias—their treatment of economic inequality—and whether systematic or not I will let the reader decide. In recent years the number of authors contributing to the discussion of economic inequality has swelled to include economists (such as Thomas Piketty, with his foundational effort *Capital in the Twenty-First Century*), historians, philosophers, political scientists, psychologists, and sociologists concerned with economic inequality's adverse effects on society. Thus, in addition to the utopian authors this book discusses are writers from diverse fields whose insights bring clarity and context to what otherwise appears (to some) an intractable problem—vast and growing income and wealth inequality.

One can view the history of moral progress as the gradual recognition of existing conditions as harmful to society. The fight for religious freedom, the anti-slavery movement, the battle for women's suffrage, the labor union movement, the feminist movement, the campaigns for civil rights, disability rights, gay rights (including same-sex marriage), and gender recognition rights were—and to the extent they are ongoing, are—further examples of the tortured path of moral progress. Whether, and to what degree, economic inequality exacerbated each of these moral struggles illustrates Frankfurt's point noted earlier. Sociologist Howard Becker explains that "Even though a practice may be harmful in an objective sense to the group in which it occurs, the harm needs to be discovered and pointed out. People must be made to feel that something ought to be done about it."[9] Sociologist Stephen Pfohl notes that this is how child abuse became a recognized problem in the 1960s. "Despite documentary evidence of child beating throughout the ages, the 'discovery' of child abuse as deviance and its subsequent criminalization are recent phenomena."[10] Thomas More's *Utopia* (1516) memorialized the recognition of economic inequality as

8 Simon Zadek, *An Economics of Utopia: Democratising Scarcity* (Aldershot, England: Avebury, 1993), 106–107n164.

9 Howard Becker, *Outsiders: Studies in the Sociology of Deviance* (New York: The Free Press, 1963), 162.

10 Stephen Pfohl, "The 'Discovery' of Child Abuse," *Social Problems* 24 (February 1997), 310. "In a four-year period beginning in 1962," he says, "the legislatures of all fifty states passed statutes against the caretaker's abuse of children."

a problem: "However abundant goods may be," declares his narrator, "when everyone, by whatever pretexts, tries to scrape together for himself as much as he can, a handful of men end up sharing the whole pile, and the rest are left in poverty."[11] Though economic inequality is a ubiquitous and longstanding problem, it took moral advocates, including utopians, to point out the harm that the extremes of wealth and poverty produce in society—and to pose innovative and often practical solutions.

This book's multiplicity of topics and their transdisciplinary treatment limit the depth of coverage available for any particular subject. To promote continuity I have chosen authors, when possible, who treat of more than one topic. William Morris, for example, appears in the discussions of education, the dignity of work, the physical environment, and revolution in utopia. Like the curator of a museum of ideas, I have tried to make the inclusion of an author's original words—especially those from an earlier age—as inobtrusive as possible, balancing aesthetic and substantive considerations. When paraphrasing, I have tried to follow H. G. Wells's advice not to turn "good and beautiful English into bad."[12]

Though perhaps curious for utopian scholarship, this work's emphasis on economic inequality led me to specify a contemporary context for pecuniary amounts appearing in the past. I have indexed English Pounds and US Dollars for inflation as of 2023. For consistency I have converted English Pounds to US Dollars at the average exchange rate for 2022 of 1.237. The purpose of this exercise is not economic precision but instilling a sense of scale for the magnitude of economic inequality across time. Thus, $1,000 in an 1887 utopia would be worth $32,300 in 2023. For converting English Pounds in the past to their current equivalent I have used the Bank of England's inflation calculator: <https://www.bankofengland.co.uk/monetary-policy/inflation/inflation-calculator> For converting US Dollars in the past to their current equivalent I have used the calculator at Measuring Worth, Purchasing Power Today—US $: <https://www.measuringworth.com/calculators/uscompare/>

11 Thomas More, *Utopia*, trans. Robert M. Adams (Cambridge: Cambridge University Press, 1975), bk.1, 38.

12 H. G. Wells, *Mankind in the Making* (New York: Charles Scribner's Sons, 1904), 137.

CHAPTER I

Inequality: Context and Problems

> "Am I right in supposing that the effect of your economy is to establish insuperable inequalities among you, and to forbid the hope of the brotherhood which your polity proclaims?"[1]
>
> —William Dean Howells, *A Traveler from Altruria* (1894)

"Inequality was the price of civilization." This was Emmanuel Goldstein's conclusion in Orwell's *Nineteen Eighty-Four* (1949).[2] In our own time, Goldstein's declaration is a commonplace with which many people unflinchingly agree. Economist John Maynard Keynes (1883–1946) affirms, however, that among the "outstanding faults of the economic society in which we live" is the "arbitrary and inequitable distribution of wealth and incomes."[3] In this he echoes Thomas Paine (1737–1809) who declared the "rugged face of society, checkered with the extremes of affluence and want, proves that some extraordinary violence has been committed upon it, and calls on justice for redress."[4] The theme of economic inequality has permeated utopian literature from its inception. Thomas More's *Utopia*

1 William Dean Howells, *A Traveler from Altruria* (New York: Sagamore Press, 1957), 65.

2 George Orwell, *Nineteen Eighty-Four* (New York: PLUME/Penguin/Harcourt Brace, 2003), 209. This claim occurs in Goldstein's treatise, *The Theory and Practice of Oligarchical Collectivism.*

3 John Maynard Keynes, *The General Theory of Employment, Interest, and Money* (New York: A Harvest Book, Harcourt, 1964), 372.

4 Thomas Paine, "Agrarian Justice," in *The Thomas Paine Reader* (New York: Penguin Books, 1987), 484. For a discussion of Paine's status as a utopian see, Mark Jendrysik, "Tom Paine: Utopian?," *Utopian Studies* 18, no. 2 (2007): 139–157.

(1516), for example, depicts a society that has eliminated both poverty and personal wealth, as well as their measuring rods—money and gold.[5]

The extent and significance of economic inequality in our own age invites frequent comparison to that of the of the Gilded Age of the late nineteenth century. For this reason, perhaps an outsized share of the utopian explorations of economic inequality discussed in this book were written during the late nineteenth and early twentieth centuries.[6] One benefit of this almost 150-year look-back is the perspective it permits regarding which issues of economic inequality are transient and time-bound and which are stubborn and enduring; how far have we come and how much lies ahead? In exploring utopian solutions to economic inequality, I follow the stipulation by Debra Satz and Stuart White that economic inequality is usually understood in terms of inequality of income and wealth, such that "'income' refers to the flow of pecuniary benefit derived from work or ownership of an asset" during a given period of time, while "'wealth' refers to a stock of value."[7] As economist Branko Milanović specifies, income is an annual measure in contrast to wealth, which is "measured at one point in time," and is the result of the "accumulation of savings, returns on investment, and inheritance over the years."[8] Wealth, observes Milanović, is "much more"

5 Gold and silver still exist in Utopia but are not used as domestic money—though "immense quantities" are stored for international contingencies. Thomas More, *Utopia,* trans. Robert M. Adams (Cambridge University Press, 1975), bk. 2, 59–60. In this More follows Plato's *Laws* whose object is that "our people should be supremely happy and devotedly attached to one another." Accordingly, the citizens "must have neither gold nor silver." Plato, *Laws*, trans., A. E. Taylor, in *Plato*: *The Collected Dialogues*, ed. Edith Hamilton and Huntington Cairns (New York: Pantheon Books, 1961), bk. 5, 743.

6 For a discussion of utopian production from 1870 to 1914, see Matthew Beaumont, "The Party of Utopia: Utopian Fiction and the Politics of Readership 1880–1900," in *Exploring the Utopian Impulse*, ed. Michael J. Griffin and Tom Moylan (Oxford: Peter Lang, 2007), 145–162.

7 Debra Satz and Stuart White, "What Is Wrong with Inequality?," in *Inequality*: *The IFS Deaton Review*, The Institute for Fiscal Studies (September, 2021): 1–29, 4. <https://ifs.org.uk/inequality/what-is-wrong-with-inequality/>

8 Branko Milanović, *Global Inequality*: *A New Approach for the Age of Globalization* (Cambridge, MA: The Belknap Press of Harvard University Press, 2016), 39.

unequally distributed than income.[9] One reason for this disparity, as economist Thomas Piketty explains, is that the flow of income, "is necessarily constrained to respect the subsistence of the poorest members of society." For, he says, it is possible "to live without owning anything, but not without eating."[10] And though Piketty warns that "When we discuss the issue of 'extreme' inequality, we need to distinguish between the distribution of property and the distribution of income,"[11] for this discussion I make no attempt to impose greater precision on these topics than expressed by the utopian authors who form the basis of this study; this is not an economic treatise but an exploration in social philosophy in its utopian expressions.

Northrop Frye notes that "Utopian thought is imaginative, with its roots in literature, and the literary imagination is less concerned with achieving ends than with visualizing possibilities."[12] Utopian programs for rectifying the extremes of affluence and want are diverse and instructive. Though no single solution has achieved universal acceptance and some proposed solutions have fallen out of favor, exposing the spectrum of utopian options offers a richer understanding of the problem and a stimulus to the moral imagination. The development of "new, alternative perspectives," affirms philosopher Paul Ricoeur, "defines utopia's most basic function."[13]

The recent influx of studies addressing income and wealth inequality reflects a concern for the future of values such as democracy, liberty, equality, and fraternity—if the trend toward greater economic inequality continues at its current pace. In his novel *Equality* (1897), Edward Bellamy's spokesperson Dr. Leete proclaims: "All human beings are equal in rights and

9 Milanović, *Global Inequality*, 39.

10 Thomas Piketty, *Capital and Ideology*, trans. Arthur Goldhammer (Cambridge, MA: The Belknap Press of Harvard University Press, 2020), 266. Piketty, says Milanović, "has revolutionized the field of income distribution by the use of fiscal sources and by his focus on top income shares. Branko Milanović, "The Return of 'Patrimonial Capitalism': A Review of Thomas Piketty's *Capital in the Twenty-First Century*," *Journal of Economic Literature* 52, no. 2 (2014): 519–534, 530.

11 Piketty, *Capital and Ideology*, 265.

12 Northrop Frye, "Varieties of Literary Utopias," in *Utopias and Utopian Thought*, ed. Frank E. Manuel (Boston: Houghton Mifflin Company, 1966), 31.

13 Paul Ricoeur, *Lectures on Ideology and Utopia* (New York: Columbia University Press, 1986), 16.

dignity, and only such a system of wealth distribution can therefore be defensible as respects and secures those equalities."[14] While Bellamy's formulation implies that such a system of distribution exists, the sample of utopias exposed here displays a prism of alternatives.

Inequality Generally

> "It is clear that you are not a man of our time, Mr. Burnham. Poor people! Rich people! Laborers' quarters! There are no such terms in the year 2000."[15]
>
> —Paul Devinne, *The Day of Prosperity: A Vision of the Century to Come* (1902)

The "central problem with most approaches to utopianism," advises Lyman Tower Sargent, "is the attempt to use a single dimension to explain a multidimensional phenomenon."[16] For utopians concerned with the management of inequality—though viewing it from diverse perspectives—equality is an essential measure of the general welfare. Contrary views on equality, however, frame disparate utopias, as there is little agreement on which dimensions of equality merit promotion. Equal income? Gender equality? Racial equality? Equal dignity? Political equality? Equality of accountability? Equality of opportunity? Equality in the eyes of God or the law?

In a discussion of egalitarianism, political philosopher Norberto Bobbio observes, "the concept of equality is relative, not absolute. ... Between whom?, Of what?, On the basis of which criteria?"[17] Amartya Sen expands this argument noting that "every plausibly defendable ethical

14 Edward Bellamy, *Equality,* 3rd ed. (New York: D. Appleton and Company, 1897), 87.

15 Paul Devinne, *The Day of Prosperity: A Vision of the Century to Come* (New York: G. W. Dillingham Company, 1902), 59.

16 Lyman Tower Sargent, "The Three Faces of Utopianism Revisited," *Utopian Studies* 5, no. 1 (1994): 1–37, 3.

17 Norberto Bobbio, *Left and Right: The Significance of a Political Distinction*, trans. Allan Cameron (Chicago: The University of Chicago Press, 1993), 60–61.

theory of social arrangements tends to demand ... [equal] treatment of individuals in some significant respect. ... For example, 'libertarians' [Ayn Rand, Robert Nozick] are concerned with equal liberties; 'economic egalitarians' [Thomas More, Edward Bellamy] argue for equal incomes or wealths."[18] This implies that while More and others have designated answers—to "between whom?," "of what?," and "on the basis of which criteria?"[19]—these answers have denied equality in some other realm, for example, equal liberties, property rights, or Robert Nozick's "right to choose what to do with what one has."[20] Psychologist Pascal Boyer notes, however, that the term "egalitarian" may be misleading. People do not want equal roles in decision making, for example; rather, the egalitarian motivation is "to circumscribe hierarchical decision making so that it does not lead to political exploitation."[21] To this philosopher Thomas Nagel adds that the egalitarian priority system "counts improvements to the welfare of the worse off as more urgent than improvements to the welfare of the better off."[22]

"Extreme social inequality," reports Gregory Claeys, "both harms individual well-being and ultimately undermines any society. Utopia," Claeys continues, "stands for the avoidance of plutocracy, the limiting of inequality, and the management of common recourses for the common good."[23] Barbara Goodwin reports five principal ills utopians link to economic inequality, (1) poverty, (2) inegalitarian methods of production, (3) class structures limiting opportunity, (4) threats to human dignity, and (5)

18 Amartya Sen, *Inequality Reexamined* (Cambridge, MA: Harvard University Press, 1992), 130.

19 Bobbio, *Left and Right*, 60–61.

20 Robert Nozick, *Anarchy, State and Utopia* (New York: Basic Books, 1974), 167.

21 Pascal Boyer, *Minds Make Societies* (New Haven, CT: Yale University Press, 201), 199.

22 Thomas Nagel, "Equality," in *Mortal Questions* (Cambridge University Press, 1979), 106–127, 117–118.

23 Gregory Claeys, "The Five Languages of Utopia: Their Respective Advantages and Deficiencies; with a Plea for Prioritising Social Realism," in *Spectres of Utopia: Theory, Practice, Conventions*, ed. Artur Blaim and Ludmila Gruszewska-Blaim (Frankfurt am Main: Peter Lang, 2012), 28–31, 30.

intrinsic injustice.[24] "There have been utopians," affirms Goodwin, "who considered that inequality was rooted in human nature to such an extent that the ideal society had to build on it constructively."[25] A popular criticism of utopias, however, is that they do not confront people as they really are but as the author wishes they might be. The counterargument is that once economic, social, or political conditions are altered we will finally see people "as they really are." In an essay on human nature, John Dewey argues that "those who hold that proposals for social change, even of rather a profound character, are impossible and utopian because of the fixity of human nature, confuse the resistance to change that comes from acquired habits with that which comes from original human nature."[26] Fortunately for a discussion of economic inequality, "Economic institutions and relations," Dewey suggests, "are among the manifestations of human nature that are most susceptible of change."[27]

Thomas Hobbes (1588–1679) assumes our natural inequalities are offsetting; men are "by nature equal." One man's guile and experience, for example, will counterbalance another man's stamina and physical strength.[28] Jean-Jacques Rousseau (1712–1778) in his discourse on the subject distinguishes moral or political from natural inequality. Moral or political inequality refers to hegemonic disparities in privilege, social class, and wealth; natural inequality denotes differences in age, physical strength, and "qualities of mind."[29] Rousseau traces the advent of economic inequality to

24 Barbara Goodwin, "Economic and Social Innovation in Utopia," in *Utopias*, ed. Peter Alexander and Roger Gill (London: Duckworth, 1984), 69–83, 70.

25 Goodwin, "Economic and Social Innovation in Utopia," 71.

26 John Dewey, "Does Human Nature Change?," in *John Dewey: The Later Works: 1925–1953*, vol. 13: 1938–1939 (Carbondale: Southern Illinois University Press, 1991), 291. For a discussion of the utopian quality of John Dewey's work see, John Freeman-Moir, "Crafting Experience: William Morris, John Dewey, and Utopia," *Utopian Studies* 22, no. 2 (2011).

27 Dewey, "Does Human Nature Change," 290.

28 Thomas Hobbes, *Leviathan: Or the Matter, Forme and Power of a Commonwealth Ecclesiasticall and Civil*, ed. Michael Oakeshott (London: Collier-Macmillan, 1962), first part, chap. 13, 98.

29 Jean-Jacques Rousseau, *Discourse on the Origin and Foundations of Inequality Among Men*, in *Rousseau's Political Writings*, trans. Julia Conway Bondanella (New York: Norton, 1988), 8–9. In our own time, Nagel expands the list to five sources of

the formation of society—to "the moment any one man needed help from another"[30]—and to the resulting division of labor. At that point, Rousseau asserts, differences in talent, strength, skill, and ingenuity meant people performing the same work did so with varying results. Working an equal time, he notes, "one earned a great deal, while the other had barely enough to live on."[31] Amplifying Rousseau's concerns, Bolivar in Marge Piercy's *Woman on the Edge of Time* (1976) proclaims, "I see the original division of labor, that first dichotomy, as enabling later divvies into haves and have-nots, powerful and powerless, enjoyers and workers, rapists and victims.'"[32]

Inequality "goes far deeper than just income and wealth," sociologist Thomas Shapiro observes. "It determines who can overcome obstacles: some have them cleared from their path, while others have trouble recovering from even minor mishaps." At its heart, stresses Shapiro, "inequality is about access, opportunity, and just rewards."[33] Inequality in the historical context of egalitarian political movements, reports Elizabeth Anderson, "referred not so much to distributions of goods as to relations between superior and inferior persons. Those of superior rank were though entitled to inflict violence on inferiors, to exclude or segregate them from social life."[34] This is the theme of William Godwin's novel, *The Adventures of Caleb Williams* (1794), discussed in Chapter 4. Slavery is the ultimate model of inequality. Describing American slavery's damaging influence on society, for example, sociologist and historian W. E. B. Du Bois (1868–1963) affirms: "The mere fact that a man could be, under the law, the actual master of the mind and body of human beings had to have disastrous effects."[35]

---

inequality, (1) "hereditary advantage" (moral or political), (2) "variation in natural abilities" (natural), (3) "intentional discrimination" (racism), (4) "effort," and (5) "bad luck." Thomas Nagel, *Equality and Partiality* (New York: Oxford University Press, 1991), 102–103.

30 Rousseau, *Discourse on the Origin and Foundations of Inequality Among Men*, 40.

31 Rousseau, *Discourse on the Origin and Foundations of Inequality Among Men*, 41.

32 Marge Piercy, *Woman on the Edge of Time* (New York: Ballantine Books, 1976), 229.

33 Thomas M. Shapiro, *Toxic Inequality* (New York: Basic Books, 2017), 218.

34 Elizabeth S. Anderson, "What is the Point of Equality?," *Ethics* 109, no. 2 (January, 1999): 287–337, 312.

35 W. E. B. Du Bois, *Black Reconstruction in America* (New York: The Free Press, 1998), 52. Disastrous effects on both the slave and the master, notes Du Bois.

Income and Wealth Inequality

> "The search for a distribution of wealth acceptable to the majority of people is a recurrent theme in all periods and all cultures."[36]
>
> —Thomas Piketty, *Capital and Ideology* (2020)

The narrator of Étienne Cabet's *Travels in Icaria* (1847) asks, "Should reason and society not repair the inequality produced by blind chance?"[37] In the US during the three decades after 1979, relates Christopher Hayes, "the top 10 percent captured *all* of the income gains, while incomes for the bottom 90 percent declined."[38] The US Federal Reserve reports that between 1989 and 2021 the share of the country's wealth the top 1 percent of the population owned grew from roughly 5 percent to 46 percent.[39] In 2019 the average income of the top 1 percent was $1,614,468; the average income of the bottom 50 percent was $18,425, a factor of 88 times.[40] A 2019 *Washington Post* article notes that "Income inequality in the United States has hit its highest level since the Census Bureau started tracking it more than five decades ago."[41] The Brookings Institution in its 2022 "World Inequality Report"[42] determined that "53 million Americans between the ages of 18–64—accounting for 44% of all workers—qualify as 'low-wage.' Their median hourly wages are $10.22, and median annual

36 Piketty, *Capital and Ideology*, 576–77.

37 Étienne Cabet, *Travels in Icaria*, trans. Leslie J. Roberts (Syracuse, NY: Syracuse University Press, 2003), 83.

38 Christopher Hayes, *Twilight of the Elites: America After Meritocracy* (New York: Crown Publishers, 2012), 219 (italics in original).

39 Board of Governors of the Federal Reserve System, <https://www.federalreserve.gov/releases/z1/dataviz/dfa/distribute/table/>

40 Tax Foundation <https://taxfoundation.org/publications/latest-federal-income-tax-data/>

41 Taylor Telford, "Income Inequality in America Is the Highest It's Been since Census Bureau Started Tracking It, Data Shows," *Washington Post*, September 26, 2019.

42 Lucas Chancel, Thomas Piketty, and others, "World Inequality Report 2022," *World Inequality Lab*. <https://wir2022.wid.world/www-site/uploads/2021/12/Summary_WorldInequalityReport2022_English.pdf>

earnings are about $18,000."[43] Anthropologist David Harvey reports, "The incredible concentrations of wealth and power that now exist in the upper echelons of capitalism have not been seen since the 1920s.[44] "Indeed," says Piketty, "socioeconomic inequality has increased in all regions of the world since the 1980s."[45]

Economic inequality, Goodwin observes, is "fundamentally linked to the division of labor."[46] This understates the case, however, as the division of labor (together with the notions of ownership and property) is the headwaters of economic inequality, for, as Rousseau asserts, the division of labor yields to "competition and rivalry on the one hand, conflicts of interest on the other, and always the hidden desire to profit at the expense of others."[47] While a few utopians promote the division of labor based on free markets, inherent principles, and spontaneous order (Ayn Rand, Robert Nozick), most utopians seek to regulate the division of labor for the benefit of society; to rein in its unfettered outcomes—blunting their effects on economic inequality—through the disparate schemes this book describes. The zenith of this regulation is exemplified by the Director of Hatcheries and Conditioning in Aldus Huxley's *Brave New World*, who reports, we "predestine and condition." "We decant our babies as socialized human beings, as Alphas or Epsilons,"[48] ensuring the required division of labor to perform society's work at any one of five levels (or fifteen, when augmented with plusses and minuses).

When viewed as a problem, economic inequality has been identified with factors such as private property, inherited wealth, racism, capitalism,

43 Martha Ross and Nicole Bateman, "Low-wage Work Is More Pervasive Than You Think, and There Aren't Enough 'good jobs' to Go Around," *The Brookings Institution*, November 21, 2019. <https://www.brookings.edu/blog/the-avenue/2019/11/21/low-wage-work-is-more-pervasive-than-you-think-and-there-arent-enough-good-jobs-to-go-around/>

44 David Harvey, *A Brief History of Neoliberalism* (Oxford: Oxford University Press, 2005), 119.

45 Piketty, *Capital and Ideology*, 1.

46 Goodwin, "Economic and Social Innovation in Utopia," 71.

47 Rousseau, *Discourse on the Origin and Foundations of Inequality*, 42.

48 Aldous Huxley, *Brave New World* (New York: Harper Collins 2004), 23.

and IQ. But components of equality—equality before the law or income equality, for example—are often interdependent or inextricably bound together, as noted. Reducing some forms of inequality, therefore, can result in increasing others.[49] Providing equalizing public benefits such as universal health care or basic income, for instance, may require an unequal (progressive) tax régime—taxing the rich at higher rates than the masses. As Thomas More explains, "Suppressing the disease in one place causes it to break out in another, since you cannot give something to one person without taking it away from someone else."[50]

While measuring equality based on income or wealth allows for a "single linear measure for relative social position" and thus of "who is well-off and not well-off," as philosopher Martha Nussbaum observes, it ignores further dimensions of well-being—including self-respect, justice, health, and the ability to navigate the physical environment.[51] Inequality, explains Piketty, "is neither economic nor technological: it is ideological and political."[52] "Every human society must justify its inequalities," continues Piketty; "unless reasons for them are found, the whole political and social edifice stands in danger of collapse."[53] In his book *Equality: The Impossible Quest* (2015) however, historian Martin van Creveld insists that "nothing could be *less* self-evident than the idea that everybody was, or ought to be, equal."[54]

49 Martin van Creveld, *Equality: The Impossible Quest* (Kouvola, Finland: Castalia House, 2015), 170; Sen, *Inequality Reexamined*, 130.

50 More, *Utopia*, trans. Adams, bk. 1, 38.

51 Martha C. Nussbaum, *Frontiers of Justice: Disability, Nationality, Species Membership* (Cambridge, MA: The Belknap Press of Harvard University Press, 2006), 114–115. "A person who uses a wheelchair," Nussbaum notes, "may have the same income and wealth as a person with 'normal' mobility, and yet be much less well-off in terms of ability to get around." The "Disability and the Utopia" exhibit at the Whitworth art gallery of the University of Manchester featured a December 9, 2020 blog post highlighting this issue. "It's rare to see a vision of a better world that actually includes disabled people without erasing them, shaming them or requiring them to go above and beyond what they're actually able to do in order to survive." <https://aplacebetweenthetrees.com/2020/12/09/3091/>

52 Piketty, *Capital and Ideology*, 7.

53 Piketty, *Capital and Ideology*, 1.

54 van Creveld, *Equality*, 183 (italics in original).

In contrast political economist Vilfredo Pareto (1848–1923) argues, "The subjective concept of the equality of man is a fact of great importance, and one which acts powerfully in determining the changes that society undergoes."[55] Hence, the utopian challenge.

Utopian Directions

> "If we are to have any Utopia at all, we must have a clear common purpose, and a great and steadfast movement of will to override all the incurably egotistical dissentients."[56]
>
> —H. G. Wells, *A Modern Utopia* (1905)

In his monograph on definitions Richard Robinson distinguishes lexical from stipulative definitions.[57] Lexical definitions of *utopia* invariably trace its meaning to Thomas More (no place or nowhere). By *stipulative* definition, says Robinson, "I mean establishing or announcing or choosing one's own meaning for a word."[58] Contemporary utopian scholarship is bountiful with stipulative definitions (and classifications) often seeking to capture some unique aspect of utopia as a point of emphasis or elaboration.[59] In this work I use *utopia* in its broadest signification to include eutopias, dystopias, critical utopias, utopian satires, and so on, as any of

55 Vilfredo Pareto, *Manual of Political Economy*, ed. Aldo Montesano and others (Oxford University Press, 2014), 63. Pareto's "optimality criterion" may be used for judging the acceptability of a particular policy change. "Basically," says Milanović, "somebody has to gain and nobody must lose." But, Milanović clarifies, "Finding economic policies (changes) of this kind is all but impossible because almost invariably somebody loses." Branko Milanović, *The Haves and the Have-Nots* (New York: Basic Books, 2011), 87.

56 H. G. Wells, *A Modern Utopia* (New York: Digireads Publishing, 2011), 53.

57 Richard Robinson, *Definition* (London: Oxford University Press, 1954), 19.

58 Robinson, *Definition*, 19.

59 See Lyman Tower Sargent's compilation of utopian terminology under "definitions" at <https://openpublishing.psu.edu/utopia/content/definitions> or his "The Three Faces of Utopianism Revisited," 9.

these forms may illustrate a society that is both nowhere and sheds light on the problem of economic inequality.[60]

When I speak of "the problem" of economic inequality, the scope of my inquiry includes both the extent to which people claim there is a problem and an understanding of what type of problem it is. That is, from the author's perspective "the problem of economic inequality" should be understood as a moral placeholder and not the proclamation of a particular moral stance, for example, egalitarian or utilitarian.[61] For the purpose of this study—though it may strike some as question begging—the meaning of the phrase will arise from the utopians who attempt to provide answers to the problem; the nature of the problem will emerge in the context of the solution(s). This accords with Ruth Levitas's claim that as material is selected for inclusion in a utopian commentary it "provides an implicit definition of the utopian object."[62]

Utopian solutions to the problems of economic inequality require either a fixed social structure or one permitting change and evolution—such as John Partington usefully terms static and kinetic utopias, respectively.[63]

60 The Manuels' historical overview includes the facts that the term *utopia* "could always be used either positively or pejoratively," and that by the seventeenth century utopia "also came to denote general programs and platforms for ideal societies, codes, and constitutions that dispensed with the fictional apparatus." Frank E. Manuel and Fritzie P. Manuel, *Utopian Thought in the Western World* (Cambridge, MA: The Belknap Press of Harvard University Press, 1979), 3–4.

61 For a discussion of the contrast between egalitarian and utilitarian views of equality, see Nagel, "Equality," in *Mortal Questions*. While More and Bellamy present egalitarian utopias, an explicitly utilitarian utopia—where the goal is "the greatest good for the greatest number"—is Stewart E. Bruce, *The World in 1931* (New York: F. L. Searl and Co., 1921), 134–135.

62 Ruth Levitas, *The Concept of Utopia* (Oxford: Peter Lang, 2011), 11.

63 John S. Partington, "The Death of the Static: H. G. Wells and the Kinetic Utopia," *Utopian Studies* 11, no. 2 (2000): 96–111; John S. Partington, "The Time Machine and a Modern Utopia: The Static and Kinetic Utopias of the Early H. G. Wells," *Utopian Studies* 13, no. 1 (2002): 57–68. Dahrendorf adds a layer of complexity to this distinction by referring to "intra-system processes, i.e., changes that are actually part of the design of utopia, and historical change, the direction and outcome of which are not predetermined." Ralf Dahrendorf, "Out of Utopia: Toward a Reorientation of Sociological Analysis," *American Journal of Sociology* 64, no. 2 (September, 1958): 115–127, 115n1.

Thomas More's *Utopia* (1516), John Macnie's *Diothas* (1883), and Edward Bellamy's *Looking Backward* (1888) provide examples of fixed orders;[64] Albert Chavannes's *The Future Commonwealth* (1892), Fayette Stratton Giles *Shadows Before or A Century Onward* (1893), and H. G. Wells's *A Modern Utopia* (1905) all by contrast feature societies stressing adaptation and change. In addition, utopias based on a "theory of history such as those of Marx, Saint-Simon and Fourier," argue Goodwin and Taylor, "predict change and improvement even in utopias."[65] While Sargent argues that "Utopia suggests that change for the better is always possible,"[66] marshalling the forces of economic change is difficult, as Thorstein Veblen (1857–1929) observed, for paradoxically, both the rich and the poor foster a conservative bent. "The abjectly poor," says Veblen, "are conservative because they cannot afford the effort of taking thought for the day after to-morrow; just as the highly prosperous are conservative because they have small occasion to be discontented with the situation as it stands to-day."[67] Dewey points to another problem hindering the utopian urge. He argues that historically people have limited themselves in their strivings for a better life "because they have waited upon some power external to themselves and to nature to do the work they are responsible for doing."[68]

Of his utopian *Icaria* (1840), Étienne Cabet says, "Let others set forth better organizational schemes, better models ... the nation will certainly learn to correct and perfect the system, just as later generations will know

64 "More's utopia," says Manuel, "is not even subject to the natural decay that Plato considered inevitable for his Republic." Frank E. Manuel, "Toward a Psychological History of Utopias," in *Utopias and Utopian Thought*, ed. Frank E. Manuel (Boston, MA: Houghton Mifflin Company, 1965), 75.

65 Barbara Goodwin and Keith Taylor, *The Politics of Utopia: A Study in Theory and Practice* (Oxford: Peter Lang, 2009), 111.

66 Lyman Tower Sargent, "Theorizing Utopia/Utopianism in the Twenty-First Century," in *Spectres of Utopia: Theory, Practice, Conventions*, ed. Artur Blaim and Ludmila Gruszewska-Blaim (Frankfurt am Main: Peter Lang, 2012), 13–25, 22.

67 Thorstein Veblen, *The Theory of the Leisure Class* (Oxford University Press, 2007), 135. For a discussion of similarities between Veblen and Bellamy see, Rick Tilman, "The Utopian Vision of Edward Bellamy and Thorsten Veblen," *Journal of Economic Issues* 19, no. 4 (December, 1985): 879–898.

68 John Dewey, *A Common Faith* (New Haven, CT: Yale University Press, 1934), 46.

how to modify and perfect it even more."[69] But a utopia that permits change, it has been argued, cannot be a true utopia—for while change may produce improvement it may also produce decay. For this reason some commentators emphasize the static quality of utopia—where "change and development," as Wells proclaimed, are "dammed back by invincible dams forever."[70] This static quality is necessary, maintains Elizabeth Hansot, if utopia "is to remain a simplified, schematic construct through which the author can investigate the implications of his ideal."[71] But a state "without the means of some change," warned Edmund Burke (1729–1797), is a state "without the means of its conservation."[72] And though Hansot asserts that the "type of thought experiment that occurs in the process of creating a utopia remains characteristic of the entire utopian tradition," she questions the efficacy of such experiments that attempt to incorporate change. In contrast, however, Catherine Stimpson asks, "Why bother to project a new world if it is to be only a toy that tinkers with the old?"[73]

A counterexample to Hansot's claim is *The Future Commonwealth or What Samuel Balcom Saw in Socioland* (1892). It is Albert Chavannes's attempt to ground utopia, Socioland, on experimentation as a means for attenuating economic inequality. "More dissatisfaction is felt among us on account of the inequality in the distribution of wealth," says Samuel Balcom his narrator, "than from any other cause."[74] Chavannes's aim was

69 Cabet, *Travels in Icaria*, lix.

70 Wells, *A Modern Utopia*, 8.

71 Elizabeth Hansot, *Perfection and Progress: Two Modes of Utopian Thought* (Cambridge, MA: The MIT Press, 1974), 19. In the case of Wells's *A Modern Utopia*, for example—where his narrator proclaims, "the world is for experiment,"—Hansot says Wells "had great difficulty explaining why innovation and creativity are to be valued in utopia." Hansot, *Perfection and Progress*, 150. Wells's response is that "Our business here is to be Utopian, to make vivid and credible, if we can, first this facet and then that, of an imaginary whole and happy world." Wells, *A Modern Utopia*, 8, 39.

72 Edmund Burke, *Reflections on the Revolution in France* (Oxford: Oxford University Press, 1993), 21.

73 Catherine R. Stimpson, "Feminism and Utopia," *Utopian Studies* 3 (1991): 1–6, 2.

74 Albert Chavannes, *The Future Commonwealth or What Samuel Balcom Saw in Socioland* (New York: True Nationalist Publishing Company, 1892), 10.

the experimental quest for a means of reversing these inegalitarian trends. In Socioland they believe in a social science, "which they claim is something different from political economy. They study this science ... to experiment in new lines of public co-operation whenever they seem to lead in the right direction."[75] Chavannes's vision also clashes with Melvin Lasky's claim that "The rigidity of almost all utopias, their authoritarianism and paternal perfectionism, are almost incomprehensible, seen against the whole record of the human imagination."[76] With respect to perfection, however, as Sargent advises, "perfection has never been a characteristic of utopian fiction."[77]

Thomas Nagel affirms that "Political theory has always been concerned to design systems which generate the psychological conditions of their own stability."[78] A utopia, I submit—whether static or dynamic—must include a mechanism of internal cohesion or centripetal force that continually draws society back to its unifying values—whether liberty, equality, fraternity, individuality, abundance, leisure, order, peace, or harmony with nature.[79] But, "how is it that human societies cohere?" is what sociologist Ralf Dahrendorf calls "the most puzzling problem of social philosophy."[80] While the citizens' solidarity or homogeneity may animate this mechanism, alternately, a utopia's centripetal force may arise from a

75 Chavannes, *The Future Commonwealth*, 5.

76 Melvin J. Lasky, *Utopia and Revolution: On the Origins of a Metaphor* (Chicago: University of Chicago Press, 1976; republished, New Brunswick, NJ: Transaction Publishers, 2004), 10.

77 Sargent, "The Three Faces of Utopianism Revisited," 6.

78 Nagel, *Equality and Partiality*, 149.

79 See Sargent's discussion of changing "dominant values" in utopias in, Lyman Tower Sargent, "Authority and Utopia: Utopianism in Political Thought," *Polity* 14, no. 4 (Summer 1982): 565–584, 573. Order in utopias is frequently maintained by what Goodwin and Taylor call "mutual control." Goodwin and Taylor, *The Politics of Utopia*, 59. In More's *Utopia*, Greenblatt notes, order results from the "intense communal pressure of honor and blame," or "shaming." Stephen Greenblatt, *Renaissance Self-Fashioning: From More to Shakespeare* (The University of Chicago Press, 1980), 47–48.

80 Ralf Dahrendorf, *Class and Class Conflict in Industrial Society* (California: Stanford University Press, 1959), 157.

"unity of opposites"[81]—opposing forces holding each other in check.[82] Durkheim suggests the division of labor itself may render this function as "the worker … does not lose sight of his collaborators," in their mutual "struggle for existence."[83] Society's method of internal cohesion is a function of its DNA though it excludes, as Sargent explains, the "continual use of force."[84] Reflecting Paine's sense that "[t]he more perfect civilisation is, the less occasion has it for government,"[85] Ricoeur affirms, utopia "is always an attempt to replace power by something else."[86] The result of my stipulation is a self-regulating and self-perpetuating society whose governing principles preclude the exploitation by one order of citizens, as Adam Smith demands, for "no other purpose but to promote that of some other."[87] To the extent such exploitation derives from the system governing the division

81 Moylan describes Piercy's *Woman on the Edge of Time*, for example, as expressing a "unity of opposites as it seeks to be both politically engaged and aesthetically multi-dimensional." Though Moylan's comment is addressed to the novel itself and not its utopia Mattapoisett, Moylan also notes the unity of opposites Piercy achieves through Mattapoisett's "collective activism that preserves the importance of the individual person" as illustrated, for example, by the eternal conflict between the genetic "shapers" and the "mixers" (referenced in Chapter 4). Tom Moylan, *Demand the Impossible: Science Fiction and the Utopian Imagination*, ed. Raffaella Baccolini (Oxford: Peter Lang, 2014), 145–146.

82 Dahrendorf lists two sociological models suggested to account for the relative stability or homeostasis of society. One is the "value consensus" model and the other is the "conflict" model. "Indeed," he says, "it may well be that society, in a philosophical sense, has two faces of equal reality: one of stability, harmony, and consensus, and one of change, conflict, and constraint." Dahrendorf, "Out of Utopia," 127.

83 Émile Durkheim, *The Division of Labor in Society* (1893), trans. George Simpson (N.p.: Digreads.com Publishing, 2019), 217, 291. Grabb explains that for Durkheim "the function of the division of labor is to provide solidarity on the basis of *dis*similarity, on the fact that highly specialized individuals … are no longer self-sufficient." Edward G. Grabb, *Social Inequality: Classical and Contemporary Theories* (Toronto: Holt, Rinehart and Winston of Canada, 1984), 77.

84 Sargent, "Authority and Utopia," 569; Sargent, "The Three Faces of Utopianism Revisited," 24.

85 Thomas Paine, *Rights of Man* (Mineola, NY: Dover Publications, 1999), 108.

86 Ricoeur, *Lectures on Ideology and Utopia*, 288.

87 Adam Smith, *Wealth of Nations* (Amherst, NY: Prometheus Books, 1991), bk. 4, chap. 8, 436.

of labor—as the division of labor is the basis of economic inequality, as noted—modifications to that system become the moral end of procedures directed at reducing economic inequality.

Utopian Quest

> "A measure of the goodness of a state is the degree in which it relieves individuals from the waste of negative struggle and needless conflict and confers upon him positive assurance and reinforcement in what he undertakes."[88]
>
> —John Dewey, *The Public and Its Problems* (1927)

"The concept of utopia in every age," declares Gregory Claeys, "is some variation on an ideal present, an ideal past and an ideal future, and the relation between the three."[89] Utopias, Dahrendorf observes, are "an intensely moral and polemical branch of human thinking."[90] George Kateb proposes that *utopia* should only apply to an ideal society "in which the welfare of all its inhabitants is the central concern, and in which the level of welfare is strikingly higher, and assumed to be more long-lasting, than that of the real world."[91] This embraces utopias tackling problems of economic inequality. In *Capital in the Twenty-First Century* (2014) Piketty explains, "The history of inequality is shaped by the way economic, social, and political actors view what is just and what is not, as well as by the relative power of those actors and the collective choices that result."[92] Accordingly, he warns, the "intellectual and political debate about the distribution of wealth has long been based on an abundance of prejudice

88 John Dewey, *The Public and Its Problems* (Chicago: The Swallow Press, 1927), 72.

89 Gregory Claeys, *Searching for Utopia: The History of an Idea* (London: Thames and Hudson, 2011), 7.

90 Dahrendorf, "Out of Utopia," 122.

91 George Kateb, *Utopia and Its Enemies* (New York: The Free Press, 1963), 6n6.

92 Thomas Piketty, *Capital in the Twenty-First Century*, trans. Arthur Goldhammer (Cambridge, MA: The Belknap Press of Harvard University Press, 2014), 20.

and a paucity of fact."[93] Furthermore, cautions economist Amartya Sen, since "we do not seem to get very much help in studying inequality from the main schools of welfare economics,"[94] this study has been left to others—historians, philosophers, political scientists, psychologists, sociologists, and utopians.

Darko Suvin characterizes Utopia as a "formal inversion of significant and salient aspects of the author's world, an inversion which has as its ultimate purpose the recognition that the author (and reader) truly live in an axiologically inverted world."[95] Utopian writers are those who diagnose systemic problems in society and envision solutions for their remediation or reform, or project the path of society's evolution and demise if no such measures are forthcoming. Assuming income and wealth inequality are subject to "repair by reason and society," the initial questions confronting utopians are: What repairs are necessary and possible, and by what means? What are the instruments, methods, or techniques to enlist?

Utopias that tackle economic inequality do so from either of two basic perspectives, each described in its place. The first calls for economic leveling, for equalizing the economic status of all members of a society (discussed in Chapter 6). Edward Bellamy's *Looking Backward* is an example. The second calls for eliminating poverty and restricting the means for accumulating vast personal wealth while tolerating measures of economic inequality seen as potentially beneficial to society (discussed in Chapters

93 Piketty, *Capital in the Twenty-First Century*, 2. In Robinson's *The Ministry for the Future* we find this indictment: "The whole field and discipline of economics, by which we plan and justify what we do as a society, is simply riddled with absences, contradictions, logical flaws, and most important of all, false axioms and false goals." Kim Stanley Robinson, *The Ministry for the Future* (New York: Orbit, 2020), 166.

94 Sen, *On Economic Inequality*, 23. One reason for this lack of help, as Schumpeter notes, is that, "Economists have been strangely slow in recognizing the phenomenon of social classes. ... Social classes, however, are not the creatures of the classifying observer but live entities that exist as such." Joseph A. Schumpeter, *Capitalism, Socialism and Democracy* (New York: Harper and Row Publishers, 1976), 14.

95 Darko Suvin, *Metamorphoses of Science Fiction: On the Poetics and History of a Literary Genre*, ed. Gerry Canavan (Bern, Switzerland: Peter Lang, 2016), 262.

2–4).[96] H. G. Wells's *A Modern Utopia* is an example.[97] These two concepts of equality, as Keith Taylor notes, differ in their treatment of property.[98]

Utopias, affirms Sargent, deal with problems that are both perennial and contemporary.[99] The problem of economic inequality is not restricted to the fact that a few people possess immense wealth while the masses work simply to get by. Wealth, observes sociologist Georg Simmel (1858–1918), "is often regarded as a kind of moral merit, as is indicated by the term 'respectability' and by popular reference to the well-to-do as 'upright citizens.'"[100] This is a central theme of philosopher Michael Sandel's 2020 *The Tyranny of Merit* (discussed in Chapter 3). The counterpart of this phenomenon, says Simmel, is "the fact that the poor are treated as if they were guilty."[101]

Income and wealth inequality harm society—when they do—by rewarding and often aggrandizing some members of society at the cost of degrading the lives of others. These others find their life-chances curtailed and their gifts unacknowledged. In Thomas More's *Utopia* (1516), narrator Raphael Hythloday proclaims (as noted in this book's introduction), "However abundant goods may be, when everyone, by whatever pretexts, tries to scrape together for himself as much as he can, a handful of men end up sharing the whole pile, and the rest are left in poverty." The result, says

96 Though poverty may be either relative or absolute, utopians expressing a desire to end poverty should be understood as addressing absolute poverty. Absolute poverty is the condition of a person whose resources fail to meet their basic needs including, "housing, educational opportunities, and political participation," as well as healthy food, safe drinking water, and preventative healthcare. Relative poverty, by contrast, is a measure of welfare where "the poverty income line would fluctuate with the fortunes of the of the rest of society." Charles E. Hurst, *Social Inequality: Forms, Causes, and Consequences*, 5th ed. (Boston: Pearson, 2004), 352–352.

97 Frankfurt argues that "to show of poverty that it is compellingly undesirable does nothing whatever to show the same of inequality." Harry G. Frankfurt, *Inequality* (Princeton, NJ: Princeton University Press, 2015), 44.

98 Keith Taylor, *The Political Ideas of the Utopia Socialists* (England: Frank Cass and Company, 1982), 12.

99 Sargent, "Theorizing Utopia/Utopianism in the Twenty-First Century," 14.

100 Georg Simmel, *The Philosophy of Money* (1900), trans. Tom Bottomore and David Frisby (Boston: Routledge and Kegan Paul, 1978), 217.

101 Simmel, *The Philosophy of Money*, 217–218.

Hythloday, embraces "two sorts of people: the rich are rapacious, wicked and useless, while the poor are unassuming, modest men, whose daily labor benefits the public more than themselves.[102] George Orwell had a different take on poverty which he saw as more than a financial calamity. Poverty, says Orwell, frees the poor "from ordinary standards of behavior, just as money frees people from work."[103]

For some observers the troubling aspect of economic inequality is the trajectory of the problem. This concern was voiced by the followers of Charles Fourier (1772–1837)—one of the founders of utopian socialism—as John Stuart Mill (1806–1873) describes. Mill, acting as "a mere reporter of the opinion of others,"[104] observes that for the Fourierists, "the tendency of the present order of society is to a concentration of wealth in the hands of a comparatively few immensely rich individuals or companies, and the reduction of all the rest of the community into a complete dependence on them."[105]

Citing Orwell's "The Lion and the Unicorn" Richard White says, "as long as there are gross inequalities in society people will never feel a sense of solidarity or of belonging to the same social project—for equality is the condition for fraternity or community with others."[106] In his book *Justice* (2009) Michael Sandel observes that "too great a gap between rich and poor undermines the solidarity that democratic citizenship requires."[107] As inequality deepens, he continues, "rich and poor live increasingly separate lives."[108] The result is a pair of separate and unequal societies since the "affluent secede from public places and services, leaving them to those

102 More, *Utopia*, trans. Adams, bk. 1, 38.
103 George Orwell, *Down and Out in Paris and London* (New York: A Harvest Book, Harcourt, Inc., 1961), 7.
104 John Stuart Mill, "Essays on Economics and Society," in *Collected Work of John Stuart Mill*, vol. 5 (Toronto: University of Toronto Press: Routledge and Kegan Paul, 1967), 716.
105 Mill, "Essays on Economics and Society," 726–727.
106 Richard White, "George Orwell: Socialism and Utopia," *Utopian Studies* 19, no. 1 (2008): 73–95, 77.
107 Michael J. Sandel, *Justice: What's the Right Thing to Do?* (New York: Farrar, Straus and Giroux, 2009), 266.
108 Sandel, *Justice*, 266.

who can't afford anything else."[109] Thorstein Veblen stressed this theme a century earlier in *The Theory of the Leisure Class* (1899). The leisure class, says Veblen, with its "pecuniary culture" is directed by a "narrowly self-regarding habit of mind" toward "individual expediency in a life looking to invidious success."[110] What happens when the wealthy live "increasingly separate lives" is described in the context of Cory Doctorow's *Walkaway* and Octavia Butler's *Parable of the Sower* in Chapter 7. In *Walkaway*, for example, the ultra-rich (called "zottas") are seen as trying to "secede from humanity." As one character reports, "They don't see their destiny as tied to ours."[111]

Economist Joseph Stiglitz warns, in *The Price of Inequality* (2012), "The more divided a society becomes in terms of wealth, the more reluctant the wealthy are to spend money on common needs."[112] "The rich don't need to rely on government for parks or education or medical care or personal security," declares Stiglitz. "They can buy all these things for themselves."[113] Though writers like economist Robert Frank assert that "the same roads are used by the rich as well as the poor,"[114] this is not always the case. As Frank subsequently remarks, deteriorating paved roads in some parts of the United States are giving way to "gravel or other rough surfaces as counties struggle with tight budgets."[115] Since it is not the rich who drive these deteriorating roads, this condition is broadly emblematic of the middle class's relative economic decline.

109 Sandel, *Justice*, 266.

110 Veblen, *The Theory of the Leisure Class*, 179.

111 Cory Doctorow, *Walkaway* (New York: Tom Doherty Associates, 2017), 66–67.

112 Joseph E. Stiglitz, *The Price of Inequality* (New York: W. W. Norton and Company, 2012), 117.

113 Stiglitz, *The Price of Inequality*, 117.

114 Robert H. Frank, *The Darwin Economy* (Princeton, NJ: Princeton University Press, 2011), 1.

115 Frank says, "Counties in Alabama and Pennsylvania have begun downgrading asphalt roads to cheaper chip-and-seal roads, also known as 'poor man's pavement.'" Frank, *The Darwin Economy*, 52; citing Lauren Etter, "Economic Crisis Forces Local Governments to Let Asphalt Roads Return to Gravel," *The Wall Street Journal* (July 17, 2010).

The state, says Aristotle (384–322 BCE), comprises "the very rich; the very poor; and the middle class which forms the mean."[116] Aristotle acknowledges the middle class as most capable of listening to reason and affirms that the best form of political society is one where "power is vested in the middle class." Aristotle notes further that good government is attainable only "in those states where there is a large middle class."[117] But in our own time, as Milanović observes, the middle class is being "hollowed out" and "the existence and function of the middle class is under attack by rising inequality."[118] So it is not simply the disparity between the rich and the poor—as a matter of luck or of distributive justice—but the practical inability without an economically vibrant middle class to retain an interdependent society.

"What has destroyed every previous civilization," warns political economist Henry George (1839–1897), "has been the tendency to the unequal distribution of wealth and power.[119] George viewed the progression of wealth inequality as leading ultimately to despotism. This "transformation of popular government into despotism of the vilest and most degrading kind," George warns, "must inevitably result from the unequal distribution of wealth."[120]

When Jesus made his enigmatic claim that "the poor will always be with you," he exposed a controversy that continues to this day.[121] Is economic inequality an inevitable dimension of the human condition or a critical problem with a practical (or utopian) solution? Left-leaning utopians More, Bellamy, Morris, Wells, and London, among others, address income (or wealth) inequality as a soluble problem. Perhaps the most explicit attempt to ensure equal incomes is Edward Bellamy's *Looking Backward* (1888) where everyone

116 Aristotle, *Politics*, trans. Ernest Barker (Oxford University Press, 1958), 4, 11, 1295b, § 4. On Hythloday's fourth voyage to *Utopia*, the "packet of books" he delivers to the Utopians includes "most of Plato's works and more of Aristotle's." More, *Utopia*, trans. Adams, bk. 2, 75. For a discussion of Aristotle's influence on More's *Utopia*, see Thomas I. White, "Aristotle and Utopia," *Renaissance Quarterly* 29, no. 4 (Winter, 1976): 635–675.

117 Aristotle, *Politics*, trans. Barker, 4, 11, 1295b, § 10.

118 Milanović, *Global Inequality*, 194.

119 Henry George, *Progress and Poverty* (New York: Robert Schalkenbach Foundation, 1953), 528.

120 George, *Progress and Poverty*, 533.

121 Matt. 26:12; Mark 14:7.

receives their equal share of "the annual product of the nation."[122] More recently Octavia Butler's *Parable of the Sower* and Cory Doctorow's *Walkaway* (discussed in Chapter 7) project the dismal outcome of unchecked income and wealth inequality.

In his *Agrarian Justice* (1797) Thomas Paine proclaims, "I care not how affluent some may be, provided that none be miserable in consequence of it."[123] When income and wealth inequality are seen as damaging to society, one class or faction of society, as noted, is benefiting at the expense of another. But economic inequality is frequently linked to prosperity as its nourishing ground. This connection was long-ago celebrated in Bernard Mandeville's *Fable of the Bees* (1714) where the machine of prosperity demands a "multitude of laborious poor"[124] and a pronounced disparity between rich and poor—both in material resources and in intellectual horizons. Regarding the laboring class, Mandeville—a champion of economic inequality—holds that while the poor "ought to be kept from starving, so they should receive nothing worth saving."[125] Emmanuel Goldstein in Orwell's *Nineteen Eight-Four* (1949) concurred: "In the long run, a hierarchical society was only possible on a basis of poverty and ignorance."[126] Like Orwell's proles (the "submerged masses"[127]) who are "without the power of grasping that the world could be other than it is,"[128] "great numbers" of the underclass, Mandeville affirms, "should be ignorant, as well as poor."[129]

In his moral teachings Adam Smith (1723–1790) touted what he called "the hardest of all the lessons of morality"—to act "with some sort of impartiality between ourselves and others."[130] Accordingly, Smith warned that "To

122 Edward Bellamy, *Looking Backward: 2000–1887* (New York: Penguin Books, 1982), 83.
123 Paine, *Agrarian Justice*, 482.
124 Bernard Mandeville, *The Fable of the Bees*, vol. 1 (Oxford: Clarendon Press, 1924; Reprint, Indianapolis: The Liberty Fund, 1988), 287.
125 Mandeville, *The Fable of the Bees*, 193.
126 Orwell, *Nineteen Eighty-Four*, 194.
127 Orwell, *Nineteen Eighty-Four*, 196.
128 Orwell, *Nineteen Eighty-Four*, 216.
129 Mandeville, *The Fable of the Bees*, 287–288.
130 Adam Smith, *The Theory of Moral Sentiments* (Indianapolis: Liberty Fund, 1976), 139.

hurt, in any degree, the interest of any one order of citizens, for no other purpose but to promote that of some other, is evidently contrary to that justice and equality of treatment which the sovereign owes to all the different orders of his subjects."[131] Smith's concern was not with the *fact* of economic inequality, but with government policies advancing the interests and opportunities of one order of citizens by impairing those of another. Whether this applies to situations where "it is the better placed who are being sacrificed and the worst placed who are being helped," as Thomas Nagel notes, is a pertinent question in the discussion of economic inequality.[132]

Smith's fear found expression in William Morris's *News From Nowhere* (1890), where the function of government before the civil war was protecting the rich from the poor.[133] Morris, specifying the object of this protection says, "society is divided into two classes, one of which is *privileged* to be kept by the labour of the other—that is, it forces the other to work for it and takes from this inferior class everything that it *can* take, and it uses the wealth so taken to keep its own members in a superior position, to make them beings of a higher order."[134] This condition was condemned in John Greene's *The Ke Whonkus People* (1890), where Professor Kumtux, the most knowledgeable Ke Whonkian citizen, explains that "special privileges to any class of people must certainly be a curse to any nation on earth or elsewhere."[135]

As the reader may have observed, utopians are inconsistent in describing their primary concern as either income *or* wealth inequality.[136] For the most part, they make no fine distinctions regarding the effects of income inequality on wealth inequality or the other way around, though these are obviously

131 Smith, *Wealth of Nations*, bk. 4, chap. 8, 436.

132 Thomas Nagel, "The Policy of Preference," in *Mortal Questions* (Cambridge University Press, 1979), 91–105, 103.

133 William Morris, "News from Nowhere," in *News from Nowhere and Other Writings* (New York: Penguin Books, 1993), 110.

134 William Morris, "Useful Work Versus Useless Toil," in *Political Writings of William Morris* (New York: International Publishers, 1973), 94 (italics in original).

135 John O. Greene, *The Ke Whonkus People: A Story of the North Pole Country* (Indianapolis, IN: Vincent Publishing Co., 1893), 234.

136 Wealth inequality, Scheidel suggests, is more difficult to measure than income inequality. Walter Scheidel, *The Great Leveler: Violence and the History of Inequality* (Princeton, NJ: Princeton University Press, 2017), 424.

interrelated. Henry George is an exception. George defines wealth in terms of the community—the common wealth. Accordingly, only items with exchange value that add to the common wealth, he believes, constitute wealth. Many things which in relation to a particular person are spoken of wealth are not, he says, because they benefit one person or class at the expense of another. His examples include (1) mortgages and bonds, since they embody an asset to one party and a liability to another; (2) slaves "whose value represents merely the power of one class to appropriate the earnings of another class;"[137] and (3) land (discussed in Chapter 4).[138] Wealth, says George, "consists of natural products that have been secured, moved, combined, separated, or in other ways modified by human exertion, so as to fit them for the gratification of human desires."[139]

Arguments Favoring Economic Inequality

> "The three richest people in the world possess more financial assets than all the people in the forty-eight poorest countries added together."[140]
>
> —Kim Stanley Robinson, *The Ministry for the Future* (2020)

The utopian discussion of economic inequality springs from the right as well as the left. "The belief that a good society can be built on the basis of inequality and private property," observes Sargent, "is certainly not uncommon."[141] Conrad Wilbrandt's *Mr. East's Experiences in Mr. Bellamy's World* and Ayn Rand's *Atlas Shrugged* are examples. These authors defend (or display) the advantages they perceive for economic inequality—individual freedom, incentives for technological progress, and competitive meritocracy.[142] In a pioneering exploration of right-wing utopias, Peter Fitting addressed a cluster of candidates including

137 George, *Progress and Poverty*, 40.
138 George, *Progress and Poverty*, 40.
139 George, *Progress and Poverty*, 41–42.
140 Robinson, *The Ministry for the Future*, 74.
141 Lyman Tower Sargent, "Capitalist Eutopias in America," in *America as Utopia*, ed. Kenneth M. Roemer (New York: Burt Franklin and Company, 1981), 201–202.
142 Piketty, *Capital and Ideology*, 712–713.

Ayn Rand's *Atlas Shrugged* that he notes challenged his conception of utopia.[143] Right-wing utopias are utopian to the class that desires to free itself from the burdens of those they seek to exclude from their ideal social order. Robert Nozick, for example, stipulates in *Anarchy, State and Utopia* that no one shall receive admittance to his utopias who will take more than they give.[144] Regarding those left behind—the poor—inequality advocates hype the trickledown benefits from the rich—such that "wealth is a blessing … for it will crowd out poverty as light dispels darkness."[145]

Characteristic of right-leaning utopians (Rand, Nozick) is a preference for freedom over equality. G. A. Cohen submits, "It is a familiar right-wing claim that freedom and equality are conflicting ideals … Most leftists," however, "reply either that there is no real conflict between equality and freedom … or that to the extent that there indeed is one, freedom should give way to equality."[146] Reconciling these claims, Cohen believes, requires acknowledging that "to have money is to have freedom,"[147] and its corollary: "poverty restricts freedom itself."[148]

In *Our Industrial Utopia and Its Unhappy Citizens* (1895), David Wheeler defends the economic status quo of industrialized capitalism. The progress resulting from inventions and the efficiencies stemming from modern industrial society achieve what he sees as a utopian ideal. It is not perfect, he asserts, but it is an ideal worth pursuing. "We are living in Utopia," Wheeler stresses, "the only Utopia there is or can be."[149] "And in

143 Peter Fitting, "Utopias Beyond Our Ideals: The Dilemma of Right-Wing Utopia," *Utopian Studies* 2, no. 1/2 (1991): 95–109.

144 Nozick, *Anarchy, State, and Utopia*, 301.

145 Conrad Wilbrandt, *Mr. East's Experiences in Mr. Bellamy's World*, trans. Mary J. Safford (New York: Harper and Brothers, 1891), 6. Piketty is skeptical of the trickledown argument: "If it were possible to wait until growth diffuses wealth, we would have seen the effects long ago: that argument falls flat." Thomas Piketty, *A Brief History of Equality*, trans. Steven Rendall (Cambridge, MA: The Belknap Press of Harvard University Press, 2022), 159.

146 G. A. Cohen, *Self-Ownership, Freedom, and Equality* (Cambridge: Cambridge University Press, 1995), 111.

147 Cohen, *Self-Ownership, Freedom, and Equality*, 58.

148 Cohen, *Self-Ownership, Freedom, and Equality*, 58n23.

149 David Hilton Wheeler, *Our Industrial Utopia and Its Unhappy Citizens* (Chicago: A. C. McClurg and Company, 1895), 10.

our Utopia," he insists, "this abundance is widely distributed among a people so fortunately free and enlightened that the old forms of inequality gradually disappear and only those remain which are ordained and maintained by nature and moral law."[150] This perspective, says Piketty, "often served as a cover for the country's inequalities and plutocratic excesses, especially in the period 1990–2020."[151] But every society, Piketty continues, "has no choice but to make sense of its inequalities, and the claim that inequality serves the common good is effective only if it has some degree of plausibility and some embodiment in durable institutions."[152]

Sociologist Émile Durkheim (1858–1917) suggests that "the development of man" may be conceived in two entirely different ways. Of these he asks: "Is it our duty to seek to become a thorough and complete human being, one quite sufficient unto oneself; or, on the contrary, to be only a part of a whole, the organ of an organism?"[153] Proponents of economic inequality advocate Durkheim's first alternative—people as individualized and self-sufficient—to stress their view that without economic inequality there would be little incentive for people to strive and achieve. As to Durkheim's second alternative Ayn Rand claims, "there is no such entity as 'society,' since society is only a number of individual men."[154] This view, as Claeys notes, is characteristic of traditional liberalism that "has often denigrated 'society,' or the existence of any common or public good."[155]

For right-leaning utopians like Rand, economic inequality is a function of unfettered freedom, free markets, and spontaneous order stemming from government non-interference. "The aim of interference," says Austrian economist F. A. Hayek, "is always to bring about a particular result which is different from that which would have been produced if the mechanism had

150 Wheeler, *Our Industrial Utopia and Its Unhappy Citizens*, 10. Inequality "ordained and maintained by nature and moral law" is a reference to social Darwinism, discussed in Chapter 4.

151 Piketty, *Capital and Ideology*, 153.

152 Piketty, *Capital and Ideology*, 411.

153 Durkheim, *The Division of Labor in Society*, 53.

154 Ayn Rand, *The Virtue of Selfishness* (New York: Signet Books, 1964), 14–15.

155 Claeys, *Searching for Utopia*, 10.

been allowed unaided to follow its inherent principles."[156] Such a system, Rand asserts, is a "free, productive, rational system ... which is, obviously, laissez-faire capitalism."[157] Anthropologist/economist Karl Polanyi is critical, however, of what he calls "the utopian principle of a self-regulating market" since, he affirms: "There was nothing natural about laissez-faire; free markets could never have come into being merely by allowing things to take their course ... [as] laissez-faire itself was enforced by the state."[158]

A Smudged Blueprint

> "Any discourse ought to be constructed like a living creature, with its own body, as it were; it must not lack either head or feet; it must have a middle and extremities so composed as to suit each other and the whole work."[159]
>
> —Plato (429?–347 BCE), *Phaedrus*

Utopias, says Goodwin, "are often written, like allegories, to influence people's way of thinking, and do not always demand the implementation of the utopian blueprint *in toto*." While utopias may "contribute to the formation of a climate of opinion," she admits, "there is, obviously, a general problem about detecting, tracing or quantifying the impact of utopian ideas."[160] Utopian arguments for moderating, minimizing, or eliminating economic inequality and for eradicating poverty rest on the idea of society as more than a throng of individuals; the individual is seen as a part of a whole. A city-state emerges, observes Socrates, because

156 Friedrich A. Hayek, *Law, Legislation and Liberty*, vol. 2 (Chicago: University of Chicago Press, 1979), 129.

157 Ayn Rand, *The Romantic Manifesto* (New York: Signet Books, 1971), 157 (italics in original).

158 Karl Polanyi, *The Great Transformation: The Political and Economic Origins of Our Time* (Boston: Beacon Press, 1944), 145, 157.

159 Plato, *Phaedrus*, trans. R. Hackforth in *Plato: The Collected Dialogues*, ed. Edith Hamilton and Huntington Cairns (New York: Pantheon Books, 1961), 510, (364c).

160 Goodwin, "Economic and Social Innovation in Utopia," 69 (italics in original).

none of us is self-sufficient.[161] Conceiving society as a unit, system, or organism for benefiting all of its members sparks the desire to ameliorate the extremes of economic inequality and ensure that everyone's dignity is preserved—but not mere dignity, argues Nussbaum: "it is the *equal dignity* of human beings that demands recognition."[162] Economic inequality sets arbitrary limits on whose contributions will benefit society, thereby squandering talent, limiting opportunities, and stifling competition—capriciously restricting the pool of competitors—by class or gender or race or religious belief. It also discounts the cumulative benefits of past generations' knowledge and experience—the "standing on the shoulders" of others who came before—and promotes the perceived individualization of success—the "self-made man" illusion inherent in what Sandel calls the "meritocratic faith."[163] "How did you come to be possessors of this knowledge and this machinery, which represents nine parts to one contributed by yourself in the value of your product?" asks Bellamy's Dr. Leete. "You inherited it, did you not?"[164] Speaking of the wealthy whose fortunes are largely a function of "vast current and past public investments in infrastructure, education, and institutions," Robert Frank argues that "no matter how talented and industrious they are, they wouldn't have had any significant wealth ... if they'd grown up in a country like Nepal or Somalia."[165]

Modern utopias, affirms Elizabeth Hansot, are "rooted in the inadequacies of a particular historical situation which they are designed to overcome."[166] Utopians who diagnose problems of income and wealth inequality

161 Plato, *Republic*, trans. Benjamin Jowett (New York: Vintage Classics a division of Random House), bk. 2, 369b, 60.

162 Nussbaum, *Frontiers of Justice*, 292 (italics in original). Kateb argues that human dignity has two components, (1) "all individuals are equal," and (2) "no other species is equal to humans." George Kateb, *Human Dignity* (Cambridge, MA: The Belknap Press of Harvard University Press, 2011), 6.

163 "Much of the appeal of the meritocratic faith consists in the idea that our success is our own doing." Michael J. Sandel, *The Tyranny of Merit: What's Become of the Common Good*? (New York: Farrar, Straus and Giroux, 2020), 123.

164 Bellamy, *Looking Backward: 2000–1887*, 112.

165 Frank, *The Darwin Economy*, 120–121

166 Hansot, *Perfection and Progress*, 110.

propose solutions reflecting diverse views of justice, morality, and human nature—however flawed.[167] "The utopian mode," says J. C. Davis, "is one which accepts deficiencies in men and nature and strives to contain and condition them through organizational controls and sanctions."[168]

The next three chapters explore organizational controls and sanctions—instruments of change—such as universal basic income and compulsory education, often recommended in clusters. Topics addressed are economic (Chapter 2), social (Chapter 3), and political (Chapter 4) reforms—though most topics overlap categories. Each chapter presents subjects with an assortment of advocates earlier and leaves those with only a smattering of backers until the end. Within each topic authors appear chronologically to expose an idea's historical progression. Chapter 5 addresses utopias, such as *Caesar's Column*, that view violence or revolution as the only means for defeating economic inequality. Chapter 6 describes utopias including More's and Bellamy's featuring (peaceful) economic leveling. Chapter 7 presents the mostly dystopic alternative economic futures on display in the writings of H. G. Wells, Kurt Vonnegut Jr, Kim Stanley Robinson, Octavia Butler, and Cory Doctorow.

Barbara Goodwin observes, "If we take the individual proposals made by utopians, particularly those of the nineteenth century, we find that many of them have been partially implemented." Most Western societies, she continues, "have progressive taxation, minimum wages, social security provisions and other welfare services; such policies are intended to reduce inequalities."[169] Additional innovations utopians advocate to combat the

167 On flawed conceptions of human nature, Pfaelzer notes, for example, that utopian authors including Bellamy, Howells, Donnelly, and Bradford Peck "describe working people with either fear, pity, or contempt. This paternalism," she says, "creeps into their utopian structures in various forms: an aristocracy of experts, a fear of social or economic equality, and the maintenance of an intellectual elite." Jean Pfaelzer, "The Impact of Political Theory on Narrative Structures," in *America as Utopia*, ed. Kenneth M. Roemer (New York: Burt Franklin and Company, 1981), 126.

168 J. C. Davis, *Utopia and the Ideal Society: A Study of English Utopian Writing 1516–1700* (Cambridge University Press, 1981), 370.

169 Goodwin, "Economic and Social Innovation in Utopia," 76. Taylor reports that "between 1888 and 1900 there appeared altogether over sixty Utopias ... which deal specifically with the abuse and possible reform of society." Walter Fuller

extremes of economic inequality include, in Chapter 2, alternate allocations of surplus labor including allocations to the general welfare, public ownership of essential businesses, workers' cooperatives and associations, and labor exchanges, as well as universal basic income, debt and interest relief, other non-progressive wealth taxes, curtailing business cycles, capping wealth or income, and cryptocurrency; in Chapter 3, free universal compulsory education, labor unions, gender equality in the workplace, dignity of work—revaluing work in relation to society, expunging racism, motherhood as a paying job, and public housing; in Chapter 4, public transparency (economic and political), property and the land question, population control, eugenics and marriage restrictions, equalizing opportunity, equalizing the physical environment for health and beauty, eliminating unemployment, reimagining marriage and divorce, patents as monopolies, labor conscription, the expanding universe of universal suffrage, universal healthcare, restricting immigration, liquor as a cause of poverty, and ending war to end poverty. These instruments of change reflect Marcel Proust's (1871–1922) spirit when he wrote, "Like a kaleidoscope which is every now and then given a turn, society arranges successively in different orders elements which one would have supposed to be immovable, and composes a fresh pattern."[170] The chapters that follow provide utopian illustrations of these instruments of change—stressing fresh patterns of elements and their anticipated connection to reducing income and wealth inequality.

Taylor, *The Economic Novel in America* (Chapel Hill, NC: The University of North Carolina Press, 1942), 206.

170 Marcel Proust, *Remembrance of Things Past*, vol. 1 "Within a Budding Grove," trans. C. K. Scott Moncrieff and Terrence Kilmartin (New York: Vintage Books, 1981), 556.

CHAPTER 2

Instruments of Change: Economic Reforms

> "Romances of the future, however fantastic they may be, have for most of us a perennial if mild interest, since they are born of a very common feeling—a sense of dissatisfaction with the existing order of things, combined with a vague faith in or hope of a better one to come."[1]
>
> —W. H. Hudson, *A Crystal Age* (1887)

Utopia, Tom Moylan argues, is "foremost a process" and cannot be "reduced to its *content*."[2] "There can be no *Utopia*," the same author suggests, but there can be utopian explorations that "shatter" society's present achievements and "point to that which is not yet experienced in the human project of fulfillment and creation."[3] Ruth Levitas views utopian thought as a method for exploring potential frontiers of human flourishing entailing "holistic thinking about the connections between economic, social, existential and ecological processes in an integrated way."[4] Utopias as practical political philosophy, explains Peter Stillman, "investigate, compare, and analyze ends, means, and existing conditions in order to encourage and enhance judicious and effective human activity."[5] Though *utopian* often serves as a term of derision, there can be nothing wrong with utopias when their purpose is to explore alternatives

1 W. H. Hudson, "Preface," in *A Crystal Age* (New York: E. P. Dutton and Company, 1917) [1887], v.

2 Moylan, *Demand the Impossible*, 38 (italics in original).

3 Moylan, *Demand the Impossible*, 27.

4 Ruth Levitas, *Utopia as Method: The Imaginary Reconstruction of Society* (New York: Palgrave Macmillan, 2013), xi, 18–19.

5 Peter G. Stillman, "'Nothing is, but what is not': Utopias as Practical Political Philosophy," in *The Philosophy of Utopia*, ed. Barbara Goodwin, 9–24 (London: Routledge, Taylor and Francis Group, 2001), 20.

to conditions—like extreme income or wealth inequality—that threaten the functioning of society. Societies will continue to evolve and change; regarding the direction of this change, B. F. Skinner asks, "Are we to be controlled by accident, by tyrants, or by ourselves in effective cultural design?"[6]

The instruments of change displayed in this chapter are labeled *economic* though they certainly promote changes to the social order (Chapter 3) and may require political action (Chapter 4). The economic reforms described here are aimed at reducing economic inequality by altering the financial incentives to which people respond.

Alternate Allocations of Surplus Labor

> "Once capitalism had died, and markets were freed from private ownership, a different kind of value took over. Instead of judging something's worth by its exchange value—what it would fetch in return for something else—the Other Now judged worth according to experiential value—the benefit the thing brought to the person who used it."[7]
>
> —Yanis Varoufakis, *Another Now* (2021)

"The rich have grown in number and wealth and are drawing everything into their hands, while the poor, growing more intelligent and better educated, realize more and more that they do not receive the full reward of their labors."[8] This was Samuel Balcom's assessment in Albert Chavannes's *The Future Commonwealth or What Samuel Balcom Saw in Socioland* (1892). What portion of a person's labor belongs to that person? This is a central issue for understanding income inequality, as the extent to which society permits one person to appropriate the value of another's labor is an essential variable. But even the phrase "belongs to that person"

6 B. F. Skinner, *Cumulative Record*, 3rd ed. (New York: Appleton-Century-Crofts, 1959), 11.

7 Yanis Varoufakis, *Another Now* (Brooklyn: Melville House, 2021), 150.

8 Chavannes, *The Future Commonwealth*, 11–12.

requires qualification. Does it belong to that person in an individual capacity? (Locke, Nozick)? Or does it belong to that person as a member of society? (More, Bellamy).[9]

Karl Marx contends that under capitalism surplus labor is the extra time a worker "must add to the working-time necessary for his own maintenance ... in order to produce the means of subsistence for the owners of the means of production."[10] Surplus labor is thus the work performed that extends beyond the worker's subsistence; it is labor that produces value for the capitalist but for which the worker is uncompensated (at least directly[11]). Labor that produces a surplus is what Marx calls "productive labor."[12] When the owners of capital appropriate this surplus, it means the worker's share of the revenue is fixed but the capitalist's share is variable—a driver of economic inequality. "Economically speaking," says

9 The question of not receiving the full value of one's labor is raised in a parallel issue by those who argue that taxation of labor is or "is on a par with forced labor," Nozick, *Anarchy, State, and Utopia*, 169, as well as those like Tolstoy who view taxation as "theft." Count Lev N. Tolstoy, *What Shall We Do Then*?, ed. and trans. Leo Wiener (Boston: Dana Estes and Company, 1904), 156. Taxation's relation to economic inequality is discussed later in this chapter.

10 Karl Marx, *Capital: A Critical Analysis of Capitalist Production*, vol. 1, trans. Samuel Moore and Edward Aveling (Ware, Hertfordshire: Wordsworth Editions Limited, 2013), vol. 1, part 3, chap. 10, sec. 3, 163. In Rosewater's *Utopia*, we read that "In its very origin CAPITAL IS A SURPLUS PRODUCT *representing an excess of labor sold by the capitalist, as compared with the poverty of the working classes which represent a deficiency in the sale or preservation of their property in labor*." Frank Rosewater, *Utopia: A Romance of Today Presenting A Solution of the Labor Problem, A New God and A New Religion* (London: F. Tennyson Neely Publisher, 1987), 125–126 (emphasis capitalization and italics in original).

11 Indirect benefits of labor (employment) are described in the section on eliminating unemployment in Chapter 4.

12 Karl Marx, *Theories of Surplus Value*, part 1 (London: Lawrence and Wishart, 1969), 152. Marx argues that the "workman's labour-time resolves itself into two parts: one for which he has received an equivalent, his wages, from the capitalist; the other which he gives to [the capitalist] gratis and which constitutes the *profit*" (81) (italics in original).

Kurt Heinzelman, "the commodity made by the laborer replaces *him*; *its* money value is greater than his."[13]

The workers in William Morris's *News from Nowhere* present one extreme on a continuum of surplus labor; they are not required to add *any* extra time to "the working time necessary" for their own maintenance. "A state is surplus-free," says Julius Sensat, "if in that state everyone ... gets back ... the amount of labor he contributes."[14] Slave labor occupies the other extreme on this continuum where the lion's share of a slave's working time *is* "extra time" that extends beyond the time necessary for the slave's own meager livelihood.[15] The slaves in More's *Utopia* thus (presumably) work more than the required six-hour day. In *Black Marxism* (1983), historian Cedric Robinson ties capitalism's early exploitation of surplus labor to slave labor noting, "historically, slavery was a critical foundation for capitalism."[16] For Robinson, slavery is a source of Marx's "primitive accumulation"—capital acquired outside the capitalist framework—furnishing the tinder of capitalism.[17]

In a discussion of exploitation in *An Economics of Utopia*, Simon Zadak argues that from More's *Utopia*, to Orwell's *1984*, to Piercy's *Woman on the Edge of Time*, utopia as a literary genre "has one central preoccupation, how one group oppresses another, and visions of how that might not be so."[18] Utopians have largely rejected the capitalist's free-market solution

13 Kurt Heinzelman, *The Economics of the Imagination* (Amherst: The University of Massachusetts Press, 1980), 183 (italics in original).

14 Julius Sensat, "Exploitation," *Noûs* 18, no. 1 (1984): 21–38, 24.

15 Du Bois reports the cost to maintain a slave in the American south was about $19 a year ($19 in 1850 is equivalent to $747 in 2023). Du Bois, *Black Reconstruction in America*, 9.

16 Cedric J. Robinson, *Black Marxism* (Chapel Hill: The University of North Carolina Press, 1983), 116.

17 Robinson, *Black Marxism,* 121–122. Since slaves may be acquired by purchase (exchange) within a capitalist system or acquired by force outside a capitalist framework, Marx's term "primitive accumulation" applies to the slaves acquired by force who formed the foundation of capitalist accumulation. This, as Marx notes, avoids circularity by positing "an accumulation not the result of the capitalistic mode of production, but its starting point." Marx, *Capital*, vol. 1, part 7, chap. 26, 501.

18 Simon Zadek, *An Economics of Utopia* (Brookfield, VT: Ashgate Publishing Company, 2007), 152–153.

of maximizing profits for the owners of capital—and its wearying defense of trickledown benefits—as a divisive and morally defective system.[19] This system, says Karl Polanyi, "has been the outcome of a conscious and often violent intervention on the part of government which imposed the market organization on society for noneconomic ends."[20] This structure, some believe, guarantees an asymmetry permitting the owner of capital to expand his portion of the surplus by squeezing out an unconscionable measure of the workers' share with what Marx calls the "lynx eye of Capital."[21]

Figure 1: "Industry, female workers, factory, Birmingham, wood engraving, 1851."

Utopians have evolved alternate methods for appropriating surplus labor based on diverse understandings of the problem. Suggested replacements for capitalism discussed in the following sections include allocating surplus labor to the general welfare, public ownership of essential businesses, workers' cooperatives, and labor exchanges.

19 With a few exceptions. See Fitting, "Utopias Beyond Our Ideals: The Dilemma of Right-Wing Utopia;" Alan Clardy, "Galt's Gulch: Ayn Rand's Utopian Delusion," *Utopian Studies* 23, no. 1 (2012): 238–262; Sargent, "Capitalist Eutopias in America."

20 Polanyi, *The Great Transformation*, 258.

21 Marx, *Capital,* vol. 1, part 3, chap. 10, sec. 6, 198.

Allocating Surplus Labor to the General Welfare

"Oh yes," said the Altrurian. "At one time, just before we emerged from the competitive conditions, there was much serious question whether capital should not own labor, instead of labor owning capital."[22]

—William Dean Howells, *A Traveler from Altruria* (1894)

In socialist (or communist) utopias, like those of More and Bellamy, the work of the laboring citizens supplies not only their own needs but generates a surplus allocated to the general welfare. In More's *Utopia* this surplus supports ambassadors, governors, scholars, priests, and magistrates ("syphogrants"); in Bellamy's *Looking Backward* it funds residents of either gender if under 21 or over 45, and women raising families. Goodwin explains that in moneyless utopias, including those of More and Bellamy, where pecuniary taxation is not an option for endowing the general welfare, "'tax' in essence"—what Goodwin calls *pre-taxation*—"consists of labour above and beyond that needed for self-subsistence."[23]

Marx's concern with surplus labor was in the context of capitalism's "boundless thirst" for production.[24] But, Marx affirms, "Capital has not invented surplus labor," which, in a capitalist economy, as noted, each worker, "must add to the working-time necessary for his own maintenance ... in order to produce the means of subsistence for the owners of the means of production."[25] But it is clear, he says, in any "economic formation of society, where not the exchange value but the use-value of the product predominates, surplus-labour will be limited by a given set of wants ... and ... no boundless thirst for surplus labour arises from the nature of production itself."[26] This is the case in More's Utopia—as well of those of Bellamy,

22 Howells, *A Traveler from Altruria*, 152.

23 Barbara Goodwin, "Taxation in Utopia," *Utopian Studies* 19, no. 2 (2008): 313–331, 317–318. In another work I refer to this system as *constructive taxation*, constructive in the sense of "construed." See *Taxation in Utopia: Required Sacrifice and the General Welfare* (Albany, NY: SUNY Press, 2020), 34–37.

24 Marx, *Capital*, vol. 1, part 3, chap. 10, sec. 2, 163.

25 Marx, *Capital*, vol. 1, part 3, chap. 10, sec. 2, 163.

26 Marx, *Capital*, vol. 1, part 3, chap. 10, sec. 2, 163.

Morris, Skinner, and others—where surplus labor is self-limiting since "the use-value of the product predominates," and the set of wants is limited.[27] In Cabet's *A Voyage to Icaria*, for example, since Icarians are "associates and equals," explains Dinaros the spokesperson, "they all must practice a trade and work for the same number of hours." The Icarian's solution for the allocation of surplus labor means that all "work instruments and materials are provided through shared capital, and all agricultural and industrial products are deposited in public warehouses."[28] Glen Nagely and J. Max Patrick describe *Icaria* as "one of the most comprehensive communist utopias ever written."[29]

Utopia: A Romance of Today

In what Kenneth Roemer calls "a confusing fantasy,"[30] Frank Rosewater's *Utopia: A Romance of Today* (1897) offers a nuanced parsing of surplus labor—what Rosewater calls the "co-operative gain." Rosewater, a social reformer, describes a failing dystopia and a budding eutopia and their contentious economic standoff.[31] The protagonists—Ross Allison and Dr. Giniwig—traveling by balloon from Paris, make an impromptu landing in Lukka, Africa. They learn that in the dystopian capitalist society of Tsor (the eastern capital of Lukka),

27 Marx, *Capital,* vol. 1, part 3, chap. 10, sec. 2, 163. The *use-value* of a product for Marx expresses a relation between the consumer and what is consumed and contrasts with its *labor-value* or its *market-value* in a capitalist economy.

28 Cabet, *Travels in Icaria*, 31–32.

29 Glenn Negley and J. Max Partick, *The Quest for Utopia* (New York: Henry Schuman, 1952; Reprint, Garden City, New York: Anchor Books, Doubleday and Company, 1962), 288.

30 Kenneth M. Roemer, *The Obsolete Necessity: America in Utopian Writings, 1888–1900* (Kent, Ohio: The Kent State University Press, 1976), 197. Bleiler says the story "is almost unintelligible." Everett F. Bleiler, *Science Fiction: The Early Years* (Kent, Ohio: The Kent State University Press, 1990), §1856, 640.

31 Tsmoul (the western capital of Lukka) asserts that its debts to Tsor (the eastern capital of Lukka) should be paid in labor or goods while Tsor believes these debts should be paid in money. Rosewater, *Utopia: A Romance of Today*, 49.

> Employment is a loan disguised
> In which the worker
> Borrows shop and tools from the rich
> And as price of the loan
> Surrenders all he earns
> Above the wages agreed?
> The price of that loan is theft—
> For employment is due
> And should neither be sold
> Nor denied."[32]

More explicitly, Zuzo, one of the leaders of the laboring class explains that the laborer, who is the borrower,

> must wait on the lender [employer] for the privilege of selling his service. The lender, however, only grants this privilege for a consideration and lives from the proceeds [surplus labor]. ... Meanwhile the total service the combined capitalists will buy ... is no more than what the workmen require for their transient needs.[33]

By contrast, in Rosewater's eutopian society of Tsmoul (the western capital of Lukka), the spokesperson (Minister Aggra) notes, production "*being a co-operative process, the co-operative gain of the worker is not at once placed in his hand.* Only his own strictly private and personal gain goes directly to him."[34] The "cooperative gain"—effectively the surplus labor—is placed in the hands of society rather than in the hands of either the worker or the capitalist (as in Tsor). In contrast to the capitalist allocation of surplus labor to profits, funding the general welfare with a portion of the workers' labor benefits the worker indirectly—supporting "the perpetuation of houses, factories and publicly held private properties."[35] The surplus labor (cooperative gain) is thus delegated to society, explains the minister, as the individual worker cannot be trusted as a "custodian of the future;"[36] such trusteeship "experience has demonstrated ... is liable to gross abuse."[37]

32 Rosewater, *Utopia: A Romance of Today*, 171.
33 Rosewater, *Utopia: A Romance of Today*, 178.
34 Rosewater, *Utopia: A Romance of Today*, 159 (italics in original).
35 Rosewater, *Utopia: A Romance of Today*, 159.
36 Rosewater, *Utopia: A Romance of Today*, 159.
37 Rosewater, *Utopia: A Romance of Today*, 159.

The Richest Man on Earth

The Richest Man on Earth (1931) presents an enhancement to Rosewater's concept of "cooperative gain"[38] or surplus labor through what author Test Dalton calls "cooperative competition,"[39] based on the economic theory of "competition in producing for use instead of for profit."[40] This is the distinction Marx drew, noted earlier, "where not the exchange value but the use-value of the product predominates."[41] The book's publisher Lowe Shearon, propounds this theory through his appearance as the character T. Square in the novel.[42] "The fiction in this book," says Shearon, "was written by Test Dalton. I supplied most of the facts."[43] The narrator Wendell Thomas is a playwright and newspaper journalist who is assigned by his employer to track down reports of recent gold discoveries on the west coast of Africa. On his journey to the site of the rumored discoveries Thomas learns of the "richest man on earth" who he discovers is an old acquaintance from New York, the actor Maitland Delafield. Before his mysterious disappearance Delafield appeared in one of Thomas's plays. In Africa, Delafield has taken the name John Napier. Napier is a convert to the economic theory of T. Square (Lowe Shearon) and has applied its utopian principles to the new Plateau Republic he founded in Africa. Napier tells Thomas, "T. Square's theory was thoroughly implanted in my mind when I came out to the West Coast of Africa."[44] The cooperative competition that results from the theory ensures there is no exploitation,

38 Rosewater, *Utopia: A Romance of Today*, 159.

39 Test Dalton, *The Richest Man on Earth* (New York: Lowe Shearon, 1931), 91.

40 Dalton, *The Richest Man on Earth*, 91.

41 Marx, *Capital*, vol. 1, part 3, chap. 10, sec. 2, 163.

42 Dalton, *The Richest Man on Earth*, 58. In a handwritten margin note in a copy of the novel annotated by the publisher, Shearon has written, "This is merely a name used by Test Dalton. It refers to myself. L.S" (58). Copy available at Arthur O. Lewis Society for Utopian Studies Papers, Rare Books and Manuscripts, Special Collections Library, Pennsylvania State University.

43 A handwritten margin note in a copy of the novel annotated by the publisher (5). Copy available at Arthur O. Lewis Society for Utopian Studies Papers, Rare Books and Manuscripts, Special Collections Library, Pennsylvania State University.

44 Dalton, *The Richest Man on Earth*, 100.

speculation, or performance bonuses for executives, and so promotes economic equality.

When Napier originally relocated to Africa from New York he purchased a small tract of land that he subsequently discovered contained diamonds within its borders.[45] With the proceeds from the sale of these diamonds in the European markets, Napier reports, he purchased a thousand square miles of land (the size of Rhode Island). He then acquired modern mining equipment and hired "the finest experts in mineralogy," to whom he paid "large sums for their services and their secrecy."[46] With his newfound wealth Napier financed building projects comprising cement roads and other infrastructure as well as houses and factories. "One-half of the inhabitants of the Plateau Republic are steadily engaged in building operations."[47] "The building of houses and roads," Napier tells the journalist, "is the most important work in the world."[48]

In Napier's Plateau Republic, "a single standard for the distribution of wealth is observed [and] there is enough for all always and too much for none ever."[49] Underlying the remarkable success of Napier's republic is its adherence to T. Square's economic theory of cooperative competition. As Napier explains to Thomas the reporter, "In every other country in the world there is poverty and unemployment solely because of unlimited profits and an unfair double standard for the distribution of wealth."[50] Poverty is thus a crime, says Napier, "just as murder is a crime—crimes by those responsible for them—not by those who suffer from them."[51] Of all the elements that combine to produce a company's profit, it is only the proprietor's share that is not determined and disclosed in advance. The proprietor's profit is a wild

45 Dalton, *The Richest Man on Earth*, 100.
46 Dalton, *The Richest Man on Earth*, 100.
47 Dalton, *The Richest Man on Earth*, 112.
48 Dalton, *The Richest Man on Earth*, 111.
49 Dalton, *The Richest Man on Earth*, 145.
50 Dalton, *The Richest Man on Earth*, 223. T. Square's theory provides that "wages, determined by advance agreement, and unlimited profits [for the owners] constitute an unfair double standard for the distribution of wealth that is economically unsound" (5).
51 Dalton, *The Richest Man on Earth*, 69.

card while all the other factors, including labor, materials, and financing are negotiated in advance.[52] Rectifying this unfair competition, Napier argues, requires the managers (CEOs, CFOs and other executives) of industrial enterprises to "state in advance a rate of compensation with which they will content themselves."[53] This is what rank and file employees do who agree to a wage before engaging in their work. Once all the elements of the enterprise have stipulated their stake in advance, declares Napier, "All surplus earnings should be prorated among the consumers."[54] At the end of the year the surplus above the proprietor's required return—the "unearned increment"—is prorated and paid back to the consumers on the basis of the amount of their purchases using coupons issued at the time of purchase.[55] For wholesale merchants prices are reduced on orders for the next season. This share-the-profits scheme stimulates the economy (more people have more money), reduces unemployment, and acts as a buffer against economic inequality. According to Napier it is the best method for distributing wealth fairly among all the elements who produced it.[56]

Public Ownership of Essential Businesses

> "If you own the things men must have, you own the men who must have them."[57]
>
> —Edward Bellamy, *Equality* (1897)

"If you sit down quietly by yourself," submits H. G. Wells (a socialist), "and try and imagine things being 'owned by all and controlled by all for the good of all,' you will presently arrive at the valuable discovery in social

52 Dalton deflects the neoliberal argument that the owner of capital is the risk taker and so entitled to the maximum profit. Dalton, *The Richest Man on Earth*, 69–70.

53 Dalton, *The Richest Man on Earth*, 88.

54 Dalton, *The Richest Man on Earth*, 88–89.

55 Dalton, *The Richest Man on Earth*, 150.

56 Dalton, *The Richest Man on Earth*, 165.

57 Bellamy, *Equality*, 82.

and political science that the phrase means nothing whatever."[58] Kenneth Roemer reports that only 20 percent of a sample of 160 utopists he surveyed, "even recommended socialism." More than 50 percent, he says, "envisioned combinations of business cooperation and governmental regulation."[59] This aligns with Keynes's view that "many big undertakings, particularly Public Utility enterprises and other business requiring a large fixed capital, still need to be semi-socialised."[60] A common definition of socialism holds that the state owns the means of production. But the means of production of what?—Certainly not war! Utopians discussed in this section recommend a range of alternatives while leaving the mass of businesses in private hands. Their proposals envision what Goodwin calls "improved capitalism" requiring "better control of industry (possibly via government takeover of key or of the most profitable industries)."[61]

The Future Commonwealth

In *The Future Commonwealth* (1892), declare Negley and Partick, Albert Chavannes "clearly considered economic adjustment to be the panacea for all social ills."[62] Chavannes, a philosopher and sociologist, describes a social order in 1950—Socioland, Africa—resting on principles looking to minimize the type of economic inequalities appearing in the United States at the end of the nineteenth century. The question the novel poses is that of what organizational steps will both eliminate poverty and truncate the accumulation of vast personal fortunes without scotching personal incentive? The novel is framed as a memoir that visitor Samuel

58 H. G. Wells, *Mankind in the Making* (New York: Charles Scribner's Sons, 1904), 373–374. In the Appendix Wells describes diverse forms of Socialism and indicates to which brand he adheres. 372–373.

59 Kenneth M. Roemer, "Contexts and Texts: The Influence of Looking Backward," *The Centennial Review* 27, no. 3 (Summer, 1983): 204–223, 215.

60 John Maynard Keynes, *The End of Laissez-Faire* (N.p.: BN Publishing, n.d. [1926]), 39.

61 Goodwin, "Economic and Social Innovation in Utopia," 73–74.

62 Negley and Partick, *The Quest for Utopia*, 138.

Balcom has written for a friend, recounting his conversations with a series of Socioland residents. As Mr. Walter, Chavannes's spokesperson contends, immense fortunes, "are not the result of individual economy or persistent labor; they are the result of the cumulative power of capital."[63] Private wealth, he continues, "is the result of social causes which encourage and reward the cumulative power of capital."[64]

The challenge Socioland faced was to limit excessive private wealth without at the same time limiting the advantages of capital's cumulative power by, for example, direct redistribution to the poor. "We cannot despoil the rich for the benefit of the poor," affirms Mr. Walter, "for it would destroy the accumulation of capital and diminish production." Furthermore, he claims that redistributing capital to "untrained and incompetent persons" would lead to its squandering and "the impoverishment of the whole country" without at the same time improving the condition of the poor.[65] For these reasons Socioland has ruled out taxation as both unjust and unnecessary.[66]

Rather than taxes, the commonwealth operates the "most extensive and profitable" businesses, "with the avowed object of making money to be spent for the good of the whole people."[67] These businesses require extensive capital, while their size and profitability mean large profits for the owners.[68] The commonwealth, according to Mr. Walter, by operating these businesses "earns money by legitimate means, and spends it for the benefit of all."[69] All governments, advises the spokesperson, are "somewhat socialists, some a little more, others a little less. We are a little more, and have entrusted the Commonwealth with the accumulation and use of a portion of our capital for the benefit of our people."[70] As a result, confirms Mr. Walter, the society is now rich and has placed all its citizens "above

63 Chavannes, *The Future Commonwealth*, 28.
64 Chavannes, *The Future Commonwealth*, 12.
65 Chavannes, *The Future Commonwealth*, 12.
66 Chavannes, *The Future Commonwealth*, 26–27.
67 Chavannes, *The Future Commonwealth*, 28.
68 Chavannes, *The Future Commonwealth*, 28.
69 Chavannes, *The Future Commonwealth*, 26.
70 Chavannes, *The Future Commonwealth*, 13–14.

want."[71] Such a system, he continues, "brings all classes together and equalizes their chances."[72] Thus, Socioland features a mixed economy with essential services carried on for public profit while retail and other business establishments are privately owned.

Among the nationalized businesses are delivery services ("letters, parcels, merchandise and persons"), utilities, the banks and life and casualty insurance companies, as well as mines and "a portion of the manufactures."[73] These are establishments that when left in private hands create the private wealth that exacerbates society's economic inequality. By placing these businesses in the public sphere, the wealth that formerly accrued to a few individuals now accumulates for the use of the state and its citizens. Socioland's more general distribution of wealth means that "great accumulations of property are not possible, and poverty is practically unknown."[74]

From the Earth's Center

The importance of "industries of a public nature" for controlling the excesses of economic inequality receives a new twist in S. Byron Welcome's *From the Earth's Center* (1895). For these industries, including "railroads, telegraph lines, the express and postal service, [and] public schools,"[75] explains Mr. Larkin to the traveler Mr. Spencer, Centralia (the Earth's Center) has designated the government as regulator-auctioneer rather than owner-operator. Kenneth Roemer says Welcome envisioned a utopia "in which everything including schools and hospitals was regulated by fierce competition."[76]

The Centralians have identified monopolies as a primary cause of extreme economic inequality because monopolies eliminate competition.

71 Chavannes, *The Future Commonwealth*, 32.
72 Chavannes, *The Future Commonwealth*, 32.
73 Chavannes, *The Future Commonwealth*, 29.
74 Chavannes, *The Future Commonwealth*, 48.
75 S. Byron Welcome, *From the Earth's Center: A Polar Gateway Message* (Chicago: Charles H. Kerr and Company, 1895), 89.
76 Roemer, *The Obsolete Necessity*, 91.

They believe that competition keeps the economic system in check, curtailing huge accretions of personal wealth. The public functions which, if left to individuals, would result in monopolies are, in Centralia, "assumed by the public and let at auction once a year to the competitor who offers to serve us on the best terms."[77] In this way "private individuals have taken the place of public officials."[78] Thus, while private corporations operate the essential businesses, a powerful financial incentive compels their effective operation for the benefit of the public.

A similar system is applied in the Plateau Republic in Test Dalton's *The Richest Man on Earth* (1931) where Napier, the richest man on earth, explains, "the republic itself will never be the operator of a mine or a water power supply, but it will let such privileges to the persons or concerns that contract to operate them to the best advantage of the public."[79]

A Modern Utopia

H. G. Wells, affirms John Partington, "was a prolific writer, an educator, and a world statesman; he was a socialist and a cosmopolitan."[80] Largely self-educated, Wells was the son of a shopkeeper and studied biology under T. H. Huxley where he "learned to regard mankind not as the spoiled daring of God," reports Jack Williamson, "but as only another endangered species, threatened by the evolution of its own brain."[81] Wells's utopian planet in *A Modern Utopia* (1905) is identical to our earth in geography and population but more direct in unifying the interests of its citizens, both present and future. The World State owns and controls

77 Welcome, *From the Earth's Center*, 114.

78 Welcome, *From the Earth's Center*, 89.

79 Dalton, *The Richest Man on Earth*, 227–228.

80 John S. Partington, "H. G. Wells: A Political Life," *Utopian Studies* 19, no. 3 (2008): 517–576, 569. "Wells's early socialism," says Partington, "represented the abolition of class barriers. He wished for free competition between individuals in society regardless of their social backgrounds" (519).

81 Jack Williamson, *H. G. Wells, Critic of Progress* (Baltimore, MD: The Mirage Press, 1973), 2.

all the planet's land and physical resources.[82] The energy producing resources—including "the exploitation of coal and electric power, and the powers of wind and wave and water" are available "for the work of life."[83] The State, says Wells's narrator, "will pour out this energy by assignment and lease."[84] By its control of the planet's energy, the World State funds its operations of education, transportation, and welfare.

Pacific Edge and *New York 2140*

The attack on income inequality in Kim Stanley Robinson's *Pacific Edge* (1990) results in a system requiring "nationalizing energy, water and land."[85] In Robinson's *New York 2140* (2018), in the context of systemic bank failures like those of 2008 and 2066, the banks crash again in 2142. The financial institutions, expecting another government bailout, are surprised when Congress refuses to capitulate. Banks are offered a choice of bankruptcy or permitting the Treasury Department to become the majority shareholder.[86] The initial refusal by Goldman Sachs is met by the Treasury Department declaring it insolvent and arranging its sale to the Bank of America. Seeing this, "Citibank took the deal offered by Treasury and Fed, and in rapid order all the other banks and investment firms also took the deal. Finance was now for the most part a privately-operated public utility."[87]

82 Wells, *A Modern Utopia*, 41.
83 Wells, *A Modern Utopia*, 39.
84 Wells, *A Modern Utopia*, 39.
85 Kim Stanley Robinson, *Pacific Edge* (New York: A Tom Doherty Associates Book, 1988), 284.
86 Kim Stanley Robinson, *New York 2140* (New York: Orbit, 2018), 601.
87 Robinson, *New York 2140*, 602–603.

Other Brief Examples

Though not foremost to their utopian schemes a number of late-nineteenth and early twentieth century utopias recommended state operation of essential businesses. Alvarado Fuller's character Rawolle, in *A. D. 2000* (1890), explains to Junius Cobb, a visitor from an earlier time, that the US government operates all railroads as well as telegraph and postal systems in the year 2000 as a source of revenue for the nation.[88] Nationalizing railroads and communication services is also suggested in Richard Michaelis's 1890 anti-utopian sequel to Bellamy's *Looking Backward*, *Looking Further Forward* (discussed in Chapter 6).[89]

To railroads and communication services Paul Devinne's *The Day of Prosperity* (1902), adds a government takeover of electric plants and farming.[90] In Stewart Bruce's *The World in 1931* (1921), the government believes that "transportation is as vital to the people as air, land or sunshine," and accordingly manufactures inexpensive cars—"made for comfort and utility"—that sell at cost for $125 ($2,080 in 2023).[91] The state also operates the railroads, oil wells, and public utilities "for the benefit of all."[92]

Workers' Cooperatives and Associations

> "Male and female minds construe cooperation in different ways and recruit different brain circuits to manage it. More generally, women tend to construe social relations primarily as between persons, while men readily view them as between groups."[93]
>
> —Pascal Boyer, *Minds Make Societies* (2018)

88 Alvarado M. Fuller, *A. D. 2000* (Chicago: Laird and Lee Publishers, 1890), 270.

89 Richard C. Michaelis, *Looking Further Forward* (Chicago: Rand, McNally and Company, 1890), 103–105.

90 Devinne, *The Day of Prosperity*, 168. "Finally, all private undertakings passed into the hands of the government."

91 Bruce, *The World in 1931*, 124–125.

92 Bruce, *The World in 1931*, 181.

93 Boyer, *Minds Make Societies*, 152.

A popular utopian solution to the problem of capitalist surplus labor is the formation of workers' cooperatives or mutual associations. Cooperatives aim to distribute their earnings directly to the workers, not on an equal basis (as in Bellamy's *Looking Backward*) but as a measure of each worker's contribution. Richard Michaelis, for example, in his 1890 response to Bellamy, *Looking Further Forward* (discussed in Chapter 6), has his spokesperson, Mr. Forest, tell Julian West, "The fact that your workingmen did not possess sufficient enterprise, mental discipline and independence, to establish mutual producing associations has driven humanity into communism."[94] The workers of the nineteenth century, Mr. Forest protests, "instead of sacrificing enormous sums in strikes, [should have] organized one trade after another into co-operative associations."[95] Another Bellamy sequel, Ludwig Geissler's *Looking Beyond* (1891) took the other side. Answering Michaelis directly, Geissler explains that "[a]ny co-operation of working men could be and was easily crushed by a combination of capitalists."[96]

Freeland

Five constitutional doctrines govern Theodor Hertzka's utopian Freeland, the second of which deals directly with remediating the pernicious effects of economic inequality, the foremost being poverty. Hertzka believed he had discovered a market system without the exploitation of workers that Marx associated with capitalism's surplus labor.[97] In *Freeland* (1891) Hertzka laid out his program in torturous detail (precis below and in Chapter 3). To effect this system the workers formed self-controlling economic units called associations, from which, explains Henry Ney the narrator, they claim the "full produce of their

94 Michaelis, *Looking Further Forward*, 100.

95 Michaelis, *Looking Further Forward*, 34.

96 Ludwig A. Geissler, *Looking Beyond: A Sequel to "Looking Backward," by Edward Bellamy, and an Answer to "Looking Further Forward," by Richard Michaelis* (London: William Reeves, 1891), 60.

97 Marx, *Capital*, part 3, chap. 7, sec. 2, 127.

labour,"[98] not as capitalists but as workers in a cooperative venture.[99] In this way, proclaims Mr. Clark, Freeland's central bank director, we "have guaranteed to labor the whole of what it assists to produce."[100]

Altneuland: The Old-New-Land

In *Altneuland: The Old New Land* (1902), Theodor Herzl describes the evolution of a Jewish state in Palestine during a twenty-year period (1902–1922) from a poor and stagnant nation into a prosperous and politically sound community. The catalyst for the transformation is a worldwide call for Jews to unite in a nondenominational social contract linking equal opportunity, state ownership of land, and an economic system centering on worker cooperatives.

"The whole merit of our New Society," explains David Littwak—a central figure and eventual president of its "New Society"—"is merely that it fostered the creation and development of the co-operatives."[101] Cooperatives limit the "boundless thirst" for production by reducing the incentive for unlimited personal gain while promoting general prosperity and eliminating poverty.[102] The cooperative society, notes Uri Zilbersheid, "aspires to abolish capitalist exploitation specifically, and all forms of exploitation generally."[103]

Their economic model follows the Irish experience in Ralahine. ("Rahaline" in the novel). At the beginning of 1831, explains Littwak, "the distress in Ireland was very great."[104] Seeking a mutually beneficial solution to the general economic misery, John Vanderleur ("Mr. Vandaleur" in the

98 Theodor Hertzka, *Freeland: A Social Anticipation*, trans. Arthur Ransom (University of California Libraries; London: Chatto and Windus, 1891), 95.

99 Hertzka, *Freeland*, 95.

100 Hertzka, *Freeland*, 246.

101 Theodor Herzl, *Altneuland: The Old-New-Land* (N.p.: n.d. [1902]), 69.

102 Herzl, *Altneuland: The Old-New-Land*, 96.

103 Uri Zilbersheid, "The Utopia of Theodor Herzl," *Israel Studies* 9, no. 3 (Fall 2004): 80–114, 96.

104 Herzl, *Altneuland: The Old-New-Land*, 117–118.

novel), a landlord acting under the inspiration of Robert Owen, reconstituted his business operation as a cooperative venture with his workers.[105] "The aims of this co-operative were; to work with a common capital, to extend mutual aid to the members, to improve the standard of living, and to educate the children."[106]

On the general strategy for limiting economic inequality, explains Littwak, "the individual is neither ground between the millstones of capitalism, nor decapitated by socialistic leveling."[107] Herzl's utopia embraces mutualism, affirms Zilbersheid, "the middle ground between socialism and capitalism."[108] The cooperative organizations sell products to the other cooperative organizations comprising "large department stores, mail order houses, and export firms" and their workers.[109] With the cooperative arrangement the laborers, "who had been living in the deepest poverty, began to prosper suddenly." At the end of each week they received as much as they had "actually earned,"[110] based on a record of the hours each man worked and "of the amount of work accomplished."[111] In establishing this new economic order, Littwak crows, "We did not have to ruin anyone in order to ease the lot of our masses."[112]

105 The Ralahine community, explains Claeys, "took place on the estate of John Scott Vanderleur, a convert to Owen's views," lasting from 1831 to 1833. Gregory Claeys, *Citizens and Saints: Politics and Anti-politics in Early British Socialism* (Cambridge University Press, 1989), 134. Geoghegan relates that Vanderleur assigned the task of operating the workers' community to Edward Craig, who was "deeply involved in the growing cooperative movement." Craig, however, notes Geoghegan, "was not a slavish disciple of Owen." He "modified and ignored Owen's strictures when he felt it necessary." One such modification was Craig's acceptance of phrenology which led to his belief—in opposition to Owen—"that some people were unreformable." Vincent Geoghegan, "Ralahine: An Irish Owenite Community (1831–1833)," *International Review of Social History* 36, no. 3 (1991): 377–411, 387.

106 Herzl, *Altneuland: The Old-New-Land*, 118.

107 Herzl, *Altneuland: The Old-New-Land*, 72.

108 Zilbersheid, "The Utopia of Theodor Herzl," 104–105.

109 Herzl, *Altneuland: The Old-New-Land*, 96.

110 Herzl, *Altneuland: The Old-New-Land*, 117–118.

111 Herzl, *Altneuland: The Old-New-Land*, 117–118.

112 Herzl, *Altneuland: The Old-New-Land*, 70.

Hertzka's influence on Herzl is apparent, observes Ulrich Bach, in the "cooperative economic order, which mediates between individualism and collectivism."[113] Yet Herzl calls Hertzka's *Freeland* a "brilliant bit of magic."[114] Herzl contrasts his Utopia to those of Bellamy and Hertzka proclaiming them two "noble lovers of humanity" who nevertheless "based their ingenious schemes on a false premise ... that humanity had already achieved that degree of maturity and freedom of judgment which is necessary for the establishment of a new social order."[115] The problem Herzl finds with Bellamy's proposal in *Looking Backward* is that "the human beings are no longer human."[116] In contrast, Herzl's protagonist David Littwak declares, "We made the New Society not because we were better than others, but simply because we were ordinary men with the ordinary human needs."[117]

The Making of a Millennium

In his 1908 *The Making of a Millennium*, Frank Rosewater adds a twist to the operation of the cooperative ventures in his utopian Temploria. These ventures, called industrial temples, issue non-tradable ("inalienable") stock to each new member as his "craft patrimony"—"gauged according to his earning capacity and subject to future alteration on that basis."[118] In addition to the worker's fixed compensation, which his "craft fellowship" or profession adjusts, the temple stock issues two forms of dividends. The first, called a "wage surplus" is an amount held back from the worker's pay in case the worker's "actual earning fell behind the fixed wage standard." The second, called a "superwage ... consists in the amount the worker earned over and above the fixed standard."[119] Though stock

113 Ulrich E. Bach, "Seeking Emptiness: Theodor Hertzka's Colonial Utopia Freiland (1890)," *Utopian Studies* 22, no. 1 (2011): 74–90, 8.

114 Herzl, *Altneuland: The Old-New-Land*, 115.

115 Herzl, *Altneuland: The Old-New-Land*, 115–116.

116 Herzl, *Altneuland: The Old-New-Land*, 115.

117 Herzl, *Altneuland: The Old-New-Land*, 116.

118 Frank Rosewater, *The Making of a Millennium* (Omaha, NE: Century Publishing, 1908), 63–64.

119 Rosewater, *The Making of a Millennium*, 64.

ownership in capitalist economies is associated with economic inequality, "this allotment of stocks among the producers," observes the narrator/traveler, meant "their wealth was kept thoroughly diffused—as much so as if owned collectively."[120]

Another Now

Corporations in Yanis Varoufakis's *Another Now* (2021) are democratic and non-hierarchical. "Our new laws and participatory institutions have put an end to the private ownership of corporations, of land, of credit and money creation."[121] Employees are issued one share each of non-transferable stock entitling them to a stake in the corporate profits and the "right to participate on equal terms in the decision-making of the company."[122] "No one could own shares in the company unless they worked for it."[123] Costa the narrator learns from his other self (Kosti) in the utopian Other Now, that a corporation's revenue is divided into five slices. "One slice, 5 per cent of all revenues," explains Kosti, is remitted to the state. The remaining 95 percent is collectively divided on a "a one-person-one-vote basis."[124] The second slice covers the fixed costs (rent, utilities, interest), a third portion is allocated for research and development, a fourth goes to equal salaries ("basic payments to staff"), and the fifth slice is allotted to performance dividends to employees—"determined via the preferential voting algorithm" on an incorruptible democratic basis.[125] The result was that "everyone shared the firm's net revenues, albeit in proportion to the average opinion of their contribution."[126]

120 Rosewater, *The Making of a Millennium*, 64.
121 Varoufakis, *Another Now*, 164–165.
122 Varoufakis, *Another Now*, 50.
123 Varoufakis, *Another Now*, 49.
124 Varoufakis, *Another Now*, 45.
125 Varoufakis, *Another Now*, 43, 45.
126 Varoufakis, *Another Now*, 47.

Labor Exchanges

> "Poverty is in fact the utopianist's great auxiliary, it is the matter he works in, the substance on which he feeds his thoughts, the providence of his obsessions."[127]
>
> —E. M. Cioran, *History and Utopia* (1960)

Robert Owen's (1771–1858) "largest and best known" labor exchange, says A. L. Morton, was the National Equitable Labour Exchange, "set up by Owen himself in 1832."[128] In the labor exchanges, says Claeys, "shoemakers, carpenters, cabinet-makers, and other artisans"[129] exchanged products using Labor Notes, bypassing the accumulation of surplus labor. The Labor Notes, Wells affirms, in denominations of "one hour, five hours, or twenty hours,"[130] represented work-hours expended in production. The valuation of labor for this time-based currency required some finessing however, as G. D. H. Cole explains, since "one man might take twelve hours to make what another would make in six."[131] As a result, says Morton, "some articles were valued much above and others much below the normal market price."[132] The labor exchanges Owen inspired were short lived, with the National Equitable Labour Exchange closing in 1834.[133]

When everyone suddenly becomes rich in Adeline Knapp's *One Thousand Dollars a Day* (1894) no one is willing to work and commerce slams to a halt. Rather than do without their accustomed goods and services, however, the citizens spontaneously form a labor exchange, working to supply the needs money will no longer purchase.[134] People likewise

127 E. M. Cioran, *History and Utopia* (The University of Chicago Press, 1960), 81.

128 A. L. Morton, *The Life and Ideas of Robert Owen* (London: Lawrence and Wishart, 1962), 39–40.

129 Gregory Claeys, Introduction to *A New View of Society and Other Writings*, by Robert Owen (New York: Penguin Classics, 1991), xviii,

130 H. G. Wells, *The Outline of History* (N.p.: n.d. [1920]), 423.

131 G. D. H. Cole, *Robert Owen* (Boston: Little, Brown, and Company, 1925), 198–199.

132 Morton, *The Life and Ideas of Robert Owen*, 40.

133 Morton, *The Life and Ideas of Robert Owen*, 40.

134 Adeline Knapp, *One Thousand Dollars a Day* (N.p.: n.d. [1894]), 7.

conduct business via labor exchanges and concomitant "organized consumption" in A. O. Grigsby and Mary P. Lowe's (Jack Adams, pseud.) *Nequa or The Problem of the Ages* (1900). As MacNair, a spokesperson for Nequa's subterranean civilization of Altruria, explains, "A given number of hours of labor in one branch of useful service to society is worth just the same number of hours of labor in some other branch."[135] Accordingly, in this system "the sale of products of all kinds are credited and debited as given amounts of labor"[136] evidenced by labor notes (called "New Occasion Notes"[137]). This scheme is part of a broader endeavor to eliminate capitalist intermediaries and their weapons—debt, gold, interest, money, profit, rent, and wages—revealing itself in the direct sale of products through mutual exchanges. "Under this system of distribution, products passed directly from the producer to the consumer and were never handled but once."[138] Because the Altrurian state owns all land and industries in *Nequa*, notes Barbara Quissell, "wealth can be equitably distributed."[139]

Labor notes reappear in Stewart Bruce's *The World in 1931* (1921) where "All government expenditures were to be met by Labor Certificates in denominations of one to fifty dollars, based on actual labor performed for the State"[140] The state pays each laborer's wages in these certificates; the workers then exchange Labor Certificates for "like services, as represented by products."[141]

135 A. O. Grigsby and Mary P. Lowe, *Nequa or The Problem of Ages* (Newton, KS: Mennonite Press, 2015; original publication Topeka, KS: Equity Publishing Company, 1900), 187.
136 Grigsby and Lowe, *Nequa*, 187.
137 Grigsby and Lowe, *Nequa*, 254–255.
138 Grigsby and Lowe, *Nequa*, 185.
139 Barbara C. Quissell, "The New World That Eve Made: Feminist Utopias Written by Nineteenth-Century Women," in *America as Utopia*, ed. Kenneth M. Roemer (New York: Burt Franklin and Company, 1981), 148–174, 165.
140 Bruce, *The World in 1931*, 140.
141 Bruce, *The World in 1931*, 143.

Redistribution of Income or Wealth: Progressive Taxation (Graduated Rates)

> "The rise in power of strongly progressive taxation seems in no way to have discouraged innovation or productivity."[142]
>
> —Thomas Piketty, *A Brief History of Equality* (2022)

Barbara Goodwin notes that "some form of redistribution is essential to the elimination of economic and social injustice."[143] In his *Politics*, Aristotle declares that "it is equally the interest of all classes," that "the proceeds of the public revenues should be accumulated and distributed among the poor," since "extreme poverty lowers the character of democracy."[144] In his lectures on redistribution, Bertrand De Jouvenel denies that "redistributionism" is "descended from socialism."[145] Land, he advises, has been redistributed for thousands of years.[146] The purpose of redistribution, says R. H. Tawney, is the "pooling" of society's "surplus resources by means of taxation" and their use to make "accessible to all ... the conditions of civilization which, in the absence of such measures, can be enjoyed only by the rich."[147] Progressive taxation—a key tool for redistribution—evolved from the principle that citizens should contribute to society in proportion to their ability ("faculty"), where *ability* referred first to property and later to income. Termed the "faculty theory," says Edward Seligman, this rationale emerged as a proportional tax in the

142 Piketty, *A Brief History of Equality*, 139.

143 Goodwin, "Economic and Social Innovation in Utopia," 72.

144 Aristotle, *Politics*, trans. Benjamin Jowett (New York: The Modern Library, 1943), bk. 6, ch. 5, 1320a § 35.

145 Bertrand De Jouvenel, *The Ethics of Redistribution* (Cambridge: Cambridge University Press, 1951), 3.

146 De Jouvenel, *The Ethics of Redistribution*, 3–4. Lycurgus (c. 800–730 BCE), for example, in response to Sparta's "extreme inequality," says Plutarch, introduced his "most hazardous" reform requiring citizens "to renounce their properties, and to consent to a new division of the land." Plutarch, *Plutarch's Lives*, the Dryden translation (New York: The Modern Library, 2001), 59.

147 R. H. Tawney, *Equality* (London: Unwin Books, 1931), 122.

middle ages,[148] and later in Adam Smith's request that people "contribute towards the support of the government ... in proportion to the revenue which they respectively enjoy under the protection of the state."[149] "It was not until the beginning of the twentieth century," observes Piketty, "that progressive taxes were established more or less everywhere within the space of a few years."[150]

Taxation is a device for reducing or intensifying economic inequality. In *The Decline and Fall of the Roman Empire* (1776) Edward Gibbon observed that the "millions of a great empire have much less to dread from the cruelty than from the avarice of their masters; and their humble happiness is principally affected by the grievance of excessive taxes, which, gently pressing on the wealthy, descend with accelerated weight on the meaner and more indigent classes of society."[151] Gibbon's reference to taxes descending with accelerating weight describes a *regressive* tax system. A tax is regressive if the proportion of taxes (or sacrifice) to income rises as income (or means) decreases—contributing to economic inequality. A *progressive* tax (graduated rates), by contrast, accelerates the rate of sacrifice as income or wealth rises. Progressive taxation is one of the widely shared utopian remedies for combatting economic inequality that has found its way into practice.

148 Edward R. A. Seligman, *Progressive Taxation in Theory and Practice*, 2nd ed. (American Economic Association Quarterly, 3rd series, 9, no. 4, 1908), 206–208. The English poll tax of 1379, for example, was imposed at different rates depending on one's class. While the lowest rate should have fallen on the peasants, says Seligman, in practice the poll taxes "were levied chiefly on the poor."

149 Smith, *Wealth of Nations*, bk. 5, ch. 2, pt. 2, 198.

150 Piketty, *A Brief History of Equality*, 131.

151 Edward Gibbon, "The Decline and Fall of the Roman Empire," in *Great Books of the Western World*, ed. Robert Maynard Hutchins and Mortimer Adler, vol. 40 (Chicago: Encyclopaedia Britannica, 1952), vol. 1, chap. 17, 251–252.

Figure 2: "Bread Line at the Bowery Mission, New York, 1928."

"Governments in advanced economies have historically mitigated inequality through public policy," affirms the International Monetary Fund, "primarily [using] progressive taxes and social transfers such as public retirement benefits."[152] With progressive taxation wealthier taxpayers pay (in theory[153]) not only a greater absolute amount of tax than their middle-class colleagues, but they pay at least part of that tax at a higher rate. Progressive taxation implements a vision of justice holding that individuals are increasingly responsible for contributing to the general welfare in proportion to the benefits they received that enabled their success—"the vast current and past public investments in infrastructure, education, and

152 International Monetary Fund, "Causes and Consequences of Income Inequality: A Global Perspective," June 2015, 21.

153 During the Carter administration in the US, reports Hayes, the top marginal rate was reduced from 70 percent to 35 percent sharply reducing the system's progressivity. As a result, while the richest 400 taxpayers paid an average tax rate of 16.6 percent, the middle fifth of taxpayers paid an average rate of 22 percent. Hayes, *Twilight of the Elites*, 226.

institutions."[154] Furthermore, this increased tax rate on higher income or wealth, as John Dewey argued, is compensation to fellow citizens for "the burdens that politicians subservient to great wealth have piled on the heads of the helpless consumer."[155] These burdens include a reluctance to apply the same progressive tax rates to corporations as to humans, as De Jouvenel affirms.[156]

In *Taxing the Rich,* political scientists Kenneth Scheve and David Stasavage observe that "Countries have gone the farthest in taxing the rich when there have been compensatory arguments for doing so. The most important context for compensation has been mass mobilization for war."[157] The compensatory argument works during wartime because it promotes the ideal of an equal sacrifice; it seeks to balance the risks to life and body young soldiers assume against the financial interest of the wealthy who stay at home. In Albert Van Petten's *The Great Man's Life: 1925–2000 A. C.* (1959), for example, the protagonist reflecting on his time in the Korean War says, the "work and tax-load of the home folks" should have been increased to equal the efforts of the soldiers. "If the people wanted to be defended, they could damn well pay for it."[158] However, most utopias avoid war, rendering this argument less decisive.

Progressive taxes are seen as a safeguard preventing society from splitting in two, with the emergence of an indifferent plutocracy controlling the fate of the poor. Kurt Vonnegut's *Player Piano* (1952), for example (discussed in Chapter 7), pictures such a scenario where a cadre of wealthy

154 Frank, *The Darwin Economy*, 120.

155 John Dewey, "The President and the Special Session," *People's Lobby Bulletin* 1 (June 1931): 1; in *John Dewey: The Later Works*: 1925–1953, vol. 6: 1931–1932 (Carbondale: Southern Illinois University Press, 1989), 345.

156 De Jouvenel, *The Ethics of Redistribution*, 60–62. In the US in 1943, for example, corporations paid 39.8 percent and individuals paid 27.1 percent of total income taxes. By 2011 corporations paid only 7.9 percent while individuals paid 47.4 percent. Donald Morris, "A Case for Company-Specific Public Disclosure of Corporate Tax Returns," *Accounting and the Public Interest 15*, no. 1 (2015): 1–21.

157 Kenneth Scheve and David Stasavage, *Taxing the Rich* (New York: Russell Sage Foundation and Princeton: Princeton University Press, 2016), 76.

158 Albert Archer Van Petten, *The Great Man's Life: 1925 to 2000 A. C.* (New York: Utopian Publishers, 1959), 13–14.

engineers and managers, assisted by computers, ensure that those across the bridge in Homestead remain poor. The aim of taxing the "super rich" at higher rates, explains Branko Milanović, is less about raising revenue and more about curbing political power.[159] Accordingly, observes Piketty, the reduction in the top marginal income tax rates over recent decades has "led to an explosion of very high incomes, which then increased the political influence of the beneficiaries of the change in the tax laws."[160] While top CEOs received an average of twenty times the typical worker's pay in 1965, their compensation had increased to 278 times by 2019.[161] Marginal tax rates like 90 percent, Milanović argues, will dissuade corporate managers from requesting "another million" when they know that 90 percent will go to the government.[162] "But with a marginal tax rate of 25 percent," he says, "the story is entirely different." In his utopian tract, "A Program of Radical Democracy" (1912), J. McKeen Cattell says no one deserves "more than four times the average income," amending Plato's four-class proposal in the *Laws*.[163] Even though a man's services may be worth more than that, Cattell stipulates, the ability to provide those services is "made possible by the organization of society."[164]

It was the "widespread emergence of a system of progressive taxation," notes Piketty, "that contributed to the reduction of inequality in the twentieth century."[165] This reduction was visible in the US between 1940 and 1945, Walter Scheidel notes, when the top tax rates for income and estates

159 Milanović, "The Return of 'Patrimonial Capitalism,'" 528.

160 Piketty, *Capital in the Twenty-First Century*, 335.

161 Lawrence Mishel and Julia Wolfe, "CEO Compensation Has Grown 940% since 1978," *Economic Policy Institute* (August 14, 2019). <https://www.epi.org/publication/ceo-compensation-2018/>.

162 Milanović, "The Return of 'Patrimonial Capitalism,'" 528.

163 J. McKeen Cattell, "A Program of Radical Democracy," *Popular Science Monthly* 80 (June 1912), 5. Plato divided society into four economic classes. Plato's narrator declares, "there must be no place for penury in any section of the population, nor yet for opulence." Accordingly, he says, "the legislator must now specify the limit in either direction." *Laws*, trans. Taylor, bk. 5, 744.

164 Cattell, "A Program of Radical Democracy," 5.

165 Piketty, *Capital and Ideology*, 31.

stood at 94 percent.[166] During the past fifty years, however, in both in the US and in Europe, the trend has been toward less progressive tax rates, rekindling the tendency toward greater economic inequality. This policy reversal, says Piketty, is evidenced by the "very strong growth of the largest fortunes and the explosion of remunerations for top executives."[167] For this reason, Piketty proposes that the "ideal policy for avoiding an endless inegalitarian spiral and regaining control over the dynamics of accumulation would be a progressive global tax on capital." This tax, he says, "would promote the general interest over private interests while preserving economic openness and the forces of competition." He admits, however, that "a truly global tax on capital is no doubt a utopian ideal."[168]

The Age of Progress

"We have found that the wide inequality in men's worldly circumstances, is the principal occasion of the vice and suffering of which we complain as a present evil." With this statement David Moore's spokesperson in *The Age of Progress* (1856) affords the setting for a particularly progressive tax law.[169] The problem the speaker identifies is the increase in crime, indolence, and vice that has split the society deeply—with many more people falling into poverty while the few enjoy their growing wealth.[170] Moore's goal is to break down the "bars of separation which Gold has erected in Society."[171] The tax, "shall be levied and collected from such estates, belonging to individuals and corporations, as shall exceed in value the sum of twenty thousand dollars [$724,000 in 2023]." Estates that exceed that amount by ten thousand dollars ($362,000 in 2023), he continues, "shall pay double the proportion of taxes paid by the smaller estates. For each

166 Scheidel, *The Great Leveler*, 149.
167 Piketty, *A Brief History of Equality*, 153.
168 Piketty, *Capital in the Twenty-First Century*, 471.
169 David Moore, *The Age of Progress; or a Panorama of Time* (New York: Sheldon, Blakeman and Co., 1856), 244.
170 Moore, *The Age of Progress*, 244–245.
171 Moore, *The Age of Progress*, 251.

additional ten thousand dollars the rate of taxation shall be increased 'geometrically!'"[172] Commenting on this arrangement, Sargent says, "clearly he wishes to limit wealth severely, but property is still held privately and great fortunes can still be accumulated."[173] Even so, a graduated tax increasing geometrically would doubtless mitigate the most pernicious extremes of economic inequality.

The Ke Whonkus People

John O. Greene's *The Ke Whonkus People* (1890) describes a subterranean civilization at the North Pole, circa 1886. The utopian depiction is sandwiched between two romantic adventures involving the narrator Sampson De Lilly's travels to and from the North Pole. The explorers embark on their voyage aboard the Polar Star. The ship's captain claims he had learned from spirits that there was a "fine climate" and a "highly civilized people" at the North Pole.[174] De Lilly and his party travel to an old volcanic crater encircled by a permanent layer of fog (the "fog hole").[175] Exploring the crater the travelers discover a passageway leading to a three-mile long tunnel. The end of the tunnel reveals a valley below containing a number of houses and a "portion of the city."[176] The adventurers had arrived at an 11,000-year-old underground civilization. The country hosts a population of four-and-a-half million, living on two hundred and sixteen thousand square miles (twice the size of Nevada).[177] Their society is conducted by the principle that there is no best form of government in the abstract, but that the relative ignorance, superstition, or education of the citizens determines the appropriate form of government.

172 Moore, *The Age of Progress*, 254 (the original is in italics and numbers capitalized).
173 Sargent, "Capitalist Eutopias in America," 196.
174 Greene, *The Ke Whonkus People*, 31.
175 Greene, *The Ke Whonkus People*, 51.
176 Greene, *The Ke Whonkus People*, 53–54.
177 Greene, *The Ke Whonkus People*, 69–70.

Because of its duration, the Ke Whonkian civilization has passed through assorted governmental structures suitable to its citizens' needs at various times. It was once ruled by a limited monarchy followed by an oligarchy under the control of the three powers, "priest-craft, wealth-craft and male-craft."[178] During this phase, which ended over a hundred years ago with their last revolution,[179] private corporations formed into combinations, "so as to cut off competition, and to monopolize all the most profitable branches of business for their own benefit."[180] From this locus of power the corporations controlled both the price they paid for labor and the price they charged for their products.[181] Over time the citizens divided into two distinct classes, "the very rich and the very poor," a process economic forces propelled with the aid of "class legislation."[182]

A regressive tax system exacerbated their economic inequality by placing a "heavy tax" on the "common necessaries of life to meet public expense." The fate of the laboring classes as a result of this system was that of "almost incessant toil and squalid poverty."[183] Their present government, a form of republicanism and democracy, explains Ke Whonkus Professor Kumtux, has mixed in a degree of socialism[184] and gives equal rights to all, "both male and female."[185]

Regarding their current progressive tax system, the professor explains that in order to retain wealth (the result of labor) "in the hands of those who create it ... taxes should be levied lightly, if at all, on the poor." The poor should be permitted to retain their wages "on which to support their families as well as possible." This income tax system, explains Kumtux, is designed to "gradually fall heavier on incomes as they increase in amount;

178 Greene, *The Ke Whonkus People*, 235.
179 Greene, *The Ke Whonkus People*, 237.
180 Greene, *The Ke Whonkus People*, 235.
181 Greene, *The Ke Whonkus People*, 236.
182 Greene, *The Ke Whonkus People*, 236–237.
183 Greene, *The Ke Whonkus People*, 237.
184 Greene, *The Ke Whonkus People*, 234.
185 Greene, *The Ke Whonkus People*, 237–238. The current year is 100 AER (after equal rights).

and it answers a double purpose," he says. "It not only draws the revenue from those most able to spare it, but it, at the same time, prevents too much of the wealth of the country from drifting into the possession of a few persons."[186]

Ten Men of Money Island

Ten Men of Money Island (1891) surveys the economic lessons ten explorers garner in founding a utopian community. These lessons include the usefulness of a medium of exchange and the dangers of unregulated monetary policies. A succession of booms and busts focuses the ten men's attention on the causes of economic inequality. "One of the first things to be accomplished," notes Seymour Norton and Robert Cowdrey's narrator, "was the adoption of some law which should equalize the conditions of the different members of the community as much as the natural abilities and qualities of men would permit, and thus restore them to their former estate of equality."[187] One of the innovations applied to avoid the extremes of economic inequality, he continues, is the introduction of a graduated income tax. The men agreed that a new system of taxation should insulate the poor from taxation, while the rich "should bear the most of the burden."[188] After much debate, reports the narrator, "It was enacted that every man should pay into the treasury a certain per cent of what he made every year in his business—the amount being increased, even, as the income increased."[189] The scheme, the narrator explains, for both income and land was one of graduated tax rates.[190] In this system of progressive taxation, while the poor "escaped taxation," the burden on the rich meant not only that they paid most of the taxes but their ability

186 Greene, *The Ke Whonkus People*, 241–242.

187 Seymour Francis Norton and Robert H. Cowdrey, *Ten Men of Money Island* (New York: Columbia University, 1891), 25.

188 Norton and Cowdrey, *Ten Men of Money Island*, 25.

189 Norton and Cowdrey, *Ten Men of Money Island*, 25.

190 Norton and Cowdrey, *Ten Men of Money Island*, 25.

to accumulate wealth was "most materially curtailed."[191] In this way, the narrator relates, the engagement of progressive taxation brought about "conditions of affairs most essential to the well-being of a truly republican form of government—viz., a state of comparative equality of wealth; at least, a state where enormous wealth on the one hand and monstrous poverty on the other does not exist."[192]

Philip Dru: Administrator

In *Philip Dru: Administrator* (1912) Edward Mandell House—a diplomat and advisor to US President Woodrow Wilson—proposes a series of reforms designed to temper economic inequality. In 1920 Dru "saw many indications that the social, financial and industrial troubles that had vexed the United States ... were about to culminate in civil war. Wealth had grown so strong, that the few were about to strangle the many."[193] The civil war (described in Chapter 5) concludes with Dru serving an eight-year term as Administrator of the US (until a new president is elected). Administrator Dru's guiding principle holds that while "heretofore the laws had been made for the judges, for the lawyers and for those whose financial or political influences enabled them to obtain special privileges," in the future, "the whole legal machinery was to be run absolutely in the interest of the people."[194] Accordingly, Dru announces, "The strong will help the weak, the rich will share with the poor, and it will not be called charity, but it will be known as justice."[195]

Under Administrator Dru's graduated income tax "exempting no income whatsoever,"[196] progressive rates tax incomes of up to one thousand

191 Norton and Cowdrey, *Ten Men of Money Island*, 25.
192 Norton and Cowdrey, *Ten Men of Money Island*, 25–26.
193 Edward Mandell House, *Philip Dru Administrator: A Story of Tomorrow 1920–1935* (New York: B. W. Huebsch, 1912), 1.
194 House, *Philip Dru: Administrator*, 174–175.
195 House, *Philip Dru: Administrator*, 66.
196 House, *Philip Dru: Administrator*, 179.

dollars a year ($32,000 in 2023) with a "nominal tax of one-half of one per cent." The tax rates increase gradually, from 1–2 to 5 percent at lower income levels. But at Dru's direction, the rates for higher-earning taxpayers were rapidly increased until they reached a maximum of 70 percent on incomes that were "ten million dollars [$317 million in 2023], or above."[197] An inheritance tax, graduated at the same rate as in the income tax, supplemented the latter. Parrington notes, "Few reformers have had more power than Mr. House—and no other American utopia has come so close to being brought to life."[198]

Other Brief Proposals

Richard Michaelis's 1890 *Looking Further Forward* (discussed in the next section and in Chapter 6) suggests taxing both gifts and inheritances progressively at the same rates, "from one percent up to fifty."[199] In Chauncey Thomas's 1891 *The Crystal Button* (discussed in Chapter 4), reports Allyn Forbes, "heavy income taxes were imposed for the avowed purpose of striking at inequalities of wealth."[200] Specifically, professor Prosper explains to protagonist and engineer Paul Prognosis that laws impose a tax on individual possessions judged "unduly great," designed "ultimately to re-absorb into the public purse any incomes that are excessive beyond all reason."[201]

John Roberts's 1893 response to Bellamy, *Looking Within: The Misleading Tendencies of "Looking Backward"* (discussed in Chapter

197 House, *Philip Dru: Administrator*, 179–180.

198 Vernon Louis Parrington, Jr, *American Dreams: A Study of American Utopias* (New York: Russell and Russell, 1964), 191. Though House's novel was not responsible for the New Deal, Parrington says, "one can find ... many similarities between the programs of Franklin Roosevelt and Philip Dru-House."

199 Michaelis, *Looking Further Forward*, 110.

200 Allyn B. Forbes, "The Literary Quest for Utopia, 1880–1900," *Social Forces* 6, no. 2 (December, 1927): 179–189, 185.

201 Chauncey Thomas, *The Crystal Button, or Adventures of Paul Prognosis in the Forty-Ninth Century* (Boston: Houghton, Mifflin and Company, 1891), 122–123.

6), includes a graduated income tax as a means of relieving economic inequality. The progressive tax falls on a family's income exceeding $1,000 ($34,000 in 2023). The tax rate beginning at 1 percent rises with each thousand dollars of income until the rate is 50 percent for incomes above $50,000 ($1,700,000 in 2023).[202]

A progressive wealth tax is enacted in Archibald Forsyth's 1897 *Rapara* (discussed in Chapter 4) to reduce economic inequality. The graduated tax is imposed with eight rates from 1/8 penny per pound (0.05 percent) to 1 penny per pound (0.4 percent) annually.[203] An exemption from the wealth tax was fixed at £50 (£50 in 1883 = £4,821 or $5,964 in 2023). The three-tier progressive tax scheme in Bruce's *The World in 1931* (1921) entails "no levy on incomes up to three thousand, five hundred dollars [$58,000 in 2023]. On larger incomes," however, "50 percent was levied on the first additional five hundred; then 99 per cent on all in excess of four thousand dollars" ($4,000 in 1931 = $78,000 in 2023).[204]

A more recent utopian (or dystopian) application of progressive taxation appears in Kim Stanley Robinson's 1990 *Pacific Edge* (discussed in Chapter 7). As part of a strategy to reduce economic inequality—in conjunction with a personal income floor (discussed on pp. 79–80)—residents are taxed "more and more heavily as they approach the personal income cap [$100,000]."[205] However, they can direct 60 percent of their taxes "to whatever services they support the most."[206] Those

202 John W. Roberts, *Looking Within: The Misleading Tendencies of "Looking Backward" Made Manifest* (New York: A. S. Barnes and Company, 1893), 268–269.

203 Archibald Forsyth, *Rapara or The Rights of the Individual in the State* (London: T. Fisher Unwin, 1897), 234–235. Before converting to the decimal system in 1971 there were 240 pennies per pound. University of Nottingham <https://www.nottingham.ac.uk/manuscriptsandspecialcollections/researchguidance/weightsandmeasures/money.aspx>

204 Bruce, *The World in 1931*, 155.

205 For an overview of the complexities of calculating an income ceiling and floor, see De Jouvenel, *The Ethics of Redistribution*, 23–27.

206 Robinson, *Pacific Edge*, 91.

who have reached the cap are called "hundreds"[207] (earning $100,000 in 1990 = $228,000 in 2023). Businesses are subject to the same sort of graduated tax system.[208] In Robinson's *New York 2140* (2018), a financial crisis leads to a "so-called Piketty tax,"[209] a progressive tax levied on both incomes and on wealth. The tax "ranged from zero for assets less than ten million dollars to twenty percent on assets of one billion or more."[210]

Universal Basic Income

> "There is enough for all. So there should be no more people living in poverty. ... Enough should be a human right, a floor below which no one can fall; also a ceiling above which no one can rise. ... Arranging this situation is left as an exercise for the reader."[211]
>
> —Kim Stanley Robinson, *The Ministry for the Future* (2020)

Universal basic income (UBI) affords each adult with a fixed payment per year, regardless of employment, explains Madeline Schwartz, thereby "decoupling economic status and employment."[212] Philippe Van Parijs specifies that universal basic income is not about the distribution of income, rather it is about "the power to decide what sort of life one wants to live. ... It is about the power to say yes to activities

207 Tom Moylan, "'Utopias is when our lives matter': Reading Kim Stanley Robinson's *Pacific Edge*," *Utopian Studies* 6, no. 2 (1995): 1–24, 10.

208 Robinson, *Pacific Edge*, 91.

209 Robinson, *New York 2140*, 602.

210 Robinson, *New York 2140*, 602.

211 Robinson, *The Ministry for the Future*, 58.

212 Madeline Schwartz, "Less Work, More Time," in *The Feminist Utopia Project*, ed. Alexandra Brodsky and Rachel Kauder Nalebuff (New York: Feminist Press, 2015), 180.

that are poorly paid or not paid at all, but are nonetheless attractive."[213] Andy Stern, a union leader, stresses that technology will increasingly eliminate middle-class jobs leaving a growing residuum of workers living in poverty (this problem is discussed in Chapter 4). The solution Stern proposes in *Raising the Floor* (2016) is universal basic income; giving people "cash, not a job."[214] Every citizen, explains Stern, would receive "a certain amount of money on a regular basis without having to do anything to be eligible for that money."[215] He suggests paying $1,000 per month to all adults between the ages of 18 and 64 and to those 65 and over who do not receive at least $1,000 per month in Social Security.[216] According to Schwartz, such a system, "would begin to eradicate poverty and minimize income inequality."[217]

The distinction between universal basic income and the equalized income of Bellamy's *Looking Backwards* is a matter of intent and scale. While universal basic income accrues unconditionally to every member of society—working or not, rich or poor—its level of support is rudimentary—aiming to raise people out of indigence. As Annie Lowrey notes, its goal is to "lop off the bottom" of Abraham Maslow's hierarchy of needs[218]—providing the needs of the physiological domain. This is what Kim Stanley Robinson does in *Pacific Edge* (discussed below and in Chapter 7) where his character Tom says, "We chopped the pyramid off and left only the constituent parts down at the base," comprising a universal basic income.[219] Bellamy's equal payment, by

213 Philippe Van Parijs, "The Universal Basic Income: Why Utopian Thinking Matters, and How Sociologists Can Contribute to It," *Politics and Society* 41, no. 2, 171–182, 174.

214 Andy Stern, *Raising the Floor* (New York: PublicAffairs, 2016), 165.

215 Stern, *Raising the Floor*, 165–166.

216 Stern, *Raising the Floor*, 201.

217 Schwartz, "Less Work, More Time," 178–179.

218 Annie Lowrey, *Give People Money: How a Universal Basic Income Would End Poverty, Revolutionize Work, and Remake the World* (New York: Broadway Books, 2018), 69.

219 Robinson, *Pacific Edge*, 285.

contrast, is conditioned on a universal work requirement and provides a "comfortable maintenance" compatible with certain "luxuries and elegancies of life."[220]

The notion of a universal basic income evolved from earlier expressions of economic equality. Thomas Paine, observe J. E. King and John Marangos, "asserts the right to a universal and unconditional Basic Income."[221] In *Agrarian Justice* (1797) Paine proposed a one-time universal equalizing payment (at age 21) of "fifteen pounds sterling" (£1,495 or $1,850 in 2023) financed by a 10 percent tax on inherited property,[222] "an idea," says Piketty, "that was far ahead of its time."[223] "The great mass of the poor," Paine observes, "are become an hereditary race, and it is next to impossible for them to get out of that state of themselves."[224] For Paine, says Jendrysik, there is no reason for human beings "to accept the inequality of the social world as 'natural.'"[225]

The poor, as John Stuart Mill explains, are "chained to a place, to an occupation and to conformity with the will of an employer, and debarred by the accident of birth both from the enjoyment, and from the mental and moral advantages, which others inherit without exertion and independently of desert."[226] As a social concern, at least to utopians,

220 While *Looking Backward* provides no monetary benchmark for this "comfortable maintenance" (85), Dr. Leete explains that a man who works half of his twenty-four-year industrial army commitment can take early retirement (at age 33) "provided he accepts for the rest of his life one half the rate of maintenance other citizens receive. It is quite possible to live on this amount," says Dr. Leete, "though one must forego the luxuries and elegancies of life." Bellamy, *Looking Backward*, 133.

221 J. E. King and John Marangos, "Two Arguments for Basic Income: Thomas Paine (1737–1809) and Thomas Spence (1750–1814)," *History of Economic Ideas* 14, no. 1 (2006): 55–71, 63.

222 Paine, *Agrarian Justice*, 477–478.

223 Piketty, *Capital and Ideology*, 118–119. See the US Social Security Administration commentary at <https://www.ssa.gov/history/tpaine3.html>

224 Paine, *Agrarian Justice*, 484.

225 Mark Jendrysik, "Tom Paine: Utopian?," *Utopian Studies* 18, no. 2 (2007): 139–157, 153.

226 John Stuart Mill, *Socialism* (N.p.: S. M. B., Special Edition, n.d. [1879]), 10. Claeys notes that in Mill's later writings he discussed themes such as population control

poverty implies influences beyond the impoverished individual's control, but perhaps within society's command. A perennial impediment to receiving society's support, however, as Aristotle notes, is that "to secure gentle treatment for the poor is not an easy thing, since a ruling class is not always humane."[227] Bernard Mandeville (1670–1733) expressed this class's contempt for the "undeserving poor," referring to those who "for want of spirit, hug themselves in their sloth, and will rather starve than stir."[228]

Mill traces one form of basic income to Charles Fourier (1772–1837). In the distribution of what is produced, Mill explains, "a certain minimum is first assigned for the subsistence of every member of the community, whether capable or not of labor."[229] Under this system "each poor member," says Fourier, receives "an advance of one year's clothing, food and lodging."[230] A fundamental difference between the Fourierist "minimum," however, and universal basic income, explain Van Parijs and Vanderborght, is that basic income is paid in cash and not in the form of "food, shelter, clothes, and other consumer goods."[231]

But it is not only socialist or left-leaning writers who advocate universal basic income. Right-leaning economist F. A. Hayek suggested a

---

and poverty that formed the "foundations of his utopianism." Claeys clarifies that this "circumscribed" use of *utopian* refers to "the pursuit of a society based upon enhanced sociability and increasingly common resources." Gregory Claeys, *Mill and Paternalism* (Cambridge University Press, 2013), 25, 137n74.

227 Aristotle, *Politics*, trans. Jowett, 4:13.

228 Mandeville, *The Fable of the Bees*, vol. 1, 242.

229 John Stuart Mill, *The Principles of Political Economy*, abridged by J. Laurence Laughlin (New York: D. Appleton and Company, 1884), 166. See also Mill, *Socialism*, 71.

230 Charles Fourier, *The Utopian Vision of Charles Fourier*, trans. Jonathan Beecher and Richard Bienvenu (Boston: Beacon Press, 1971), 250–251.

231 Philippe Van Parijs and Yannick Vanderborght, *Basic Income* (Cambridge, MA: Harvard University Press, 2017), 12. The same authors report, "Fourier's chief disciple and founding father of the Fourierist school was the French philosopher and economist Victor Considerant (1808–1893)" who wrote, "Forwarding the minimum is the basis of freedom and the guarantee of the emancipation of the proletarian. No freedom without minimum" (77, 271n32).

"sort of floor below which nobody need fall"[232] while Charles Murray, a sociologist and co-author of *The Bell Curve*, proposed a $10,000 a year basic income.[233]

The World a Department Store

Bradford Peck's *The World a Department Store* (1900) describes a cooperative society in 1925 providing universal basic income. The society is a "copartnership" animated by cooperation rather than competition.[234] In this Cooperative Association, explains a treasury department official Mr. Mathew to the visitor Mr. Brantford, each person receives a "coupon check book" to which deposits are made "as long as they shall live."[235] When a child is born, the official continues, the treasury department assigns them a number and then deposits one hundred and twenty dollars a year in an account which the mother "can draw or allow to remain to the child's credit on deposit." At age 4 the annual deposit is increased to $180; at age 6 to $300 at which point, says Mr. Mathew, the child is "taught to pay its own expenses"[236] ($300 in 1925 = $5,500 in 2023). "Every man and woman member, as long as they live," receives deposits of at least fifteen hundred dollars annually ($1,500 in 1925 = $25,500 in 2023).[237] "We look upon our members as our capital," Mr. Brantford is told, "each human being is considered as an investment."[238]

232 Hayek, *Law Legislation and Liberty*, 55.
233 Stern, *Raising the Floor*, 177. Stern suggests that the left-leaning proponents of UBI "believe we need a safety net for everyone," while the right-leaning proponents are "people who believe in smaller government" (207).
234 Bradford Peck, *The World a Department Store: A Story of Life Under a Cooperative System* (Boston: Bradford Peck, 1900), 310.
235 Peck, *The World a Department Store*, 33.
236 Peck, *The World a Department Store,* 37.
237 Peck, *The World a Department* Store, 37–38.
238 Peck, *The World a Department Store,* 37.

The financial support for this arrangement arises from a division of labor based on cooperative departments that deal directly with the consumer. The Cooperative Association abolished all work aiding and abetting competition, including advertising and salespeople (Peck supplies four pages of tables listing the competitive jobs abolished and the resulting annual savings).[239] This effectively purged the waste that had resulted from capitalist competition.[240] The cumulative savings goes to fund the payments to each worker's account.

The Great Man's Life: 1925 to 2000 A. C.

Universal basic income is the central theme of Albert Van Petten's *The Great Man's Life: 1925 to 2000 A. C.* (1959). George Mann the protagonist is a single-minded political activist on a mission to effect a permanent level of prosperity. "I think," says Mann, "that we ought to be able to have an almost unlimited prosperity—an almost continual improvement—bounded only by our willingness to work."[241] After forming an independent political party in Kentucky, Mann's strategy was to back candidates who would take a pledge to support his economic plan. In the November election of 1958, Mann reports, "of all the candidates whom we endorsed, only one or two were defeated."[242] With the support of these pledged officials, enhanced by Mann's unrelenting lobbying efforts, a "Prosperity Fund" was enacted from which each person in Kentucky over the age of 12 receives $10 a week ($100 in 2023).[243] When these payments commenced people had more money to spend which stimulated commerce and created new jobs. The increasing economic activity also meant wages for unskilled labor increased "from one dollar per hour to three dollars per hour

239 Peck, *The World a Department Store*, 160–163.

240 Peck, *The World a Department Store*, 85–86.

241 Van Petten, *The Great Man's Life*, 46. A. C. in the title is a reference to "after Christ," 10.

242 Van Petten, *The Great Man's Life*, 67.

243 Van Petten, *The Great Man's Life*, 47–48, 73.

within six months" ($10 to $30 an hour in 2023) and the poor were "spared the desperate anguish of complete poverty."[244]

The "wealth tax" enacted to support the Prosperity Fund was designed to encourage property owners to put their property to its most effective use. "All real wealth ought to produce services ... to provide income,"[245] explains Mann. The tax is "proportional" to the amount of each person's "real wealth"[246] with exemptions for those on the lower end of the economic spectrum.[247] Mann says of the tax, "we'll collect most of the money from the persons who are using their wealth least efficiently.[248]

Kentucky's success led other states and the federal government to adopted similar measures. In 1960, "Congress passed legislation to effect the Prosperity Fund on a national scale," paying citizens of the US $10 a week ($100 in 2023).[249] For those receiving both state and federal payments this amounted to $10,400 a year (adjusted to 2023 dollars). In addition to ensuring a general prosperity, the Prosperity Fund's operations prevented the nation's wealth "from drifting into the control of only a few people."[250]

Pacific Edge

The law regulates income extremes in Kim Stanley Robinson's *Pacific Edge* (1990), with a federal floor and ceiling.[251] As Oscar the town

244 Van Petten, *The Great Man's Life*, 79.
245 Van Petten, *The Great Man's Life*, 49.
246 Van Petten, *The Great Man's Life*, 48. In another work Van Petten explains that his wealth tax will tax only "idle" or "paper" wealth. Rather than taxing the market value of a person's house, for example, this tax would only tax the owner's equity in the house, the value minus any mortgage owed to the bank. Albert Archer Van Petten, *The Prosperity Plan* (Utopian Publishers, 1972), 15, 203.
247 Van Petten, *The Great Man's Life*, 233.
248 Van Petten, *The Great Man's Life*, 48.
249 Van Petten, *The Great Man's Life*, 96, 99.
250 Van Petten, *The Great Man's Life*, 18.
251 Robinson, *Pacific Edge*, 52.

attorney explains, the system in El Modena, similar to other California towns, is a mix of local communalism with features of the federal model providing an income base—a universal basic income. Land and public utilities are owned in common while residents are required to perform ten hours a week for town-owned businesses ("town work" described in Chapter 3). A "town share" of the income of the town-owned businesses goes back out to the citizens, amounting to "about twice the national income floor"[252] of ten thousand dollars a year[253] ($10,000 in 1990 = $22,800 in 2023). (*Pacific Edge* is described more fully in Chapter 7.)

Another Now

Yanis Varoufakis's *Another Now* (2021) features an unconditional monthly payment ("dividend") to each citizen. The dividend is "a *return* to every citizen for their partial *ownership* of society's capital."[254] Its purpose, says Kosti (the alternate narrator) is to "liberate everyone from the fear of destitution but also from the demeaning and cruel means testing of the welfare state." The state payment is funded by a 5 percent corporate revenue tax (noted above). "It provides people who do not care to engage in business activity," explains Kosti, "with sufficient income to provide priceless contributions to society that no market can properly value," for example "environmental conservation or non-commercial art."[255]

252 Robinson, *Pacific Edge*, 91–92.
253 Robinson, *Pacific Edge*, 52.
254 Varoufakis, *Another Now*, 54 (italics in original).
255 Varoufakis, *Another Now*, 54.

Minimum Wage Laws

> "It is curious how people take it for granted that they have a right to preach at you and pray over you as soon as your income falls below a certain level."[256]
>
> —George Orwell, *Down and Out in Paris and London* (1933)

"In the English Lower House," relates Karl Marx (1867), "for more than 400 years laws had been made for the maximum, beyond which wages absolutely must not rise."[257] In his 1884 *Principles of Political Economy*, J. S. Mill asks, "By what means, then, is poverty to be contended against? How is the evil of low wages to be remedied?"[258] He answers, "The simplest expedient which can be imagined for keeping the wages of labor up to the desirable point would be to fix them by law."[259] Adam Smith (1723–1790) argued that a "man must always live by his work, and his wages must at least be sufficient to maintain him."[260] Workers' wages must support their families as well, says Smith, otherwise "the race of such workmen could not last beyond the first generation."[261] This view is contrary to the seventeenth century mercantilist "utility of poverty doctrine" which, explain economists Jon Wisman and James Smith, "legitimated state-enforced maximum wages"[262] maintaining the workers' mere subsistence. Bernard Mandeville (1670–1733) promoted the doctrine that only workers on the brink of starvation possess the requisite motivation to work.[263]

256 Orwell, *Down and Out in Paris and London*, 181.

257 Marx, *Capital*, vol. 1, part 8, chap. 28, 517–519. Roman Emperor Justinian (485–562 BCE) enacted the earliest known attempt to curb wage growth with government action. Scheidel, *The Great Leveler*, 326, 321–322.

258 Mill, *The Principles of Political Economy*, 200.

259 Mill, *The Principles of Political Economy*, 193.

260 Smith, *Wealth of Nations*, 72.

261 Smith, *Wealth of Nations*, 72.

262 Jon D. Wisman with James F. Smith, "Legitimating Inequality: Fooling Most of the People All of the Time," *American Journal of Economics and Society* 70, no. 4 (October, 2011): 974–1013, 981–982.

263 Mandeville, *The Fable of the Bees*, vol. 1, 366.

When the poor are "well managed," Mandeville declares, "who as they ought to be kept from starving, so they should receive nothing worth saving."[264] By the middle of the eighteenth century, reports philosopher John Herman Randall, Jr, the merchant and manufacturing class's demand for government protection of the "rights of property and contract" and "freedom in all else" provided a justification for "profit-seeking and for the continuance of poverty" that have remained, says Randall (in 1926), "with little change to the present day."[265]

In the United States, the first state to adopt a minimum wage was Massachusetts in 1912. A national minimum wage (with critical exceptions[266]) was adopted in 1938 at 25 cents an hour (equivalent to $5.28 in 2023).[267] Though this rate was periodically adjusted by Congress, it has lost 40 percent of its purchasing power over the past forty years.[268] The *New York Times* reported in 2020 that "If the federal minimum wage in 1968 had kept up with inflation and productivity, it would now be $22 an hour. Instead, it's $7.25."[269] Piketty reports a similar result in France where wages increased "only 8 percent" between 1983 and 1995 trailing well behind price inflation.[270] This exemplifies a trend in Western countries that exacerbates economic inequality, as Piketty also observes: that of excluding low-wage workers from benefits afforded to the unemployed poor.[271]

264 Mandeville, *The Fable of the Bees*, vol. 1, 193.

265 John Herman Randall Jr, *The Making of the Modern Mind: A Survey of the Intellectual Background of the Present Age* (Boston: Houghton Mifflin, 1926), 322–323.

266 US Department of Labor list of exceptions <https://webapps.dol.gov/dolfaq/go-dol-faq.asp?faqid=218>

267 The US Fair Labor Standards Act.

268 Binyamin Applebaum, *The Economist's Hour* (New York: Back Bay Books, Little, Brown and Company, 2019), 325. For the history of the minimum wage see US Department of Labor <https://www.dol.gov/agencies/whd/minimum-wage/history/chart>

269 Nicholas Kristof and Sheryl WuDunn, "Who Killed the Knapp Family?," *New York Times* (January 9, 2020).

270 Thomas Piketty, *The Economics of Inequality*, trans. Arthur Goldhammer (Cambridge, MA: The Belknap Press of Harvard University Press, 2015), 50.

271 Piketty, *The Economics of Inequality*, 105.

Figure 3: "Front view of houses—Wild Court, in the Seven Dials district of London, notorious as one of the most dangerous slums. From a sketch in Report of Common Lodging Houses presented to both Houses of Parliament, 1855."

Caesar's Column

Ignatius Donnelly's *Caesar's Column* (1890), report Negley and Patrick, is a "combination of almost all the variations on the utopian theme."[272] Though it is remembered largely for its apocalyptic images of furious urban warfare in New York—"Civilization is gone, and all the devils are loose!"[273]—there are two endings, notes Pfaelzer: "the secular and the utopian."[274] The secular ending (discussed in Chapter 5) "discloses the existence of an angry class," says Pfaelzer, "which because of its perverted development, destroys society as a whole.[275] The utopian ending—in what Philip Wegner describes as the "Oz-like, isolated, agrarian" Uganda[276]—promises legal reforms, including a minimum wage. In narrator Gabriel Weltstein's journal we read, "Congress shall have the right to fix the rate of compensation for all forms of labor, so that wages shall never fall below a rate that will afford the laborer a comfortable living, with a margin that will enable him to provide for his old age."[277] In fixing compensation rates, Weltstein continues, "We shall not seek to produce uniformity of recompense for all kinds of work; for we know that skilled labor is intrinsically worth more than unskilled; and there are some forms of intellectual toil that are more valuable to the world than any muscular exertion."[278]

272 Negley and Partick, *The Quest for Utopia*, 23.

273 Ignatius Donnelly, *Caesar's Column: A Story of the Twentieth Century* (N.p.: n.d. [1890]), 161.

274 Jean Pfaelzer, *The Utopian Novel in America* (University of Pittsburgh Press, 1984), 138. There are two expressions of utopia in the novel. The first occurs in the chapter "Gabriel's Utopia," and the second in Uganda after Gabriel's escape from New York.

275 Pfaelzer, *The Utopian Novel in America*, 133.

276 Phillip E. Wegner, *Imaginary Communities: Utopia, The Nation, and the Spatial Histories of Modernity* (Berkeley: University of California Press, 2002), 123.

277 Donnelly, *Caesar's Column*, 192.

278 Donnelly, *Caesar's Column*, 193. Noto's *The Ideal City* uses a graded system as well where "recompense in all the great divisions of human labor is made nearly equal." Professors, for example, receive the same salary regardless of their field of specialization. Cosimo Noto, *The Ideal City* (New York, 1903), 321.

For Donnelly, however, the benefits of a minimum wage could not ignore its effects on trade with countries whose workers live in poverty or work for a lower rate of pay ("impoverished labor"). Trade with such countries is prohibited as it would inevitably drag down the workers' wages in Donnelly's more prosperous Ugandan utopia.[279]

A Modern Utopia

The world H. G. Wells describes in *A Modern Utopia* (1905) encourages employment and a minimum standard of living for all its citizens.[280] "Wells aims, through his minimum standard," writes John Partington, "to eliminate the struggle for the basics of life; housing, food, clothing and amenities such as heating and fresh, warm water."[281] Wells terms it "unjust and cruel" to permit "any one be fully employed at a rate of payment at which a wholesome, healthy, and ... reasonable happy life is impossible."[282] Wells's modern Utopia features a worldwide minimum wage adequate to "cover the cost of a decent life."[283] Expectations for full participation in society include, however, sufficient personal initiative enticing citizens to exceed the minimum wage. As a consequence, explains the narrator (the "Voice"), "to be moneyless will be clear evidence of unworthiness."[284] Satisfaction with the minimum wage disqualifies a person for marriage and hence for legal reproduction (discussed in Chapter 4). Fortunately, says Wells, "the inducements to men and women to raise their personal value above the minimum wage will be very great indeed."[285] The aim of the minimum wage, the narrator continues, is "not to rob life of incentives

279 Donnelly, *Caesar's Column*, 192.

280 Wells, *A Modern Utopia*, 57.

281 Partington, "The Time Machine and a Modern Utopia," 64. Partington notes, however, that "negative eugenics had an important role to play in establishing that minimum standard" (66). Wells's eugenic views are discussed in Chapter 4.

282 Wells, *Mankind in the Making*, 100.

283 Wells, *A Modern Utopia*, 57.

284 Wells, *A Modern Utopia*, 61.

285 Wells, *A Modern* Utopia, 63.

but to change their nature, to make life not less energetic, but less panic-stricken and violent and base."[286] Since the world government provides education and training, opportunities to advance beyond the minimum wage are abundant (discussed in Chapter 4 in *Equalizing Opportunity*).

A Romance of Two Centuries: A Tale of the Year 2025

Kenneth Guthrie was an American mystic and classical scholar.[287] His 1919 utopian *A Romance of Two Centuries: A Tale of the Year 2025* follows the adventures of its male protagonist into a future world where a series of female characters provide him assistance and emotional support. As the narrator approvingly reports, the central (and universal) values in the world of 2025 are "personal loyalty, culture, and spirituality."[288] The proposed solution to the problem of economic inequality is not through "leveling down" but through "leveling up." For, as the narrator explains, while the "well-to-do remained the same, those whose living had been precarious now had a firm standing-ground."[289] This standing-ground was the result of a personal ledger card that is punched with shapes indicating the type of expenditure or the amount of credit earned through work. The card is credited with any form of "approved day's work," with adjustment for an "efficiency rating."[290] The corresponding wage is proportional to the "physical, social and intellectual needs of the average individual." In this way, explains the narrator, "all persons received equivalent pay"[291]—arguably a form of minimum wage.

286 Wells, *A Modern* Utopia, 63.
287 Bleiler, *Science Fiction: The Early Years*, 315.
288 Kenneth Sylvan Guthrie, *A Romance of Two Centuries: A Tale of the Year 2025* (India: Pranava Books, n.d. [1919]), 265.
289 Guthrie, *A Romance of Two Centuries*, 59.
290 Guthrie, *A Romance of Two Centuries*, 58.
291 Guthrie, *A Romance of Two Centuries*, 168.

Debt and Interest Relief

> "It's precisely when the money changes hands, when the debt is canceled, that equality is restored and both parties can walk away and have nothing further to do with each other."[292]
>
> —David Graeber, *Debt: The First 5,000 Years* (2011)

Plato declares in the *Laws* that in his ideal society all purchases are to be made in the marketplace and exchanges effected with "money for goods, and goods for money, neither party giving credit to the other."[293] Debt, says Scheidel, "has certainly been a driver of inequality, forcing farmers to sell their land and cutting into disposable incomes." At least in theory, he continues, "the reduction or cancellation of debt might have helped to improve the position of poor borrowers at the expense of wealthy lenders." In practice, however, the same author concedes, "there is no good evidence that any such measures made a real difference."[294] Laws against usury, observes Keynes, are "amongst the most ancient economic practices of which we have record."[295] Francis Bacon argues, however, that "to speak of the abolishing of usury is idle. All states have ever had it. ... So as that opinion must be sent to Utopia."[296]

"[T]he great redeeming feature of poverty," Orwell declares, is "the fact that it annihilates the future."[297] The burden of debt is one tool in this process, as John Vernon notes in *Money and Fiction* (1984) since debt

292 David Graeber, *Debt: The first 5,000 Years* (Brooklyn, NY: Melville House, 2011), 122.

293 Plato, *Laws*, trans. Benjamin Jowett in *Great Books of the Western World*, vol. 7, ed. Robert Maynard Hutchins and Mortimer J. Adler (Chicago: Encyclopaedia Britannica, 1952), bk. 8, 849.

294 Scheidel, *The Great Leveler*, 359.

295 Keynes, *The General Theory of Employment, Interest, and Money*, 351.

296 Francis Bacon, "Of Usury," in *The Essays or Counsels Civil and Moral*, ed. Brian Vickers (Oxford University Press, 1999), 94.

297 Orwell, *Down and Out in Paris and London*, 20.

is a "means of arresting the future."[298] For those living in poverty, report psychologists Sendhil Mullainathan and Eldar Shafir, the acquisition of debt is often a tempting short-term solution—a consequence of the narrowly focused thinking associated with scarcity. "People short on money," their research shows, "patch together short-term solutions. ... And as the patches accumulate ... so do long-term costs."[299]

Caesar's Column

In an otherwise dystopian depiction of the working class's battle with an "unbridled plutocracy,"[300] a chapter titled "Gabriel's Utopia" offers a welcome respite in Donnelly's *Caesar's Column* (1890). Gabriel Weltstein the narrator, is asked what steps he would take if the "reformation of the world" came into his hands. First, says Weltstein, "I should do away with all interest on money. Interest on money is the root and ground of the world's troubles. It puts one man in a position of safety, and thereby at once creates a radical distinction in human society."[301] Usury, he says, "kills off the enterprising members of a community by bankrupting them, and leaves only the very rich and the very poor."[302] The reason for this, the narrator explains, is that "every dollar the employers of labor pay the lenders of money," comes directly out of the workers' pockets. Usury, he concludes, is "the cause of the first aristocracy, and out of this grow all the other aristocracies."[303] The necessity to borrow, says narrator Weltstein, "is one of the results of borrowing. That disease produces the symptoms."[304]

298 John Vernon, *Money and Fiction: Literary Realism in the Nineteenth and Early Twentieth Centuries* (Ithaca, NY: Cornell University Press, 1984), 112.
299 Sendhil Mullainathan and Eldar Shafir, *Scarcity* (New York: Picador, Henry Holt and Company, 2013), 116.
300 Donnelly, *Caesar's Column*, 60.
301 Donnelly, *Caesar's Column*, 66–67.
302 Donnelly, *Caesar's Column*, 67–68.
303 Donnelly, *Caesar's Column*, 67–68.
304 Donnelly, *Caesar's Column*, 67.

Freeland

Theodore Hertzka, a Viennese political economist and journalist, calls his *Freeland* (1891) "an economic romance" that "keeps to the firm ground of the soberest reality."[305] In *Freeland*, says Joyce Hertzler "we have an economist's attempt to counteract the deficiencies of the present economic and social order."[306] Hertzka' Freeland eliminates poverty ("we have no poor at all"[307]) while promoting the benefits of personal initiative and individual freedom. The "fiercest competition," says Arthur Ransom, is combined with "nationalization of land and capital,"[308] resulting in what Frank Manuel terms a "state-capitalist" utopia.[309] "Hertzka's novel," asserts Elun Gabriel, "illustrates the ambiguous nature of an enduring liberal belief that a free market system will end social and cultural inequalities."[310]

The utopian state of Freeland develops in a region of central east Africa proximate to Lake Victoria. The new residents are largely European men emigrating in search of opportunity in what they see as a less developed land.[311] Like many utopians, Hertzka saw himself as offering practical solutions to crucial social problems of his day. But the solutions to these problems, he insists, are not found in "an absolutely good order of society, but in that of the relatively best."[312]

305 Theodor Hertzka, Introduction to *Freeland: A Social Anticipation*, trans. Arthur Ransom (University of California Libraries; London: Chatto and Windus, 1891), xxii.

306 Joyce Oramel Hertzler, *The History of Utopian Thought* (New York: The Macmillan Company, 1926), 236.

307 Hertzka, *Freeland*, 204.

308 Arthur Ransom, "A Competitive Utopia," *The Gentleman's Magazine* 271 (London: Chatto and Windus, 1891), 45.

309 Manuel, "Toward a Psychological History of Utopia," 85.

310 Elun Gabriel, "Utopia, Science, and the Nature of Civilization in Hertzka's *Freiland*," *Seminar* 48, no. 1 (February 2012): 9–29, 12.

311 Bach notes that Hertzka was a product of his time and, "was seemingly blind to the similarities in the plight of the Viennese working poor with that of the Maasai whose land he sought to colonize." Bach, "Seeking Emptiness," 87.

312 Hertzka, introduction to *Freeland*, xvii–xviii.

Central to Hertzka's message in *Freeland*, suggests Gabriel, is "the growing confidence in a triumph over social inequality … through peaceful reform."[313] Ulrich Bach claims that Hertzka's utopia is "of more than mere historical interest to a present-day reader."[314] Negley and Patrick report that "Hertzka's [*Freeland*] is indeed perhaps the 'best-laid' plan of all utopian blueprints. His attention to the details of economic, political, and technical organization is fascinating."[315] For his part, however, Kateb affirms that "any serious utopian thinker will be made uncomfortable by the very idea of a blueprint of detailed recommendations concerning all facets of life."[316]

The bank director Mr. Clark explains that in Freeland anyone may charge as high a rate of interest as they please. However, he says, "you will find no one willing to pay it you, because everyone can get as much capital as he needs without interest."[317] Hertzka claims to have discovered a previously overlooked principle of political economy—"*that interest, though not unjust, will nevertheless in a condition of economic justice become superfluous and objectless.*"[318] From the engineer-narrator Henry Ney's journal, we learn that the "Free Society undertook to place [capital] at the disposal of everyone who wished for it, and that without interest, on condition that it was reimbursed out of the proceeds of production."[319] Thus in Freeland, rather than usury laws or proscribed interest, the state supplies interest-free loans.[320]

313 Gabriel, "Utopia, Science, and the Nature of Civilization in Theodor Hertzka's *Fieiland*," 16.
314 Bach, "Seeking Emptiness," 89.
315 Negley and Patrick, *The Quest for Utopia*, 108.
316 George Kateb, "Utopia and the Good Life," in *Utopias and Utopian Thought*, ed. Frank E. Manuel (Boston: Houghton Mifflin Company, 1966), 239.
317 Hertzka, *Freeland*, 258.
318 Hertzka, Introduction to *Freeland*, xvii–xviii, xxi (italics in original).
319 Hertzka, *Freeland*, 93.
320 Hertzka, *Freeland*, 258.

Other Non-progressive Wealth Taxes

> "Because we can't or won't redistribute through the tax system, we're forced to attend to the interests of the poor in other, more costly ways."[321]
>
> —Robert Frank, *The Darwin Economy* (2011)

Inheritance, says Thomas Shapiro in *Toxic Inequality*, "could be characterized as the nemesis of equal opportunity, meritocracy ... and quite possibly democracy itself."[322] Inheritance is rarely limited to property; frequently it portends superior education, outsized political influence, and claims to a favorable career. Inherited assets, Shapiro advises, "give those who receive them a huge head start in life and provide incalculable, unearned advantages."[323] Thomas Paine stressed the importance of this fact when he espoused what Claeys terms the "principle of progress,"[324] that no person "ought to be in a worse condition when born under what is called a state of civilization, than he would have been had he been born in a state of nature."[325] For this reason, in addition to land reform (of which in its place), Paine recommends a 10 percent inheritance tax falling "at the moment that property is passing by the death of one person to the possession of another." At that time, he says, "the bequeather gives nothing: the receiver pays nothing."[326]

321 Frank, *The Darwin Economy*, 112.

322 Shapiro, *Toxic Inequality*, 146.

323 Shapiro, *Toxic Inequality*, 123.

324 Gregory Claeys, *Thomas Paine: Social and Political Thought* (Boston: Unwin Hyman, 1989), 201.

325 Paine, *Agrarian Justice*, 477–478.

326 Paine, *Agrarian Justice*, 478–480. Piketty muses, "Imagine a system of inheritance redistribution that enabled everyone to receive a minimal inheritance." Piketty, *A Brief History of Equality*, 160.

The Diothas

John Macnie's *The Diothas* (1883), observes Walter Taylor, is "one of the very few really significant works among the now-forgotten romances of the Gilded Age."[327] Macnie's guide Utis Estai explains to the visitor/narrator Ismar Thiusen (Macnie's pen name) that "At a very early period it was found that the excessive accumulation of wealth in certain families led to very serious evils."[328] Among the rich whose wealth was inherited "without any merit or exertion on their part," notes Estai, the majority are "mere drones inflated with the idiotic pride of uselessness, besides many actively noxious by their vices." For this reason, law limited the power of bequest. No person could legally bequeath to any other person more than a specified amount. This value was set at $20,000 [$613,000 in 2023]."[329] In this way society forbids the well-heeled to employ their wealth in a way that experience has shown to be harmful to society.[330] As Vernon Parrington, Jr notes, under Macnie's system, "men had the opportunity to become neither wealthy beyond other men, nor poor beyond other men."[331]

Looking Within: The Misleading Tendencies of "Looking Backward" Made Manifest

John Roberts's 1893 *Looking Within: The Misleading Tendencies of "Looking Backward"* (discussed in Chapter 6) recommends a 10 percent wealth tax. This is suggested by Robert's spokesperson and farmer Mr. Acre who opposes Bellamy's scheme. "Those who possessed wealth," says

327 Taylor, *The Economic Novel in America*, 189.

328 John Macnie, *The Diothas, or, a Far Look Ahead* (New York: G. P. Putnam's Sons, 1883), 115.

329 Macnie, *The Diothas*, 115.

330 Macnie, *The Diothas*, 116. The result of this law was that people of great wealth would "leave the residue for some public object," or parcel it out in smaller lots to a greater number of people resulting in a "more equal diffusion of wealth."

331 Parrington, Jr, *American Dreams*, 60.

Mr. Acre, "could much better have devoted a tenth of it to provide for the poor than to lose it all." A preferable approach, argues Mr. Acre, would have been to retain the old system while using the tax to help the poor by "providing employment in industry though subsidized by government."[332]

Other Brief Examples

In Alexander Craig's *Ionia* (1898), to preserve the Ionians from plutocracy, explains the ambassador, no person may receive an inheritance of more than £50,000 [£5,154,000 or $6,375,000 in 2023].[333] Any amount greater than £50,000 escheats to the state. In Wells's *A Modern Utopia* (1905) a tax falls at death on that which the deceased used to make a living, primarily business and investment properties. These assets face heavy taxes since, as Wells says, the government takes the "lion's proportion."[334] Robert Frank's *Social* Integration (1935) employs a confiscatory estate tax geared at limiting economic inequality. "[W]hatever property the individual may accumulate during his lifetime will, upon his death, automatically become government property."[335] The state in Albert Van Petten's *The Great Man's Life: 1925 to 2000 A. C.* (1959) levies a wealth tax to fund his scheme of universal basic income.[336]

332 Roberts, *Looking Within*, 181.

333 Alexander Craig, *Ionia: Land of Wise Men and Fair Women* (Chicago: E. A. Weeks Co., 1898), 200, 202.

334 Wells, *A Modern Utopia*, 41.

335 Robert Frank, *Social Integration: A Brief Fictional History of the United States During the Period*, 1935–1945 (Boston, MA: The Christopher Publishing House, 1935), 158.

336 Van Petten, *The Great Man's Life*, 71–72.

Curtailing Business Cycles

> "A lot of people think that we must have cycles between prosperity and depression; they think that those cycles are unavoidable, but the reasoning doesn't seem logical to me."[337]
>
> —Albert Van Petten, *The Great Man's Life: 1925 to 2000 A. C.* (1959)

Panic selling, business failures, mortgage foreclosures, price gouging, bankruptcies, recessions, depressions, and the widespread unemployment of "hard times" are visible manifestations of business cycles.[338] One of the functions of central banks around the world is to soften the effects that otherwise accompany the boom or bust nature of economic activity. In the United States, for example, the Federal Reserve modifies the interest rates it charges in response to what it perceives as unfavorable changes in inflation and unemployment.[339]

One feature of John Macnie's *The Diothas* (1883), Louis Kern observes, is that by the ninety-sixth century "business cycles need no longer be feared."[340] Though a regulated economy, as the guide Utis Estai explains to the visitor Ismar Thiusen, their system is not communism, as "each is the owner of whatever property he acquired, whether by gift or his own exertion."[341] Both the supply of goods required and of labor needed for specific

337 Van Petten, *The Great Man's Life*, 46.

338 Fischer distinguishes between relatively short business cycles and much longer "great waves" which he says "appear on the surface of the evidence." Discovering these great waves, he says, requires a skill that is "immensely difficult for many academic scholars ... to look the evidence in the face, without fixed ideological, theoretical or epistemological preconceptions." David Hackett Fischer, *The Great Wave: Price Revolutions and the Rhythm of History* (Oxford University Press, 1996), 9.

339 "The Federal Reserve performs key functions in the public interest to promote the health of the U.S. economy and the stability of the U.S. financial system." <https://www.federalreserve.gov/aboutthefed/the-fed-explained.htm>.

340 Louis J. Kern, "Evangelical Environmentalism and the New Commonwealth: Visions of Labor, Urban Culture, and Technological Transformation in Futuristic Fiction, 1883–1903," *Utopian Studies* 4 (1991): 42–54, 53.

341 Macnie, *The Diothas*, 12.

jobs are coordinated through access to statistics on consumption. These statistics, the guide explains, "enable us to estimate, not only the amount of any product on hand at a given time, but also the number of new producers of any class that will be required within a given number of years."[342] Their vocational education program uses this data to guide students into the proper careers and thus avoid the "waste of misdirected effort, resulting in the overcrowding of callings."[343] In this way the correct number of new workers in any calling is "assigned to each district every year, and divided among the boys [and girls] of the proper age."[344] Yet, "none is made to adopt a trade to which he has a decided objection."[345]

Capping Wealth or Income

> "The beginning of reform is not so much to equalize property as to train the nobler sort of natures not to desire more, and to prevent the lower from getting more; that is to say, they must be kept down, but not ill-treated."[346]
>
> —Aristotle, *Politics*

A handful of utopians have tackled economic inequality by imposing a maximum on wealth or income. Alvarado Fuller's *A. D. 2000* (1890) restricts corporate profits to 20 percent a year.[347] Ignatius Donnelly's Ugandan utopia in *Caesar's Column* (1890) limits the amount of money or land a person can own. "All above that must be used, either by the owner or the government, in works of public usefulness."[348] Stewart Bruce's *The World in 1931* (1921) (effectively) confines personal income to

342 Macnie, *The Diothas*, 119–120.

343 Macnie, *The Diothas*, 119.

344 Macnie, *The Diothas*, 119–120. "Boys and girls have an equal right to enter any employment" (121).

345 Macnie, *The Diothas*, 119–120.

346 Aristotle, *Politics*, trans. Jowett, bk. 2, chap. 7, 1267b.

347 Fuller, *A. D. 2000*, 268.

348 Donnelly, *Caesar's Column*, 191–193.

$4,000 annually ($78,000 in 2023) as noted in the discussion of progressive income taxes.[349] The union-based government in Jack Wagner's 1979 *The Great Change* (discussed in Chapter 3) caps personal income at $500 a month ($2,050 in 2023).[350] Kim Stanley Robinson's 1990 *Pacific Edge* (discussed in Chapter 7) curbs annual income at $100,000 ($228,000 in 2023), as noted;[351] Robinson's *Ministry for the Future* (2020) restricts personal income to ten times the "universal necessary income,"[352] echoing Orwell's "ten to one"[353] counsel cited in this book's introduction.

Cryptocurrency

> "One percent of all electricity created is burned to make bitcoins."[354]
>
> —Kim Stanley Robinson, *The Ministry for the Future* (2020)

Alternatives to government currencies play a significant role in utopian history; labor notes (Owen), pasteboard credit cards (Bellamy), personal ledger cards (Guthrie), international paper money (Donnelly),[355] centry (Rosewater),[356] digital carbon coins (Robinson),[357] and the digital

349 Bruce, *The World in 1931*, 155.
350 Wagner, *The Great Change*, 49.
351 Robinson, *Pacific Edge*, 91.
352 Robinson, *The Ministry for the Future*, 478.
353 George Orwell, "The Lion and the Unicorn: Socialism and the English Genius," in *Essays* (New York: Everyman's Library, 1998; Alfred A. Knopf, 1968), 336.
354 Robinson, *The Ministry for the Future*, 80. The amount of electricity required to operate Bitcoin computers in the US "is as if another New York City's worth of residences were now drawing on the nation's power supply." The result is environmental damage from fossil fuel-generated electricity and higher electric costs for other consumers. "The Real-World Costs of the Digital Race for Bitcoin," Gabriel J. X. Dance, *New York Times* (April 9, 2023).
355 Donnelly, *Caesar's Column*, 71.
356 Described in Chapter 4. Rosewater, *The Making of a Millennium*, 10, 125.
357 Digital carbon coins employed for environmental remediation feature in Robinson's *The Ministry for the Future*, 172–173.

currency Kosmos (Varoufakis)[358] are examples. Technology brings the hope of solving even unforeseen problems. Plato warned, however, that that inventors of technology are not the best judges of "what measure of harm and of profit they have for those that shall employ them."[359] The blockchain technology animating cryptocurrency did not arise as a tool for aiding the poor, but its true believers see this as one of its benefits.[360] For the populations of poor living in economically less developed countries, for example, some perceive Bitcoin and other cryptocurrencies as a viable substitute for a banking system that is either absent or out of reach. A recent paper in the journal *Utopian Studies* acknowledges the utopian aspirations of its staunchest proponents that "cryptocurrency could become a universal currency."[361] One outcome of such a digital revolution, as Robinson envisions in *The Ministry for the Future* (2020), is an increase in financial transparency contributing to economic equality (described in Chapter 4).

358 Kosmos, a digital currency used for regulating international trade, appears in Varoufakis's *Other Now*, 132. Sargent's database, "Utopian Literature in English," affords additional sources including, for example, a utopia where cash is eliminated and all transactions are made using a national credit card that permits purchases only of an approved nature. J. B. Ball, *The Handbook of the Universal Monetary System of National Credit Control: An Advanced Theory of Government and Finance* (Regina, SK, Canada, 1956). <https://openpublishing.psu.edu/utopia/content/universal-monetary-system-national-credit-control-financial-revolution-nationalized>

359 Plato, *Phaedrus*, 520 (274e).

360 ShareCast advertisement, "How Bitcoin Can Benefit the Poor in the Developing Countries" <https://www.sharecast.com/promoted/cryptocurrencies/how-bitcoin-can-benefit-the-poor-in-the-developing-countries.html>. An opinion piece in *Bitcoin Magazine* proclaims, "Bitcoin is the Solution to the World's Economic Inequality Problem." January 17, 2023. <https://bitcoinmagazine.com/culture/bitcoin-solves-global-economic-inequality>

361 John Mark Robinson, "The Neoliberal Utopianism of Bitcoin and Modern Monetary Theory," *Utopian Studies* 33, no. 1 (2022): 127–143, 131.

CHAPTER 3

Instruments of Change: Social Reforms

> "It is the reformer who is anxious for the reform, and not society, from which he should expect nothing better than opposition, abhorrence, and even mortal persecution."[1]
>
> —M. K. Gandhi, *An Autobiography* (1927)

My categorization of certain reforms as social in contrast to those I have classified economic or political, though necessarily arbitrary, rests on my assumption that social reforms nurture fundamental cultural changes. Some of the topics I discuss in this chapter, such as universal compulsory education or labor unions, have important economic consequences and may also require governmental action, but their nature marks a shift in how members of society view one another and signals a change in the underlying sense of society. While economic reforms are aimed at altering people's conduct by changing the financial incentives to which they respond and political reforms modify conduct by enacting new laws and their sanctions, social reforms aim at more "permanent" alterations in the forces that create and maintain an ideal society.

Free Universal Compulsory Education

> "Even the pretense of having an educated populace was ending. Politicians shook their heads and said sadly that universal education was a failed experiment."[2]
>
> —Octavia E. Butler, *Parable of the Talents* (1998)

1 M. K. Gandhi, *An Autobiography or The Story of My Experiments with Truth*, trans. Mahadev Desai (Ahmedabad: Navajivan Publishing House, 1927), 200.

2 Octavia E. Butler, *Parable of the Talents* (New York: Grand Central Publishing, 1998), 365.

Education for utopians, asserts Hertzler, "was one of society's main instruments for realizing its destiny."[3] "Universal education" affirms reformer Ignatius Donnelly (1831–1901), "is the basis of all progress."[4] Education, however, observes J. S. Mill, "is one of the most difficult of all arts." Any progress is slow and difficult, he contends, because "the future generation is educated by the present, and the imperfections of the teachers set an invincible limit to the degree to which they can train their pupils to be better than themselves."[5] Aggravating this restriction, as Dewey explains, is the fact that "the subject-matter as well as standards of proper conduct are handed down from the past."[6] The alternative to this backward-looking (and anti-utopian) educational philosophy is, Dewey believes, the "systematic utilization of scientific method as the pattern and ideal of intelligent exploration and exploitation of the potentialities inherent in experience."[7] Such education, Dewey submits, "arouses curiosity, strengthens initiative, and sets up desires and purposes"[8]—the grist of utopian visions.

Education is "at the heart of all utopian imagining," argues Michael Robertson. "Utopia depends on the notion of human plasticity, the idea that humans can be, if not perfected, then at least brought closer to an ideal."[9] For utopians struggling with the problem of economic inequality, however, it is not the perfectibility of humans but the elimination of class-, gender-, and race-biased educational structures that is assigned the highest priority. These structures favor one group with educational blessings they deny to others, thereby preserving the educationally deprived group in its perpetually disadvantaged position. In the US, for example, as Nussbaum observes, students in a "rich school district may have as much as 75 or 100

3 Hertzler, *The History of Utopian Thought*, 292.

4 Donnelley, *The Golden Bottle*, 246.

5 Mill, *Socialism*, 60.

6 John Dewey, "Experience and Education," in *John Dewey: The Later Works: 1925–1953*, vol. 13: 1938–1939 (Carbondale: Southern Illinois University Press, 1991), 6.

7 Dewey, *Experience and Education*, 58.

8 Dewey, *Experience and Education*, 20–21.

9 Michael Robertson, *The Last Utopians* (Princeton, NJ: Princeton University Press, 2018), 259.

times as much spent on them as is spent on students in a poor district."[10] Michael Sandel in *The Tyranny of Merit* adds, "most colleges and universities do less to expand opportunity than to consolidate privilege."[11] "By bringing full educational opportunities within reach of all," affirms Hertzler, "society would be enabled to capitalize all of its latent assets of human capacity."[12]

"Equality of educational opportunity," argues sociologist Ralf Dahrendorf, "is a basic right of every citizen, because education is both a prerequisite and a dimension of full social and political participation."[13] Education is invaluable in the battle against economic inequality not merely because better educated citizens will have more paths to economic (or other) success, but also, as Piketty observes, because "the thirst for fiscal justice grows stronger as people become better educated and better informed."[14] In the long run, Piketty continues, "it is access to skills and diffusion of knowledge that allow inequality to be reduced both within countries and at the international level."[15] The most significant tool in this process, according to Piketty, is compulsory elementary education.[16] Herbert Gans, a sociologist who studies education as a means of overcoming poverty explains, however, that while education has been conceived as a means to escape from poverty, his research suggests that education, "at least for the poor, is not a causal agent in the achievement of mobility, but one of its effects. ... Economic success leads to educational success, not the other way around."[17] This implies that educational reforms require implementation *along with* reforms such as universal basic income to effectively combat

10 Nussbaum, *Frontiers of Justice*, 294.

11 Sandel, *The Tyranny of Merit*, 169.

12 Hertzler, *The History of Utopian Thought*, 293.

13 Ralf Dahrendorf, *Life Chances: Approaches to Social and Political Theory* (University of Chicago Press, 1979), 127.

14 Piketty, *Capital and Ideology*, 577.

15 Piketty, *Capital and Ideology*, 534.

16 Piketty, *The Economics of Inequality*, 80. For a discussion of the distinction between educational compulsion and educational coercion in its utopian context, see Sarah Otterson, "Diversity, Change, Violence: Octavia Butler's Pedagogical Philosophy," *Utopian Studies* 19, no. 3 (2008): 433–456, 443.

17 Herbert J. Gans, *People, Plans, and Policies: Essays on Poverty, Racism, and Other National Urban Problems* (New York: Columbia University Press, 1993), 231–232.

the ravages of poverty and other dimensions of economic inequality. As King Timoleon, in Alexander Craig's *Ionia* (1898), informed his citizens, "the best school system which could be devised would fail to educate the children of parents who were unable to find bread for their families."[18]

Education in this discussion is viewed more broadly than the acquisition of knowledge; utopians see education either as a way of molding character and altering society (Robert Owen, Albert Chavannes), or of maintaining the spirit of an ideal society (Étienne Cabet, Edward Bellamy).[19] A common theme of utopian educational reform is removing children from their parents' harmful influence. Utopian writers as diverse as Robert Owen, Charlotte Perkins Gilman,[20] and B. F. Skinner[21] have expressed this concern. The sea captain-narrator in Tommaso Campanella's *City of the Sun* (1602) explains, "since individuals for the most part bring forth children wrongly and educate them wrongly," the Solarians "commit the education of the children ... to the care of magistrates."[22] This mistrust of parental judgment extends to expectant mothers in Girgsby and Lowe's *Nequa* (1900) where the education of unborn children is coordinated in "Matron's homes." These homes, which Parrington calls "the sole original contribution of *Nequa*,"[23] provide a controlled environment for the "scientific adaption of pre-natal influences to specific purposes," since pre-natal influences are "the commencing point in the education of every child."[24]

18 Craig, *Ionia: Land of Wise Men and Fair Women*, 207. The historical Timoleon, a Greek statesman and general who died in 337 BCE, features in *Plutarch's Lives*, 325–335.

19 Gutek reports that Bellamy "did not believe that formal education could change the social order." What education delivers is "socially-educated" people who can understand the benefits of working in concert rather than in competition. Gerald Gutek, "An Analysis of Formal Education in Edward Bellamy's Looking Backward," *History of Education Quarterly* 4, no. 4 (December, 1964): 251–263, 260–261.

20 Child rearing is entrusted only to the most skilled teachers. Charlotte Perkins Gilman, *Herland* (Mineola, NY: Dover Publications, 1998), 70.

21 Skinner's spokesperson Frazier asserts, "We have to attenuate the child-parent relation." B. F. Skinner, *Walden Two* (New York: Macmillan Publishing Co., 1976), 131.

22 Tommaso Campanella, "The City of the Sun," trans. Thomas W. Halliday, in *Ideal Commonwealths* (London: The Colonial Press, 1901), 156.

23 Parrington, *American Dreams*, 101.

24 Grigsby and Lowe, *Nequa*, 230–231.

"Universal" Education

One caveat Shapiro poses in *Toxic Inequality* affects the term *universal* itself. Whether speaking of universal education, universal basic income, or universal health care, observes Shapiro, when a "politician calls a process or policy universal, we generally take this to mean that everybody is equally eligible."[25] But an ambiguity in the phrase *equally eligible* arises from the distinction between universally qualified and universally provided. When eligibility incorporates considerations of means—everyone who can afford it is eligible—universality is restricted by design. Jack Wagner emphasizes this distinction in *The Great Change* (1979), where they "don't just say that everyone is entitled to an education, but that the government *must* set up an education system so that every child has access to it free of charge."[26]

Robert Owen

Robert Owen (1771–1858) was a Welsh textile manufacturer and managing partner in a New Lanark, Scotland mill employing "about two thousand people."[27] There he championed a form of universal compulsory education ("infant schools") designed to mold the character of his ideal citizens such that they would understand the importance of character formation in developing people capable of living a cooperative, modest, and peaceful life.

Owen decreed that our character is formed in early childhood, not as a result of a person's own efforts but through exposure to external factors of training and education. "In every known region of the earth," Owen recites, "man has been compelled from infancy to acquire the peculiar notions of some sect, some class, some party, and of some country. In consequence, each individual has been surrounded by four

25 Shapiro, *Toxic Inequality*, 190.
26 Jack Wagner, *The Great Change* (Trinidad, CA: Trinidad Press, 1979), 212 (italics in original).
27 Wells, *The Outline of History*, 432.

dense atmospheres of error and prejudice."[28] For Owen, says Claeys, education "was eventually to end the unconscious determination of character by circumstances."[29] In articulating what he calls his "discovery," Owen offers the following proclamation: "'That the character is formed *for* and not *by* the individual,' is a truth to which every fact connected with man's history bears testimony."[30] For Owen, notes John Harrison, education "was to be the lever, first for dealing with the problem of the poor, but soon for effecting change throughout the whole of society."[31] Owen's goal was to transform education by ensuring that everyone is exposed to the same *enlightened* notions—a universal curriculum taught by uniformly trained teachers—including the proper view of character formation. "This focus on character and reasoning," explains David Leopold, "was central to Owen's criticism of contemporary educational theory and practice."[32] Owen's work, report John Lawson and Harold Silver, "helped to create a confidence in the possibility of overcoming the problems of industrialization and change."[33]

Owen believed it possible to create "any general human character, good, bad, or indifferent,"[34] in any population—but especially in children[35]—"yet preserving always the organic peculiarities of each individual."[36] In asserting this, Claeys explains, Owen "never implied that

28 Robert Owen, *A New View of Society and Other Writings* (New York: Penguin Classics, 1991), 161.

29 Claeys, *Citizens and Saints*, 120.

30 Owen, *A New View of Society*, 305 (italics in original).

31 John F. C. Harrison, *Utopianism and Education* (New York: Teachers College Press, Teachers College, Columbia University, 1968), 33.

32 David Leopold, "Education and Utopia: Robert Owen and Charles Fourier," *Oxford Review of Education* 37, no. 5 (October, 2011): 619–635, 626.

33 John Lawson and Harold Silver, *A Social History of Education in England* (London: Methuen and Co., Ltd., 1973), 247.

34 Robert Owen, *The Revolution in the Mind and Practice of the Human Race* (London: Effingham Wilson, Publisher, 1849), 22.

35 Owen, *A New View of Society and Other Writings*, 19.

36 Owen, *The Revolution in the Mind*, 22.

any character could be 'given' to every individual, only that groups could be educated to share certain characteristics in common."[37]

It was the infant school, notes Lawson and Silver, "that established Owen's reputation," giving rise to an infant-school movement.[38] Owen boasts in his autobiography, "The New Rational Infant School which I had invented, and its unheard of results, were blazed abroad, and excited great interest."[39] The means of instruction, reports Leopold, "were designed to make learning a pleasure and delight to children," who were "encouraged to ask questions and seek clarification."[40] The infant schools "were original enough in their educational techniques," posits Raymond Williams, "but they were far more innovating in their humanity and kindness."[41]

This form of education, Owen assumed, would facilitate society's transformation into a harmonious series of self-governing, self-supporting townships (discussed below and in Chapter 6).[42] In this way, says Wells, Owen supposed that "What could be done for one industrial community could be done ... for every industrial community in the country."[43] Ultimately, Owen's leveling scheme would place all children under the care of the township of their birth.[44] "The single family arrangements," Owen decrees, "will be broken up, and everything connected with them."[45] The physical removal of children is necessary, he explains, because their parents' affections for them are "too strong for their judgments."[46] As a result, Owen

37 Claeys, Introduction to *A New View of Society and Other Writings,* by Robert Owen, xxiv.

38 Lawson and Silver, *A Social History of Education in England*, 247.

39 Robert Owen, *The Life of Robert Owen Written by Himself* (London: Effingham Wilson, 1857), 188.

40 Leopold, "Education and Utopia: Robert Owen and Charles Fourier," 625.

41 Raymond Williams, *Culture and Society: 1780–1950* (New York: Columbia University Press, 1983), 28.

42 Owen, *The Revolution in the Mind*, 43.

43 Wells, *The Outline of History*, 432.

44 Owen, *The Revolution in the Mind*, 61.

45 Robert Owen, *Lectures on an Entire New State of Society* (London: J. Brooks, 1830), 141.

46 Owen, *The Revolution in the Mind*, 78.

directs, "All children in the same Township shall be trained and educated together, as children of the same family."[47]

Travels in Icaria

Étienne Cabet's *Travels in Icaria* (1840), says Hertzler, "was a community and equality of goods and work, of duties and rights, of burdens and benefits and enjoyments."[48] Born in Dijon France, Cabet worked as a lawyer, social reformer, and publisher of an antigovernment newspaper, *Le Populaire*. Cabet's "increasingly radical outlook," relates Keith Taylor, resulted in his prosecution and a five-year exile, most of which was spent in England where his political views shifted from republicanism to communism.[49] Historian Marie Berneri observes that it was probably the influence of Robert Owen that led Cabet to found Icarian communities in America.[50] In 1847, reports Taylor, Cabet contacted Owen for advice on possible US sites,[51] the most durable of which was Nauvoo, Illinois on the Mississippi River (1849–1856[52])—a little over 300 miles from Owen's then defunct New Harmony, Indiana community (1825–1827).

Icaria reveals the importance of universal compulsory education in promoting economic equality. "Being that we consider education to be the basis and foundation of society," reports Dinaros a young Icarian historian, "the republic provides it to all its children equally, just as it gives them equal nourishment.'"[53] This includes the same general or elementary education, "without differentiation by sex or profession

47 Owen, *The Revolution in the Mind*, 80.
48 Hertzler, *The History of Utopian Thought*, 206.
49 Taylor, *The Political Ideas of the Utopian Socialists*, 162.
50 Marie Louise Berneri, *Journey Through Utopia* (Freeport, NY: Books for Libraries Press, 1969), 221–222.
51 Taylor, *The Political Ideas of the Utopian Socialists*, 164.
52 Cabet and some of his followers left in 1856 for St Louis. The Nauvoo colony ended in 1860.
53 Cabet, *Travels in Icaria*, 32 (capitalization in original removed).

... which encompasses the basic elements of all human knowledge."[54] Parents are charged with educating their children until the age of 5 regarding personal and family matters.[55] After the age of 3 children mingle informally with their peers exposing them "to sociability, equality, and fraternity."[56] At the age of 5, "communal education" begins and continues until "seventeen [girls] or eighteen [boys]."[57] This communal instruction, notes Cabet's spokesperson, is "delegated to national instructors in national schools."[58]

The universal format of Icarian education means that what is taught and learned is "exactly the same for each person, and each person is encouraged to teach others what he or she knows."[59] Because agriculture is the country's most important industry, explains Valmor, an Icarian spokesperson, they desire that all citizens be educated in farming[60] (as in More and Campanella[61]). At 17 years of age for girls and 18 for boys specialized education begins giving each citizen the theoretical and practical knowledge necessary "to excel in his or her scientific or industrial profession."[62] "Imagine, if you can," Dinaros exclaims, "the salutary consequences of this revolution in the education of women."[63]

54 Cabet, *Travels in Icaria*, 61, 123.
55 Cabet, *Travels in Icaria*, 61, 65.
56 Cabet, *Travels in Icaria*, 73.
57 Cabet, *Travels in Icaria*, 65.
58 Cabet, *Travels in Icaria*, 61.
59 Cabet, *Travels in Icaria*, 62.
60 Cabet, *Travels in Icaria*, 123.
61 More, *Utopia*, trans. Adams, bk. 2, 43–44; Tommaso Campanella, *The City of the Sun*, trans. Daniel J. Donno (Berkeley: University of California Press, 1981), 43, 49.
62 Cabet, *Travels in Icaria*, 67.
63 Cabet, *Travels in Icaria*, 67.

Figure 4: "Equality/Lectures in Physics for girls at the Sorbonne, Paris, 1867"

The Diothas

In Everett Blieler's assessment, *The Diothas* is "perhaps the second most important American nineteenth-century ideal society."[64] Diotha is a family name passed down from mother to daughter.[65] Riva Diotha is one of the residents the traveler/narrator meets on his visit to utopia in the ninety-sixth century. In *The Diothas* (1883), writes Vernon Parrington, Jr, John Macnie "was rebelling against the poverty of his age, a poverty which economists bred to Malthusian economics insisted was an inevitable corollary of the capitalistic system of free enterprise."[66] Macnie's utopian goal was to present a mixed economy where people had the opportunity to become successful—though not excessively rich—without

64 Bleiler, *Science Fiction: The Early Years*, 735.

65 Macnie, *The Diothas*, 58–59.

66 Parrington, Jr, *American Dreams*, 60.

fear of poverty.[67] In achieving this goal education is regarded as "the main business of life."[68]

The dual purpose of education is occupational training and building society's cohesiveness.[69] "The fundamental training imparted in the schools and academies," explains narrator Ismar Thiusen, "was so thorough, that upon it any superstructure could be raised."[70] Boys and girls attend the same classes until age 17, though after age 12 their mode of dress is altered and they are seated apart.[71] Each course of study, the narrator continues, has a "well-defined purpose ... in which the balance was nicely adjusted between the desirable and the attainable."[72] Training the young is regarded as the "one great duty, both of the family and of the State."[73] In the selection of their careers, boys and girls may enter the same professions.[74] Because a "sound, equally developed body" is viewed as fundamental to their educational curriculum, they provide the "youth of both sexes a twofold physical training"—athletic and industrial.[75] The athletic training is such that tends to "impart activity and grace."[76] The industrial training includes "the use of tools and instruments as shall make the hands the reliable servants of the brain."[77] Their instructional philosophy holds that knowledge acquired from books, "though by no means neglected," is the "least important branch of education."[78]

67 Parrington, Jr, *American Dreams*, 60.
68 Macnie, *The Diothas*, 131.
69 Macnie, *The Diothas*, 113–114.
70 Macnie, *The Diothas*, 131.
71 Macnie, *The Diothas*, 150.
72 Macnie, *The Diothas*, 131.
73 Macnie, *The Diothas*, 117.
74 Macnie, *The Diothas*, 121.
75 Macnie, *The Diothas*, 114.
76 Macnie, *The Diothas*, 114.
77 Macnie, *The Diothas*, 114.
78 Macnie, *The Diothas*, 117.

Looking Backward and *Equality*

The "first effect of economic equality," Dr. Leete explains to Julian West in *Equality* (the 1897 expansion of *Looking Backward*), "was to provide equal educational advantages for all and the best the community could afford."[79] Universal education is provided in *Looking Backward* (1888) until age 21. Specialized education or training in professional schools is available until age 30.[80] Bellamy's *Equality* adds the dimension of free lifetime learning in the form of "elective post-graduate courses of study in every branch of science."[81] The significance of this education, especially for "middle-aged fathers and mothers," is the fact that during youth the mind is not yet prepared for the study of the "most important branches of knowledge," which the more mature mind is able to grasp and appreciate.[82]

The Ke Whonkus People

Professor Kumtux in John O. Greene's 1890 *The Ke Whonkus People* (introduced in Chapter 2), declares: "I would maintain free, public secular schools, with free text books and compulsory attendance for all children. … Because, education of the masses is the only means of smothering out superstition which enslaves them; and also of advancing civilization and developing the race."[83]

The Future Commonwealth

Socioland, Africa (referenced in Chapter 2) is the country in Albert Chavannes's *The Future Commonwealth* (1892) where they hold that "equal advantages in education are necessary to maintain equal chances of success

79 Bellamy, *Equality*, 248.
80 Bellamy, *Looking Backward*, 75.
81 Bellamy, *Equality*, 249.
82 Bellamy, *Equality*, 249.
83 Greene, *The Ke Whonkus People*, 234.

in society."[84] In the tradition of Robert Owen, Chavannes emphasizes the role of childhood education for developing character and preparing citizens for the benefits of a noncompetitive social order. "I realize fully," explains the visitor/narrator Samuel Balcom, "that the progress they have made is due to the development of their character which enables them to place in the hands of the Commonwealth many of its most important industries, while at the same time they have been able to safely withdraw government control from the departments of morals and religion."[85]

The Socioland schools teach the importance of work, explains Balcom's guide Miss Bell, and "all the advantages we enjoy here are the result of man's and woman's labor."[86] As a result of their education, Miss Bell continues, they learn that they will, in turn, become "useful members of society."[87] Another character, Mr. Wilton, advises the visitor that children in Socioland, rather than learning the biblical lesson that labor is a curse following the fall of Adam, learn that it is only through labor that "all that which makes life worth living has been attained" and that their continued progress will result from "labor intelligently directed." This is only possible, Mr. Wilton declares, "when the right kind of spirit animates the whole population."[88]

Contrary to societies offering fixed social structures and craving political stability, "We care nothing for these things," explains another spokesperson Mr. Bell. "We are trying to improve our condition in life, and are ready to change every day if we are better satisfied thereby."[89] Because of Socioland's emphasis on experimentation and change, "very little compulsion is ever used." We learn that if we "desire to attain certain ends, certain means must be used," but we are free to use those means "or neglect them as we choose."[90] These principles presumably apply to their education as well.

84 Chavannes, *The Future Commonwealth*, 30.
85 Chavannes, *The Future Commonwealth,* 114.
86 Chavannes, *The Future Commonwealth*, 91.
87 Chavannes, *The Future Commonwealth*, 91.
88 Chavannes, *The Future Commonwealth*, 57–58.
89 Chavannes, *The Future Commonwealth*, 98.
90 Chavannes, *The Future Commonwealth*, 90.

Shadows Before or A Century Onward

Central to the compulsory educational curriculum in *Shadows Before or A Century Onward* (1893) is Fayette Stratton Giles's elimination of religious teachings in the schools and their replacement with science and natural law. In the prior century, as his narrator professor Busbey notes, religion controlled education and opposed the teachings of science.[91] In particular, Darwin's theory of natural selection and Spencer's teachings on the survival of the fittest were "bitterly opposed by our vested educational and theological institutions."[92] Giles's ideal curriculum, based on Spencer's synthetic philosophy, explains the professor, includes, "showing the necessary and inseparable continuity of all the sciences and the invariable laws governing all matter, animate and inanimate, and man's relation to them."[93] Education, as Iolas, one of the guides explains, "is entirely free and compulsory."[94] "We all feel that the children of the rich and poor, should have equal facilities in preparation for the struggles incident to life and for the enjoyment of life's pleasures."[95]

News from Nowhere

William Morris, in *News from Nowhere* (1890), took a contrary view on compulsory education, claiming the process cuts across our nature's grain; Morris's utopia entrusts education to experience and personal interest. His

91 Fayette Stratton Giles, *Shadows Before or A Century Onward* (India: Pranava Books, n.d. [1893]), 26.
92 Giles, *Shadows Before*, 26.
93 Giles, *Shadows Before*, 21, 61 Spencer's synthetic philosophy—which spans biology, psychology, sociology, and morality (in their interconnectedness)—is his attempt to "compare all opinions of the same genus; to set aside ... elements in which opinions disagree; to observe what remains after the discordant constituents have been eliminated; and to find from this remaining constituent that ... which holds true." Herbert Spencer, *Synthetic Philosophy*: *First Principles* (New York: D. Appleton and Company, 1890), 11, 127–128.
94 Giles, *Shadows Before*, 65–66.
95 Giles, *Shadows Before*, 66.

character old Hammond satirizes compulsory education as "something to be swallowed by the beginner in the art of living whether he liked it or not, and was hungry for it or not."[96] Hammond claims that such education was an outgrowth of poverty rather than a solution. During the nineteenth century society was so "miserably poor ... that real education was impossible for anybody." The theory of "so-called education," he says, "was that it was necessary to shove a little information into a child, even if it were by means of torture." With traditional compulsory education, Hammond continues, children are enrolled in school when they reach a certain age, regardless of their "varying faculties and dispositions." This procedure, he explains, ignores differences of growth, "bodily and mental." No one, he fears, "could come out of such a mill uninjured."[97]

Morris's opposition to compulsory education was in line with his general view of decentralized social relations (discussed in Chapters 5 and 6). He encourages education—though not traditional classroom instruction—to allow people to discover the types of work they will find enjoyable and fulfilling. Hammond explains to William Guest, "our children learn, whether they go through a 'system of teaching' or not. ... They all of them know how to cook; the bigger lads can mow; many can thatch and do odd jobs as carpentering; or they know how to keep shop. I can tell you they know plenty of things."[98]

Labor Unions

> "Unless we banded ourselves together and as one body against this Leviathan which 'hires and fires,' we were helpless, crushed piecemeal, having no voice as to ourselves and our work. And so I went in for the union."[99]
>
> —W. E. B. Du Bois, *Dark Princess* (1928)

96 Morris, *News from Nowhere*, 97.
97 Morris, *News from Nowhere*, 97.
98 Morris, *News from Nowhere*, 66.
99 W. E. B. Du Bois, *Dark Princess* (Oxford University Press, 2007), 202.

"Organized originally to sustain wages and restrict intolerable hours," reports H. G. Wells, the "Trade Union movement was at first something altogether distinct from socialism."[100] Robert Owen (1771–1858), states Morton, was an early inspiration for the English Trade Union movement. Owen viewed the movement as a vehicle for "establishing his socialist commonwealth."[101] By the middle of 1833, Cole affirms, "Owen had become established as the recognized leader of the Trade Union movement."[102]

Figure 5: "The farm labourers' lock-out—trades' union demonstration at Manchester in favor of the labourers, 1874."

100 Wells, *The Outline of History*, 433.

101 Morton, *The Life and Ideas of Robert Owen*, 43.

102 Cole, *Robert Owen*, 203–204. Kropotkin reports that "when Robert Owen started his Grand National Consolidated Trades' Union, it mustered half a million members in a few months." Peter Kropotkin, *Mutual Aid: A Factor in Evolution* (McClure, Philips and Company, 1902), 143.

Labor unions, declares Jack Wagner in *The Great Change* (1979) are an "equal force to offset Big Business in the halls of government; two equal forces with Labor protecting the rights and the welfare of the people."[103] Growing economic inequality during recent decades in the US correlates with a steady decline in union membership. "The widening of the pay distribution," notes economist Anthony Atkinson, "has coincided with a decline in the role of trade unions."[104] In the US, says Piketty, "the virulence of politicians opposed to labor unions and the collapse of the federal minimum wage have been decisive in the fall of the lowest incomes."[105] Spanning the past forty years union membership for Americans has dropped from one out of five workers to one out of ten workers.[106] During the 1950s one out of three workers were members of a union.[107] Government programs of social security and unemployment compensation, notes economist Mancur Olson, "have made union insurance schemes much less useful for attracting members."[108] "The power of unions, Applebaum reports, has also been "eroded by the antipathy of elites and by the government's tolerance for corporate concentration, which shifted bargaining power to employers."[109] In recent years, however, union organizers have seen limited success at employers such as Apple, Amazon, Google, and Starbucks, and US approval of

103 Wagner, *The Great Change*, 15.

104 Anthony B. Atkinson, *Inequality: What Can Be Done?* (Cambridge: Harvard University Press, 2015), 93.

105 Piketty, *A Brief History of Equality*, 152.

106 US Department of Labor, Bureau of Labor Statistics, union membership <https://www.bls.gov/news.release/pdf/union2.pdf>. The same agency reports that "nonunion workers had median weekly earnings that were 83 percent of earnings for workers who were union members."

107 Lowrey, *Give People Money*, 41.

108 Mancur Olson, *The Logic of Collective Action: Public Goods and the Theory of Groups* (Cambridge: Harvard University Press, 1965), 75.

109 Applebaum, *The Economists' Hour*, 325. Gross describes multiple anti-union strategies employed by corporations to either discourage union formation or promote the dissolution of existing unions. Bertram Gross, *Friendly Fascism: The New Face of Power in America* (Montreal: Black Rose Books, 1980), 244–245.

labor unions is at its highest point since 1965 (71 percent).[110] Janet Yellen, former chair of the US Federal Reserve and Secretary of the Treasury told reporters. "Unions can contribute to reversing the stark increase in inequality we've seen in recent decades, promoting economy-wide growth."[111]

Labor unions appear as a force in the struggle for economic equality in Bellamy's *Looking Backward* (1897) and Morris's *News from Nowhere* (1890), though only as a transitional stage. Before his extended sleep Bellamy's Julian West lived in Boston in 1887 where labor problems were endemic and any resolution seemed illusory.[112] Walter Taylor notes that novels of the period "emphasize the disorder, the suffering, and the brutality caused by strikes."[113] Regarding the "frequent episodes of labor-capital violence," reports Edward O'Donnell, "the years 1880–1900 alone witnessed nearly 37,000 strikes."[114] *Philip Dru: Administrator* (1912) proposes union representation on the boards of corporations to neutralize the oligarchy's thumb on the scale. Edward House balances this requirement, however, with an obligation of the unions not to strike, but to submit their grievances to arbitration, thus neutralizing the unions' most potent weapon.[115] In what Parrington, calls Philip Dru's "most radical proposal,"[116] a revised Franchise Law called for members of labor unions to "share a certain percentage of the earnings above their wages" after the owners received a fixed return on their capital.[117] While the utopias described below tout the benefits of

110 The Gallup Organization, "U.S. Approval of Labor Unions at Highest Point Since 1965," August 20, 2022, conducted August 1–23, 2022, with a random sample of 1,006 adults.

111 Dave Jamieson, "Janet Yellen Argues Unions Help Reduce Income Inequality," *HuffPost*, August 28, 2023.

112 Bellamy, says Tilman, "believed that labor unions as such could not fundamentally transform society because their social base as merely class organizations was too narrow." Rick Tilman, "The Utopian Vision of Edward Bellamy and Thorsten Veblen," *Journal of Economic Issues* 19, no. 4 (December, 1985): 879–898, 885.

113 Taylor, *The Economic Novel in America*, 73.

114 Edward T. O'Donnell, *Henry George and the Crisis of Inequality* (New York: Columbia University Press, 2015), xix.

115 House, *Philip Dru: Administrator*, 183.

116 Parrington, Jr, *American Dreams*, 189.

117 House, *Philip Dru: Administrator*, 183.

unions as an equalizing force, this feeling was not unanimous as Sargent notes.[118] Fullers's *A. D. 2000* (1890), for example, features laws "against combined strikes, intimidation of the employed, etc."[119] while Rosewater's *The Making of a Millennium* (1908) excluded "aggressive labor movements," rendering "open shops ... perfectly safe and harmless."[120]

Philip Meyer's Scheme

"American unionism made its first major and lasting advance on a national scale between 1897 and 1904. In that period," says Olson, "the number of unionized workers increased from 447,000 to 2,072,000."[121] In a novel dedicated to "the author of 'Looking Backward,'" Archibald McCowan (pseudonym Luke A. Hedd) reveals his plan to empower the union movement of the early twentieth-century. In *Philip Meyer's Scheme* (1892), the eponymous narrator and protagonist, is a member of the Typographical Union and a foreman in the composing room of a printing company. He has written a plan to convince workers that the only way they can achieve economic equality is by organizing all the existing unions into one "Universal Union" and encouraging workers who are not members of a union to join. Having read both Bellamy's *Looking Backward* and Donnelly's *Caesar's Column*, Meyer's concern is that a "privileged class" is forming in the United States "to whom the great mass of the people would be virtually slaves."[122]

Meyer's scheme calls for every working person in the United States to contribute one half of 1 percent of their wages to the union fund. In 1901, Myers reports, the workers' collective earnings were $150 million a week (equivalent to $5.4 billion in 2023) and their contribution to the

118 Sargent, "Capitalist Eutopias in America," 199.

119 Fuller, *A. D. 2000*, 268.

120 Rosewater, *The Making of a Millennium*, 63.

121 Olson, *The Logic of Collective Action*, 77. "Labor made its most notable gains between 1935 and 1945" (79).

122 Archibald McCowan, *Philip Meyer's Scheme: A Story of Trades Unionism* (New York: J. S. Ogilvie, 1892), 12, 17.

fund would be $750,000 a week ($27 million in 2023). Meyer calculates that out of their weekly contributions the "Universal Brotherhood" fund could support "40,000 men on strike and pay them full wages."[123] With this system in place, however, as Meyer acknowledges, "strikes would cease, because the bosses would grant the men their rights, knowing that it would be impossible to replace them if the men were forced to strike."[124] In spite of sporadic resistance, momentum for his project flourished and within three years "his scheme had been tried and had proven a success."[125] Sargent notes that "While not a utopia itself, the novel is about how active trade unions will be able to bring about Bellamy's Nationalism."[126]

The Iron Heel

Jack London's *The Iron Heel* (1908) is offered as a memoir Avis Everhard had written recounting the "turbulent period embraced between the years 1912 and 1932."[127] The manuscript's focus is the rise of the oligarchic Iron Heel and Avis Everhard's husband Ernest's role as a revolutionary leader. "In all the world were hard times, labor troubles, perishing middle classes, armies of unemployed, clashes of economic interests in the world market, and mutterings and rumblings of a socialist revolution."[128] The novel describes the initial stages in a battle between labor and capital that continues for three centuries until labor ultimately triumphs. It portrays the extremes of economic inequality in the United States as a totalitarian oligarchy exploits its economic and political power to enslave the laboring classes—the "people of the abyss"[129]—threatening

123 McCowan, *Philip Meyer's Scheme*, 17, 26.
124 McCowan, *Philip Meyer's Scheme*, 26.
125 McCowan, *Philip Meyer's Scheme*, 65.
126 Lyman Tower Sargent <https://openpublishing.psu.edu/utopia/content/philip-meyer's-scheme-story-trades-unionism>.
127 Jack London, *The Iron Heel* (New York: The Macmillan Company, 1908), 3.
128 London, *The Iron Heel*, 140.
129 London, *The Iron Heel*, 104. The phrase "people of the abyss," according to London's narrator "was struck out by the genius of H. G. Wells in the late nineteenth

"the whine of machine-guns."[130] Their condition was "pitiable," notes the narrator: they lived "like beasts in great squalid labor-ghettos, festering in misery and degradation. ... They were labor-slaves."[131] Of the revolution required to overthrow the despotic forces of the oligarchy—the Iron Heel—the narrator proclaims: "Thus do we poor humans attain our ends, striving through carnage and destruction to bring lasting peace and happiness upon the earth."[132] London, says Tony Barley, "sees class struggle as inescapable, informing all aspects of social existence."[133] Philip Wegner affirms the influence of Ignatius Donnelly's 1890 *Caesar's Column* (discussed in Chapter 5) on London's novel.[134]

As the labor unrest continued, it progressed into a revolution of the working class against their capitalist masters.[135] Like Marx, writes Gorman Beauchamp, "London believed that power is never relinquished from above, but must always be wrested from below."[136] Avis's husband Ernest Everhard, one of the organizers of the worldwide labor opposition, describes the battle between capitalism and labor for control of the means of production ("the machines").[137] The battle is the result of the fact, as Ernest explains, that regardless of the division of surplus labor assigned between capital and labor, labor will consume its portion of the surplus while capital will not. The result is an expanding unconsumed capital surplus.[138] If capital eventually wins this conflict, Ernest tells his audience of

---

century A.D.," 169n92. "People of the abyss" is used repeatedly by Wells in his 1901 *Anticipations.*

130 London, *The Iron Heel*, 68.

131 London, *The Iron Heel*, n202.

132 London, *The Iron Heel*, 7.

133 Tony Barley, "Prediction, Programme and Fantasy in Jack London's *The Iron Heel*," in *Anticipations: Essays on Early Science Fiction and Its Precursors*, ed. David Seed (Syracuse, NY: Syracuse University Press, 1995), 159.

134 Wegner, *Imaginary Communities*, 122.

135 London, *The Iron Heel*, 117.

136 Gorman Beauchamp, "Jack London's Utopian Dystopia and Dystopian Utopia," in *America as Utopia*, ed. Kenneth M. Roemer (New York: Burt Franklin and Company, 1981), 91–107, 93.

137 London, *The Iron Heel*, 97–104.

138 London, *The Iron Heel*, 102.

small businessmen, "you and labor, and all of us, will be crushed under the iron heel of a despotism as relentless and terrible as any despotism that has blackened the pages of the history of man."[139]

In this battle, "Black Hundreds" challenge the growth of the labor and socialist movements. The tactics of this counter-revolutionary force comprise "[r]iot, arson, and wanton destruction of property"[140]—under the guise of patriotism. As part of the "hard times" of 1912, the labor unions suffered a "decisive defeat"[141]—originally at the hands of paid strikebreakers ("private soldiers of the capitalists"[142])—but subsequently by soldiers of the US Army.[143] Initially this setback resulted from the strikebreakers' application of physical force, but ultimately it took the form of bribes to the most powerful unions. The oligarchy subsidized higher wages for the workers in the powerful railroad, steel, and machinists' unions. Without the support of the most powerful unions, Ernest predicts, the unions of unskilled workers, including the coal miners, "will be ground out of existence."[144] In the wake of these events, what Ernest foresaw was "the defection of the great labor unions and the rise of the castes."[145]

"The Iron Heel had triumphed in open warfare," Everhard's manuscript reports, "but we held our own in the new warfare, strange and awful and subterranean. … All was unseen, much was unguessed; … and yet through it all was order, purpose, control."[146] The manuscript was completed during the final days of preparation for the Second Revolt in 1932.[147] "'The tortuous and distorted evolution of the next three centuries would compel a Third Revolt," relates Anthony Meredith, London's utopian historian writing 700 years in the future, "and many revolts, all drowned in seas of blood, ere the

139 London, *The Iron Heel*, 104.

140 London, *The Iron Heel*, 115. The "Black Hundreds" was the name of the Russian reactionary, nationalist, pro-Tsarist movement in the early twentieth century. See also, London, *The Iron Heel*, 113n69.

141 London, *The Iron Heel*, 139.

142 London, *The Iron Heel*, 115n71.

143 London, *The Iron Heel*, 115–116.

144 London, *The Iron Heel*, 148–149.

145 London, *The Iron Heel*, 146.

146 London, *The Iron Heel*, 166–167.

147 London, *The Iron Heel*, 5.

world movement of labor should come into its own."[148] The manuscript was not discovered until four hundred years after the establishment of the new order under labor's control—the Brotherhood of Man. In this new world, London projects, "instead of being crushed by the machines," life will be "fairer, and happier, and nobler" and everyone will participate in the "equitable distribution of the products of the wonderful machines."[149]

Social Integration

Robert Frank's *Social Integration* (1935), written from the perspective of 1945, recounts fictive social and geological changes in the US during the previous decade. Adding to the troubles precipitated by the Great Depression, in 1935 a powerful earthquake strikes the western coast of the US, resulting in a Pangeatic event. Three quarters of the country, comprising western and midwestern states, submerges at the "rate of about ten feet per day" triggering a massive eastward migration.[150] On the east coast a large area of the ocean bottom (2.8 million square miles[151]—five times the size of Alaska) rises above sea level as thousands of acres appear daily revealing the continent of Atlantis—now an extension of the United States.[152]

The social, economic, and physical changes resulting from these calamities include political realignments, with the traditional Democratic and Republican parties losing favor while three new parties emerge—the Government Conformist Party, the National Socialist Party, and the United

148 London, *The Iron Heel*, 6.

149 London, *The Iron Heel*, 104.

150 Frank, *Social Integration*, 16.

151 Frank, *Social Integration*, 24.

152 Plato's writings on Atlantis describe an advanced civilization existing nine thousand years earlier. Plato's spokesman Critias reports Atlantis is an "island larger than Libya and Asia together." Plato, *Critias*, trans. A. E. Taylor, in *Plato: The Collected Dialogues*, ed. Edith Hamilton and Huntington Cairns (New York: Pantheon Books, 1961), 1213, 108e–110d.

Labor Party.[153] Formed in 1936, the United Labor Party combined forty-two previously existing unions and professional societies."[154]

The central focus of the political debate of the day was the politico-economic allocation of the new landmass adjoined to the east coast—Atlantis, approximately two-thirds of the reconfigured country—and the fate of the (surviving and impoverished) former residents of the water-logged western and midwestern states.[155] These questions are addressed in "The Land Sales and Allotment Plan" under consideration by a special session of Congress called by President Roosevelt. During the six months following the earthquake, however, "no constructive legislation had been accomplished because of the deadlock in Congress."[156]

Frank employs a didactic literary mechanism comprising a series of speeches by experts in economics, sociology, religion, engineering, and psychology presented at the convention of the United Labor Party to flesh out the scope of the nation's problems. Stressing the importance of union leadership in addressing economic inequality, the engineer reminds the audience that "a large share of the earnings which might have been set aside to provide for all employees has been paid to stockholders as extra dividends, and to the officers of the company as bonuses."[157] At the conclusion of the speeches, the chairman of the party announces that "rapidly growing revolutionary sentiment" has created "economic and political conditions so unsound, and social conditions so unbearable, that people, generally, are receptive to any constructive change."[158] In consequence of the union's nationwide organizing efforts, the chairman informs his audience, "the government of the United States is now ... under the temporary control and direction of the United Labor Party."[159] In accord with this new authority the United Labor Party's "council of committeemen" form

153 Frank, *Social Integration*, 31–32.
154 Frank, *Social Integration*, 34.
155 Frank includes a map of the resulting North American landmass. Frank, *Social Integration*, 21.
156 Frank, *Social Integration*, 29–30.
157 Frank, *Social Integration*, 106.
158 Frank, *Social Integration*, 159–160.
159 Frank, *Social Integration*, 161.

a provisional government replacing the president and his cabinet as well as the members of congress. Martial law is declared as the military has joined the union efforts.[160] "The people of the United States, generally, and the world at large were stunned at the sudden developments, namely, the establishing of the provisional government," explains the narrator, and the "firm measures taken to ratify the new government by popular vote."[161] The Party's aspirations call for a centralized (largely socialist) government, an emphasis on education, and a plan for a popular election to ratify the United Labor Party's authority or else reinstate the former government, as the voters decide.[162]

The Great Change

All utopias, submits Ricoeur, "try to show ways people may be governed other than by the state."[163] The "Great Change" refers to the turn of events when the country's political authority was remarkably ceded to a union-inspired egalitarian Enterprise. Before becoming the title of Jack Wagner's 1979 novel, the phrase, "the great change" appeared in both Bellamy's *Looking Backward* and Morris's *News from Nowhere.*[164] Jack Shaw, Wagner's protagonist, like Wagner, was a union official in San Francisco until 1961 when he retired. As the result of a plane crash near the North Pole, Shaw had frozen in a block of ice for over fifty years.[165] When he awakes in a hospital in San Francisco Shaw learns he is now 119 years-old in the year 2022.[166]

The Great Change had occurred in August, 1991 in Chicago. "America had not been a pretty sight in 1991," explains Dr. Betty Carsons, a history professor at "Cal."[167] "About twenty tremendously large conglomerates

160 Frank, *Social Integration*, 161–162.
161 Frank, *Social Integration*, 171.
162 Frank, *Social Integration*, 155–158, 161–170.
163 Ricoeur, *Lectures on Ideology and Utopia*, 298.
164 Bellamy, *Looking Backward*,122; Morris, *News from Nowhere*, 199.
165 Wagner, *The Great Change*, 31.
166 Wagner, *The Great Change*, 31.
167 Wagner, *The Great Change*, 53.

created through many mergers"[168] then owned industrial America. These multinational corporations controlled the country's physical production and distribution system.[169] Unemployment was high.[170] The arms race had bankrupted the nation.[171] Welfare, reports Dr. Carsons, "was far below subsistence." Interest on small loans, the professor continues, "was as high as 25 percent a month."[172] Corruption was endemic and no one trusted the government or the politicians. "The question was, how long before the powder keg blows up?"[173]

The catalyst for The Great Change was a speech by Dr. Charles Walker, Professor of Political Economy at the University of Chicago to tens of thousands of people who had marched on City Hall on a Saturday morning in August.[174] The professor "pointed out in simple terms how poverty could be ended, how everyone could have a job, how the burden of taxes could be lifted, how everyone could have ample medical care. How all could make a worthwhile contribution to a society in which there were no loan sharks to threaten your lives."[175] "By six o'clock that evening Chicago had a functioning militia of two million men and women."[176] "By ten o'clock Saturday night a Planning Commission was approved and at six o'clock Sunday night the Planning Commission came on the air with a temporary program for Chicago."[177] News from Chicago rapidly spread as "[o]ne city after another fell."[178] Four months later England adopted the same economic model.[179]

At the core of the governing Enterprise was the National Economic and Planning Committee that monitored supply and demand of all products and services throughout the country. For each industry the Committee

168 Wagner, *The Great Change*, 53.
169 Wagner, *The Great Change*, 61.
170 Wagner, *The Great Change*, 53.
171 Wagner, *The Great Change*, 61.
172 Wagner, *The Great Change*, 53.
173 Wagner, *The Great Change*, 60.
174 Wagner, *The Great Change*, 56.
175 Wagner, *The Great Change*, 57.
176 Wagner, *The Great Change*, 59.
177 Wagner, *The Great Change*, 66.
178 Wagner, *The Great Change*, 60.
179 Wagner, *The Great Change*, 241.

determines the need to establish a centralized industrial complex of between five thousand and thirty thousand workers.[180] The national shipbuilding Enterprise, for example, located in San Francisco, employs twenty thousand workers. Scale is important for an industrial complex because in addition to providing work, it also supplies housing, meals, and recreation for all of its employees in accordance with the union mandate. The shipbuilding complex includes facilities necessary to maintain a "civilized community—housing, cultural facilities, schools, libraries, everything essential to the welfare of the employees."[181]

A union-sanctioned maximum wage ensures relative economic equality—and a measure of leveling. No one may earn more than $500 a month, as noted in Chapter 2 ($2,050 in 2023). Workers in all professions receive the same benefits and social status, though their pay ranges from $76 to $275 a month depending on the requirements of the job. Adjustments are made for educational level and additional responsibilities. In an ironic equivalence Professor Carsons, for example, receives $25 a month as chair of her department and an equal amount for her medical degree.[182] "You can imagine people's consternation in learning they couldn't earn more than five hundred dollars and their base pay would be seventy-six dollars a month," explains Professor Carsons.[183] The discontent subsided, however, when people learned that a new system of prices had gone into effect, leaving them with more money for luxuries than they had before.[184] This was effected by reducing the value of the "old money" by 99.85 percent.

The profit from each Enterprise is divided into three equal parts. One third goes to the Enterprise for plant and equipment maintenance as well as employee housing or recreational facilities, "or anything beneficial to the Enterprise."[185] Another third goes to the Cultural Committee, for paid vacations, recreation, theater tickets, and "everything that contributes to the

180 Wagner, *The Great Change*, 141.
181 Wagner, *The Great Change*, 153.
182 Wagner, *The Great Change*, 83.
183 Wagner, *The Great Change*, 69.
184 Wagner, *The Great Change*, 69.
185 Wagner, *The Great Change*, 97, 165.

good, rich, full life of the workers."[186] The Enterprise issues the last third as equal bonuses to the workers.[187] Union organizations, as Jack Shaw observes, "are now a very important, perhaps the most important part" of the Great Change society,[188] to which Dr. Carsons adds: unions are "really, the heart of the system."[189]

Prior to his fifty-year sleep, Jack admits he had little faith in the "so-called leaders," of the union movement to which he had given his life.[190] The rank-and-file's natural distrust of their leaders, says sociologist Robert Michels (1876–1936), results from the leaders' advancing their own priorities over the workers' needs.[191] The organizational phase of the Enterprise met this challenge when Dr. Walker requested the dissolution of the old unions and the reorganization of their members into industrial unions.[192] "No more craft unionism with its racism, elitism and corruption."[193] Union leaders would be "paid by the Enterprise like every other worker."[194]

186 Wagner, *The Great Change*, 97–98.

187 Wagner, *The Great Change*, 99, 165.

188 Wagner, *The Great Change*, 74.

189 Wagner, *The Great Change*, 75.

190 Wagner, *The Great Change*, 64.

191 Michels coined the phrase "Iron Law of Oligarchy" to reflect the fact that once members are elected to oversee their union's operations, those members demonstrate a "detachment ... from the class which it represents," entailing a "necessary conflict with the interests of the collectivity." Robert Michels, *Political Parties: A Sociological Study of the Oligarchical Tendencies of Modern Democracy* (1915), trans. Eden and Cedar Paul (New York: The Free Press, 1962), 70, 285, 342, 353.

192 Wagner, *The Great Change*, 75.

193 Wagner, *The Great Change*, 75. In a discussion of the racist history of the US labor movement, Du Bois reports that a National Labor Union meeting in Philadelphia in 1869, "contrary to all labor philosophy," determined to "divide labor by racial and social lines and yet continue to talk of one labor movement." Du Bois, *Black Reconstruction in America*, 356–357.

194 Wagner, *The Great Change*, 75.

Gender Equality in the Workplace

> "Most utopianists simply assume that sex roles, the status of women and the attitudes toward them, will remain the same in the future good society as they are in the present bad society."[195]
>
> —Lyman Tower Sargent, "Women in Utopia" (1973)

In all the Western countries, Piketty reports, the participation of women in the labor market rose from 10–20 percent in 1950 to more than 50 percent in the 1980s.[196] As one recent report notes, however, "All the women on Earth make about half as much money as the men."[197] The World Economic Forum's Global Gender Gap Report measures the number of years it will take to achieve gender parity for earnings. In their 2021 global report, "the average distance completed to parity was 68%." Based on the current trajectory, the report predicts "it will take 135.6 years to close the gap worldwide."[198] Questions of gender equality, however, relate not to pay only but to occupational access and career advancement.

Plato sought gender equality in the workplace for the Guardians of his Republic, a small minority of the citizens. Plato has his spokesperson Socrates argue that people "of the same nature" are qualified to undertake the same pursuits. Just as a cobbler who is bald and one who is hairy are of the "same nature," Socrates explains, so a man and woman are of the same nature with respect to education and career choice.[199] Accordingly, in the *Laws* Plato declares "nothing can be more absurd than the practice which prevails in our own country, of men and women *not* following the same

195 Lyman Tower Sargent, "Women in Utopia," *Comparative Literature Studies* 10, no. 4 (December, 1973): 302–316, 306.

196 Piketty, *The Economics of Inequality*, 87.

197 Jason Lalljee and Madison Hoff, *Business Insider*, December 10, 2021. <https://www.businessinsider.com/how-much-women-make-compared-men-wealth-changed-over-time-2021-12>.

198 World Economic Forum <https://www.weforum.org/agenda/2022/03/international-womens-day-gender-gap-inequality/>

199 Plato, *Republic,* trans. Jowett, bk. 5, 454.

pursuits with all their strength and with one mind, for thus the state, instead of being a whole, is reduced to a half."[200] In *The Subjection of Women* (1869) J. S. Mill affirms this contention, arguing that we ought "not to ordain that to be born a girl instead of a boy, any more than to be born black instead of white, or a commoner instead of a nobleman, shall decide the person's position through all life."[201]

City of the Sun

Tommaso Campanella's *City of the Sun* (1602) is an expression of monastic economic equality. Campanella wrote the *City of the Sun*, says Berneri, "with his mind and limbs still aching from the tortures of the Inquisition."[202] Though Campanella trained in the Dominican order from age 14, the Inquisition arrested him in 1599 for spreading heretical ideas. His imprisonment in Naples continued for almost thirty years.[203] In the City of the Sun, says Genoese, Campanella's seafaring narrator, men and women "perform the same tasks, whether of a mental or a mechanical nature"[204] and "each individual is assigned to the work he has the greatest aptitude for."[205] Each person's "particular inclination" explains Genoese, is determined from his date of birth because those "born under the same constellation ... tend to be alike in ability."[206] Because labor is "equitably distributed," in the City of the Sun, "no one need work more than four hours each day."[207] And though "no one is assigned to things

200 Plato, *Laws*, trans. Jowett, bk. 7, 805 (emphasis added).
201 John Stuart Mill, *The Subjection of Women* (Mineola, NY: Dover Publication, 1997), 18.
202 Berneri, *Journey Through Utopia*, 88.
203 Claeys, *Searching for Utopia*, 118; Daniel J. Donno, "Introduction," in *The City of the Sun*, ed. Tommaso Campanella, trans. Daniel J. Donno (Berkeley: University of California Press, 1981), 10.
204 Campanella, *The City of the Sun*, trans. Donno, 49.
205 Campanella, *The City of the Sun*, trans. Donno, 81.
206 Campanella, *The City of the Sun*, trans. Donno, 59, 81.
207 Campanella, *The City of the Sun*, trans. Donno, 65.

that are destructive of his individuality,"[208] both sexes, says Genoese, perform "military service and work in the fields and pastures."[209]

Gender Equality Placed on a Pedestal

In her *Invisible Women* (2019), Caroline Criado-Perez notes that "men picture a man 80% of the time they think of a 'person.'"[210] This may explain the frequently flawed execution of utopian attempts to include gender equality as a force in undercutting the causes of economic inequality. Many nineteenth-century utopian solutions to gender inequality are no more than Victorian head fakes. In W. W. Satterlee's *Looking Backward and What I Saw* (1890) (discussed in Chapter 6), for example, equality for women includes suffrage to allow "woman's superior purity and quick perception of moral issues be utilized for the blessing of the nation."[211] This supports Pfaelzer's observation on nineteenth-century utopias that women citizens were "pious, modest, and maternal creatures" and that "utopian authors did not understand that social and economic equality would imply new forms of female characterization."[212] In particular, Pfaelzer explains, women's roles as unpaid domestic laborers went unquestioned though there were efforts to lighten their burden in this "lonely and degrading work" as utopian authors "introduced new technology for household labor."[213] Economic equality, however, demands women's economic independence, as Alice Ilgenfritz Jones and Ella Merchant's *Unveiling a Parallel* (1893), for example, illustrates.

208 Campanella, *The City of the Sun*, trans. Donno, 81.
209 Campanella, *The City of the Sun*, trans. Donno, 81.
210 Caroline Criado-Perez, *Invisible Women: Data Bias in a World Designed for Men* (New York: Abrams Press, 2019), 95.
211 W. W. Satterlee, *Looking Backward and What I Saw* (New York: Arno Press and the New York Times, 1971), 147.
212 Pfaelzer, "The Impact of Political Theory on Narrative Structures," 123.
213 Pfaelzer, "The Impact of Political Theory on Narrative Structures," 123.

Digression on Labor and Work

"Women have always worked," observes Criado-Perez. "They have worked unpaid, underpaid, underappreciated, and invisibly, but they have always worked."[214] For domestic work "*not* to involve the exploitation and oppression of women," advises Ruth Levitas, "it is necessary simultaneously to challenge the sexual division of labour, and insist on the skill and value of domestic work."[215] Levitas uses the term "domestic work" rather than "domestic labor." "'Labor,'" says Heinzelman, "has an emotive charge which will not be straitened by scientific objectivity. The word," he says, "retains its experiential subjectivity, whether we are speaking of the work of men's hands, child-bearing, or the mental exertions occasioned by the imagination."[216] In her discussion of labor and work, Hannah Arendt traces the etymology of the two terms and finds characteristic of "labor," understood as a noun, that it "never designates the finished product."[217] Historically, she notes, "To labor meant to be enslaved by necessity."[218] For Arendt, says Kateb, labor comprises "those activities that have to do with maintaining mere biological existence," as "the laborer produces for consumption."[219] The worker, notes Kateb, is "above" the laborer since while the laborer produces for consumption, the worker "contrives and fabricates for use."[220] Work and its product, says Arendt, "bestow a measure of permanence and durability upon the futility of mortal life."[221] Challenging the sexual division of labor accordingly requires reconciling the moral dignity of labor and work (discussed in the next section).

214 Criado-Perez, *Invisible Women*, 142.

215 Ruth Levitas, "'Who Holds the Hose?' Domestic Labour in the Work of Bellamy, Gilman and Morris," *Utopian Studies* 6, no. 1 (1995): 65–85, 83.

216 Heinzelman, *The Economics of the Imagination*, 142.

217 Hannah Arendt, *The Human Condition*, 2nd ed. (Chicago: The University of Chicago Press, 1958), 80.

218 Arendt, *The Human Condition*, 83.

219 Kateb, "Utopia and the Good Life," 250–251.

220 Kateb, "Utopia and the Good Life," 251.

221 Arendt, *The Human Condition*, 8.

Travels in Icaria

"I wrote the 'Voyage to Icaria' to place before the world the example of a great nation having a community of goods."[222] For Étienne Cabet, notes Leslie J. Roberts, the sufferings of humanity are "the consequence of bad social organization, and in particular inequality."[223] Cabet, writes Berneri, "belonged to that type of social reformer whose love of humanity is as boundless as their faith in their own power to work out its salvation."[224] Dinaros, a young historian in Cabet's *Travels in Icaria* (1840), affirms: "Man distinguishes himself from all other animate beings by his reason, his perfectibility, and his sociability." There can be no happiness, he explains, "without association and equality." For this reason Icarians formed their society "based on perfect equality,"[225] with all citizens "equal in rights and in duties." Icarians comprise, "but a single family," Dinaros continues, "whose members are united by the bonds of fraternity."[226] In light of this moral foundation the Icarians decreed, for example, that there would be "as many female as male doctors and surgeons."[227] In spite of these claims, however, Icarian women are designated "chief homemakers" and "exempted from the workshops because looking after home and hearth is yet another occupation useful to the republic."[228]

Looking Backward and Equality

In *Looking Backward* (1888), though the nation's annual net income is divided equally among all its citizens, Bellamy evinced reluctance in

222 Étienne Cabet quoted in Moritz Kaufmann, *Utopias: Or, Schemes of Social Improvement from Sir Thomas More to Karl Marx* (London: C. Kegan Paul and Co., 1879), 126.

223 Leslie J. Roberts, Preface to the 2nd ed., Cabet, *Travels in Icaria*, trans. Roberts, lvii.

224 Berneri, *Journey Through Utopia*, 219.

225 Cabet, *Travels in Icaria*, 31 (capitalization in original removed).

226 Cabet, *Travels in Icaria*, 31 (capitalization in original removed).

227 Cabet, *Travels in Icaria*, 94.

228 Cabet, *Travels in Icaria*, 84.

promoting equality of opportunity for women. When Julian West asks Dr. Leete if, under the new economic conditions, women have been reduced to cultivating "their charms and graces," Dr. Leete replies that women "have quite too much spirit to consent to be mere beneficiaries of society." Rather than stipulating their equality in the industrial army, however, Dr. Leete explains that women "are under an entirely different discipline … and constitute rather an allied force than an integral part of the army of the men."[229] Because women are "inferior in strength to men, and further disqualified industrially," Dr. Leete continues, "under no circumstances is a woman to follow any employment not perfectly adapted, both as to kind and degree of labor, to her sex."[230] Sargent notes that Bellamy was chastised for these paternalistic sentiments "and the attitude toward women they represent."[231] In *Equality* (1897), Bellamy reverses his earlier posture, as Levitas explains, "and abandons the sexual division of labour in the public sphere."[232] With respect to the Industrial Army, Bellamy has Edith Leete declare: "There is not a trade or occupation in the whole list … in which women do not take part."[233] Unable to get out of his own way, however, Bellamy then prompts Edith to explain that this is primarily a function of the perfected machinery they now employ. "As we have grown stronger," Edith proclaims, "all sorts of work have grown lighter … machines do all, and we only need to guide them."[234] Thus the sexual division of domestic labor remains intact while questions of its legitimacy, as Levitas suggests, are swept under the carpet.[235]

229 Bellamy, *Looking Backward*, 184–185.
230 Bellamy, *Looking Backward*, 185.
231 Lyman Tower Sargent, "Edward Bellamy's Boston in 2000 from 1888 to 1897: The Evolution of Bellamy's Future Boston from *Looking Backward* Through *Equality*," *Utopian Studies* 27, no. 2 (2016): 152–181, 161, 172.
232 Levitas, "Who Holds the Hose?," 68.
233 Bellamy, *Equality*, 43.
234 Bellamy, *Equality*, 44.
235 Levitas, "Who Holds the Hose?," 68–69.

Shadows Before or a Century Onward

Set in New York City in 1996 and influenced by Herbert Spencer and social Darwinism, gender equality in Fayette Stratton Giles's *Shadows Before or A Century Onward* (1893) arose gradually through changes in the environment to which natural selection fashioned a response. "Until recently," asserts Giles's professor-character Busbey, "women have been educated either to be the drudges or the toys of men, or else to be looked up to as angels above them. It remained for justice to see that they were neither the one nor the other."[236] Throughout the evolution of the species, explains the professor, conditions of environment "operating unequally upon the sexes, making unequal mental and physical demands upon them at different stages of evolution, tended each to evolve and perpetuate bodily and mental differences between the sexes."[237]

The elimination of war was the catalyst for the evolution of gender equality. The wars of the past, which Giles presumes were a male activity, meant the survival of the fittest men took place in a very different environment than the survival of the fittest women. It took the termination of war to create overlapping environments to which both men and women respond to bring forth an equal survival response.[238] "The abolition of war has replaced militancy by industrialism," explains the professor, "and so made possible similar occupations for both sexes."[239] This stage of human evolution has facilitated a conscious effort to further equalize the environments to which both genders respond. "In our present social stage of universal peace," the professor continues, "the giving to women of equal rights, political and civil, with equal liberties, is required by that first prerequisite to the greatest happiness: [Spencer's] law of equal freedom conditioned by the law of right."[240] In a just society, Spencer proclaimed, everyone's freedom must be equal. This is implemented by his "law of right social relationships,"

236 Giles, *Shadows Before*, 186.
237 Giles, *Shadows Before*, 185–186.
238 Giles, *Shadows Before*, 185–186.
239 Giles, *Shadows Before*, 187.
240 Giles, *Shadows Before*, 184.

which states: "Every man has freedom to do all that he wills, provided he infringes not the equal freedom of any other man."[241]

Other Brief Examples

Mary Griffith's *Three Hundred Years Hence* (1836), explains Barbara Quissell, deals with women's "need to understand business methods and their ability to control their own finances."[242] As Griffith notes, "people are respected in proportion to their wealth."[243] For Griffith, says Parrington, "money matters" were more important in achieving equality than the vote.[244] The protagonist's dream portends the time when women are "trained to the comprehension of mercantile operations," earning them "respect from men."[245]

The Diothas (1883) is John Macnie's egalitarian vision of the ninety-sixth century where for the "first time in the history of our race, the influence of woman made itself directly felt in legislation."[246] Upon concluding their education, since all work is morally equal, "boys and girls have an equal right to enter any employment."[247]

Women's wages were doubled and then quadrupled in Ignatius Donnelly's *The Golden Bottle* (1892) when they organize a Women's Cooperative Association.[248] The Association established its own stores

241 Herbert Spencer, *Social Statics* (New York: D. Appleton and Company, [1850] 1865), 106, 121 (original italics eliminated).

242 Quissell, "The New World That Eve Made," 160.

243 Mary Griffith, *Three Hundred Years Hence* (N.p.: n.d. [1836]), 54.

244 Parrington, *American Dreams*, 18–19.

245 Griffith, *Three Hundred Years Hence*, 69. The women who were accorded Griffith's solution specifically excluded African Americans as the "whole of the negro population" was "transplanted" to Liberia (71). Citing Griffith's novel, Sargent notes that, with a few exceptions, "U.S. utopian fiction … is, until the second half of the twentieth century, racist." Lyman Tower Sargent, "African Americans and Utopia: Visions of a Better Life," *Utopian Studies* 33, no. 1 (2020): 27–96, 28.

246 Macnie, *The Diothas*, 147.

247 Macnie, *The Diothas*, 121.

248 Ignatius Donnelly, *The Golden Bottle: The Story of Ephraim Benezet of Kansas* (India: Pranava Books, n.d. [1892]), 101.

which sell the goods women manufacture directly to consumers "without the intervention of middlemen."[249] As the Association's organizer Sophie explains, "you will get the goods you purchase at the same price you pay now; the only difference will be that all the profits of the labor of thousands of workers will not be absorbed, as it is now, by a score or so of middlemen."[250]

Lola, an Altrurian spokesperson in Grigsby and Lowe's *Nequa* (1900), explains to the visitors, "Here, both sexes are placed upon terms of absolute equality, and every individual has an opportunity to find the place that is best suited to his or her inclinations."[251] (*Nequa*'s system of commerce is discussed in Chapter 2.)

"In our democracy," relates Lilac in Kenneth Guthrie's *A Romance of Two Centuries: A Tale of the Year 2025* (1919), gender equality is a foundational principle; "men and women share alike in everything."[252] Accordingly, "all persons received equivalent pay."[253]

Dignity of Work—Revaluing Work in Relation to Society

> "Ask yourself why the man who makes your plow, or tills your ground, should be inferior to you who muddle your lives away in counting-rooms or offices?"[254]
>
> —Marie Howland, *Papa's Own Girl* (1874)

The utopian goal with respect to work is not merely that work (or labor) should have dignity (in contrast to leisure, for example), nor that all work should confer dignity on the worker, but that all types of work should bestow equal dignity; work itself should create a moral equivalence for its contribution to the ideal state. In *The Theory of the Leisure Class* (1899),

249 Donnelly, *The Golden Bottle*, 90.
250 Donnelly, *The Golden Bottle*, 94.
251 Grigsby and Lowe, *Nequa*, 105.
252 Guthrie, *A Romance of Two Centuries*, 119.
253 Guthrie, *A Romance of Two Centuries*, 168.
254 Marie Howland, *Papa's Own Girl: A Novel* (New York: John P. Jewett, 1874), 361.

sociologist Thorstein Veblen reports: "The institution of a leisure class is the outgrowth of an early discrimination between employments, according to which some employments are worthy and others unworthy."[255] Thomas More's goal of equalizing the moral value of work is a recurrent utopian theme. More's aim was a hierarchy-free division of labor—"there is no sort of trade that is in great esteem among them," affirms narrator Hythloday.[256] In Cabet's *Icaria* (1840) the host Valmor explains to the traveler, "All professions are honored equally, the shoemaker as much as the doctor."[257] *The Coming Race* (1871) affords a system that while "admitting different degrees of wealth, yet establishes perfect equality in rank"—"a shopkeeper being of exactly the same grade in estimation as the large landed proprietor."[258] Dr. Leete in Bellamy's *Looking Backward* (1888) asserts, "there is recognized no sort of difference between the dignity of the different sorts of work required by the nation."[259] A Martian host in Jones and Merchant's *Unveiling a Parallel* (1893) tells her guest, "We do not regard any work as mean.... We do not require people to do anything for us which we would not do for ourselves, or for them."[260] Connie, the time traveler to Mattapoisett in Marge Piercy's *Woman on the Edge of Time* (1976) asks, "'Well, if a person can do something ... important, why should they chop onions and pick caterpillars off tomato plants?' 'Eating isn't important?' Luciente scowled with amazement."[261]

255 Veblen, *The Theory of the Leisure Class*, 11.

256 Thomas More, *Utopia*, ed. Henry Morley (Project Gutenberg <https://www.gutenberg.org/files/2130/2130-h/2130-h.htm>)

257 Cabet, *Travels in Icaria*, 83.

258 Edward Bulwer-Lytton, *The Coming Race* (N.p.: Loki's Publishing, n.d. [1871]), 47, 90.

259 Bellamy, *Looking Backward*, 126.

260 Alice Ilgenfritz Jones and Ella Merchant, *Unveiling a Parallel* (New York: Syracuse University Press, 1991), 124–125.

261 Piercy, *Woman on the Edge of Time*, 291 (ellipsis in original).

Work, the Division of Labor, and Inequality

The relation between work and economic inequality is complex and unsettled. Work arrayed across a spectrum of dignity—based on hegemonic criteria such as social class, family history, or brain vs. muscle labor—is one source of economic inequality. One of the aims utopians pursue is establishing the division of labor on principles unrelated to accidents of birth—wealth, poverty, gender, class, or race. In his *Philosophy of Money* (1900), sociologist Georg Simmel notes, "We are well aware that countless work activities in the 'higher professions' in no way place higher claims upon the subject than they do upon 'lower' ones; that workers in coal mines and factories must often possess a circumspection, a capacity for resignation, a defiance of death which raises the subjective value of their achievement far above that of many bureaucratic occupations or those requiring education."[262]

Making all forms of work honorable releases workers from the artificial inducements of prestige and the stigma of labor supposed degrading. Initially this process requires eliminating those employments inimical to society's ideal. Thomas More, for example, abolishes "useless trades" such as attorneys, loan sharks, and marketing directors. The remaining forms of labor in Utopia are morally equivalent as each requires six hours a day in support of More's ideal society.

The Divine Hierarchy of Work

Samuel Balcom the traveler in Albert Chavannes's *The Future Commonwealth or What Samuel Balcom Saw in Socioland* (1892), explaining the conditions of his homeland to his guide, Miss Bell, says, "The dissatisfaction with the inequalities in conditions is becoming greater every year."[263] Over the centuries, Balcom continues, the poor have been taught that God created the existing social hierarchy where some are rich

262 Simmel, *The Philosophy of Money*, 416.

263 Chavannes, *The Future Commonwealth*, 65–66.

and powerful and others are poor and submissive, and that "any attempt to change these social relations was an act of rebellion against the decrees of an all-wise Providence.[264] This outlook, notes historian John Herman Randall, stems from the medieval view of society as "a great hierarchy of ascending orders, in which every man has his God-appointed function and recognized obligations."[265] "Knight or peasant, monk or doctor, each in his own way does God's bidding, each can attain perfection in his station." This scheme, says Randall, represents "complete harmony between the individual and the social."[266] Arthur Lovejoy describes this "plan and structure of the world" in *The Great Chain of Being* (1936), a work that Lasky calls a "masterful study in intellectual history."[267] It was this conception, Lovejoy affirms, which through the Middle Ages and down to the late eighteenth century "many philosophers, and most men of science, and, indeed, most educated men, were to accept without question."[268] The twentieth century reimagined the dignity of work and its hierarchical composition as three accounts appeared that rejected the Great Chain of Being and its natural or spiritual origins: exploit, merit, and IQ.

Dignity and Exploit

Thorsten Veblen's discussion of the moral quality of work traces its dignity to its character as exploitative. The extent to which a person's work exploits nature or other people was an historical measure of its dignity.

264 Chavannes, *The Future Commonwealth*, 65–66. Accordingly, we learn that in the past "the poor were kept quiet by alternate doses of charity and promises of eternal bliss in the world to come" (2).

265 Randall, *The Making of the Modern Mind*, 58.

266 Randall, *The Making of the Modern Mind*, 60.

267 Lasky, *Utopia and Revolution*, 595

268 Arthur O. Lovejoy, *The Great Chain of Being* (New York: Harper and Row, 1936), 59. John Locke, for example, notes, "when we consider the infinite power and wisdom of the Maker ... it is suitable ... that the species of creatures should also, by gentle degrees, ascend upward from us toward his infinite perfection, as we see they gradually descend from us downwards." John Locke, *An Essay Concerning Human Understanding* (New York: Dover, 1959), vol. 2, 68; 3:6:10.

To exploit, says Veblen, is to acquire "by seizure."[269] Those employments, he continues, "which are to be classed as exploit are worthy, honourable, noble; other employments, which do not include this element of exploit, and especially those which imply subservience or submission, are unworthy, debasing, ignoble."[270] "Veblen," says Charlotte Perkins Gilman, shows how labor, "being first performed by women and then by conquered opponents made slaves, was despised by the early mind."[271]

Dignity and Merit

Michael Sandel, in *The Tyranny of Merit* (2020), urges that "To renew the dignity of work, we must repair the social bonds the age of merit has undone."[272] The "age of merit" is a reference to the time that extends from the present back to (roughly) the First World War. Michael Young (1915–2002), a sociologist and Labour Party leader who coined the term *meritocracy*, assigned 1914 as the start of this period which he prolongs to 2034 in a utopian (or dystopian) projection that allows him to expand his "historical analysis" seventy-five years after the publication of his book: *The Rise of the Meritocracy* (1958).[273] During this 120-year span society aspired to honor work based on merit—a meritocracy (intelligence and effort comprising merit[274])—replacing the older measures of dignity: age, class, and wealth.[275] A meritocracy ushers the most capable workers in every field into positions where they can exercise their talents for the benefit of all. "In the course of a mere hundred years," writes Young, "we have come

269 Veblen, *The Theory of the Leisure Class*, 15.

270 Veblen, *The Theory of the Leisure Class*, 15.

271 Charlotte Perkins Gilman, *Human Work* (Lanham, MD: AltaMira Press, 2005), 179.

272 Sandel, *The Tyranny of Merit*, 222.

273 Michael Young, *The Rise of the Meritocracy* (London: Routledge Taylor and Francis Group, 2017), xi, xv, 4, 93. Sandel notes that Young, when he coined the term *meritocracy* in 1958, "described a dystopia, not an ideal." Sandel, *The Tyranny of Merit*, 116.

274 Young, *The Rise of the Meritocracy*, 84.

275 Young, *The Rise of the Meritocracy*, 69, 82.

close to realizing at one stroke the ideal of Plato"[276]—in whose *Republic* the dignity of work was ensured as each person practiced "one of the functions in the city, that one for which his nature made him naturally most fit."[277]

The logic of meritocracy, proclaims Christopher Hayes, "is ironclad putting the most qualified, best equipped people into positions of greater responsibility and import."[278] But the ideal of a meritocracy, says Sandel, "in which jobs and pay perfectly reflected people's efforts and talents," degenerated into a system of honoring one's own talents as deserved and equating success with personal effort ("our success is our own doing"[279]) measured in financial rewards—money as a proxy for merit. The result was "hubris and anxiety among the winners and humiliation and resentment among the losers."[280] For the wealthy "zottas" in Cory Doctorow's 2017 *Walkaway* (discussed in Chapter 7), for example, "every privilege they enjoyed was deserved."[281] A competitive meritocracy, Sandel argues, is thus "a hollow political project that reflects an impoverished conception of citizenship and freedom."[282]

Dignity and the Cognitive Elite

In their controversial study *The Bell Curve* (1994), psychologist Richard Herrnstein and sociologist Charles Murray report that the twentieth century "dawned on a world segregated into social classes defined in terms of money, power, and status. The ancient lines of separation based on hereditary rank were being erased, replaced by a more complicated set of overlapping lines." In earlier times, they note, the majority of smart people were engaged in "ordinary pursuits, mingling, working, and living

276 Young, *The Rise of the Meritocracy*, 93.
277 Plato, *Republic*, trans. Allan Bloom, 2nd ed. (Basic Books, 1968), bk. 4, 433a.
278 Hayes, *Twilight of the Elites*, 217.
279 Sandel, *The Tyranny of Merit*, 222.
280 Sandel, *The Tyranny of Merit*, 120.
281 Doctorow, *Walkaway*, 465.
282 Sandel, *The Tyranny of Merit*, 120.

with everyone else. Many were housewives. Most of the rest were farmers, smiths, millers, bakers, carpenters, and shopkeepers. Social and economic stratification was extreme, but cognitive stratification was minor."[283] During that period, with respect to English society in particular, Young reports: "intelligence was distributed more or less at random. Each social class was, in ability, the miniature of society itself." "The upper classes," Young continues, "had their fair share of geniuses and morons, as did the workers."[284] One reason economic inequality is such a prominent and apparently intractable problem in today's world, argue Herrnstein and Murray, is that persons with high IQs—the *cognitive elite*—have emerged as a significant economic factor.[285] Technology, they say, has created more jobs for the cognitive elite—provoking an "invisible migration"—while revolutionizing how workers may perform these jobs.[286] Membership in this new class is gained by high IQ; "neither social background, nor ethnicity, nor lack of money will bar the way."[287] Though this practice promotes cultural diversity—at least in the workplace—it also ensures the stigmatization of jobs that do not require above average intelligence. This result occurs in Young's meritocratic dystopia of 1988, where due to their lack of intelligence, "about a third of all adults were unemployable in the ordinary economy ... and needed some form of sheltered employment."[288] Kurt Vonnegut's *Player Piano* (discussed in Chapter 7) depicts a society stratified by IQ, where engineers and managers have captured all

283 Richard J. Herrnstein and Charles Murray, *The Bell Curve: Intelligence and Class Structure in American Life* (New York: Free Press, 1994), 25, 27. For background on the controversy see, *The Bell Curve Debate*, ed. Russell Jacoby and Naomi Glauberman (New York: Times Books, 1995).

284 Young, *The Rise of the Meritocracy*, 4.

285 "Perhaps," says Nagel, "someone will discover a way to reduce the socially produced inequalities (especially the economic ones) between the intelligent and the unintelligent ... without limiting the availability of opportunities. ... But in the absence of such a utopian solution, the familiar task of balancing liberty against equality will remain with us." Nagel, "The Policy of Preference," 105.

286 Herrnstein and Murray, *The Bell Curve*, 511. Herrnstein and Murray shy away from the term *meritocracy*, preferring instead, "what people often call merit" (512).

287 Herrnstein and Murray, *The Bell Curve*, 510.

288 Young, *The Rise of the Meritocracy*, 110.

the high-paying jobs, and machines have eliminated manual labor. As a result, one of the characters grouses, "Used to be there was a lot of damn fool things a dumb bastard could do to be great, but the machines fixed that."[289]

News from Nowhere

A notable feature of William Morris's *News from Nowhere* (1890) is the lack of an occupational hierarchy. All work is of equal dignity and no occupation is honored above another. Each person works at that craft they can enjoy and find fulfillment in. The "absence of artificial coercion," explains old Hammond, means that each person can do "what he can do best, joined to the knowledge of what productions of labor we really want."[290] Furthermore Hammond says, "There is no difficulty in finding work which suits the special turn of mind of everybody; so that no man is sacrificed to the wants of another."[291] In spite of this apparent occupational flexibility, however, more than one commentator discerns a gender-driven division of labor. Philip Steer, for example, notes that while *News from Nowhere* "focuses on sexual equality" it does so "without disturbing gender roles."[292] In "Who Holds the Hose?" Levitas argues that for Morris "the sexual division of labor is intact." Although women are "not exclusively confined to domestic labour," she contends, "the range of work they undertake is narrower than that of man."[293] To the contrary, John Bellamy Foster observes that "When we are introduced for the first and only time in the text to an example of higher craftsmanship, and of

289 Kurt Vonnegut, Jr, *Player Piano* (New York: The Dial Press, 2006), 207.

290 Morris, *News from Nowhere*, 123.

291 Morris, *News from Nowhere*, 127.

292 Philip Steer, "National Pasts and Imperial Futures: Temporality, Economics, and Empire in William Morris's *News from Nowhere* (1890) and Julius Vogel's *Anno Domini 2000* (1889)," *Utopian Studies* 19, no. 1 (2008): 49–72.

293 Levitas, "Who Holds the Hose?," 78.

the most strenuous kind, it is an occupation filled by a woman [Mistress Philippa the stonemason]."[294]

For Morris the mutual interdependence of occupations further protects their moral equality. Thus, "wares which we make are made because they are needed: men make for their neighbours' use as if they were making for themselves."[295] Ultimately, all work which "would be irksome to do by hand is done by immensely improved machinery; and in all work which it is a pleasure to do by hand machinery is done without."[296]

The Future Commonwealth or What Samuel Balcom Saw in Socioland

Albert Chavannes's *The Future Commonwealth or What Samuel Balcom Saw in Socioland* (1892) promotes economic equality by making all forms of work honorable.[297] The goal of their society in Socioland is the experimental design of alternatives to the flawed systems the utopia's founders left behind in America. In establishing Socioland in Africa, "we had no settled plan," Mr. Walter insists, "but we had a very clear idea of the results we were going to strive for."[298] Those results were not the leveling of society but the discovery of principles to eliminate the causes of poverty. "As wealth cannot be created by individual effort alone but is the result of the combined industry of the whole people," observes another Socioland spokesperson, "it is but common justice that as far as possible the whole nation should profit by its increased production."[299]

294 John Bellamy Foster, "William Morris's Romantic Revolutionary Ideal: Nature, Labour and Gender in *News from Nowhere*," *The Journal of William Morris Studies* 22, no. 2 (2017).

295 Morris, *News from Nowhere*, 127.

296 Morris, *News from Nowhere*, 127.

297 Chavannes, *The Future Commonwealth*, 57.

298 Chavannes, *The Future Commonwealth*, 7.

299 Chavannes, *The Future Commonwealth*, 80.

From the Earth's Center

All work is valuable and equally esteemed in Centralia in S. Byron Welcome's *From the Earth's Center* (1895). The story follows the travels of Ralph Spencer who leaves America with two friends for an adventure at the earth's center. The society they find there is described as "the acme of civilization."[300] Among the narrator's early observations is that there is no "down-trodden class here—in fact, there is but one class."[301] Celia, one of his hosts, explains that people here loathe titles of distinction like "honorable" and are not ashamed to "have it known what occupation they follow."[302] "They have no titles, no uniforms, no manner or kind of social mark or distinction."[303] A human being, explains Spencer the narrator, "man or woman—is of far more consequence than any possible position or title whatever."[304] To his surprise, Spencer discovers that *even farmers* "live among other people, dress like other people, and cannot be distinguished from other people, except when at work."[305] "Bankers and street-car conductors, railroad presidents and brakemen, judges and laborers, lawyers and policemen, the chief executive and the poorest citizen—all mingle together and mutually respect one another—all attend the same theaters, the same balls, the same concerts, the same card parties, and dine at the same tables."[306] Everyone here, asserts the narrator, "without respect to condition" is equal and enjoys the "privileges and pleasures, that under a less perfect system of economic government would be restricted to a chosen few!"[307]

300 Welcome, *From the Earth's Center*, 56.
301 Welcome, *From the Earth's Center*, 72.
302 Welcome, *From the Earth's Center*, 172.
303 Welcome, *From the Earth's Center*, 72.
304 Welcome, *From the Earth's Center*, 72.
305 Welcome, *From the Earth's Center*, 71–72.
306 Welcome, *From the Earth's Center*, 72.
307 Welcome, *From the Earth's Center*, 56.

Expunging Racism

> "Political equality does not imply social equality, or physical equality, or race equality."[308]
>
> —Ignatius Donnelly, *Donnelliana: An Appendix to Caesar's Column* (1892)

Racism, writes John Lovchik, is "a system of ranking human beings for the purpose of gaining and justifying an unequal distribution of political and economic power."[309] Satterlee's *Looking Backward and What I Saw* (1890), one of numerous rebuttals to Bellamy's *Looking Backward*, references an early twentieth-century race war between African Americans "whose ancestors had suffered the tortures of the hell of slavery" and some of the "most fiendish and brutal ... in whose veins there flowed a portion of Anglo-Saxon blood."[310] This was part of a larger struggle lasting twenty-five years (described in Chapter 6) and culminating in Bellamy's industrial army.

Journalist and novelist George S. Schuyler's *Black No More* (1931) pictures the chaotic social and economic consequences of a Harlem-based African American physician, Dr. Junius Crookman, discovering a "revolutionary machine," says Tarshia L. Stanley, "capable of turning African-Americans into Caucasians."[311] The doctor's procedure—"only one of three solutions to the problem of racism"[312]—involves inducing severe

308 Ignatius Donnelly, *Donnelliana: An Appendix to Caesar's Column* (Chicago: Francis J. Schulte and Company, 1892), 183.

309 John Lovchik, *Racism: Reality Built on a Myth* (Eugene, OR: Resource Publications, 2018), 3.

310 Satterlee, *Looking Backward and What I Saw*, 54–55.

311 Tarshia L. Stanley, "Re-read and Recover: Afrofuturism as a Reading Practice in George S. Schuyler's *Black No More* and Octavia E. Butler's 'The Book of Martha,'" (243–260) in *Race and Utopian Desire in American Literature and Society*, ed. Patricia Ventura and Edward K. Chan (Palgrave MacMillan, 2019), 247. Although *Black No More* "has been labeled *anti-utopian* literature in recent critiques," notes Stanley, "Schuyler has crafted what for many African-Americans would have been a utopia" (247–248).

312 Stanley, "Re-read and Recover: Afrofuturism as a Reading Practice," 248. The other two methods are "get out" or "get along."

vitiligo—an autoimmune disease that targets pigment-producing cells called melanocytes. The depigmentation results in white areas on the skin—in this case covering the entire body. As the treatment becomes widespread "the very foundation of civilization, white supremacy, was threatened."[313] Stanley observes that "What begins in Crookman's mind as a solution to the race problem quickly reveals itself to be the upending of a society built on race prejudice and economic divides."[314] "Schuyler," says Zamalin, "wanted Americans to know that white supremacy was nothing but a powerful fantasy, whose elimination could only be undertaken by whites."[315]

In a 2020 study, nonprofit Inequality.org reports, "The racial wealth divide is where the past shows up in the present. The glaring gap in wealth reflects the multigenerational history of white supremacy in the United States and the systematic denial of wealth-building opportunities to Black people."[316] "Here in America," announces Matthew Townes, protagonist of W. E. B. Du Bois's *Dark Princess* (1928), "black folk must help overthrow the rule of the rich by distributing wealth more evenly first among themselves and then in alliance with white labor, to establish democratic

313 George S. Schuyler, *Black No More* (Victoria, BC, Canada: Must Have Books, 2021), 84. "Schulyer's satires in the vein of Jonathan Swift, Alexander Pope, and Voltaire were unlike anything in the utopian tradition." Alex Zamalin, *Black Utopia: The History of an Idea from Black Nationalism to Afrofuturism* (New York: Columbia University Press, 2019), 65.

314 Stanley, "Re-read and Recover: Afrofuturism as a Reading Practice," 247.

315 Zamalin, *Black Utopia*, 72.

316 Chuck Collins, Omar Ocampo, Dedrick Asante Muhammad, and Darrick Hamilton, "White Supremacy Is the Pre-existing Condition," *INEQUALITY.ORG*, June 2020. <https://inequality.org/our-inequality-work/reports-2/> "No group of working Americans has paid a steeper price for income inequality in the tax-cutting past four decades than African Americans. ... Over the decades, 'next to no progress has been made in closing the black-white income gap,' concluded a report for the Federal Reserve Bank of Minneapolis in 2018. 'The typical black household remains poorer than 80 percent of white households.'" James B. Steele, "How Four Decades of Tax Cuts Fueled Inequality," *The Center for Public Integrity*, November 29, 2022 <https://publicintegrity.org/inequality-poverty-opportunity/taxes/unequal-burden/how-four-decades-of-tax-cuts-fueled-inequality/>

control of industry. During this process," Townes continues, "they must keep step and hold tight hands with the other struggling darker peoples."[317]

A Modern Utopia, says H. G. Wells, "is a Utopia as wide as Christian charity, and white and black, brown, red and yellow, all tints of skin, all types of body and character, will be there … [though functioning under] an entirely different set of traditions, ideals, ideas, and purposes."[318] In *The Racial Horizons of Utopia* (2016) Edward Chan writes, "It has been easy enough to imagine a mono-racial utopia, a collection of homogenous 'citizens of nowhere' as the basis for a future or alternative social formation free from racial conflict." But, he asks, "what of attempts to envision a utopia that includes racial difference at its very core?"[319] Bellamy overtly skirted the issue in *Equality* (1897), holding that while the "many millions of recently freed negro slaves" were assimilated into the industrial army, this procedure "involved no more commingling of races than the old had done. It was perfectly consistent with any degree of race separation in industry which the most bigoted local prejudices might demand."[320] Wells's characterization of the racial mix in *A Modern Utopia* (1905) offers an ambiguous attempt to bridge the gap of racial difference. While external "racial markers" remain, a combination of education, training (manners), and eugenics has eliminated racial conflicts. Chan notes a comparable result in Piercy's *Woman on the Edge of Time* (1976), which still exhibits "racial signifiers" although "racial meaning no longer exists."[321] In Piercy's utopian Mattapoisett, Connie (Consuelo Ramos) the protagonist inquires, "You saying there's no racism left? Paradise on earth, all God's children are equal?" Luciente, Connie's Mattapoisett guide replies, "Our mems [immediate

317 Du Bois, *Dark Princess*, 185. *Dark Princes*, says Zamalin, "painted an image of utopian possibility where people of color had autonomy of their lives. … Unlike his utopian predecessors, Du Bois both expanded the tradition to more explicitly include interracial democracy and Afro-Asian solidarity and introduced a self-consciously critical understanding of utopia." Zamalin, *Black Utopia*, 51.

318 Wells, *A Modern Utopia*, 15.

319 Edward K. Chan, *The Racial Horizon of Utopia: Unthinking the Future of Race in Late Twentieth-Century American Utopian Novels* (Bern: Peter Lang, 2016), 85.

320 Bellamy, *Equality*, 364–365.

321 Chan, *The Racial Horizon of Utopia*, 103.

community], our children, our friends include people of differing gene mixes. Our mothers also." But, she continues, "There's no genetic bond."[322] "[W]e broke the bond between genes and culture," affirms Luciente, "broke it forever. We want there to be no chance of racism again."[323]

Chan's challenge of "a utopia that includes racial difference at its very core?"[324] is confronted in Hertzka's *Freeland* (1891) where the European settlers to Africa (described in Chapter 2) engage in educating "the black and brown natives that they would become more and more useful associates in our great work."[325] "Much of the initial work of building the Freeland colony," notes Gabriel, "is done with the use of African labourers, who work voluntarily and are well paid with European goods."[326] As the indigenous (Maasai) workers are educated—"We took considerable pains," asserts narrator Ney, to teach them to read and write—those who succeed are rewarded with citizenship rights including the right to vote.[327] Thus as Gabriel observes, "Hertzka's emphasis on economic reorganization as the key to civilization's progress undercut the increasingly rigid discourse of scientific racism that justified European domination of non-European peoples."[328]

Motherhood as a Paying Job

> "Were twenty shillings to be given immediately on the birth of a child to every woman who should make the demand ... it might relieve a great deal of instant distress."[329]
>
> —Thomas Paine, *Rights of Man* (1792)

322 Piercy, *Woman on the Edge of Time*, 109.
323 Piercy, *Woman on the Edge of Time*, 108–109.
324 Chan, *The Racial Horizon of Utopia*, 85.
325 Hertzka, *Freeland*, 72.
326 Gabriel, "Utopia, Science and the Nature of Civilization in Theodor Hertzka's *Fieiland*," 21.
327 Hertzka, *Freeland*, 141–142.
328 Gabriel, "Utopia, Science and the Nature of Civilization in Theodor Hertzka's *Fieiland*," 26.
329 Paine, *Rights of Man*, 173.

In her book *Invisible Women*, Criado-Perez challenges the "male default" model of work that renders "women's work" invisible and unaccounted for. "The work women do," she says, "paid and unpaid, is the backbone of our society and our economy."[330] A number of utopias have tackled the question of paying women for raising children. Women in Bellamy's *Looking Backward* (1888) earn their equal share of the national income whether working in conjunction with the industrial army or caring for their children. In one of numerous Bellamy continuations, *Young West: A Sequel to Edward Bellamy's Celebrated Novel, Looking Backward* (1894), Solomon Schindler has Julian West's son explain that "the nation does not begrudge a woman her support during the time in which she withdraws from the [industrial] army in order to devote herself to the holiest of all her obligations, to give to the community citizens who will take up the work where it must pass from our hands."[331]

Freeland

Though the first settlers to the African colony described in Theodor Hertzka's *Freeland* (1891) are men (as noted in Chapter 2), women were soon recruited as teachers and wives.[332] Though Hertzka's spokesperson Henry Ney declares, "our principles secured perfect liberty to woman"—he clarifies that women "must be altogether withdrawn from the struggle for the necessities of life."[333] Women's primary function is motherhood and early childhood education. The "special duty of the mother,"[334] which she "seldom needs to be taught,"[335] Ney explains, is "the intellectual and physical development of the young."[336]

330 Criado-Perez, *Invisible Women*, 142.

331 Solomon Schindler, *Young West: A Sequel to Edward Bellamy's Celebrated Novel, Looking Backward* (Boston: Arena Publishing Company, 1894), 197–198.

332 Hertzka, *Freeland*, 115.

333 Hertzka, *Freeland*, 140.

334 Hertzka, *Freeland*, 230.

335 Hertzka, *Freeland*, 231.

336 Hertzka, *Freeland*, 140. Exceptions are made, however, as Freeland women are "not forbidden to engage in any occupation, and isolated instances have occurred

In exchange for this gender-specific division of labor Freeland women have a right to a "competent maintenance, fairly proportionate to the level of the average wealth of the community."[337] Maintenance is also provided to children, old men, and men incapable of work. Maintenance is justified by the fact that the wealth of a nation, says Hertzka, "is the result of the intellectual labour of numberless previous generations, *whose bequest belongs as much to the weak and helpless as to the strong and capable*."[338] Gregory Claeys refers to this perspective as the "theory of 'social debt' by which the rich always owed some portion of their wealth to society at large."[339] J. E. King and John Marangos affirm that the "social debt" undercuts "objections to measures that redistribute income (and wealth) from rich to poor."[340] For married women maintenance is based on the principle that "even the wife ought not to be thrown upon the husband for maintenance and made dependent upon him."[341] Hertzka provides a table pegging this maintenance based on the number of children in the family.[342] As a baseline, the maintenance for "independent" women was fixed at 75 percent of that for men. This pecuniary gender disparity, notes the narrator, is because the "*requirements* of a woman are less than those of a man" and "not an expression of any lower estimate of the *claim* of woman."[343] For independent women with two children the maintenance was the same as for a man; one child a little less (7/8ths), three children a little more (9/8ths). The source of this maintenance is Freeland's ≈ 30 percent income tax on labor.[344]

---

of women doing so, particularly in intellectual callings ... when special gifts justified such actions."

337 Hertzka, *Freeland*, 137.

338 Hertzka, *Freeland*, 138 (italics in original).

339 Gregory Claeys, "Paine's *Agrarian Justice* (1796) and the Secularization of Natural Jurisprudence," *Bulletin of the Society for the Study of Labour History* 52, pt. 3 (November, 1987): 21–31, 21; reprinted in *Thomas Paine*, ed. Bruce Kuklick (London: Ashgate Publishing, 2006; reissue Oxfordshire, UK: Routledge, Taylor and Francis Group, 2018), 173.

340 King and Marangos, "Two Arguments for Basic Income: Thomas Paine (1737–1890) and Thomas Spence (1750–1814), 63.

341 Hertzka, *Freeland*, 141.

342 Hertzka, *Freeland*, 141.

343 Hertzka, *Freeland*, 140–141 (italics in original).

344 Hertzka, *Freeland*, 109, 161, 260.

Utopia: A Romance of Today

Men in Frank Rosewater's *Utopia: A Romance of Today* (1897), explains Minister Aggra—of the eutopian society of Tsmoul (the western capital of Lukka noted in Chapter 2)—to the guests, "are rewarded here according to ability and skill, industry or merit, but not until the other members of the household have been rewarded on an equitable basis."[345] Since mothers "serve humanity, and their welfare cannot be gaged entirely by the peculiar skill or ability of the husband," continues the minister, every mother "who has the care of home and the home education of children" receives an independent income.[346] The work mothers are compensated for does not include cooking or laundry, however, as the homes feature neither a kitchen nor a laundry. Meals are procured at public restaurants in each neighborhood.[347] These arrangements, observes the minister, are "by no means communistic, but rather individualistic." Paying the mothers separate incomes gives them "a distinct individuality and standing in the household and in the community."[348] This system, stresses the minister, protects the work women perform against being "falsely and inequitably absorbed"[349] into the wages of the men.

A Modern Utopia

H. G. Wells's *A Modern Utopia* (1905) provides maintenance to women who are caring for their *legitimate* children—children born to parents legally married—having passed the state's eugenic screening requirement (described in Chapter 4). A modern Utopia equalizes matters between the sexes: "women are to be as free as men." This is effected in the "only possible way," explains the narrator, by insisting that motherhood is a

345 Rosewater, *Utopia: A Romance of Today*, 156 (italics and capitalization in original removed).
346 Rosewater, *Utopia: A Romance of Today*, 156.
347 Rosewater, *Utopia: A Romance of Today*, 150.
348 Rosewater, *Utopia: A Romance of Today*, 157.
349 Rosewater, *Utopia: A Romance of Today*, 156–157.

"service to the State and a legitimate claim to a living."[350] Thus, a woman who is, or is becoming, a mother, "is as much entitled to wages above the minimum wage ... as a policemen, a solicitor-general, ... a Government professor, or anyone else the state sustains."[351]

Public Housing

> "The first result of the Social Palace ... is to ameliorate the condition of the laborer; to create for the benefit of the masses a sum of advantages which will lighten the hardships of toil, and meanwhile, by the education of the young, to prepare for the social regeneration of the rising population."[352]
>
> —Jean Baptiste André Godin, *Social Solutions* (1871)

Public housing in the US emerged as part of President Roosevelt's New Deal in 1934. Its appointed goals included creating jobs and affordable housing while clearing away slums.

Thomas More's *Utopia* (1516) mandates fungible public housing for all citizens as a facet of its economic leveling scheme (discussed in Chapter 6). Though it is public housing, the Utopians are "not only quick to repair deterioration but foresighted in preventing it."[353]

The social transformation Robert Owen envisaged (discussed in Chapter 6) includes the emergence of uniform communities or townships (nuclei or home colonies) with a standardized physical layout and architecture including public housing. "Experience," Owen wrote, "will probably prove that the best general form for the domestic and educational dwellings, will be a square, sufficiently large" to house the "maximum population"[354] of 2,000 people. Each square will enclose an area of

350 Wells, *A Modern Utopia*, 75.
351 Wells, *A Modern Utopia*, 75.
352 Jean Baptiste Andre Godin, *Social Solutions* (New York: John W. Lovell Company, Publishers, 1886), 264.
353 More, *Utopia*, trans. Adams, bk. 2, 52.
354 Owen, *The Revolution in the Mind*, 44.

"about sixty-five acres" (65 acres = 1/10 sq. mile ≈ 2 city blocks), within an estate of "about 2,000 or 3,000 acres"[355] (2,560 acres = 4 square miles). Four square buildings housing the community's educational endeavor anchor each township's square.[356] Four "magnificent buildings" project into the center of the square "attached to which, will be the kitchens."[357] Between these buildings enclosing the square will be 144 "private dwelling-houses."[358] Each five-story building—in what Frank Manuel describes as Owen's "barrackslike monastic communism"[359]—includes a basement, apartments for the workers and a top story housing the children's dormitories. "The manufactures and trades which may be necessary to make the township self-supporting, may also be arranged at some convenient distance from the first square, also in the form of square."[360]

Each community or colony, Owen stipulates, shall "be the property of a joint-stock company; who,—having purchased the land, and erected thereon the requisite buildings, and furnished the same,—shall let the whole, upon lease, to a company of tenants; the latter having power gradually to fine down the rents, and ultimately to become the owners, at a stipulated price."[361]

Marie Howland's *Papa's Own Girl* (1874) features a wealthy count (Von Frauenstein), inspired by Jean-Baptiste André Godin (1817–1888), a French industrialist and social innovator Charles Fourier had influenced.[362] Of his

355 Robert Owen, *A Development of the Principles and Plans on Which to Establish Self-Supporting Home Colonies* (London: Published by the Home Colonization Society, 1841), 38.

356 Owen, *The Revolution in the Mind*, 44–45.

357 Owen, *A Development of the Principles and Plans on Which to Establish Self-Supporting Home Colonies*, 38.

358 Owen, *A Development of the Principles and Plans on Which to Establish Self-Supporting Home Colonies*, 38 (capitalization in original removed).

359 Frank E. Manuel, *The Prophets of Paris* (New York: Harper Torchbooks, 1962), 226.

360 Owen, *The Revolution in the Mind*), 44–45.

361 Owen, *A Development of the Principles and Plans on Which to Establish Self-Supporting Home Colonies*, 37.

362 Howland, *Papa's Own Girl*, 413. Godin says of Fourier that "his views are generally worthy of study and reflection ... [and] the work of a great genius." Godin, *Social Solutions*, 42.

passion Godin writes, "I gave myself up to the study of means to reconcile the growth and progress of grand industries with the prosperity of the working-classes, that their homes might be the abodes of health, intelligence, and morality instead of centres of poverty and demoralization."[363] Following Godin's model (the Familistère, Guise, France) Howland's count proposes building a community of apartments and social and industrial facilities (the Social Palace) to provide work for the poor but ultimately to offer them a better life and a pleasant home. The benefits of such housing, according to Godin, include "the superiority of the habitation" as well as "all the advantages which surround the home"[364]—a resident-run bakery, butchery, and grocery selling products of the residents' agricultural and industrial efforts.[365] Unlike Owen's succession of square buildings, however, Godin's Familistère (Social Palace) comprised a series of parallelograms enclosing a court.[366]

The count privately financed Howland's public housing as both an investment returning 6 percent a year and, more significantly, a facility aimed at reduce poverty.[367] The count explains that "those who build it and those who come to live in it, shall buy it and own it through the rents they pay."[368] After fifteen years the count will relinquish the apartments to their renters. Once the initial capitalist-financed construction is complete, labor organizations will replicate these facilities on the same terms.[369] Each complex will house 2,000 people or 500 families on 115 acres (roughly twice the size of Owen's building complex).[370] While a silk "manufactory" is the primary industry employing the residents,[371] the housing development will offer education for the children as well as medical facilities and centralized laundry and eating accommodations.

363 Godin, *Social Solutions*, 27.
364 Godin, *Social Solutions*, 233.
365 Godin, *Social Solutions*, 270.
366 Godin, *Social Solutions*, 226.
367 Howland, *Papa's Own Girl*, 533.
368 Howland, *Papa's Own Girl*, 413.
369 Howland, *Papa's Own Girl*, 414.
370 Howland, *Papa's Own Girl*, 412.
371 Howland, *Papa's Own Girl*, 413.

The public housing Walter Mosley recommends in his 2016 utopian tract on viable human survival comprises "rudimentary" apartments of 550 square feet that will rent for 10 percent of the "person's salary" and for which "*any citizen* is qualified."[372] While an unemployed person with no salary will pay no rent for her cubicle "an investment banker making $1.5 million will pay $150,000 a year." Governments (city, state, and federal) will build and subsidize the apartments. These residences, "not comprising slums," Mosley states, will also "not define class." They will appeal to people seeking more time to "consider and enhance their work" including artisans and thinkers as well as single parents and "aged pensioners."[373]

372 Walter Mosley, *Folding the Red into the Black or Developing a Viable Utopia for Human Survival in the 21st* Century (New York: OR Books, 2016), 99 (italics in original).

373 Mosley, *Folding the Red Into the Black*, 99.

CHAPTER 4

Instruments of Change: Political Reforms

"Throughout the ages we find this belief growing in men's minds that there can be such a rearrangement of laws and powers as to give rule and order while still restraining the egotism of any ruler and of any ruling class."[1]

—H. G. Wells, *The Outline of History* (1920)

"One of the reasons why utopianism deserves to be taken seriously," affirm Goodwin and Taylor, "is that it has so often been a stimulus to political activity."[2] Political reforms are the results of government action and for that reason may be more transient than social reforms which alter the underlying culture and the structure of human interaction. Governments come and go. Direct political action has rarely been the utopian's primary choice for reform; it has rather been the presentation of a new political configuration displaying solutions to current social or economic problems.

Public Transparency—Economic and Political

"We live in full view, perpetually awash with light, in among our transparent walls, woven from sparkling air. We have nothing to hide from one another."[3]

—Yevgeny Zamyatin, *We* (1924)

1 Wells, *The Outline of History*, 432.
2 Goodwin and Taylor, *The Politics of Utopia*, 126.
3 Yevgeny Zamyatin, *We*, trans. Natasha Randall (New York: The Modern Library, 2006), 19.

The tale of Gyges's ring in Plato's *Republic* and the exploits of Griffin in H. G. Wells's *The Invisible Man* evince the public harm people passing invisibly pose—the harm of personal transparency.[4] Public transparency, by contrast, facilitates the economic equality the citizens experience in More's *Utopia* (1516)—where narrator Hythloday says, "there are no … hiding places; no spots for secret meetings.[5] The goal of More's transparency scheme is that since citizens "live in the full view of all, they are bound to be either working at their usual trades or enjoying their leisure in a respectable way."[6]

In *The Public and Its Problems* (1927), John Dewey distinguishes between actions that are private and those that are public, not on the basis of their visibility but on the basis of their consequences. A discussion among "merchants planning to monopolize a market," says Dewey, though carried out in private, "acquires a public capacity" because the resulting actions will affect "the welfare of many others."[7] Thomas Piketty speaks of the "political fear of transparency and the demands for redistribution that might result from it."[8]

While public transparency does not guarantee economic equality, utopians view a lack of transparency as a catalyst for economic inequality—hiding opportunities, skewing competition, and concealing corruption—as private financial forces inexorably seek to wrest the reins of power. Berlin-based nonprofit Transparency International conducts surveys to assess the quality of the world's governments based on a Corruption Perceptions Index (CPI). The organization defines corruption as the "abuse of entrusted power for private gain," and holds "the powerful and corrupt to account, by exposing the systems and networks that enable corruption."[9] As Robert Frank notes, the ten most transparent governments on Transparency International's list are also among the most affluent, while the

4 Plato, *Republic*, bk. 2, 359–360; H. G. Wells, *The Invisible Man* (New York: Bantam Classic, 1970).

5 More, *Utopia*, trans. Adams, bk. 2, 59.

6 More, *Utopia*, trans. Adams, bk. 2, 59.

7 Dewey, *The Public and Its Problems*, 18.

8 Piketty, *Capital and Ideology*, 678.

9 Transparency International <https://www.transparency.org/en/>

least transparent, most corrupt governments are those governing the poorest countries—with respect to their masses.[10] And, "the poorer a country," as Charles Hurst reports, "the greater is the income discrepancy between the richest and the poorest 20 percent of the population."[11]

The Crystal Button

Those who have taken an oath "to be true and honest in … every act, word, and thought"[12] wear a crystal button in Chauncey Thomas's ideal society.[13] John Costor is the "Apostle of Truth" in *The Crystal Button* (1891). Costor, says Parrington, "believed that the abolition of political deceit was the solution of all our ills."[14] As his truth movement grew, "politics gradually became honest."[15] Costor is described as a "peculiarly energetic and skillful" organizer; he recruited preachers of every persuasion and "scattered them as missionaries throughout the globe."[16] The success of Costor's truth movement is attributed to the fact that truth was seen as "an object that appealed to the sympathies of all men and women," regardless of religious, national, or other differences, "and thus afforded common ground for the adoption of an ideal and inspiration that should be universal."[17]

10 Frank, *The Darwin Economy*, 56.
11 Hurst, *Social Inequality*, 159.
12 Thomas, *The Crystal Button*, 158 (original in italics). Parrington says of *The Crystal Button*, "The plot is more perfunctory even than that of *Looking Backward*, but it is a supremely good example of a novel by an engineer." Parrington, *American Dreams*, 64.
13 Thomas, *The Crystal Button*, 163.
14 Parrington, *American Dreams*, 66.
15 Parrington, *American Dreams*, 66.
16 Thomas, *The Crystal Button*, 162–163.
17 Thomas, *The Crystal Button*, 139–140. Similarly, Altruria is "a country where truth alone is recognized as a standard for the regulation of human conduct." Grigsby and Lowe, *Nequa*, 165.

Freeland

While Hertzka's *Freeland* (1891) permits degrees of income inequality, an economic transparency policy mitigates its pernicious effects. Mr. Clark, the bank director, explains to his visitors, "the comprehensive, transparent, and detailed publicity which marked all the pecuniary affairs of Freeland."[18] The amounts of each person's income and expenditures, he says, "lie open to the day; all the world knows what everybody has and whence he gets it."[19] In this way, "The sharp light of universal publicity puts an end to the secrets and conspiracies of monopoly,"[20] a persistent source of economic inequality.

Equality

Bellamy's *Equality* (1897) promotes economic transparency with a greatly simplified accounting and record keeping system. In Julian West's Boston of 1887, explains Dr. Leete, private capitalists "sat up nights devising tricks to deceive, defeat, and overreach one another."[21] But now that the economy has been nationalized, the financial recordkeeping is "so simple and invariable" that the accounts of each individual are maintained "automatically by a machine."[22] As a result, Dr. Leete tells West, "one accountant serves where dozens were needed in your day."[23] "Such accounting is child's work,"[24] he boasts, and "debit and credit are no longer known."[25]

18 Hertzka, *Freeland*, 249.
19 Hertzka, *Freeland*, 249.
20 Manuel and Manuel, *Utopian Thought in the Western World*, 766.
21 Bellamy, *Equality*, 33.
22 Bellamy, *Equality*, 32.
23 Bellamy, *Equality*, 32.
24 Bellamy, *Equality*, 33.
25 Bellamy, *Equality*, 34.

Philip Dru: Administrator

Transparency is imperative in the governmental reforms enacted in *Philip Dru: Administrator* (1912). Regarding the tax system, for example, the people had "quickly learned the value of knowing how much and for what they were paying. This, perhaps, more than any other thing, had awakened their interest in public affairs."[26] The source of economic inequality Edward House addresses is the result of unwarranted corporate profits arising from collusion, monopolies, price fixing, and other tools for thwarting honest competition.[27] The difficulties Dru seeks to overcome ensue from a lack of public transparency, especially among corporations and between corporations and agencies of government. "When there is a monopoly or trust, it is easy to locate the offense," says Dru. But it is a different matter to police a large number of corporations and individuals, who, "under the guise of competition, have an understanding, both as to prices and territory to be served."[28]

In a discussion of their prior corrupt system, Dru explains that while politicians received kickbacks "in the most open and shameless way,"[29] businesses of a "public nature" such as grain elevators, cotton compresses, and lumber mills were influenced by financially interested railroad officials. These favored corporations received "rebates and better shipping facilities than their competitors and competition was stifled."[30] In their greed, corporations and wealthy individuals lobbied legislatures with "the most unconscionable bills, giving them land, money and rights to further exploit the public."[31]

Dru's solution is a new transparency law requiring public representation on corporate boards by agents of governments—either national, state, or

26 House, *Philip Dru: Administrator*, 292.

27 Regarding the industrial competition of the late nineteenth century, Bellamy's Dr. Leete complains, "the so-called competitive system was the ghastliest farce ... [as] there was not a particle of genuine competition in it." Bellamy, *Equality*, 395.

28 House, *Philip Dru: Administrator*, 256.

29 House, *Philip Dru: Administrator*, 187.

30 House, *Philip Dru: Administrator*, 187.

31 House, *Philip Dru: Administrator*, 187–188.

municipal[32]—and twice a year compelling corporations "to make public a full and a clear report, giving the receipts and expenditures, including salaries paid to high officials."[33] In the future, there would be "no hiding under cover," as the government's oversight of corporations meant "everything was to be done in the open, and in a way entirely understandable to the ordinary layman."[34]

The Ministry for the Future

Kim Stanley Robinson's ecocritical *The Ministry for the Future* (2020) recounts the struggles of a UN agency tasked with advocating for "the world's future generations of citizens, whose rights, as defined in the Universal Declaration of Human Rights, are as valid as our own."[35] The narrator recounts a technological twist to transparency's effect on economic inequality, encouraging the rich to pay their assigned share of taxes (noted in Chapter 2). "If all fiat money everywhere went digital and got recorded in blockchains, so that its location and transaction history could be traced and seen by all, then illegal tax dodges could be driven into non-existence."[36] Reflecting on the achievement of this digitization frontier, the narrator explains, "Of course many rich people had attempted to abscond to a safe haven with their riches, but ... the fact that all money was now blockchained and tracked, meant that all the old havens and shelters were being rooted out and eliminated."[37]

Another Now

Costa, the protagonist, in Yanis Varoufakis's *Another Now* (2021) recounts a silent revolution in the utopian Other Now precipitated by a "remarkably

32 House, *Philip Dru: Administrator*, 259.
33 House, *Philip Dru: Administrator*, 189.
34 House, *Philip Dru: Administrator*, 190.
35 Robinson, *The Ministry for the Future*, 16.
36 Robinson, *The Ministry for the Future*, 333.
37 Robinson, *The Ministry for the Future*, 478–479.

infectious" open-source computer virus.[38] The virus, named the Panopticon Code, "lay dormant and wholly undetectable" on "every computer network on the planet."[39] When the virus was eventually activated, the result was "immediate and total informational transparency.... Citizens had access to every state secret.... For the first time, the poor and the weak had the same access to information as the rich and the powerful.... Within minutes the world changed. Governments and corporations were paralyzed by the billions of eyes trained on them.... Gradually outrage at what was being revealed gave way to calls for reform."[40] The reforms—universal basic income and workers' cooperatives (described in Chapter 2)—led to a more equal distribution of income and wealth.

Transparency Through Eliminating Vested Interests from Education

The ideal of universal compulsory education was addressed in Chapter 3. But this ideal may be subverted by economic or political forces. A theme common to Edward Bellamy and Thorsten Veblen, argues Rick Tilman, is the impediment to transparency arising from the "ideological control the capitalist class has over the popular mind." Bellamy and Veblen, says Tilman, saw education as subject to "capitalist influence and made economically subservient to the vested interests." [41] Bellamy illustrates this theme in a schoolroom scene in *Equality* (1897) entitled, "How Progress Antagonized Vested Interests." There (in 2000), in response to a teacher's question about education in the time of Bellamy (1887), the student explains that higher education at that time was available to only a small class who "molded the thoughts of the people," set the standards, "and through the control of their minds dominated their material interests and determined the course of civilization."[42] Given this level of obligation, the student continues, "it was a most vital point that this elite class

38 Varoufakis, *Another Now*, 81.
39 Varoufakis, *Another Now*, 81.
40 Varoufakis, *Another Now*, 81–82.
41 Tilman, "The Utopian Vision of Edward Bellamy and Thorstein Veblen," 890.
42 Bellamy, *Equality*, 228.

should be qualified to discharge so responsible a duty in a spirit of devotion to the general weal unbiased by distracting motives."[43] However, under the system of capitalism, "which made every person and group economically dependent upon and exclusively concerned in the prosperity of the occupation followed by himself and his group," the student concludes, "this ideal was impossible of attainment." As any new idea arose that affected their source of income, the members of this class—instead of asking "whether the idea was good and true"—asked instead "how it would immediately and directly affect the set of doctrines, traditions, and institutions, with the prestige of which their own personal interests were identified."[44]

Jack London's *The Iron Heel* (1908) expresses the concern that in an increasingly oligarchic "democracy" where the elected officials' assigned role is "to give the stamp of constitutional procedure to the mandates of the Oligarchy,"[45] education would inevitably become an instrument of the oligarchic Iron Heel.[46] A professor's seditious book expressed London's fears. As the narrator explains,

> This book, "Economics and Education," ... dealt, in elaborate detail [with] ... the capitalistic bias of the universities and common schools. It was [an] ... indictment of the whole system of education that developed in the minds of the students only such ideas as were favorable to the capitalistic regime, to the exclusion of all ideas that were inimical and subversive.[47]

In our own time, Dan Sabia echoes this concern when he writes in "Democratic/Utopian Education" that "neoliberal and neoconservative

43 Bellamy, *Equality*, 228.

44 Bellamy, *Equality*, 229.

45 London, *The Iron Heel*, 168. The direction of this concern features explicitly in *The Space Merchants* where the members of congress are assigned to their primary benefactors, for example, the "senator from DuPont Chemicals" and the "senator from Disney." Frederik Pohl and C. M. Kornbluth, *The Space Merchants* (New York: Thomas Dunne Books imprint of St Martin's Griffin, [1953] 2011), 10.

46 London explores what is termed "oligarchic capture" where "Congress and the Senate were empty pretenses, farces." London, *The Iron Heel*, 168.

47 London, *The Iron Heel*, 74n51.

values and perspectives drive demands for schools to be efficient and accountable … [while] promoting … individualistic conceptions of citizens."[48]

Transparency Through the Disinterested Pursuit of Justice

William Godwin (1756–1836) was convinced that government itself precluded transparency and called for its "euthanasia."[49] Government, he proclaimed, "cannot proceed but upon confidence, as confidence on the other hand cannot exist without ignorance."[50] Secrets of state, he believed, "will commonly be found to consist of that species of information relative to the interests of a society, respecting which the chief anxiety of its depositaries is that it should be concealed from the members of that society.[51] Legislation, Godwin asserts, "is in almost every country grossly the favourer of the rich against the poor."[52] For this reason law blends into privilege as the rich are "directly or indirectly the legislators of the state,"[53] and as such, affirms Godwin, are "perpetually reducing oppression into a system, and depriving the poor of that little commonage of nature as it were, which might otherwise still have remained to them."[54] This is the theme of Godwin's *Things as They Are; or, The Adventures of Caleb Williams* (1794), which William Hazlitt praises as a "master-piece, both

48 Dan Sabia, "Democratic/Utopian Education," *Utopian Studies* 23, no. 2 (2012), 392. For a discussion of conservative billionaire-reformers' efforts to influence higher education, see Jane Mayer, *Dark Money: The Hidden History of the Billionaires Behind the Rise of the Radical Right* (New York: Anchor Books, 2016).

49 William Godwin, *Enquiry Concerning Political Justice and Its Influence on Modern Morals and Happiness*, (1798), 3rd ed. (New York: Viking Penguin, 1895), bk. 3, chap. 6, 248.

50 Godwin, *Enquiry Concerning Political Justice*, 3rd ed., bk. 3, chap. 6, 247.

51 Godwin, *Enquiry Concerning Political Justice*, 3rd ed., bk. 5, chap. 21, 539.

52 Godwin, *Enquiry Concerning Political Justice*, 3rd ed., bk. 1, chap. 3, 93.

53 William Godwin, *An Enquiry Concerning Political Justice* (1793), 1st ed. (Oxford University Press, 2013), bk. 1, chap. 5, 30.

54 William Godwin, *An Enquiry Concerning Political Justice*, 1st ed., bk. 1, chap. 5, 30.

as to invention and execution."[55] E. F. Bleiler describes *Caleb Williams* as a novel of social theory showing "the interrelations of miseducation, injustice, and the police state,"[56] while Pamela Clemit affirms the novel dramatizes "the inner workings of a hierarchical society, [and] the psychological and linguistic strategies by which inequality is maintained."[57] When Caleb's wealthy master, Mr. Falkland, "a gentleman of six thousand a year [£633,000 or $783,000 in 2023],"[58] appears before magistrates on an allegation of murder, Falkland—evincing the authority of his class—proclaims: "Conscious as I am of deserving approbation and not censure, of having passed my life in acts of justice and philanthropy, can anything be more deplorable than for me to answer to a charge of murder?"[59]—a dimension of transparency that Hayes calls "inequality of accountability."[60] Thus, says Godwin, the law was "better adapted for a weapon of tyranny in the hands of the rich than for a shield to protect the humble part of the community against their usurpations."[61]

55 William Hazlitt, *The Spirit of the AGE: Or, Contemporary Portraits* (Paris: A. and W. Galignani, 1825), 199.

56 Bleiler, "Introduction," in *Three Prophetic Novels of H. G. Wells*, ix.

57 Pamela Clemit, *The Godwinian Novel* (Oxford: Clarendon Press, 1993), 45.

58 William Godwin, *Things as They Are; or, The Adventures of Caleb Williams* (New York: Penguin Books, 1988), 286.

59 Godwin, *The Adventures of Caleb Williams*, 104. In Donnelly's *The Golden Bottle* the narrator notes, however, that "The Rich man should never forget that the honors which accompany him are not paid to himself, but to his money." Donnelley, *The Golden Bottle*, 43.

60 Hayes, *Twilight of the Elites*, 102. In *Caleb Williams* this uneven treatment is made explicit: "Six hundred a year shall protect a man from accusation; and the validity of an impeachment shall be suspended, because the author of it is a servant!" Godwin, *The Adventures of Caleb Williams*, 287.

61 Godwin, *The Adventures of Caleb Williams*, 76.

Transparency Through Eliminating the Religious Foundations of Government

Removing the religious foundations from government has appealed to some utopians as a means of encouraging transparency and thus promoting economic equality. Samuel Balcom, the narrator in Albert Chavannes's *The Future Commonwealth* (1892), acknowledges "how difficult it will be for us to make any marked advance so long as we try to follow at the same time the teachings of the Bible and the dictates of our natural desires."[62] *Shadow's Before* (1893) is Fayette Stratton Giles's vision of a society in 1993 grounded in science (noted in Chapter 3). Their current form of science-based governance was preceded by a system whose "opposition to ... scientific facts, proved that they had no criterion of truth."[63] The universities had "opposed scientific research and bitterly antagonized scientific advance," which they saw as "an attempt to dethrone God."[64] During the previous régime Herbert Spencer's 1855 *Psychology* and Charles Darwin's 1859 *On the Origin of Species* were censured by "vested educational and theological institutions."[65] But the transformation to a society grounded in science opened a "glorious epoch for the poor, suffering, enslaved man."[66]

On learning the conditions of the poor in England, Jason Delphion, the Ionian ambassador in Alexander Craig's *Ionia* (1898), explains to an English philanthropist, "Then, apparently, the church is in league with the state for the purpose of keeping the poor people where they are, and preventing them from improving their condition."[67] In Herzl's *Altneuland*:

62 Chavannes, *The Future Commonwealth*, 68.

63 Giles, *Shadows Before or A Century Onward*, 27.

64 Giles, *Shadows Before or A Century Onward*, 26.

65 Giles, *Shadows Before or A Century Onward*, 26. Dewey notes that "the 'Origin of the Species' introduced a mode of thinking that in the end was bound to transform the logic of knowledge, and hence the treatment of morals, politics and religion." John Dewey, *The Influence of Darwin on Philosophy* (New York: Henry Holt and Co., 1910), 2.

66 Giles, *Shadows Before or A Century Onward*, 113.

67 Craig, *Ionia*, 116.

The Old-New-Land (1902) "Religion had been excluded from public affairs once and for all."[68] Religious sects are seen as obstacles to "real progress and true civilization"[69] in Cosimo Noto's *The Ideal City* (1903). Their only aim, says Noto, is to use God's name as a "tyrannical tool, in order to keep people blindly submissive."[70]

Property and the Land Question

> "The first man who, having fenced off a plot of land, thought of saying 'This is mine' and found people simple enough to believe him was the real founder of civil society."[71]
>
> —Jean-Jacques Rousseau, *Discourse on the Origin and Foundations of Inequality Among Men* (1755)

"Do you mean," exclaimed Edith Leete in Bellamy's *Equality* (1897), "that if a man were only clever and unscrupulous enough he might appropriate, say, the entire territory of a country and leave the people actually nothing to stand on unless by his consent?" "Certainly," was the reply.[72] In *The Politics of Utopia*, Goodwin and Taylor write: "The major cause of social evil, utopians almost unanimously agree, is private property, which produces a variety of disruptive sentiments and desires."[73] Stipulating the ontological limits of property is a foundational utopian task: What is the nature of property? What may be owned and by whom in an ideal society?

"Property," affirms Wells, "is a purely provisional and law-made thing."[74] "The notion of property, as it has developed over centuries and as it is embodied in our legal codes," stresses economist Milton Friedman, involves

68 Theodor Herzl, *Altneuland: The Old-New-Land*, 199–200.
69 Noto, *The Ideal City*, v., 42–43.
70 Noto, *The Ideal City*, vi.
71 Rousseau, *Discourse on the Origin and Foundations of Inequality Among Men*, 34.
72 Bellamy, *Equality*, 102.
73 Goodwin and Taylor, *The Politics of Utopia*, 60; see also 136–137.
74 Wells, *Mankind in the Making*, 371.

"complex social creations rather than self-evident propositions."[75] Some utopian writers, Ayn Rand for example, take the opposing view claiming the necessity of owning property as a self-evident moral right. "Without property rights," declares Rand, "no other rights are possible."[76] Disentangling diverse conceptions of ownership (and property) is thus vital for diagnosing sources of economic inequality.

In *Utopia*, Thomas More's Hythloday argues that "unless private property is entirely abolished, there can be no fair or just distribution of goods." As long as private property remains, Hythloday continues, "by far the largest and best part of the human race will be oppressed by a distressing and inescapable burden of poverty and anxieties."[77] Later utopians singled out private ownership of *land* as the critical problem. Land in Robert Burton's utopia in *The Anatomy of Melancholy* (1621) will be publicly administered, he says, because private landowners "are many times idiots, ill husbands, oppressors, covetous, and know not how to improve their own, or else wholly respect their own, and not public good."[78] Thomas Spence in his *Constitution of Spensonia* (1807) makes this distinction: "The right of property is that which belongs to every citizen to enjoy and dispose of according to his pleasure, property, revenues, labor, and industry. Here his property in land is excepted," he stipulates, "which, being inseparably incorporated with that of his fellow parishioners, is inalienable."[79] Thomas Paine recommended countries establish funds to compensate citizens for the loss of their "natural

75 Milton Friedman, *Capitalism and Freedom* (Chicago: The University of Chicago Press, 2002), 26.

76 Rand, *The Virtue of Selfishness*, 33. See also Rand, *Atlas Shrugged*, 1062.

77 More, *Utopia*, trans. Adams, 38.

78 Robert Burton, *The Anatomy of Melancholy*, ed. Holbrook Jackson (New York: Published by the New York Review of Books, 2001), 101.

79 Thomas Spence, "The Constitution of Spensonia," in *Pig's Meat: Selected Writings of Thomas Spence, Radical and Pioneer Land Reformer* (Nottingham: Spokesman, 1982), 168. Claeys observes of Spence that virtually all his writings are a "variation on the theme of rendering land communal, under parish management, in order to eradicate poverty." Claeys, *Searching for Utopia*, 90.

inheritance, by the introduction of the system of landed property"[80] (noted in Chapter 2).

The Icarian's desire for equality in Étienne Cabet's (1840) utopia extends to their land and its resources. "All the property of the associates," says Dinaros the historian character, along with "all the products of earth and industry, form a single social capital," which belongs "indivisibly to the people."[81] In Chauncey Thomas's *The Crystal Button* (1891), "air, water, sunshine, and land are peculiarly the people's own."[82]

Late nineteenth and early twentieth century utopians— including Henry George, S. Byron Welcome, Archibald Forsyth, Theodore Herzl, and H. G. Wells—offer common ownership of land as a means for eliminating poverty. J. S. Mill summarizes the shared theme of these utopians. "The essential principle of property being to assure to all persons what they have produced by their labor and accumulated by their abstinence, this principle cannot apply to what is not the produce of labor, the raw material of the earth."[83] Though the writers this section describes sought only peaceful means for transforming society's land policies, in historical context, as Scheidel observes, land reform without violence "has rarely, if ever, been a potent means of combating inequalities of income or wealth."[84]

Henry George

"The great cause of inequality in the distribution of wealth," Henry George maintains, "is inequality in the ownership of land."[85] George's *Progress and Poverty* (1879) was a best-selling text on political

80 Paine, *Agrarian Justice*, 477–478.
81 Cabet, *Travels in Icaria*, 31.
82 Thomas, *The Crystal Button*, 246.
83 Mill, *The Principles of Political Economy*, 172.
84 Scheidel, *The Great Leveler*, 359.
85 George, *Progress and Poverty*, 295.

economy, second in sales only to the Bible during the late nineteenth century.[86] In *Progress and Poverty* George claims he has established a connection between increasing poverty and increasing wealth (and increasing wealth inequality). The problem George undertakes to explain, says George Raymond Geiger, is that while the production of wealth had increased, "the distribution of wealth had increased only the disparity between those who had and those who had not."[87]

The association of poverty with progress, George declares, is the "riddle which the Sphinx of Fate put to our civilization."[88] George sought to explain why industrial progress, while raising a few to great wealth, leaves the working poor no better off. Applying both deduction and induction, George affirms, results in the same conclusion, "that the unequal ownership of land necessitates the unequal distribution of wealth."[89] The three factors of production for George are labor, capital, and land. The resulting produce is thus divided among "the laborer, the capitalist, and the land owner."[90] "If, with an increase of production," he says, "the laborer gets no more and the capitalist no more, it is a necessary inference that the land owner reaps the whole gain."[91] As a consequence, any future advances in industrial production, George stresses, will not only fail to benefit the poor but may serve "further to depress their condition."[92]

86 Richard Fisher, "Henry George: Antiprotectionist Giant of American Economics," *Economic Insight.* Federal Reserve Bank of Dallas, vol. 10, no. 2 (2005). <https://web.archive.org/web/20120315013201/http://www.dallasfed.org/research/ei/ei0502.pdf>

87 George Raymond Geiger, *The Philosophy of Henry George* (New York: The Macmillan Company, 1933), 15.

88 George, *Progress and Poverty*, 10.

89 George, *Progress and Poverty*, 329.

90 George, *Progress and Poverty*, 222.

91 George, *Progress and Poverty*, 222.

92 George, *Progress and Poverty*, 328.

Figure 6: "Slums in Bluegate Fields, east London, a notorious breeding-ground for crime and suffering." Paul Gustave Doré 1872

George claims he has linked the "tendency of wages to the starvation point" to the fact that the "land on which and from which all must live is made the exclusive property of some."[93] When land is subject to private ownership, George explains, "The strongest and most cunning easily acquire a superior share ... and in becoming lords of the land they become necessarily lords of their fellow-men."[94] Thus for George, observes Louis

93 George, *Progress and Poverty*, 403.
94 George, *Progress and Poverty*, 350.

Wasserman, private land ownership itself, "originated in force, fraud, and conquest, and it was perpetuated by those who inherited or acquired this private power to exact rent as tribute from others."[95]

George argues that though an equal distribution of land is impossible, "anything short of that would be only a mitigation, not a cure, and a mitigation that would prevent the adoption of a cure."[96] Though George believed the government should own the land as a common resource and lease it to individuals and corporations, his practical solution to the land question was the imposition of a single tax on the unimproved value of land. This solution, he says, will "raise wages, increase the earnings of capital, extirpate pauperism, abolish poverty, ... lessen crime, ... purify government and carry civilization to yet nobler heights.[97]

From the Earth's Center

"We do not regard land as property," explains Mr. Johnson, a character in S. Byron Welcome's *From the Earth's Center* (1895). "Only those things which are produced by the hand of man can rightly be termed property." Land, Mr. Johnson continues, was here "before the advent of man."[98] Thus we assert an equal claim to the land, as we do air, water, light, and heat. It is plain, he says, "that no one can own that which [he] neither made himself nor paid any one else for making."[99] When viewing land as our natural heritage, Mr. Johnson explains, "it is self-evident, that, unless the rental value of land is paid over to the community—as Henry George has advised ... equality of natural rights cannot exist."[100]

Everyone possesses a natural right to use the land on an equal basis, Mr. Johnson tells the visitors, "and if some of us step aside and allow others

95 Louis Wasserman, "The Essential Henry George," in *Critics of Henry George*, ed. Robert V. Andelson (Malden, MA: Blackwell Publishing, 2003), 39.

96 George, *Progress and Poverty*, 327.

97 George, *Progress and Poverty*, 405–406 (italics in original.).

98 Welcome, *From the Earth's Center*, 118.

99 Welcome, *From the Earth's Center*, 118.

100 Welcome, *From the Earth's Center*, 129.

exclusive possession both of their share and our share too, is it not fair that they should pay for the privilege they enjoy?" "Our land-value tax," boasts Mr. Johnson. "is strictly speaking, no tax at all. It is a fee charged the holder of land for the use of which others are willing to pay the same fee."[101] In this way, "competition—a natural law—regulates the whole thing."[102]

Rapara

The island of Rapara is the scene of a settlement of Europeans among the indigenous Polynesian inhabitants in Archibald Forsyth's (1897) novel of the same name. Attractions of the island ("New Zealand, with changes"[103]) include its "climate, rich soil, friendly inhabitants, and unoccupied land."[104] Though several of the organizers of the settlement are introduced at the outset of this largely expository disquisition, the characters are merely placeholders for competing political positions. The bulk of *Rapara* comprises legislative debates and battling newspaper editorials detailing arguments back and forth and the resulting bills proposed and voted on.

Forsyth expresses his concern with economic inequality in the book's dedication to the "hundreds of thousands" who are "starving in the midst of plenty" and calling for the just distribution of the plenty. "Now it is plain to any intelligent person," declares the narrator, "that a large number of people have more wealth than they can use after indulging in every kind of luxury, and that a much larger number of people have insufficient wealth to provide them with the bare necessities of life while others are subjected to semi or actual starvation."[105]

101 Welcome, *From the Earth's Center*, 119.
102 Welcome, *From the Earth's Center*, 75.
103 Lyman Tower Sargent, "Australian Utopian Literature: An Annotated, Chronological Bibliography 1667–1999," *Utopian Studies* 10, no. 2 (1999): 138–173, 146.
104 Forsyth, *Rapara*, 2. In contrast to other utopias like *Freeland*, for example, the "unoccupied" land in Rapara is genuinely unoccupied, even by the island's indigenous Polynesian inhabitants.
105 Forsyth, *Rapara*, 291–292.

Under the "primitive laws and institutions of Rapara,"[106] observes the narrator, land was owned privately. But "the folly and injustice" of granting monopolies in land to a few individuals was recognized.[107] Subsequently the State Council met in 1850 and changed the law so that land is now centrally owned and leased to the citizens. An ordinance of the Land Commission declares: "All land is to be held on perpetual leasehold tenure and subject to rent appraisement every thirty years."[108] These provisions are to serve the interests of "the country and of future generations."[109]

Altneuland: The Old-New-Land

Theodor Herzl's *Altneuland: The Old-New-Land* (1902) sought to revitalize Palestine into a prosperous and politically sound community—a New Society (as noted in Chapter 2). The first people to set out for the Old-New-Land were the poor and working classes, "those who had nothing to lose and everything to gain."[110] The promise of employment and a fresh start in a new land attracted them. But, says David Littwak, one of the nation's leaders, in enticing new settlers:

> We had to think not only of the penniless masses, but of the more well-to-do elements whom we wanted to attract to Palestine. ... I followed in the steps of the Khedive Ismail of Egypt, who had offered a free building site to anyone pledging himself to erect a house. ... I did the same thing, but made the proviso that the land was to revert to the New Society after fifty years (since we had reinstituted the old jubilee year).[111]

106 Forsyth, *Rapara*, 13n1.
107 Forsyth, *Rapara*, 13n1.
108 Forsyth, *Rapara*, 29.
109 Forsyth, *Rapara*, 42.
110 Herzl, *Altneuland*, 137.
111 Herzl, *Altneuland*, 168–169. *Leviticus* 25. For a discussion of the utopian character of the jubilee year see Jonathan Kaplan, "The Levitical Jubilee as a Utopian Legal Institution," *Utopian Studies* 33, no. 3 (2022): 495–513.

As a condition for membership all existing residents must sell their land to the New Society and then lease it back.[112] In this way the increases in land values "accrue not to the individual owner, but to the public."[113]

A Modern Utopia

H. G. Wells's *A Modern Utopia* (1905), says Morton, "describes a mixed economy based largely on the ideas of Hertzka's *Freeland*, an economy in which private enterprise still operates in a framework of the public ownership of land."[114] It is a global utopia that Wegner says represents "a triumph of rational organization and centralized planning."[115] In the spirit of Thomas More, Wells's narrator declares, "we need not argue here to prove that the resources of the world and the energy of mankind, were they organized sanely, are amply sufficient to supply every material need of every living human being."[116] The result of this proposition is a World State that "presents itself as the sole landowner of the earth."[117] In holding its land, explains the narrator, the state "holds all the sources of energy, and either directly or through its tenants, farmers and agents, develops these sources, and renders the energy available for the work of life."[118] But, says the narrator, "in view of the unknown necessities of the future," the leases are limited to fifty years (as in Herzl).[119]

112 Herzl, *Altneuland*, 98.

113 Herzl, *Altneuland*, 98.

114 A. L. Morton, *The English Utopia* (London: Lawrence and Wishart, 1952; Reprint, Berlin: Seven Seas Books, 1968), 243. In *Freeland* Hertzka's narrator explains, "the land—so far as it is used as a means of production and not as sites for dwelling-houses—is absolutely masterless, free as air; it belongs neither to one nor to many: everyone who wishes to cultivate the soil is at liberty to do so where he pleases, and to appropriate his part of the produce." Hertzka, *Freeland,* 93, 257.

115 Wegner, *Imaginary Communities*, 109.

116 Wells, *A Modern Utopia*, 56.

117 Wells, *A Modern Utopia,* 39.

118 Wells, *A Modern Utopia*, 39.

119 Wells, *A Modern Utopia*, 41. See note 110.

Population Control, Eugenics, and Marriage Restrictions

> "The deliberate breeding of a strong, big field-hand stock could be carried out by selecting proper males, and giving them the run of the likeliest females. This in many Border States became a regular policy and fed the slave trade."[120]
>
> —W. E. B. Du Bois, *Black Reconstruction in America* (1935)

Aristotle warned of a connection between population growth and poverty. "If no restriction is imposed on the rate of reproduction," he argued, "poverty is the inevitable result; and poverty produces, in its turn, civic dissention and wrongdoing."[121] English cleric and political economist Thomas Malthus (1766–1834) popularized this theme in the nineteenth century. Malthus argued that the poor are and will remain poor by the interaction of natural laws. Natural cycles or "oscillations," Malthus claimed, increase the number of people "before the means of subsistence are increased."[122] During this phase the price of labor will decrease while the price of food rises. And since the population is bound to grow at a faster pace than the food supply, Malthus argued, the poor will inevitably remain poor.[123] While Malthus claimed that the food supply's check on population growth is "confined chiefly ... to the lowest orders of society,"[124] Bellamy countered that "Malthus and all his followers ... had only to open their eyes to see that wherever the poverty and squalor chiefly abounded ... humankind multiplied like rabbits."[125]

120 Du Bois, *Black Reconstruction in America*, 44.

121 Aristotle, *Politics*, trans. Barker, bk. 2, ch. 6 1265b § 13.

122 Thomas Malthus, *An Essay on the Principle of Population* (Oxford: Oxford University Press, 1993), 19.

123 Malthus, *An Essay on the Principle of Population*, 19.

124 Malthus, *An Essay on the Principle of Population*, 35.

125 Bellamy, *Equality*, 411.

Eugenics

In "Eugenics and Utopia," John Maynard Smith, declares, "There is no field of application of science to human affairs more calculated to arouse our prejudices than eugenics."[126] The aim of negative eugenics (eugenic pruning), says Walter Taylor, is that the "unlovely in human nature will be gradually eliminated."[127] Bellamy's Dr. Leete expresses the goal of positive eugenics as the transmission to posterity of the "attributes that human nature admires"—the "gifts of person, mind, and disposition."[128] Francis Galton (1822–1911) held that the object of eugenics is, "to represent each class or sect by its best specimens"[129] and to cause "the useful classes" to contribute "more than their proportion to the next generation."[130] This may be an affirmative undertaking or a matter of imposing strategies of "benign" neglect on the "less-useful" classes. A number of utopias promote eugenic practices—including Plato's *Republic*, Campanella's *City of the Sun*, Thomas's *The Crystal Button*, Gilman's *Herland*, as well as Huxley's *Brave New World*—but the role of eugenics in these works has little to do with economic equality. The utopias of Fayette Stratton Giles, Edward Bellamy, and H. G. Wells, by contrast, propose eugenic practices as a means of eliminating poverty—primarily by equalizing human capacity.

Social Darwinism

A government eugenics policy affects citizens by restricting their marriage and child-rearing choices. Eugenics garnered popular interest in the nineteenth and early twentieth centuries with the advent of social

126 John Maynard Smith, "Eugenics and Utopia," in *Utopias and Utopian Thought*, ed. Frank E. Manuel (Boston: Houghton Mifflin Company, 1965), 150–168, 150.

127 Taylor, *The Economic Novel in America*, 197.

128 Bellamy, *Looking Backward*, 191.

129 Francis Galton, "Eugenics: Its Definition, Scope, and Aims," *The American Journal of Sociology* 10, no. 1 (July, 1904): 1–25, 2.

130 Galton, "Eugenics: Its Definition, Scope, and Aims," 3.

Darwinism, encouraged by the writings of Herbert Spencer. Richard Hofstadter, in *Social Darwinism in American Thought*, identifies eugenics as the most "enduring fact of social Darwinism."[131] In what Darko Suvin calls Spencer's "liberal triumphalism,"[132] Spencer defines his social philosophy called *dynamics* as a study of "the forces by which society is advanced towards perfection."[133]

Spencer's "survival of the fittest"[134] was a passive-aggressive approach that encouraged nature to take what Spencer saw as its course without human interference, especially interference through governmental action on behalf of the poor. "The poverty of the incapable, the distresses that come upon the imprudent, the starvation of the idle," Spencer argues, "are the decrees of a large, far-seeing benevolence"[135] that demands "discipline which is pitiless in the working out of good."[136] Social Darwinists "justified economic inequality," says economic historian J. Bradford DeLong, "by claiming that inherent racial traits both accounted for their economic success and justified existing economic inequalities."[137] In his 1901 *Anticipations* H. G. Wells argues that as the public has "assimilated and understood" the theory of natural selection, "it has destroyed, quietly but entirely, the belief in human equality."[138]

131 Richard Hofstadter, *Social Darwinism in American Thought*, rev. ed. (Boston: Beacon Press, 1944), 161.

132 Suvin, *Metamorphoses of Science Fiction*, 390.

133 Spencer, *Social Statics*, 447. For Darwin, however, perfection was relative and not absolute. "Natural selection tends only to make each organic being as perfect as, or slightly more perfect than the other inhabitants of the same country with which it comes into competition." Charles Darwin, *The Origin of Species*, sixth London edition (1876), (Los Angeles: Enhanced Media Publishing Co., 2017), 130.

134 "This survival of the fittest, which I have here sought to express in mechanical terms, is that which Mr. Darwin has called 'natural selection, or the preservation of favored races in the struggle for life.'" Herbert Spencer, *The Principles of Biology*, vol. 1 (New York: D. Appleton and Company, 1888), 444–445, §165.

135 Spencer, *Social Statics*, 353–354.

136 Spencer, *Social Statics*, 353.

137 J. Bradford DeLong, *Slouching Towards Utopia* (UK: Basic Books, 2022), 112.

138 H. G. Wells, *Anticipations* (N.p.: n.d. [1901]), 101.

Looking Backward

The economic system of Bellamy's *Looking Backward* (1888) requires a meaningful contribution from each member of the industrial army. Citizens who would take more than they give, acting as a drain on society's resources, must be weeded out. Bellamy's eugenic pruning relies neither on Darwin's natural selection nor Spencer's survival of the fittest. For Bellamy, as Matthew Hartman notes, "the struggle for survival threatens the social stability upon which progress depends."[139] From its inception, therefore, Bellamy's society mitigated this struggle by sequestering the "large residuum too hopelessly perverted, too congenitally deformed, to have the power of leading a good life, however assisted."[140] Toward this population, says Bellamy's spokesperson Dr. Leete, "the new society, strong in the perfect justice of its attitude, proceed[ed] with merciful firmness."[141] The incorrigible criminals and the "morally insane," explains Dr. Leete, were segregated with "a good conscience," not as punishment but to ensure their inability to reproduce.[142] In these ways, Dr. Leete advises, society was able to rid itself of "a load of inherited depravity" within one generation following the peaceful revolution.[143]

Shadows Before or A Century Onward

Following the path of social Darwinism and the teachings of Herbert Spencer, Fayette Stratton Giles, in *Shadows Before or A Century Onward* (1893), explicitly advocates eugenic practices to promote economic

139 Matthew Hartman, "Utopian Evolution: The Sentimental Critique of Social Darwinism in Bellamy and Pierce," *Utopian Studies* 10, no. 1 (1999): 26–41, 31.

140 Bellamy, *Equality*, chap. 37, 363.

141 Bellamy, *Equality*, chap. 37, 363 Bellamy's policy meant that those who from disability or illness were truly unable to work, still received an equal allocation of the nation's prosperity as comrades in Bellamy's "brotherhood of man," not as charity but as a right.

142 Bellamy, *Equality*, chap. 37, 364.

143 Bellamy, *Equality*, chap. 37, 364

equality. "One of the principal causes which led to the unequal distribution of wealth and to class suffering," says Giles's professor character, "was the great mental and physical inequality of individuals."[144] Rather than policies for improving the lot of the poor, Giles focuses on making it more difficult for the poor to propagate by imposing marriage restrictions. "'It has been the aim of the century,' says the professor, 'to improve the conditions and the happiness of all men, and, as far as possible, to remove the causes which created and continued the classes of the miserably poor and diseased, and the disinherited."[145]

Following Herbert Spencer's advice, Giles's social order holds that in the "essentially unfit there is a tendency to extinction through progressive degeneration, unless the unwise philanthropy enable them to persist and perpetuate as parasites."[146] Philanthropy's goal, says Giles's Spencer character, should not be the myopic attempt to minimize the suffering of the poor but to "isolate the essentially and manifestly unfit, and to provide tenderly, but firmly, for their extinction."[147]

The society's "contract marriage system," explains Giles's professor, requires couples to produce certificates of "good mental and physical health," a genealogical record, and proof that they are not "perpetuating a class of criminals."[148] In addition, applicants for marriage must certify sufficient resources to support "a possible third party"—their children.[149] Under this marriage regime, which Giles terms, "conditional monogamic union," the "weak and sickly do not marry" and "leave but few or no progeny."[150]

As a result of these eugenic practices, explains the professor, the population has "eliminated the general, wide, mental, moral, physical, and material differences of other times," and "evolved a higher race type."[151] This "nearer equalization of men," both "mentally and physically," stipulates

144 Giles, *Shadows Before or A Century Onward*, 264.
145 Giles, *Shadows Before or A Century Onward*, 263.
146 Giles, *Shadows Before or A Century Onward*, 230.
147 Giles, *Shadows Before or A Century Onward*, 230.
148 Giles, *Shadows Before or A Century Onward*, 207–208.
149 Giles, *Shadows Before or A Century Onward*, 137, 212.
150 Giles, *Shadows Before or A Century Onward*, 213.
151 Giles, *Shadows Before or A Century Onward*, 265.

the professor, "makes possible a corresponding more equal production and distribution of wealth and a consequent more equal happiness among individuals at large."[152]

A Modern Utopia

In *A Modern Utopia* (1905), Wells's World State's interest in marriage is eugenic. Its concern is for the future of society and thus with the nature of its children. Accordingly, it "intervenes between the sexes only because of the coming generation."[153] The parties contracting for marriage must be "free from specific transmissible taints."[154] They must also be "sufficiently intelligent and energetic to have acquired a minimum education." Finally, "The man at least must be in receipt of a net income above the minimum wage"[155] while "holding a position of solvency and independence in the world."[156] These provisions preclude marriage, and so reproduction, by society's "idiots and madmen, its drunkards and men of vicious mind, its cruel and furtive souls."[157]

Progress depends "essentially on competitive selection,"[158] asserts Wells's narrator; "there must be a competition in life of some sort to determine who are to be pushed to the edge, and who are to prevail and multiply."[159] On the continuum of "the endless variety of men" and "their endless gradation of quality," the narrator continues, "the people of exceptional quality must be ascendant. The better sort of people … must have the fullest … opportunity of parentage."[160] In contrast, those who cannot contribute to

152 Giles, *Shadows Before or A Century Onward*, 215.
153 Wells, *A Modern Utopia*, 78.
154 Wells, *A Modern Utopia*, 77.
155 Wells, *A Modern Utopia*, 77.
156 Wells, *A Modern Utopia*, 74.
157 Wells, *A Modern Utopia*, 56.
158 Wells, *A Modern Utopia*, 73.
159 Wells, *A Modern Utopia*, 56–57.
160 Wells, *A Modern Utopia*, 56. Partington defends Wells's eugenic position against critics he says are biased. "I will discredit those recent critics … who have labeled Wells as a eugenicist and racist, accusing him of desiring to eliminate large sections

society—including minimum wage workers (discussed in Chapter 2)—must be in "the descendant phase, the species must be engaged in eliminating them.... [as] the breed of failures must not increase, lest they suffer and perish, and the race with them."[161]

In the case of illicit children, the narrator advises, the offender is under a debt to the state "that has in the last resort your liberty as a security, and, moreover, if this thing happens a second time, or if it is a disease or imbecility you have multiplied, we will take an absolutely effectual guarantee that neither you nor your partner offend again in this matter."[162] The "absolutely effectual guarantee" is a reference to forced sterilization.[163] In a discussion of Francis Galton's views on eugenics, Wells explains, "It is in the sterilization of failures, and not in the selection of successes for breeding, that the possibility of an improvement for the human stock lies."[164]

Other Brief Statements

Étienne Cabet's *Travels in Icaria* (1847) features a "Commission on Perfectibility"[165] with the authority to prohibit marriages likely to

of the poor and non-white populations of the world in order to improve the standard of life of the white, middle-class elite." Partington, "The Death of the Static," 96. Wells notes that "flaws and gaps in our knowledge" render eugenic regulation "no more than a theory and a dream," as we are "not a bit clear what points to breed for and what points to breed out." Wells, *Mankind in the Making*, 37–38.

161 Wells, *A Modern Utopia*, 56.

162 Wells, *A Modern Utopia*, 74.

163 In the name of "purifying the blood of successive generations," Thomas's *The Crystal Button* proposes "an instantaneous and painless operation," rendering the patient "forever sterile." Thomas, *The Crystal Button*, 71.

164 H. G. Wells, "Discussion," in Francis Galton, "Eugenics: Its Definition, Scope, and Aims," *The American Journal of Sociology* 10, no. 1 (July, 1904): 1–25, 11. Bloomfield observes that Wells was "the first Utopian familiar with Darwin and Galton." Paul Bloomfield, "The Eugenics of the Utopians: The Utopia of the Eugenists," *The Eugenics Review* 40 (21 new series) (April 1948–January 1949): 191–198, 193 (italics in original).

165 Cabet, *Travels in Icaria*, 100.

produce "unhealthy" children.[166] In Icaria, says Eugene in a letter to his brother, "the entire nation think and work continuously for the improvement of the human race." Accordingly, "The republic negotiates with several of the most beautiful foreign nations to obtain a great number of children of both sexes, which it adopts, raises, and marries off to its own children."[167]

One of the four laws contributing to Ionia's balanced prosperity is its Marriage Law. In Alexander Craig's *Ionia* (1898) implementation of this law requires a staff of both sexes to evaluate applicants for marriage licenses—rejecting those who are not "masters of some trade or art" that would permit them to support a family including a "certain minimum of property." Also excluded from Ionian marriages are people with hereditary diseases and "all forms of insanity," as well as "all drunkards" and those with "lax morality."[168]

Eugenics remains controversial in Piercy's *Woman on the Edge of Time* (1976). One faction in Mattapoisett, the "shapers," want to "intervene genetically [and] breed for selected traits." The contrasting side, the "mixers," do not believe people can "know objectively how people should become."[169] Which position would promote their version of economic equality is uncertain as "there's no final authority."[170] "By the novel's end," says Moylan, "the controversy is not resolved, and the utopian project remains open and uncertain on this issue."[171]

166 Cabet, *Travels in Icaria*, 99.
167 Cabet, *Travels in Icaria*, 99.
168 Craig, *Ionia*, 207–208.
169 Piercy, *Woman on the Edge of Time*, 246.
170 Piercy, *Woman on the Edge of Time*, 164.
171 Moylan, *Demand the Impossible*, 134.

Equalizing Opportunity

> "If here and there one of the lowest class by uncommon industry, and pinching his belly, lifts himself above the condition he was brought up in, nobody ought to hinder him."[172]
>
> —Bernard Mandeville, *The Fable of the Bees* (1714)

Edward Bellamy's Dr. Leete asks, "how shall an equal opportunity for the pursuit of happiness be guaranteed to all save by a guarantee of economic equality?"[173] The demand for equalizing opportunity is seen in societies attempting to balance uneven chances (fates) with, for example, equal education, health care, and minimum wage laws. In *Equality* (1931) historian R. H. Tawney affirms, however, that opportunities to "rise" require the "presence of a high degree of practical equality which can diffuse and generalize opportunities."[174] This requirement is more emblematic of affluent than of impoverished classes, however. It is an example of what sociologist Robert Merton called the Matthew Effect.[175] "For whosoever hath, to him shall be given, and he shall have more abundance,"[176] tainting the spirit of equalizing opportunity.

Opportunities are valuable occasions for achieving our goals and improving our life chances as they hold the seeds of future choices and distant possibilities. The fork in the road an opportunity poses is a time-constrained choice leading possibly to regret or remorse. Psychologist Albert Bandura observes that "forsaken opportunities figure more prominently in people's regrets than do the regrets of action."[177] People's regrets,

172 Mandeville, *The Fable of the Bees*, vol. 1, 193.

173 Bellamy, *Equality*, 17.

174 Tawney, *Equality*, 106.

175 Merton coined the term *Matthew Effect* to denote the accumulation of advantages and in particular the tendency of scientists who were already famous to become more famous. Robert K. Merton, *On Social Structure and Science* (Chicago: The University of Chicago Press, 1996), 160.

176 Bible KJV Matt.13:12.

177 Albert Bandura, *Self-Efficacy: The Exercise of Control* (New York: W. H. Freeman, 1997), 71.

says Bandura, "commonly center on educational opportunities forsaken, valued careers not pursued, interpersonal relationships not cultivated, risks not taken, and failures to exercise a stronger hand in shaping one's life course."[178]

The meaning of *equalizing opportunity* is a contentious matter and one that its advocates fail to analyze critically. Confusion (or obfuscation) regarding the meaning of equal opportunity explains why people can agree on the putative moral importance of equal opportunity yet hold ideologically contrary positions on what this entails. Michael Young, a sociologist, refers to equal opportunity as an "unpleasant term" of obscure origins.[179] "What is the purpose of abolishing inequalities in nurture," he asks, "except to reveal and make more pronounced the inescapable inequalities of Nature?"[180] But philosopher Charles Frankel declares that the notion of equality of opportunity "plays so central a role in the pantheon of contemporary social ideals that it clearly merits philosophical examination."[181] In spite of this lack of clarity and conceptual agreement, Christopher Hayes asserts, "it is inevitable that the education system will be asked to do the heavy lifting."[182]

In a discussion of equality that Amartya Sen calls a "meticulous and helpful exploration,"[183] political scientist Douglas Rae observes that the "ideological power of equal opportunity ... lies very largely ... in the wish and hope that the children of yesterday's losers may become tomorrow's winners."[184] Rae distinguishes three forms of equal opportunity.[185] In the first, chance determines which person attains a desired goal. When two people have an equal opportunity to win the lottery, he says, each person

178 Bandura, *Self-Efficacy*, 71.

179 Young, *The Rise of the Meritocracy*, 11n1.

180 Young, *The Rise of the Meritocracy*, 105.

181 Charles Frankel, "Equality of Opportunity," in *Against Equality: Readings on Economic and Social Policy*, ed. William Letwin (London: The Macmillan Press, 1983), 167–188, 169.

182 Hayes, *Twilight of the Elites*, 48.

183 Sen, *Inequality Reexamined*, 23.

184 Douglas Rae, *Equalities* (Cambridge, MA: Harvard University Press, 1981), 66–67.

185 Rae, *Equalities*, 65.

has a ticket.[186] According to his second form, two people have equal opportunities, "if each has the same instruments for attaining the opportunity.[187] This second "means regarding" sense is exemplified in situations where competing individuals are provided equal tools, equal training, and identical rules to follow—in order to demonstrate "unequal speed, agility, punching power, wit, cunning, muscle"—revealing thereby unequal talents "resulting in *un*equal prospects of success."[188] Aristotle illustrated this sense when he observed that if a number of flute-players are "equal in their art, there is no reason why those of them who are better born should have better flutes given to them."[189] The significance of these equal means, Rae stipulates, "is *not equal prospects of success, but legitimately unequal prospects of success.*"[190] Political economist Vilfredo Pareto (1845–1923)—whom Rae says was a "supreme proponent of means-regarding equal opportunity"—holds that this second form of equal opportunity benefits society because it tends to promote people of ability from the "lower strata" and demote incapable people from the "higher."[191] According to Pareto, in assessing the equality of opportunity, "It is not only the accumulation of inferior elements in a [higher] social stratum that is harmful to society, but also the accumulation in the lower strata of superior elements that are prevented from rising."[192]

Rae's first sense provides equal access to the ends, the second provides equal access to the means necessary to pursue the ends and is the focus of the utopians discussed here. In his third sense of equal opportunity, equal access to the ends comes through what Rae calls "compensatory inequality." Examples include affirmative action schemes and golf "handicaps" where players with unequal skills are assigned "handicaps" (subtractions from their actual score) to equalize their chances of "winning." Kurt Vonnegut Jr. satirized compensatory inequality in "Harrison Bergeron" (1961), where

186 Rae, *Equalities*, 66.
187 Rae, *Equalities*, 66.
188 Rae, *Equalities*, 66 (italics in original).
189 Aristotle, *Politics*, trans. Jowett, bk. 3, chap. 12, § 1282b.
190 Rae, *Equalities*, 66 (italics in original).
191 Rae, *Equalities*, 67.
192 Pareto, *Manual of Political Economy*, 196.

"the year was 2081, and everybody was finally equal."[193] Anyone excelling in appearance, intelligence, or strength, for example, is assigned an artificial handicapping device to neutralize their natural advantage.

In the context of economic inequality questions of equal opportunity affect the rich and poor in different ways—to the detriment of the poor. For someone attempting to escape from poverty, for example, says Frankel, "successful performance is urgently needed and false steps are costly."[194] Psychologists Mullainathan and Shafir report that being poor reduces a person's cognitive capacity.[195] The poor, they submit, "have lower *effective* capacity than those who are well off … not because they are less capable, but rather because part of their mind is captured by scarcity,"[196] and scarcity "encourages behaviors that make us shortsighted.[197] In this they echo Godin (1817–1888), a French social reformer, who advised that "foresight itself is, to the poor, but a new consciousness of their unfortunate condition."[198] In *A Connecticut Yankee in King Arthur's Court* (1889), Mark Twain describes a character whose mind was so disordered by her financial troubles "that when she was overborne with hunger all acts, criminal or other, swam meaningless through her brain and she knew nothing rightly, except that she was *so* hungry!"[199] These factors complicate immensely efforts to equalize opportunities. They also bolster Frankel's claim that "we cannot have real equality of opportunity unless we successfully modify those aspects of the individual's situation which prevent him from performing up to the level of his natural abilities."[200]

193 Kurt Vonnegut, Jr, "Harrison Bergeron," in *Welcome to the Monkey House* (New York: Dial Press, 1968), 7.
194 Frankel, "Equality of Opportunity," 185.
195 Mullainathan and Shafir, *Scarcity*, 13.
196 Mullainathan and Shafir, *Scarcity*, 60 (italics in original).
197 Mullainathan and Shafir, *Scarcity*, 120.
198 Godin, *Social Solutions*, 233.
199 Mark Twain, *A Connecticut Yankee in King Arthur's Court* (New York: Bantam Books, 1981), 218 (italics in original).
200 Frankel, "Equality of Opportunity," 183.

Altneuland: The Old-New-Land

Students in Theodor Herzl's *Altneuland: The Old-New-Land* (1902) come from all kinds of homes, explains a health official, yet "we do not permit distinctions of any kind in our schools, either in clothing or in anything else."[201] The only differences we recognize, says the official, "are those created by the pupils themselves through effort or natural talent."[202] "Conditions are alike for all as in a race or prize competition," the same official continues. "All must be equal at the beginning, but not at the end."[203] It is unethical, therefore, to single out children according to their parents' wealth or social rank.[204] For this reason all educational institutions are free from the elementary school to the university. In these ways, "each generation is given a new start."[205]

Though David Littwak, the eventual president of the "New Society," affirms that "women have equal rights with the men,"[206] he overlooks the fact that boys receive a different form of educational opportunity from girls. While we learn little about the girls' education, we know schools specifically exclude girls from an annual three-month educational trip around the world which these schools afford only to the "best pupils"—specifically, boys.[207] "Girls don't go on such tours ... the place of a growing girl is beside her mother."[208]

A Modern Utopia

Equalizing opportunity in *A Modern Utopia* (1905) encompasses preparation for fruitful participation in the labor force—"everyone will have had

201 Herzl, *Altneuland*: *The Old-New-Land*, 211.
202 Herzl, *Altneuland*: *The Old-New-Land*, 211.
203 Herzl, *Altneuland*: *The Old-New-Land*, 211.
204 Herzl, *Altneuland*: *The Old-New-Land*, 212.
205 Herzl, *Altneuland*: *The Old-New-Land*, 211.
206 Herzl, *Altneuland*: *The Old-New-Land*, 60.
207 Herzl, *Altneuland*: *The Old-New-Land*, 182.
208 Herzl, *Altneuland*: *The Old-New-Land*, 182.

an education," says Wells's narrator, "and a certain minimum of nutrition and training."[209] The World State encourages education and research with "great systems of laboratories ... at which research [is] conducted under the most favourable conditions."[210] Its "world-wide House of Saloman," Wells's "Utopian self" explains, employs "over a million men" engaged in discovery and invention.[211] Wells's scientists include women, since, he stipulates, the pronoun "'He' indeed is to be read as 'He and She.'"[212]

Technological Advancement and Unequal Opportunity

Walter Scheidel expresses concern that as our scientific and technological knowledge advances, economic inequality will accelerate and equality of opportunity will decline. Recent advances in gene editing, he notes, "have made it possible to delete and insert specific pieces of DNA both in Petri dishes and in living organisms with unprecedented ease."[213] The acceptance of these procedures, says Scheidel, will lead to unequal outcomes "by handing an advantage to those able to afford private treatment."[214] In the long run, he speculates, the creation of "designer babies" for the rich may curtail economic mobility, resulting ultimately in a "bifurcation into two different species," the "genetic elite,"—perhaps like the "Vril-ya" of Bulwer-Lytton's *The Coming Race* (1871)[215] or the 1 percent in Doctorow's

209 Wells, *A Modern* Utopia, 61.
210 Wells, *A Modern* Utopia, 107.
211 Wells, *A Modern* Utopia, 107.
212 Wells, *A Modern* Utopia, 75.
213 Scheidel, *The Great Leveler*, 431.
214 Scheidel, *The Great Leveler*, 431.
215 In Bulwer-Lytton's *The Coming Race* (1871) a subterranean people (the "Vril-ya") are similar to humans but larger and more beautiful, with unlimited powers derived from a force called "vril." The posthuman coming race is "destined to return to the upper world, and supplant all the inferior races now existing therein." Bulwer-Lytton, *The Coming Race*, 27–28, 32, 54.

2019 "The Masque of the Red Death"[216] (discussed in Chapter 7)—and the rest of humanity.

Equalizing the Physical Environment for Health and Beauty

> "Due regard for the health of the inhabitants not only means that their place of abode should be in a healthy locality and should have a healthy exposure: it also means that they should have the use of good water."[217]
>
> —Aristotle (384–322 BCE), *Politics*

Environmental justice, declares one of its advocacy groups, "seeks to challenge the abuse of power which results in poor people having to suffer the effects of environmental damage caused by the greed of others."[218] Economic inequality means the poor commonly live in compromised physical surroundings termed *sacrifice zones*—the stench of chemical plants, landfills, and slaughter houses; the smoke from refineries and the soot from coal-powered electric plants—in close proximity to factories, airports, and railroads.[219] Psychologists studying the effects of noise pollution on cognitive performance tested sixth grade students in a school building adjacent to a railroad yard. Tests showed that students on the

216 Cory Doctorow, "The Masque of the Red Death," in *Radicalized* (New York: Tom Doherty Associates, 2019), 251.

217 Aristotle, *Politics*, trans. Barker, 7:11, 1330b.

218 David A. McDonald, "Environmental Racism and Neoliberal Disorder in South Africa," in *The Quest for Environmental Justice: Human Rights and the Politics of Pollution*, ed. Robert D. Bullard (San Francisco: Sierra Club Books, 2005), 255–278, 259. Citing "Environmental Justice Networking Forum," *Environmental Justice Newsletter* (Autumn 1997): 1.

219 A sacrifice zone is a geographic area impaired by environmental damage. These zones most commonly exist in or around low-income and minority communities. The label, says Lerner, is "an Orwellian term coined by government officials." Steve Lerner, *Sacrifice Zones: The Front Lines of Toxic Chemical Exposure in the United States* (Cambridge, MA: The MIT Press, 2010), 2.

noisy side of the building—sidetracked by rumbling trains—were a "full year behind their counterparts on the quieter side."[220]

Whether viewed as causes or outcomes of economic inequality, our own age recognizes that poverty frequently accompanies contaminated water, air that is fouled or toxic, and land poisoned by leaking underground storage tanks. The World Health Organization estimates that one-fifth of the world's population live in areas where fresh water is scarce.[221]

Utopians have proposed various measures to rectify these environmental inequities. Plato's *Laws* for an ideal state call for a person "convicted of poisoning waters" to pay a fine and "undertake the purification of the contaminated spring or reservoir."[222] Robert Burton's utopia in *The Anatomy of Melancholy* (1621) promises "conduits of sweet and good water, aptly disposed in each town."[223] Mary Griffith's Philadelphia of 2135, in *Three Hundred Years Hence* (1836), features a "fine stream of water" running through pipes under the center of the pavement, "bursting up every twenty feet in little jets, cooling the air, and contributing to health and cleanliness."[224] Robert Owen (1771–1858) expressed concern for the health of the citizens in his ideal society with his stipulation that in each township structure "there will be four massive Towers, each 240 feet in height ... designed to carry off the smoke and effluvia of the fires below, used for heating the buildings, cooking, &c."[225] When William Guest awakes to his new surroundings in Morris's *News from Nowhere* (1890), he remarks on changes in the physical environment. The "soap-works with their smoke-vomiting chimneys were gone; the engineer's works gone; the lead-works

220 Mullainathan and Shafir, *Scarcity*, 42.

221 Abhijit V. Banerjee and Esther Duflo, *Poor Economics: A Radical Rethinking of the Way to Fight Global Poverty* (New York: PublicAffairs, Hachette Book Group, 2011), 105–106. Citing World Health Organization, Water Scarcity Fact File, 2009, available at <http://www.who.int/features/factfiles/water/en/>.

222 Plato, *Laws*, trans. Taylor, bk. 8, 845d-e.

223 Burton, *The Anatomy of Melancholy*, 99.

224 Griffith, *Three Hundred Years Hence*, 41.

225 Owen, *A Development of the Principles and Plans on Which to Establish Self-Supporting Home Colonies*, 39 (capitalization in original).

gone; and no sound of riveting and hammering came down the west wind from Thorneycroft's."[226]

Quiet and Clean and Green

Dr. Nelli, in Cosomo Noto's *The Ideal City* (1903), sounded the alarm when he proclaimed: "If the resisting power of the cells of the human body is so tremendous, what might we all not be if we could live in an uncontaminated environment, according to the laws of health!"[227] Noto's ideal society in New Orleans features physicians directing government policies aiming to prevent disease and improve the health of all citizens. In Noto's utopia, explains Louis Kern, the "management of the physical environment ... lay largely in control of hygienic conditions. The environment has first to be purified and its action on the individual organism will produce perfection."[228]

Noto's policies call for maintaining streets that are "first, clean; second, noiseless."[229] As both the physicians and landscape artists had requested, "in every street were planted trees"[230] and reservoirs installed to supply "a powerful stream of water" that periodically washed the streets and cleansed the air. In this way, says the doctor, the city "is kept as clean as possible and no dust circulates through the air."[231] During the previous era, Dr. Nelli explains to his friend Will, the noise of the city "was one of the frequent causes of the widespread disease," especially diseases of the nervous system. In the new era, wide-ranging health measures bring quiet; manufacturing, for example, was relocated beyond the city limits eliminating the din of machinery.[232]

226 Morris, *News from Nowhere*, 48.
227 Noto, *The Ideal City*, 63.
228 Kern, "Evangelical Environmentalism and the New Commonwealth," 50.
229 Noto, *The Ideal City*, 161–162.
230 Noto, *The Ideal City*, 165.
231 Noto, *The Ideal City*, 161–162.
232 Noto, *The Ideal City*, 179–180.

"The percentage of green space in people's living environment," reports a 2006 study, "has a positive association with the perceived general health of residents."[233] For the poor in cities like New York, however, prospects for accessing parks and tree-lined boulevards are limited.[234] The city of Red Cross, in Frank Rosewater's egalitarian society of Temploria (*The Making of a Millennium*, 1908), features a "series of parks—long parallel streaks of brilliant foliage, extending for miles across the entire length of the city." In addition, notes the narrator, "Glistening fountains and thousands of lesser sprays moistened the surrounding verdure and cooled the atmosphere, while scores of fantastic pavilions afforded rest and comfort for the weary."[235]

Aesthetic Considerations

While Noto had treated equalizing the physical environment for health concerns, other utopians, specifically William Morris—a painter, designer, and social reformer—stressed our constructed environment's aesthetic qualities. Morris, says Gib Prettyman, "is horrified by the effect of mass culture on aesthetic sensibilities and on expressions of uniqueness."[236] One of the first sights Morris's narrator in *News from Nowhere* (1890) awakes to in the transformed England of the twenty-second century is a new bridge on the Thames in place of the one he recalled. "I had perhaps dreamed of such a bridge," marvels William Guest, "but never seen such an one out of an illuminated manuscript. ... It was of stone arches, splendidly solid, and as graceful as they were strong."[237] People are

233 Jolanda Maas, Robert A. Verheij and others, "Green Space, Urbanity, and Health: How Strong is the Relation?," *Journal of Epidemiology and Community Health* 60, no. 7 (July): 587–592, 591.

234 In New York, under the urban planning of Robert Moses, this unequal distribution of parks was by design. See Robert A. Caro, *The Power Broker: Robert Moses and the Fall of New York*.

235 Rosewater, *The Making of a Millennium*, 45–47.

236 Gib Prettyman, "Gilded Age Utopias of Incorporation," *Utopian Studies* 12, no. 1 (2001): 9–40, 35.

237 Morris, *News from Nowhere*, 48.

now "surrounded by beautiful things of their own fashioning," explains Morris's character old Hammond.[238] What used to be called art and segregated from daily life, adds Hammond, "has become a necessary part of the labour of every man who produces."[239]

In *A Modern Utopia* (1905) Wells's narrator declares, "There is nothing in machinery, there is nothing in embankments and railways and iron bridges and engineering devises to oblige them to be ugly. ... Things made by mankind under modern conditions are ugly, primarily because our social organization is ugly."[240] Accordingly Wells segregates residential from industrial land. There will be "wide stretches of cheerless or unhealthy or toilsome or dangerous land with never a household," says Wells's narrator. "[T]here will be regions of mining and smelting, black, with the smoke of furnaces and gashed and desolated by mines." Men, he says, "will come thither and work for a spell and return to civilization again, washing and changing their attire in the swift gliding train."[241]

Eliminating Unemployment

> "An army of unemployed led by millionaires quoting the Sermon on the Mount—that is our danger."[242]
>
> —George Orwell, "The Lion and the Unicorn" (1941)

238 Morris, *News from Nowhere*, 159.

239 Morris, *News from Nowhere*, 159–160. "Like Dewey," Freeman-Mohr observes, "Morris, too, was just as scathing of art treated as the instrument of showiness of class power." John Freeman-Moir, "Crafting Experience: William Morris, John Dewey, and Utopia," *Utopian Studies* 22, no. 2 (2011), 213. "The growth of capitalism," Dewey writes, "has been a powerful influence in the development of the museum as the proper home for works of art, and in the promotion of the idea that they are apart from the common life." John Dewey, *Art as Experience* (New York: Minton, Balch and Company, 1934), 8.

240 Wells, *A Modern Utopia*, 47.

241 Wells, *A Modern Utopia*, 24.

242 Orwell, "The Lion and the Unicorn," 327.

Unemployment, says Piketty, is a "fundamental feature of contemporary inequality."[243] As Frederic Jameson observes, "Few Utopian fantasies are quite so practical and potentially revolutionary in their effects as the demand for full employment."[244] Unemployment is detrimental to social cohesion and harmful to individuals. People who are out of work, reports Applebaum, "suffer a decline in health and life expectancy." Unemployment, he submits, "is not just a lack money; it is also a lack of purpose and opportunity."[245]

Figure 7: "An unemployed man comes home, Britain. His wife, breastfeeding the baby, and his many children look towards him in concern." c.1905

The World a Department Store

Bradford Peck's *The World a Department Store* (1900) defeats unemployment by eliminating competition. Since the Cooperative Association

243 Piketty, *The Economics of Inequality*, 25.
244 Frederic Jameson, *Archaeologies of the Future: The Desire Called Utopia and Other Science Fictions* (London: VERSO, 2005), 147.
245 Applebaum, *The Economist's Hour*, 319, 329.

functions as a department store (see the discussion of universal basic income in Chapter 3), the workers are cross-trained in the work of more than one department, permitting the Association to "transfer laborers when necessary, from one department to another,"[246] thus providing "constant labor."[247] "Our children," one of the residents explains to the visitor Mr. Brantford, "have been taught the necessity of knowing how to perform more than one kind of labor."[248]

A Modern Utopia

A Modern Utopia (1905) tackles unemployment through exploiting its "delocalized" and "fluid" workforce. Wells's World State engages worldwide labor exchanges that report the "fluctuating pressure of economic demand."[249] The presumption, says Wells's narrator, is that a population "largely migratory and emancipated from locality"[250] will relocate once or twice a year, whether locally or globally as the labor exchanges direct.[251] "The State," affirms Wells's narrator, "will stand at the back of the economic struggle as the reserve employer of labor."[252] Wells addresses "the endless variety of men [and] their endless gradation of quality,"[253] consigning unskilled or displaced workers, or those who are "indecently dressed, or ragged and dirty, or publicly unhealthy"[254] to the state's care and control. Of these, the state,

246 Peck, *The World a Department Store*, 242. Similarly, Hertzka'a *Freeland* minimizes unemployment by the "regular and automatic migration of labour from one industry to another." Hertzka, *Freeland*, 267.
247 Peck, *The World a Department Store*, 310.
248 Peck, *The World a Department Store*, 296.
249 Wells, *A Modern Utopia*, 62.
250 Wells, *A Modern Utopia*, 35.
251 Wells, *A Modern Utopia*, 61.
252 Wells, *A Modern Utopia*, 57–58.
253 Wells, *A Modern Utopia*, 56.
254 Wells, *A Modern Utopia*, 57.

> will find him work if he can and will work, it will take him to it, it will register him and lend him the money wherewith to lead a comely life until work can be found or made for him, and it will give him credit and shelter him and strengthen him if he is ill. In default of private enterprises it will provide inns for him and food.[255]

The public works projects, the narrator states, "would have to be toilsome, but not cruel or incapacitating."[256]

The Making of a Millennium

The cure for unemployment in Temploria, in Frank Rosewater's 1908 *The Making of a Millennium*, was the introduction of a new currency, the centry. Their economic system, Centrism, "keeps the doors of employment always open and one's purse always filled."[257] A centret, explains the host to the travelers, is "an order on jobs" just as a dollar is "an order on commodities or services." This currency "is given to the buyer—one centret for every dollar he parts with,"[258] guaranteeing its owner a job. "When jobs are given exclusively to consumers, the jobs never run short—the consumer always creating a labor demand proportional to that he supplies with his labor."[259]

Moving the Mountain

The "socialized industries" of Charlotte Perkins Gilman's *Moving the Mountain* (1911)—emphasizing education, efficiency, and eugenics—"ensured employment to every citizen, and provided all the necessaries of life."[260] To better match people with the work they desired, "Bureaus of Employment were formed all over the country." This resulted in public

255 Wells, *A Modern Utopia*, 57.
256 Wells, *A Modern Utopia*, 57.
257 Rosewater, *The Making of a Millennium*, 52.
258 Rosewater, *The Making of a Millennium*, 10.
259 Rosewater, *The Making of a Millennium*, 12.
260 Charlotte Perkins Gilman, *Moving the Mountain* (N.p.: n.d. [1911]), chap. 12, 88.

works employment for "hitherto neglected labor" and meant "harbors were cleared, canals dug, cities rebuilt, bare hills reforested. ... And where there is work for everyone, at good wages, there is no poverty."[261]

Woman on the Edge of Time

Work in Mattapoisett's "non-growth," "steady-state"[262] economy in Piercy's *Woman on the Edge of Time* (1976) is open ended; everyone shares in it including children and the elderly.[263] Slackers are asked to leave the community, abolishing unemployment.[264]

Technological Unemployment

In *Raising the Floor* (2016) Andy Stern describes how, in our own time, we are losing increasing numbers of middle-class jobs to systems computers operate, disaggregating work into component tasks and assigning these tasks in the most efficient manner. He cites a 2013 Oxford University study concluding that "47 percent of jobs in the US are at risk of being eliminated due to software, robotics, and machines engaging artificial intelligence"[265]—technological unemployment. As one Doctorow character observes, "They knew that the world was heading to a state when the number of betas and gammas the alphas needed to keep the systems running would far exceed the demand."[266]

From our earliest recorded history, affirms Keynes, down to the beginning of the eighteenth century, "there was no very great change in the standard of life of the average man living in the civilised centers of the earth." This slow rate of development, Keynes reports, resulted from two

261 Gilman, *Moving the Mountain*, chap. 6, 45–46.
262 Moylan, *Demand the Impossible*, 122–123.
263 Piercy, *Woman on the Edge of Time*, 123, 127.
264 Piercy, *Woman on the Edge of Time*, 106.
265 Stern, *Raising the Floor*, 161.
266 Doctorow, "The Masque of the Red Death," 250.

reasons—"the remarkable absence of important technical improvements" and "the failure of capital to accumulate."[267] Some utopians express concern that technological progress will result in increasing numbers of unemployed and worsening economic inequality.

Robert Owen (1771–1858) argued that the steam engine and spinning machines have "inflicted evils on society, which now greatly overbalance the benefits which are derived from them."[268] "The key issue for Owen," says Claeys, "was ... the provision of employment for those whose labour was being displaced by machinery."[269] "Mechanism," Owen proclaimed, "which may be made the greatest of blessings to humanity, is under the existing arrangements, its greatest curse."[270] At one time Owen saw a potential solution in the return to more rudimentary farming techniques such as spade husbandry.[271] Owen's plan, advises Cole, was "a way of providing work for the unemployed, and at the same time laying the foundations of a better social order."[272] "Owen's vision of fundamental social transformation," Claeys advises, "rested upon the premise that society was being destroyed by, but could ultimately be enormously benefited by, the large-scale displacement of manual labour by machinery."[273] Ultimately, Owen proclaimed, "Machinery should be applied, to the utmost extent of its known powers, to supersede manual labor in every department, including the domestic."[274]

267 John Maynard Keynes, *Essays in Persuasion* (N.p.: Classic House Books, 2009), 194.

268 Owen, *A New View of Society and Other Writings*, 264.

269 Gregory Claeys, *Machinery, Money and the Millennium: From Moral Economy to Socialism, 1815–1860* (Princeton, NJ: Princeton University Press, 1987), 39–40.

270 Owen, *A New View of Society and Other Writings*, 194.

271 Claeys, *Machinery, Money and the Millennium*, 45–46. Owen, *A New View of Society and Other Writings*, 261.

272 Cole, *Robert Owen*, 137.

273 Claeys, *Machinery, Money and the Millennium*, 35.

274 Owen, *The Revolution in the Mind*, 45. The last century, says Owen, has given "the greatest increase ... to the power of production per individual, that has occurred in the human race: a revolution ... which places at our disposal the means of changing for the better the condition of mankind." Owen, *Lectures on an Entire New State of Society*, 156.

The dangers machines pose to society was satirized in Samuel Butler's *Erewhon* (1872) where a professor's "extraordinary book" argued that machines were "ultimately destined to supplant the race of man."[275] For this reason, inquires the professor, "Is it not safer to nip the mischief in the bud and to forbid them further progress?"[276] Interestingly, as Anna Vaninskaya observes, "distrust of the machine" is "politically neutral," embracing values common to some on the left as well as the right.[277]

More recent utopians, such as Mosley (2016), see the negative effects of technological unemployment as a reason for taxing the machines (robots). Since a cardboard folding machine, for example—that eliminated eighteen jobs—produces a greater profit for the company, that profit, says Mosley, should be taxed "to fund the other needs" of the unemployed, such as education or retraining.[278]

Reimagining Marriage and Divorce

> "Isn't it clear to you that the first requirement for the ideal state is the loosing of all the bonds that constrict man, the bonds of matrimony, religion, family, tradition, 'morality' so-called, patriotism, and class distinction?"[279]
>
> —Claire Myers Spotswood, *The Unpredictable Adventure: A Comedy of Woman's Independence* (1935)

275 Samuel Butler, *Erewhon* (Mineola, NY: Dover Publications, 2002), 44.

276 Butler, *Erewhon*, 119.

277 Anna Vaninskaya, "Janus-Faced Fictions: Socialism as Utopia and Dystopia in William Morris and George Orwell," *Utopian Studies*, 14, no. 2 (2003): 83–98, 94.

278 Mosley, *Folding the Red into the Black*, 91–93. A study by MIT economists supports a modest tax on robots as a means of reducing economic inequality. Peter Dizikes, *MIT News*, December 21, 2022. <https://news.mit.edu/2022/robot-tax-income-inequality-1221>

279 Claire Myers Spotswood, *The Unpredictable Adventure: A Comedy of Woman's Independence* (Garden City, NY: Doubleday, Doran and Company, 1935), 86.

When marriage is an impediment to economic equality, reimagining marriage (and divorce) is a utopian imperative. This reimagining results in questions of marriage's economic or practical necessity, its regulation by the state, and its bearing on the division of labor. As an observer of marriage in the early nineteenth-century, Robert Owen lamented that "under existing arrangements" the "pernicious effects" of marriage have "taken deep root in our oldest established habits, customs, and relations, and it has spread its baneful influence through all the ramifications of society."[280] Dr. Forest ("Papa") in Marie Howland's (1874) *Papa's Own Girl*, proclaims, "nothing cramps the growth of all that is best in manhood and womanhood like the forced intimacy of the marriage tie, when no deep sympathy or mutual trust exists."[281] In his 1830 "Lecture on Marriage" Owen's solution for both marriage and divorce—during "the intermediate stage of society"—was a simple public declaration of intent followed by a waiting period and a second public affirmation.[282]

Regarding the practice of marriage in utopia, says Goodwin, "even today we still display the same conservative reluctance as most earlier utopians to abandon the institution despite increasingly conclusive evidence (*vide* the divorce rate) that lifelong monogamy is an unattainable ideal, and maybe no ideal at all."[283] This conservative reluctance appears in women's utopias of the late nineteenth and early twentieth century, as Nan Bowman Albinski observes, since their attitude toward marriage is "one of reform, rather than dissolution."[284] They mention marriage, says Ablinski, "only in the context of a near-unanimous interest in easier divorce."[285] Clare's divorce from her husband Albert in *Papa's Own Girl*, for example, left her feeling "the victim of a hideous farce" as she was legally precluded from remarrying until after Albert's "actual" death.[286] Male utopians, by contrast,

280 Owen, *A New View of Society*, 323.

281 Howland, *Papa's Own Girl*, 285.

282 Owen, *A New View of Society*, 331–332. For marriage the waiting period was three months; for uncontested divorce, six months; for contested divorce an additional six months.

283 Goodwin, "Economic and Social Innovation in Utopia," 80.

284 Nan Bowman Albinski, *Women's Utopias in British and American Fiction* (London: Routledge Taylor and Francis Group, 1988), 64.

285 Albinski, *Women's Utopias in British and American Fiction*, 17 (italics in original).

286 Howland, *Papa's Own Girl*, 457.

Ablinski advises, "describe future worlds in which all social institutions *but* marriage have been radically changed."[287] William Morris is an exception. In *News from Nowhere* (1890) marriage is a personal commitment with no state involvement because there is no state. Morris's spokesperson old Hammond explains that while marriages are sometimes dissolved by either party, divorce is no longer necessary as the enforcement of property rights has since been abolished.[288]

In Florence Caroline Dixie's *Gloriana; Or The Revolution of 1900* (1890), the protagonist Gloria De Lara (disguised as Hector L'Estrange and described below in the section on universal suffrage) proclaims: "Thousands of miserable unions are yearly effected in consequence of woman's unnatural and one-sided position in Society." These marriages, she continues, are "for money, or for position, or to escape the restraints of home, or because she has no chance of making her way in the world."[289] In this Dixie concurred with Bellamy who saw marriage, says Tilman, as "an institution deformed by late-nineteenth-century capitalistic culture, in which women were little more than slaves."[290] Concerning marriage in the year 2000, however, Bellamy's Dr. Leete affirms, "The necessities of poverty, the need of having a home no longer tempt women to accept as the fathers of their children men whom they neither can love nor respect."[291] Accordingly the doctor declares, "the establishment of economic equality did in fact mean incomparably more for women than for men."[292] Similarly in the Martian country of Thursia, in Jones and Merchant's *Unveiling a Parallel* (1893), marriage, explains the Earthman traveler, "not being an economic necessity" releases women from "certain sordid motives which often actuate women in our world in their frantic efforts to avert the appalling catastrophe of missing

287 Albinski, *Women's Utopias in British and American Fiction*, 17 (italics in original).

288 Morris, *News from Nowhere*, 90–93.

289 Florence Caroline Dixie, *Gloriana; or, the Revolution of 1900* (N.p.: Mint Editions, [1890] 2021), 94.

290 Tilman, "The Utopian Vision of Edward Bellamy and Thorstein Veblen," 891.

291 Bellamy, *Looking Backward*, 191. Similarly, women in Edward House's *Philip Dru Administrator* (1912) no longer face compulsion to marry or be "a charge upon unwilling relatives or, as in desperation they sometimes did, lead abandoned lives." House, *Philip Dru: Administrator*, 219–220.

292 Bellamy, *Equality*, 132.

a husband."[293] Both Jones and Merchant and Bellamy's utopias stress women's economic independence[294] which renders divorce a mere "detail."[295] By contrast, in Giles's *Shadows Before or A Century Onward* (1893), while marriage may be contracted for any length of time longer than one year, or "for life, at the option of the contracting parties,"[296] the marriage contract must specify the responsibility of parties for "ample provision for the welfare of progeny,"[297] should the parents divorce.

Marriage is reimagined out of existence in Mattapoisett, in Piercy's *Woman on the Edge of Time* (1976). While there is no equivalent of marriage there is gender-indifferent coupling "for love, for pleasure, for relief, out of habit, out of curiosity and lust."[298] "Coupling" is unrelated to human reproduction which, as described in Chapter 5, has been transferred to "brooders."[299]

Patents as Monopolies

> "The very first official thing I did, in my administration ... was to start a patent office: for I knew that a country without a patent office and good patent laws was just a crab, and couldn't travel any way but sideways or backwards."[300]
>
> —Mark Twain, A Connecticut Yankee in King Arthur's Court (1889)

293 Jones and Merchant, *Unveiling a Parallel*, 92–93. Kolmerten calls *Unveiling a Parallel*, "one of the most clever utopian novels criticizing male ideas." Carol A. Kolmertan, "Texts and Contexts: American Women Envision Utopia, 1890–1920," in *Utopian and Science Fiction by Women*, ed. Jane L. Donawerth and Carol A. Kolmerten (New York: Syracuse University Press, 1994), 107–125, 111.

294 Gilman says, "As long as what I get is obtained by what I give, I am economically independent." Charlotte Perkins Gilman, *Women and Economics* (Mineola, NY: Dover Publications, 1988), 6.

295 Bellamy, *Equality*, 132.

296 Giles, *Shadows Before or A Century Onward*, 208.

297 Giles, *Shadows Before or A Century Onward*, 209.

298 Piercy, *Woman on the Edge of Time*, 64.

299 Piercy, *Woman on the Edge of Time*, 106.

300 Twain, *A Connecticut Yankee in King Arthur's Court*, 41.

"He that invents anything for public good in any art or science," in Robert Burton's utopia (1621), "shall be accordingly enriched, honoured, and preferred."[301] For successful inventions in H. G. Wells's *A Modern Utopia* (1905), the state pays a royalty it divides between the inventor and the educational institution that produced her.[302] But a smattering of utopians view patents as a source of undeserved personal wealth and hence a threat to economic equality. These utopians regard patents as a means of cornering markets, limiting competition, and creating monopolies, all of which may intensify economic inequality. As a form of state-sanctioned monopoly a patent grants the inventor an exclusive right for a specified time.[303] This in spite of the fact that the invention arose not as a unique individual effort, but with the benefit of a social and cultural backdrop—an application, as noted, of what Claeys calls the "theory of 'social debt.'"[304] Even Ayn Rand acknowledged this principle which applies to her hero John Galt the electrical engineer and inventor in her utopian *Atlas Shrugged* (1957). Rand concedes that "the knowledge potentially available to man is greater than any one man could begin to acquire in his own lifespan; every man gains an incalculable benefit from the knowledge discovered by others."[305] In this she echoes Bellamy's Dr. Leete who asks rhetorically, "How happened it that your workers were able to produce more than so many savages would have done? Was it not wholly on account of the heritage of the past knowledge and achievements of the race, the machinery of society, thousands of years in contriving, found by you ready-made to your hand?[306]

301 Burton, *The Anatomy of Melancholy*, 104.

302 Wells, *A Modern Utopia*, 107.

303 A US patent is currently for twenty years.

304 Claeys, "Paine's *Agrarian Justice* (1796) and the Secularization of Natural Jurisprudence," 21.

305 Ayn Rand, The Virtue of Selfishness, 32.

306 Bellamy, *Looking Backward*, 112.

Caesar's Column

Caesar's Column (1890) explores the damage patents cause to economic equality. As Gabriel Weltstein, Donnelly's narrator explains, muscle first ruled the world, then intellect, and now "cunning." The purpose of a patent is to provide incentive for new inventions while protecting intellectual property from exploitation. But the true result because of cunning, observes Donnelly's narrator, is that society produces, "one millionaire and thousands of paupers."[307] Initially, Weltstein observes, "Ten thousand men are working at a trade. One of them conceives the scheme of an invention, whereby their productive power is increased tenfold." Then a cunning capitalist entices the poor inventor to sell his invention for "a pittance" and subsequently secures a patent—"a monopoly under the shelter of unwise laws.[308] The result, as Weltstein describes, is that though the workmen can now produce ten times more goods in the same amount of time, the workers' wages remain the same and the benefit of the increased productivity accrues to the cunning owner of the patent. "The workmen still get their $1.50 per day [$51 in 2023], and Cunning pockets the remainder."[309] Since one man can now do the work of ten, Weltstein continues, this throws nine men out of employment. "But the nine men must live; they want the one man's place; they are hungry; they will work for less; and down go wages, until they reach the lowest limit at which the workmen can possibly live."[310]

From the Earth's Center

Eliminating monopolies is believed to reduce economic inequality in S. Byron Welcome's *From the Earth's Center* (1895). For the inventors in Welcome's utopia there are no patents, since patents are a form of monopoly. "Inventions are not the exclusive work of one person," asserts Mr.

307 Donnelly, *Caesar's Column*, 73.
308 Donnelly, *Caesar's Column*, 72–73.
309 Donnelly, *Caesar's Column*, 73.
310 Donnelly, *Caesar's Column*, 73.

Norton, a civil engineer who the travelers meet on their ship, "and, even if they were," he contends, the education the inventor received at the public expense would entitle the public to "a claim on the results of his discoveries."[311] A person, the same character asserts, has no claim on anything "but the product of his own efforts." But the knowledge "which enables one to make an invention is common property." And where many people have contributed their efforts, "they should be free to avail themselves of the resultant common property."[312]

Labor Conscription

> "Then we may impose the law that ... our women are not to neglect the arts of war—they must be practiced by all citizens, male and female alike."[313]
>
> —Plato (c. 429–347 BCE), *Laws*

Perceiving that market forces assign the least agreeable jobs to the least qualified workers—perpetuating economic inequality—a handful of utopians engage short-term labor conscription to promote an egalitarian perspective. This practice teaches the conscripts humility and the importance to society of even the most menial labor. While military conscription features in some early utopias, most later examples involve merely necessary but disagreeable tasks. Plato calls for women's universal military training in case their city comes under attack, as it would be a "disgrace to the state, if the women had been so miserably trained that they could not fight for their young ... and die or undergo any danger."[314] Though "both men and women carry on vigorous military training"[315] in More's *Utopia* (1516) "they take every precaution to avoid having to fight

311 Welcome, *From the Earth's Center*, 102.

312 Welcome, *From the Earth's Center*, 102–103.

313 Plato, *Laws*, trans. Taylor, bk. 7, 814c.

314 Plato, *Laws*, trans. Jowett, bk. 7, 814.

315 More, *Utopia*, trans. Adams, bk. 2, 85.

in person."[316] Farming, however, is "the one job at which everyone works, men and women alike, with no exceptions." The farming conscription is on a two-year rotation after which citizens return to their former vocations.[317] "Common to everyone," in Campanella's *City of the Sun* (1602) are "military service and work in the fields and pastures."[318]

The Diothas

In John Macnie's *The Diothas* (1883), there is "a sort of conscription in force" exacting "for public purposes the service of all young men between the ages of seventeen and twenty-five." The conscripts called "zerdars," says the narrator, perform labors "which, however useful or indispensable, are not attractive as life employments to those not compelled to follow them."[319] The tasks assigned to these young men are rotated and no form of labor is "regarded as unbecoming."[320]

Looking Backward

Upon completing their schooling at age 21, but before entering their chosen vocation, men in Bellamy's *Looking Backward* (1888) undergo a three-year boot camp working as common laborers, "assignable to do any work at the discretion of his superiors."[321] The three years, Dr. Leete explains, follow a "stringent discipline none are exempt from."[322] There is no military conscription, however, as there are no wars and the constitution omits any war powers.[323]

316 More, *Utopia*, trans. Adams, bk. 2, 90.
317 More, *Utopia*, trans. Adams, bk. 2, 43, 48.
318 Campanella, *The City of the Sun*, 81.
319 Macnie, *The Diothas*, 156.
320 Macnie, *The Diothas*, 163.
321 Bellamy, *Looking Backward*, 73.
322 Bellamy, *Looking Backward*, 73.
323 Bellamy, *Looking Backward*, 67. The issue of Bellamy's lack of military defense was addressed by Arthur Dudley Vinton in *Looking Further Backward*.

Mildred Carver, USA

The importance of working to benefit others actuates Martha Bensley Bruère's *Mildred Carver, USA* (1919), wherein Mildred is an 18-year-old woman born to wealth and privilege. "In this feminist revision of Edward Bellamy's industrial army," reports Carol Farley Kessler, a Universal Service "enlists both men and women for a year of public works."[324] The conscripts "were of every race, every complexion, every degree of prosperity."[325] As Mildred faces her one-year obligation in the Agriculture Service, "the idea of work was full of terrifying allurement. What would it be like? What would they find she was able to do?"[326] Facing the prospect of leaving her luxurious New York home—"a little aristocracy of her own" where "her family represented not the survival of the fittest but the survival of the preferred"—for a Minnesota flour mill, Mildred muses: "I wonder ... what it would be like to really work—to have to do something whether you wanted to or not."[327] Her first assignment requires sewing bags of flour closed with six stitches each, "to help provide bread for the people of all the world."[328]

The Expanding Universe of Universal Suffrage

> "There was no more reason why women should be excluded from the ballot-box, than there was why she should be denied access to the church or the school house. She was not only a human being, but the creator of human beings."[329]
>
> —Ignatius Donnelley, *The Golden Bottle* (1892)

324 Carol Farley Kessler, "Women Daring to Speak: United States Women's Feminist Utopias," *Utopian Studies* 2 (1989): 118–123, 120.

325 Martha Bensley Bruère, *Mildred Carver, USA* (New York: The MacMillan Company, 1919), 29.

326 Bruère, *Mildred Carver, USA*, 52.

327 Bruère, *Mildred Carver, USA*, 23, 52, 188.

328 Bruère, *Mildred Carver, USA*, 64.

329 Donnelley, *The Golden Bottle*, 228.

In 1914 labor activist and union organizer Mother Jones (Mary Harris, 1837–1930) declared, "I have no vote and I've raised hell all over this country."[330] Women's suffrage was the focus for a handful of utopians of the late nineteenth and early twentieth centuries including Florence Caroline Dixie (1890) and Edward Mandell House (1912).[331] Preceding this, however, were demands for men's universal suffrage. In England, influenced by Thomas Spence, reports Malcolm Chase, the London Working Men's Association—with its 1838 People's Charter—demanded election reform including universal suffrage for men.[332] Though the US emancipated four million slaves in 1863, the right of African American men to vote, reports Du Bois, was brutally disrupted even after the ratification of Fifteenth Amendment (1870).[333]

In *Equality* (1897) Bellamy's Dr. Leete explains, "There was a great stir about women's rights, but the programme then announced was by no means revolutionary. It only aimed at securing the right to vote, together with various changes in the laws about property-holding by women, the custody of children in divorces, and such details."[334] These "details" were the

330 Quoted by Elliott J. Gorn in *Mother Jones: The Most Dangerous Woman in America* (New York: Hill and Wang, 2001), 232.

331 Albinski reports that few women utopians promoted universal suffrage. Albinski, *Women's Utopias in British and American Fiction*, 57–60. Spotswood, for example, declares, "There is only one kind of independence women have ever achieved so far—and that is financial." Spotswood, *The Unpredictable Adventure*, 434. Gorn reports that Emma Goldman called the women's vote "a fetish of bourgeois society," while Mother Jones declared her antipathy to the movement. Gorn, *Mother Jones*, 230.

332 Malcolm Chase, "Paine, Spence, Chartism and 'The Real Rights of Man,'" in *Thomas Spence: The Poor Man's Revolutionary*, ed. Alastair Bonnett and Keith Armstrong (London, 2014), 13–25, 22. Chase says of the Chartist movement that the main problem they foresaw was a society "increasingly divided (politically, socially and economically) between rich and poor" (24).

333 Du Bois, *Black Reconstruction in America*, 680–690. Du Bois notes that Robert Owen's son Robert Dale Owen was instrumental in negotiating the principles of the Fourteenth Amendment to the US Constitution (1868). This Amendment, while it did not guarantee Black men the right to vote (guaranteed by the Fifteenth Amendment), set the stage by conferring citizenship on all persons born or naturalized in the United States (301).

334 Bellamy, *Equality*, 132.

subject of J. S. Mill's *The Subjection of Women* (1869) where Mill declared, "the legal subordination of one sex to the other—is wrong in itself."[335] Mill's concern was for women's equal education, occupational choice, and right to vote. "Why should any human beings—even women—be forced to obey laws in the making of which they take no part?"[336] This was Claire Myers Spotswood's query in *The Unpredictable Adventure* (1935).

The utopian aspirations of Florence Caroline Dixie in her 1890 *Gloriana; Or The Revolution of 1900*, says Albinski, lie with "emancipating her sex through education, physical exercise and discipline, and through political leadership."[337] *Gloriana* is the story of a charismatic politician's attempts to emancipate the women of England by securing their right to vote. In the guise of Hector L'Estrange, the protagonist Gloria De Lara organizes a political movement swaying public opinion in favor of her goal. As Hector D'Estrange, Gloria tells her followers, "And now my friends, we are on the eve of a great revolution."[338] After her election to Parliament, however, a scheme of intrigue and deceit truncates Gloria's political aspirations. The vengeful plot drives Gloria into exile, though she is presumed dead. Her continuing inspiration, however, leads to legislation in the House of Lords recognizing women's right to vote. Gloria later celebrates this victory upon return from her South American banishment.

In *Philip Dru: Administrator* (1912), Edward House's Dru has a "profound sympathy" for the women who seek equality with men. Dru imagines that "universal franchise without distinction of race, color or sex"[339] would lead to a society of economic equality, releasing women from their coerced economic dependence on men.[340] Dru "believed that with the franchise would come equal opportunity and equal pay for the same work."[341]

335 Mill, *The Subjection of Women*, 1.

336 Spotswood, *The Unpredictable Adventure*, 80.

337 Albinski, *Women's Utopias in British and American Fiction*, 18.

338 Dixie, Gloriana, 119.

339 House, *Philip Dru: Administrator*, 218.

340 House, *Philip Dru: Administrator*, 219–220.

341 House, *Philip Dru: Administrator*, 219–220. Universal suffrage in the US was phased in during the period: 1869–1965. See the US Department of Justice: History of Federal Voting Rights Laws. <https://archive.ph/20210106161217/https://www.justice.gov/crt/history-federal-voting-rights-laws>

Figure 8: "Victoria Woodhull (1838–1927), noted American feminist, with her sister Jennie Claflin, try to vote in the New York election of 1871, but are turned away."[342]

Universal Health Care

"Is it not enough for an individual to be tortured by disease without paying for it?"[343]

—Cosimo Noto, *The Ideal City* (1903)

342 The "flamboyant" Woodhull, says Albinski, was a candidate for the US Presidency in 1872, 1876, and 1880. Albinski, *Women's Utopias in British and American Fiction,* 58. Wells notes, *The Humanitarian* was Woodhull's monthly New York and London "organ of propaganda" promoting eugenic themes such as the "rapid multiplication of the unfit." Wells, *Mankind in the Making,* 36–37.

343 Noto, *The Ideal City*, 204.

The American Medical Association (AMA) affirms that poverty is detrimental to health. "Populations with high- and rising-income inequality are associated with lower life expectancy, higher rates of infant mortality, obesity, [and] mental illness."[344] The poor suffer more chronic health conditions than their more fortunate neighbors due in part to a dearth of preventative care and (in the US) the cost of private medical insurance. In *Shadows Before* (1893) preventative health care has largely replaced remedial treatments. Giles's spokesperson explains, "Advanced medical science recognizes the fact that its best results are obtained in using preventive rather than curative measures; that most ills may be prevented, while but few are cured, without leaving an injured system."[345]

Craig's (1898) Ionian "laws of health are so thoroughly understood and so carefully observed that disease of any kind is very rare."[346] In place of "external appliances and ingredients" Grigsby and Lowes's Alturian residents in *Nequa* (1900) "depend mainly upon arousing the internal powers of the mind and spirit, which alone can exercise any absolute control over the human organism."[347] Guthrie's *A Romance of Two Centuries: A Tale of the Year 2025* (1919) endorses preventative care; here physicians' pay is "on the basis of their efficiency in maintaining their patients' health."[348] Robert Frank's *Social Integration* (1935) calls for discontinuing all private medical practice and for "all medical organizations [to] be government owned and controlled so that medical services will be furnished the public free of charge."[349] Luciente, a resident of Mattapoisett in Piercy's *Woman on the Edge of Time* (1976) touts the benefits of universal health care in 2137. She tells Connie, the protagonist from the past, that doctors now teach people to heal themselves. "We program the local cells. Slow healing but

344 American Medical Association Press Release, June 13, 2022. <https://www.ama-assn.org/press-center/press-releases/ama-adopts-new-policy-connecting-poverty-level-wages-adverse-health>

345 Giles, *Shadows Before,* 116.

346 Craig, *Ionia*, 59.

347 Grigsby and Lowe, *Nequa*, 104.

348 Guthrie, *A Romance of Two Centuries*, 55–56.

349 Frank, *Social Integration*, 158.

better after." On the practice of surgery, Luciente explains, "We don't do much taking out. When we do, we regrow."[350]

Social Security

> "The Other Now was brimming with features that any liberal would find hard to resist: an absence of income and sales taxes; ... universal freedom from poverty, but also from a welfare state demanding that benefit-recipients surrender their dignity at the door of some social security office."[351]
>
> —Yanis Varoufakis, *Another Now* (2021)

Hythloday, the narrator in Thomas More's *Utopia* (1516), protests the plight of the working poor in England: "After society has taken the labour of their best years, when they are worn out by age, sickness and utter destitution, then the thankless commonwealth, forgetting all their sleepless nights and services, throws them out to die a miserable death."[352] In our own day, reports The International Monetary Fund, governments in advanced economies have "mitigated inequality through public policy—primarily progressive taxes and social transfers such as public retirement benefits."[353] Don Marquis's *Almost Perfect State* (1927), expresses the utopian sense of social security. In the almost perfect state, Marquis says, "every person shall have at least ten years of easy, carefree, happy living before he dies—things will be so arranged economically that this will be possible for each individual."[354]

The US Social Security Administration credits Thomas Paine with promoting the concept of public retirement

350 Piercy, *Woman on the Edge of Time*, 170.

351 Varoufakis, *Another Now*, 153.

352 More, *Utopia*, trans. Adams, bk. 2, 104–105.

353 International Monetary Fund, "Causes and Consequences of Income Inequality: A Global Perspective," June 2015, 21.

354 Don Marquis, *The Almost Perfect State* (New York: Doubleday, Page and Company, 1927), 182.

benefits.[355] In his *Agrarian Justice* (1797), Paine suggested the "sum of ten pounds per annum [£996 or $1,232 in 2023] during life, to every person now living, of the age of fifty years, and to all others as they shall arrive at that age."[356] In its initial formulation, however, the US Social Security Act of 1935, notes Shapiro, contributed to income and wealth inequality by excluding the majority of non-white citizens from its safety net.[357] This result extends Patricia Ventura's observation that "the United States was founded as a racial dystopia."[358]

The state in John W. Roberts, *Looking Within: The Misleading Tendencies of "Looking Backward" Made Manifest* (1893) supports pensioners over fifty.[359] Fayette Stratton Giles's *Shadows Before* (1893) features an insurance system in which "all workmen must insure against accidents and for old age."[360] The citizens of Bruce's *The World in 1931* (1921) receive a state pension upon reaching age 58; there is also a pension for the "care of those who, through sickness or accident, are unable to work."[361]

355 In acknowledgment of its historical debt to Paine, the US Social Security Administration website features a link to the text of *Agrarian Justice*. <https://www.ssa.gov/history/tpaine3.html>

356 Paine, *Agrarian Justice*, 678.

357 Shapiro, *Toxic Inequality*, 133. The 1935 Social Security Act excluded agricultural and domestic workers from retirement benefits and unemployment insurance. On its website the NAACP reports that "the origins of Social Security were rooted in racism. ... The exemptions were finally repealed in the 1950s, but they had significantly worsened the economic gap between Blacks and Whites." <https://naacp.org/articles/viewing-social-security-through-civil-rights-lens>

358 Patricia Ventura, "Introduction: Race and Utopian Desire," in *Race and Utopian Desire in American Literature and Society*, ed. Patricia Ventura and Edward K. Chan (Palgrave Macmillan, 2019), 1–19, 6.

359 Roberts, *Looking Within: The Misleading Tendencies of "Looking Backward" Made Manifest*, 271.

360 Giles, *Shadows Before or A Century Onward*, 137.

361 Bruce, *The World in 1931*, 178.

Restricting Immigration

> "The production and trade globalization of the late 1800s was fueled by one hundred million people leaving their continent of origin to live and work elsewhere."[362]
>
> —J. Bradford DeLong, *Slouching Towards Utopia* (2022)

Charlotte Perkins Gilman's eugenically modified US in *Moving the Mountain* (1911) restricts immigration to avoid severe economic inequality. As a result of these efforts, Gilman's character Nellie tells her brother John, in America there is "no such thing … as poverty."[363] Immigration, Nellie continues, is a "sociological process not possible to stop, but quite possible to assist and to guide to great advantage. And here in America," Nellie affirms, "we recognized our own special place—'the melting pot.'"[364] In Gilman's utopia immigrants, as they disembark at Jamaica Harbor, are sifted through a meticulous human sieve, first as to nationality and then using "the most searching and thorough—microscopic—chemical" physical exam. "We have … an idea of what people ought to be," says Nellie, "and how to make them so."[365] "No immigrant is turned loose on the community till he or she is up to a certain standard"—a melting pot for what Gilman calls the "American blend," immigrants exclusively "from a few closely connected races."[366]

Mr. Forest, the spokesperson in Richard Michaelis's *Looking Further Forward* (1890) argues, however, that "The comparatively small harm done by immigrants was largely over-balanced by the many advantages the citizens of the United States obtained through the large influx of people from

362 DeLong, *Slouching Towards Utopia*, 40.

363 Gilman, *Moving the Mountain*, chap. 2, 14–15. There is also no "labor problem," no "color problem," and no "sex problem."

364 Gilman, *Moving the Mountain*, chap. 2, 15.

365 Gilman, *Moving the Mountain*, chap. 2, 17.

366 Gilman says, "All Americans have come from somewhere else. But all persons who come from somewhere else are not therefore Americans." Charlotte Perkins Gilman, "Is America Too Hospitable?," in *Charlotte Perkins Gilman: A Nonfiction Reader*, ed. Larry Ceplair (New York: Columbia University Press, 1991), 290.

Europe." "The very fact that hundreds of thousands of able-bodied people, whose rearing and education had cost the European countries millions of dollars, landed on American shores was a great gain to the United States."[367]

Liquor as a Source of Poverty

> "One-half of the miseries of our working men would be at once relieved, if the forty million bushels of grain were made into bread instead of liquors."[368]
>
> —W. W. Satterlee, *Looking Backward and What I Saw* (1890)

During the 1920s the United States instituted a national prohibition against alcoholic beverages—their production, importation, or transportation (the Constitution's 18th Amendment, 1920–1933[369]). John Macnie's (1883) *The Diothas* (described in Chapter 5), proposes eliminating poverty through a reduction in the waste resulting from alcohol consumption. "Intemperance was made simply impossible by a total prohibition, under severe penalties, of the manufacture or possession of intoxicating beverages." This "was found to make all the difference between the existence of an ever-increasing substratum of hopeless poverty and a general diffusion of comfort and independence."[370]

In his 1893 response to Bellamy, *Looking Within: The Misleading Tendencies of "Looking Backward" Made Manifest*, John Roberts exposes what he sees as critical flaws in Bellamy's economic arrangements as they relate to Roberts's view of human nature. In Roberts's version (described in Chapter 6), by the year 2000 not only have workers largely ceased to produce as much as they once did—and not enough to sustain the

367 Michaelis, *Looking Further Forward*, 113.

368 Satterlee, *Looking Backward and What I Saw*, 151.

369 In her autobiography, written during this period, Mother (Mary Harris) Jones notes that prohibition required greater sacrifice from the working classes than from the wealthy who had access to private clubs.

370 Macnie, *The Diothas*, 148.

country—but they have developed an underground economy driven by alcohol and gambling ("There were ten thousand drunkards in Boston"[371]). The downward spiral of production resulted in shortages of food and other necessities. This forced the government to admit the experiment with Bellamy's plan had failed after two generations and call for a transition back to the system of the late nineteenth century, modified, however, to avoid the abuses that resulted in vast economic inequality including a ban on the sale of liquor except at government stores.

Ending War to End Poverty

> "And now, Mr. Prognosis, we come down to the time when the crowning glory of the new order of things is at hand,—the accomplishment of permanent and universal peace among men."[372]
>
> —Chauncey Thomas, *The Crystal Button* (1891)

Economist Branko Milanović reports that in the United States today, "wars are fought by the poor (including many who are not even US citizens), are financed by the middle class, and benefit the rich."[373] Adam Smith declared (1776): "War, and the preparation for war, are the two circumstances which, in modern times, occasion the greater part of the necessary expense of all great states."[374] In Gilman's *Moving the Mountain* (1911) we learn that war funding—which formerly consumed 70 percent of the national income—was allotted to ending poverty by creating jobs and providing education to everyone.[375]

The spokesperson for the Altrurians in Grigsby and Lowe's *Nequa* (1900) observes:

371 Roberts, *Looking Within: The Misleading Tendencies of "Looking Backward" Made Manifest*, 162.
372 Thomas, *The Crystal Button*, 168.
373 Milanović, *Global Inequality*, 163–164.
374 Smith, *Wealth of Nations*, bk. 5, chap. 2, 493.
375 Gilman, *Moving the Mountain*, chap. 9, 70.

> "When woman secured her true position in the world she put an end to war by removing the vicious commercial, financial and governmental systems that enabled one class of people to oppress another. When greedy and domineering classes could no longer have soldiers to do their bidding, poverty was abolished by securing to the whole people equal access to the unlimited productive power of the earth."[376]

376 Grigsby and Lowe, *Nequa*, 105.

CHAPTER 5

Violence and Revolution

> "Revolution does not mean red flags and street fighting, it means a fundamental shift of power. Whether it happens with or without bloodshed is largely an accident of time and place."[1]
>
> —George Orwell, "The Lion and the Unicorn" (1941)

In *Utopian Fantasy* (1955) Richard Gerber proposes that the "most admirably constructed utopia fails to convince if we are not led to believe that the danger of revolt is excluded."[2] Certain utopias, however, feature violence and revolution as requisite to achieving an ideal society from which "revolt is excluded." The three preceding chapters featured economic, social, and political schemes for relieving economic inequality. Implementation of these schemes was often left out of account, however, as the traveler was fancifully transported to the new society in a cataleptic trance, a drug coma, or a frozen state.[3] In *The Great Leveler: Violence and the History of Inequality* (2017), historian Walter Scheidel stresses the importance of "powerful shocks" that "flatten inequality." These "violent ruptures," he says, in addition to pandemics and mass mobilization warfare, include state failures and violent revolution.[4] Scheidel warns, however, that historically equality enforced by revolutions "lasted only as long

1 Orwell, "The Lion and the Unicorn," 323.

2 Richard Gerber, *Utopian Fantasy* (London: Routledge and Kegan Paul, 1955), 68.

3 "Key to all the utopian novels of the [eighteen] nineties," says Saxton, is the "question of transition to the future." Alexander Saxton, "'Caesar's Column': The Dialogue of Utopia and Catastrophe," *American Quarterly* 16, no. 2, pt. 1 (Summer, 1967): 224–238, 230.

4 Scheidel, *The Great Leveler*, 6, 174 (wars), 333 (pandemics), 251–254 (revolutions). Milanović refers to plagues and wars as "malign ways in which economic inequality can be reduced." Milanović, *Global Inequality*, 163.

as these regimes were in power.... The moment they fell ... inequality of income and wealth rapidly returned."[5]

The four utopias this chapter describes stress the necessity of violence for effecting economic equality. Applying Hannah Arendt's moral taxonomy in *On Revolution*—revolt or rebellion versus revolution (explained below)—reveals, however, that while revolution is achieved in John Macnie's *The Diothas* (1894) and William Morris's *News from Nowhere* (1890), revolution is unexpectedly aborted in Frank Rosewater's *Utopia: A Romance for Today* (1897), and the violent uprising at the core of Ignatius Donnelly's *Caesar's Column* (1890) fails to attain the moral trajectory of a revolution.

George Kateb in *Utopia and its Enemies* (1963) lists objections against utopias that require the violent overthrow of the current governing structure. Every revolution, he declares, "consumes the dreams which set it in motion."[6] Though revolution is a tactic for social change, explains Henri Saint-Simon (1760–1825), it is the "most inadequate of all methods."[7] One reason for this, observes Pierre-Joseph Proudhon (1809–1865), is that a revolution "is always split by parties and sects, which work to pervert it."[8] Adding a cynical dimension to these assessments George Orwell (1903–1950) notes that "every revolutionary opinion draws part of its strength from a secret conviction that nothing can be changed."[9]

As early as 1890, observes Pfaelzer, "a small group of utopian authors concluded that only apocalypse would deliver utopia." These utopians, she says, "doubted that consumer cooperatives, nationalized railroads, public education, and the women's vote would guarantee a prosperous future."[10] For this reason, Pfaelzer explains, "Violent revolution—punitive

5 Scheidel, *The Great Leveler*, 253.
6 Kateb, *Utopia and Its Enemies*, 48.
7 Henri Saint-Simon, *The Political Thought of Saint-Simon*, ed. Ghita Ionescu (Oxford: Oxford University Press, 1976), 124 (italics in original).
8 Pierre-Joseph Proudhon, *General Idea of the Revolution in the Nineteenth Century*, trans. John Beverley Robinson (Mineola, NY: Dover Publications, 2003), 168.
9 George Orwell, *The Road to Wigan Pier* (New York: A Harvest Book – Harcourt, 1958), 158.
10 Pfaelzer, *The Utopian Novel in America*, 112.

and redemptive—emerges as the logical consequence of the painful inequalities of the current era."[11]

The Diothas

"What sort of a revolution do you propose to carry out?"

"One that will equalize things, especially the wealth of the country."[12]

—John Roberts, *Looking Within: The Misleading Tendencies of "Looking Backward" Made Manifest* (1893)

The Diothas, report Negley and Patrick, "contains in embryo what might have been the most modern and the most profound utopia of the nineteenth century."[13] *The Diothas, or, A Far Look Ahead* (1883) depicts John Macnie's egalitarian society in the ninety-sixth century, developed out of a corrupt, oppressive, and increasingly violent régime in the United States. It illustrates Moylan's claim that in late nineteenth-century utopias, "subversive visions were relocated in a future time when the process of revolutionary, historical change brought about the utopian society."[14] The narrator, Ismar Thiusen, visiting from the past, learns from his guide and friend, Utis Estai, that the "more or less democratical forms of government ... that rose on the ruins of the decayed monarchical and aristocratical systems of your time, soon showed symptoms of decay."[15] Reacting to the "general relaxation of the bonds of law and morality" around the world, the mood in the United States, Estai says, became "stern, almost savage."[16] As a result of the "extremes of democracy and lawlessness," she says, industry died out and society "relapsed to a form

11 Pfaelzer, *The Utopian Novel in America*, 112–113.
12 Roberts, *Looking Within: The Misleading Tendencies of "Looking Backward,"* 27.
13 Negley and Partick, *The Quest for Utopia*, 51.
14 Moylan, *Demand the Impossible*, 6.
15 Macnie, *The Diothas*, 108.
16 Macnie, *The Diothas*, 111.

of barbarism."[17] From this "seething and fermenting mass," affirms the guide, new political organizations gradually evolved as the "sole refuge from anarchy."[18] Some nations of the past restored order and industry by employing despotism. Through new laws and their enforcement by severe penalties, they gradually reestablished respect for the law. Other nations, Estai explains, pursued republican forms of governance, but held their elected officials to higher standards. These efforts were finally rewarded with the elimination of the criminal classes,[19] while "the worst of the monopolists and their legislative tools" were ultimately brought to account. Macnie, claim Negley and Patrick, was "discouragingly realistic" about the "slow and tortuous" development of society through "dictatorship, world wars, and the devastation of monopolies of power."[20] In the centuries that followed, both strains of government—the despotic and the republican—attained "a high degree of material prosperity,"[21] presumably through a strict reliance on the rule of law.[22]

Ultimately, a great military genius ("a Napoleonic figure"[23]) appeared on the world stage, reports the guide, "fired with the hope of universal empire."[24] Through military conquest he reduced the world's despotic nations to "one large empire."[25] "He next attacked and overwhelmed ... the Liberal nations of the Old World." It was during this conflict, the guide observes, that London was "reduced to a heap of ruins."[26] In the final stage of his conquest the military genius attacked the United States. For nearly a year "he held the whole Atlantic region."[27] But the invader "was first checked, then driven back toward the coast ... and captured with what remained of

17 Macnie, *The Diothas*, 109.
18 Macnie, *The Diothas*, 109.
19 Macnie, *The Diothas*, 111.
20 Negley and Partick, *The Quest for Utopia*, 51.
21 Macnie, *The Diothas*, 110, 112.
22 Nagley and Patrick cite Macnie's conviction that "social order can be achieved only through law." Negley and Partick, *The Quest for Utopia*, 51.
23 Bleiler, *Science Fiction: The Early Years*, 735.
24 Macnie, *The Diothas*, 112.
25 Macnie, *The Diothas*, 112.
26 Macnie, *The Diothas*, 112.
27 Macnie, *The Diothas*, 112.

his army."[28] Despotism, declares Estai, "had received its final blow."[29] Since that time, she explains, the "progress of mankind in good government has been peaceful and continuous."[30] They have achieved a vision of economic equality where a great income provides no personal advantage. "It cannot procure a comfort beyond what all enjoy, nor does it confer an iota of social power. ... Great wealth, in fact, is neither desired nor desirable among us."[31] Their society's goal is not leveling but "a more equal diffusion of wealth." As Estai relates to the visitor, "we have no aristocracy ... if you mean a class living in idleness by the toil of others."[32] Neither is there a working class "that spends its life in toil that leaves no leisure."[33]

Caesar's Column

> "To put political power in the hands of men embittered and degraded by poverty is to tie firebrands to foxes and turn them loose amid the standing corn."[34]
>
> —Henry George, *Progress and Poverty* (1879)

In the *Politics* Aristotle warns that "the masses become revolutionary when the distribution of property is *unequal*."[35] Economist Amartya Sen contends that the "perception of inequality" depends "substantially on possibilities of actual rebellion."[36] In what Claeys calls "one of the more successful responses to Bellamy,"[37] *Caesar's Column* (1890) stands as a reminder of the permanent struggles involved in moderating

28 Macnie, *The Diothas*, 112–113.
29 Macnie, *The Diothas*, 112–113.
30 Macnie, *The Diothas*, 113.
31 Macnie, *The Diothas*, 144.
32 Macnie, *The Diothas*, 11, 24.
33 Macnie, *The Diothas*, 11.
34 George, *Progress and Poverty*, 532.
35 Aristotle, *Politics,* trans. Barker, bk. 2, ch. 8 1266b § 10, (italics in original).
36 Amartya Sen, *On Economic Inequality* (Oxford University Press, 1973), 1.
37 Claeys, *Dystopia: A Natural History*, 325.

the unequal distribution of wealth. *Caesar's Column*, says Roemer, was Ignatius Donnelly's best-selling work and "one of the four most popular utopian novels written during the late nineteenth century."[38] Saxon calls *Caesar's Column* "One of the most powerful projections of catastrophe in American literature."[39] In real life Donnelly, a product of the Philadelphia public schools, was an attorney, newspaper publisher, and Lieutenant governor of Minnesota. In his introduction to *Caesar's Column,* Donnelly asserts of his time that "the many are plundered to enrich the few," while corporations in league "depress the price of labor and increase the cost of the necessaries of existence."[40] Furthermore, Donnelly notes, as "society divides itself into two hostile camps"—the rich and the "despised" poor—their opposing forces "wait only for the drum-beat and the trumpet to summon them to armed conflict."[41] In *Caesar's Column,* report Negley and Patrick, Donnelly "takes the position that only violence and revolution can rid society of the vicious machinations of oligarchy, and he is depressingly realistic about the results of violence as a method of social change."[42]

In Donnelly's novel (action occurring in 1988), the world has devolved—under the weight of corruption and greed—into an assemblage of oligarchic dictatorships, "gigantic combinations" whose aim is to "plunder the poor; to make the miserable more miserable; to take from those who had least and give it to those who had most."[43] Donnelly, notes Barley, "prophesied an epidemic of corporate corruption causing mass immiseration and stimulating a world-wide revolt."[44] Like Jack London in *The Iron Heel*, says Wegner, "Donnelly must struggle to embody for his readers the powers that determine the shape of contemporary society."[45]

38 Roemer, *The Obsolete Necessity*, 72.
39 Saxton, "Caesar's Column," 224.
40 Donnelly, *Caesar's Column*, 7.
41 Donnelly, *Caesar's Column*, 7.
42 Negley and Partick, *The Quest for Utopia*, 23–24. Historian Scheidel reports that "Genuinely radical urban revolts were generally rare in history" and even those with a "relatively modest agenda tended to fail." Scheidel, *The Great Leveler*, 252.
43 Donnelly, *Caesar's Column*, 177–178.
44 Barley, "Prediction, Programme and Fantasy in Jack London's *The Iron Heel*," 156.
45 Wegner, *Imaginary Communities*, 122.

The story is narrated in a series of letters Gabriel Weltstein, a sheep farmer visiting New York City, has written to his brother Heinrich in a Swiss agricultural colony in Uganda. In one letter Weltstein writes that in "all the shops and factories we visited ... we saw exemplified ... that 'iron law of wages' which the old economists spoke of ... that reduction, by competition, of the wages of the worker to the least sum that will maintain life and muscular strength enough to do the work required, with such little surplus of vitality as might be necessary to perpetuate the wretched race."[46]

In a vivid depiction of the extremes of economic inequality *Caesar's Column* reveals a world divided between great masses of wretched laboring poor and a few wealthy oligarchs and their loyal followers. Donnelly, says Kumar, "saw the power of large-scale oligarchic capitalism leading inexorably to a business dictatorship."[47] The danger that most threatened the "middle-class regime" of the Gilded Age, says Taylor, "was the unremitting pressure ... which Big Business exercised on all branches of government ... [through] economic pressure, intimidation and straightout bribery."[48] The oligarchs and their enablers, says Donnelly's narrator, "corrupted the courts, the juries, the newspapers, the legislatures, the congresses, the ballot-boxes and the hearts and souls of the people. ... [T]hey drove justice from the land and installed cruelty, ignorance, despair and vice in its place."[49] In this way, says Taylor, capitalist powers "wrested the State away from the service of the general welfare."[50]

Intervening in this politico-economic divide is a cluster of men who have organized the workers into an underground armed force for revolution—the Brotherhood of Destruction—a festering organization, a political "secret society having a membership of [one hundred] millions, and extending all over the world."[51] "Every able-bodied man in the whole

46 Donnelly, *Caesar's Column*, 28.

47 Krishan Kumar, *Utopia and Anti-Utopia in Modern Times* (Oxford, UK: Basil Blackwell, 1987), 128.

48 Taylor, *The Economic Novel in America*, 27.

49 Donnelly, *Caesar's Column*, 177–178.

50 Taylor, *The Economic Novel in America*, 27.

51 Donnelly, *Caesar's Column*, 24, 26.

vast Brotherhood, in American and Europe, has been supplied with his weapon and a full accompaniment of ammunition."[52]

The hierarchical Brotherhood comprises at its base groups of ten men, none of whom knows more than nine other members.[53] The leaders of these groups are themselves organized into groups of ten, but in this second tier, "no man knows his fellow's name or face; they meet always masked." Similarly, for the group of ten above them and so on. "The highest body of all is a group of one hundred, selected out of the whole force by an executive committee."[54] The Executive Committee includes three men: Caesar Lomellini, a man of "immense size" and courage hailing from South Carolina; Maximilian Petion (Max)—believed the assumed name of Arthur Phillips, an "intelligent gentlemen" of "scholarly tastes" and advocate of socialism; and an unnamed Russian organizer of the Brotherhood of Europe who a spy reports is "the brains of the organization."[55]

While the Brotherhood is recruiting and training men for the revolution, the oligarchs "have so long held mankind in subjection that they laugh at the idea of the great, dark, writhing masses, rising up to overthrow them." Government to them is an "exquisitely adjusted piece of mechanism whose object is to keep the few happy and the many miserable."[56] As Alexander Saxton observes, however, "revolution, when it came, would serve only to substitute chaos for tyranny."[57]

Hannah Arendt in *On Revolution* distinguishes between rebellion (or revolt) and revolution. A rebellion, she says, which is "more than a mass hysteria"[58] is the "first and violent stage" of a revolution whose goal is liberation; rebellion is an "uprising against tyranny."[59] Following this uprising is a "quieter second stage" of revolution and the constitution of a new organizing body.[60] In *Caesar's Column*, however, the revolt is *not*

52 Donnelly, *Caesar's Column*, 46.
53 Donnelly, *Caesar's Column*, 78.
54 Donnelly, *Caesar's Column*, 78.
55 Donnelly, *Caesar's Column*, 81–83.
56 Donnelly, *Caesar's Column*, 112.
57 Saxton, "Caesar's Column," 229.
58 Hannah Arendt, *On Revolution* (New York: Penguin Books, 1963), 17.
59 Arendt, *On Revolution*, 30, 133.
60 Arendt, *On Revolution*, 133.

a prelude to a second stage whose end is "the foundation of freedom."[61] This is a common fate of rebellions, Arendt explains, as "there is nothing more futile than rebellion and liberation unless they are followed by the constitution of the newly won freedom."[62] This accords with Lasky's claim in *Utopia and Revolution* that "where there is no vision there is no proper preparation for the real or the desired course of human events."[63] Only where "novelty is connected with the idea of freedom," Arendt emphasizes, "are we entitled to speak of revolution."[64] This condition never materializes in *Caesar's Column*, as the organizers succumb to the wrath of their own hordes.

Figure 9: "France, French Revolution 1789, storming of the Bastille July 14, 1789, capture of Gouverneur de Launay, wood engraving after drawing by Prieur."

61 Arendt, *On Revolution*, 133.
62 Arendt, *On Revolution*, 133. However, she notes, "the turmoil of liberation has … frequently defeated the revolution."
63 Lasky, *Utopia and Revolution*, 44.
64 Arendt, *On Revolution*, 24.

All night long the "awful Bedlam raged," reports Weltstein the narrator. "The dark streets swarmed. … Fires sprang up all over the city, licking the darkness with their hideous tongues of flame, and revealing by their crimson glare the awful sights of that unparalleled time."[65] As the revolt continues, notes Saxton, "the world sinks through savagery to chaos."[66] Engaged in an "uncontrollable nihilistic orgy," proclaims Michael Fellman, the "subhuman workers destroyed every element of civilization."[67] In a scene of unfettered anarchy the members of the Executive Committee lose control of their charges. "It is the first instinct of such mobs," affirms Max, "to suspect their leaders and slay them."[68] The enraged combatants butcher two of the leaders, including Caesar Lomellini, while Max escapes. Before his death, Lomellini—whom Pfaelzer describes as "a simple peasant" turned "brutal revolutionary leader"[69]—orders the construction of a monument in Union Square "composed of the bodies of a quarter of a million of human beings, who were once the rulers, or the instruments of the rulers, of this mighty, but, alas! this ruined city."[70] This monument—Caesar's Column—proclaims Lomellini, built from corpses encased in concrete, "shall last while the earth stands." "And if there aren't enough dead to build it of, why, we'll kill some more; we've got plenty to kill."[71] The monument is dedicated to "the death and burial of modern civilization"[72] representing what Pfaelzer calls a "rite of social purification."[73]

Max, the surviving leader, foresees that civil government will not rise again out of the ruins for many centuries.[74] "Ignorance, passion, suspicion, brutality, criminality, will be the lions in the path" of rebirth

65 Donnelly, *Caesar's Column*, 176.
66 Saxton, "Caesar's Column," 234.
67 Michael Fellman, *The Unbounded Frame: Freedom and Community in Nineteenth Century American Utopianism* (Westport, CT: Greenwood Press, 1973), 141.
68 Donnelly, *Caesar's Column*, 182.
69 Pfaelzer, *The Utopian Novel in America*, 123.
70 Donnelly, *Caesar's Column*, 177–178.
71 Donnelly, *Caesar's Column*, 172.
72 Donnelly, *Caesar's Column*, 177.
73 Pfaelzer, *The Utopian Novel in America*, 136.
74 Donnelly, *Caesar's Column*, 24, 26.

and recovery. "After about three-fourths of the human family have died of hunger, or been killed," Max predicts, "the remainder, constituting, by the law of the survival of the fittest, the most powerful and brutal, will find it necessary, for self-defense against each other, to form squads or gangs."[75]

> The greatest fighter in each of these [gangs] will become chief. ... Then the history of the world will be slowly repeated. ... Gradually, and in its rudest forms, labor will begin again; at first exercised principally by slaves. Men will exchange liberty for protection. After a century or two a kind of commerce may arise. Then will follow other centuries of wars, between provinces or nations. ... And so, step by step, mankind will re-enact the great human drama, which begins always with a tragedy, runs through a comedy, and terminates in a catastrophe.[76]

Allan Axelrad reports that Donnelly "rejected the evolutionist social Darwinian notion of linear progress;"[77] he believed that history is "cyclical and catastrophic."[78] Rather than cycles that last a few years or a generation, however, *Caesar's Column* focuses on cycles extending for centuries: from civilization's destruction—the result of intractable economic inequality—to its rebirth, reestablishment, and gradual advancement. Though Jack London's *The Iron Heel* (1908) also describes a pitched battle between labor and a brutal oligarchy raging for centuries (as noted in Chapter 3), London's revolution contrasts with Donnelly's in following the spirit Arendt directs—that "through it all was order, purpose, control."[79]

75 Donnelly, *Caesar's Column,* 184.

76 Donnelly, *Caesar's Column,* 184.

77 Allan M. Axelrad, "Ideology and Utopia in the Works of Ignatius Donnelly," *American Studies* 12, no. 2 (fall 1971): 47–65, 52.

78 Axelrad, "Ideology and Utopia in the Works of Ignatius Donnelly," 52.

79 London, *The Iron Heel*, 166–167.

News from Nowhere

> "The problem is not how to construct the future upon the ruins of the past; but to demonstrate how it is now in our power to create prosperity for those deprived of the necessities of life without robbing anything from those who are rich."[80]
>
> —Jean Baptiste André Godin, *Social Solutions* (1871)

A. L. Morton argues that for William Morris utopia "is not somewhere remote in time or space but grows out of existing society through struggle, bearing clear traces of that struggle and of its whole past."[81] The past for Morris, says John Freeman-Moir, "was understood as a resource for enriching and securing the present as a step toward a better future."[82] In contrast to *Caesar's Column* with its unfocused workers' revolt, *News from Nowhere*, following Arendt's prescription, features a rebellion followed by a second stage whose end is "the foundation of freedom."[83] *News from Nowhere* portrays a post-revolutionary English society c. 2100–2150.[84] The revolution is described in a chapter titled: "How the Change Came."[85] In this chapter, says Owen Holland, Morris offered "an imagined

80 Godin, *Social Solutions*, 7.

81 Morton, *The English Utopia*, 207.

82 Freeman-Moir, "Crafting Experience: William Morris, John Dewey, and Utopia," 204.

83 Arendt, *On Revolution*, 133.

84 Whether William Guest's visit occurs two hundred years after 1952 ("the great battle," Morris, *News from Nowhere,* 78)—as Kumar assumes—or two hundred years after the end of the nineteenth century (with the "approaching destruction of commerce," Morris, *News from Nowhere*, 137) is arguable. Old Hammond says both: "You must understand ... we have changed within the last two hundred years" (Morris, *News from Nowhere*, 91), and "We have been living for a hundred and fifty years ... in our present manner" (Morris, *News from Nowhere*, 111). Krishan Kumar, "A Pilgrimage of Hope: William Morris's Journey to Utopia," *Utopian Studies* 5 no. 1 (1994): 89–107, 91.

85 Kumar praises this chapter in particular as "nothing less than a complete 'natural history' of revolution, incorporating elements of 1789, 1830, 1848, and 1871—the principal revolutions up to Morris's time ... linking the movements and ideas ...

prehistory of Nowhere consisting of a lengthy account of the social revolution that brought the utopian society into being."[86] Michael Holzman claims that Morris presents here "a clear rendering of the step-by-step dialectic of social forces resolving themselves into structural change."[87] In this chapter Morris's spokesperson old Hammond, of whom Vincent Geoghegan says his "age makes him a transitional figure,"[88] explains in great detail the 200-year progression from capitalist "wage slavery" to decentralized communism.[89] Marie Berneri describes Morris's detailed exposition saying he writes exclusively about subjects "he knows intimately and in which he is passionately interested."[90]

In mid-nineteenth century England, Hammond tells William Guest, "it was the function of government to protect the rich against the poor."[91] This protection, according to Morris, consisted in maintaining the rich in their "superior position, to make them beings of a higher order."[92] The dual role of Parliament at that time, affirms Hammond, was on the one hand to protect the interests of the upper classes and on the other hand "to delude the people into supposing that they had some share in the management of their own affairs."[93] By controlling the work available to the poor, the privileged class with the aid of government, Morris reports, forced the poor to work for it and took from this "inferior class" as much as it could.[94]

---

with a sweeping projection into the future ... when the socialist revolution finally triumphs." Kumar, "A Pilgrimage of Hope," 97–98.

86 Owen Holland, "Spectatorship and Entanglement in Thoreau, Hawthorne, Morris, and Wells," *Utopian Studies* 27, no.1 (2016): 28–52, 40.

87 Michael Holtzman, "Anarchism and Utopia: William Morris's *News from Nowhere*," ELH 51, no. 3 (Autumn, 1984): 589–603, 598.

88 Vincent Geoghegan, "The Utopian Past: Memory and History in Edward Bellamy's *Looking Backward* and William Morris's *News From Nowhere*," *Utopian Studies* 3, no. 2 (1992): 75–90, 81.

89 Hammond tells Guest, "we discourage centralization." Morris, *News from Nowhere*, 101.

90 Berneri, *Journey Through Utopia*, 259.

91 Morris, *News from Nowhere*, 110.

92 Morris, "Useful Work Versus Useless Toil," 94.

93 Morris, *News from Nowhere*, 108.

94 Morris, "Useful Work Versus Useless Toil," 94.

But, with all the changes that have occurred during the past 200 years, old Hammond confirms to Guest, the class distinctions have been dissolved away and there is no longer anything "which you ... would call a government."[95] The resulting society is Morris's expression of a new invisible hand guiding people to follow their natural talents in a communal environment of equality and freedom, producing only what is elegant, well-crafted, and which their neighbors desire.

Though initially, as old Hammond explains, the government used every means—including military force—to slow the progress of the workers seeking economic freedom, Parliament was increasingly constrained to make concessions in the form of laws protecting workers' rights and raising their wages. While it is true that the workers could hardly "conceive the happiness of a free life," Hammond tells Guest, the workers understood that their masters oppressed them, and that the workers could "do without them, though perhaps they scarce knew how."[96] When the socialist-inspired vision of communal equality and freedom arose late in the nineteenth century, Hammond affirms, "the power of the middle classes, the then tyrants of society, was so enormous and crushing" that communal life seemed but a dream.[97] For the social activists working for the change—"because they could see further than other people"[98]—the dream waited on a more effective organization of the workers and their acceptance of the words of "more enlightened men who were then called Socialists."[99] During this period—with the constitution of a new organizing body[100]—the workers had their first exposure to the teachings of socialism and continued to organize trade unions, "though in a very piecemeal way."[101] Socialism, says Polanyi, "is the solution natural to industrial workers who see no reason why production should not be regulated directly."[102]

95 Morris, *News from Nowhere*, 107.
96 Morris, *News from Nowhere*, 135.
97 Morris, *News from Nowhere*, 133–134.
98 Morris, *News from Nowhere*, 133.
99 Morris, *News from Nowhere*, 134.
100 Arendt, *On Revolution*, 133.
101 Morris, *News from Nowhere*, 135.
102 Polanyi, *The Great Transformation*, 242.

The business owners naturally resisted the measures for organizing labor, as these efforts served to upset the existing system of commerce. At the same time, notes Hammond, there was among the working classes "growing confusion, great suffering ... and, as a consequence, great discontent."[103] This phase of the workers' transition from wage slaves to a position of increasing power continued while the authority of the upper classes "lessened, as their command over wealth lessened."[104] This gradual power shift advanced one of the workers' goals which Holzman asserts was "to make capitalism so costly as to be impractical."[105] During this early period of the movement, old Hammond reports, the working classes were poorly organized despite the gains they had extracted from their employers.[106] Though the struggle for power meant the masters could no longer command their workers "to complete subjection," neither could the workers "force freedom" from their masters.[107]

The workers initially formed unions representing their individual trades and followed the "foolish tactic" of organizing only isolated strikes.[108] Throughout the country workers staged scattered labor protests, strikes, and riots that police met wielding bludgeons.[109] But, says Hammond, the police could not concentrate in any one location since the riots were everywhere.[110] Eventually, however, the unions consolidated into the Federation of Combined Workmen[111] (its revolutionary name was the Committee of Public Safety), where a strike by one group of workers had the support of all the others. It was through this Federation of "almost all the recognised wage-paid employments," relates Hammond, that the workers were now able to obtain better pay and improved working conditions.[112]

103 Morris, *News from Nowhere*, 136.
104 Morris, *News from Nowhere*, 136.
105 Holtzman, "Anarchism and Utopia: William Morris's News from Nowhere," 599.
106 Morris, *News from Nowhere*, 136.
107 Morris, *News from Nowhere*, 136.
108 Morris, *News from Nowhere*, 136.
109 Morris, *News from Nowhere*, 140.
110 Morris, *News from Nowhere*, 140.
111 Morris, *News from Nowhere*, 140.
112 Morris, *News from Nowhere*, 136.

At the end of the nineteenth century "the cry arose," old Hammond tells Guest, to compel the masters to shorten the work hours and the "masters had to yield."[113] Following a long struggle, Parliament passed a law "fixing a minimum price for labour ... supplemented by a law fixing the maximum price on the chief wares then considered necessary for a workman's life."[114] In response, the "master class" raised an uproar at the "approaching destruction of Commerce."[115] The government's attempt to avert this destruction was a socialist-inspired program "hostile to the masters," establishing government factories producing "necessary wares, and markets for their sale."[116] This state ownership of critical industries led to a period of "State Socialism," which old Hammond reports "did not work smoothly."[117] There was "growing confusion," and "great suffering" among the workers and, "as a consequence, great discontent."[118] To the "privileged classes," however, declares Hammond, "it seemed as if the end of the world were come."[119] The newspapers, reports Hammond, "almost entirely in the hands of the masters—clamoured to the Government for repressive measures."[120]

On a Sunday, on what old Hammond calls a "comparatively trifling occasion," the workers held the first in a series of meetings in Trafalgar Square. During this meeting the police attacked the assembled masses, resulting in the deaths of five workers and injuries to many others. One hundred workers went to jail. The following day the workers convened a second meeting at the same location. The crowd at this meeting was too large for the police to control, however, and ten policemen and three or four workers died in the ensuing violence.[121]

In spite of the workers' progress a hunger crisis developed. In response the workers' Committee, "on the one hand afraid of general unorganized

113 Morris, *News from Nowhere*, 137.
114 Morris, *News from Nowhere*, 137.
115 Morris, *News from Nowhere*, 138.
116 Morris, *News from Nowhere*, 138.
117 Morris, *News from Nowhere*, 135–136.
118 Morris, *News from Nowhere*, 136.
119 Morris, *News from Nowhere*, 138.
120 Morris, *News from Nowhere*, 140.
121 Morris, *News from Nowhere*, 140.

pillage, and on the other emboldened by the wavering conduct of the authorities," facilitated the workers' looting "two or three big provision stores in the centre of the town."[122] These actions were carried out peacefully, "the police assisting in keeping order at the sack of the stores, as they would have done at a big fire."[123]

Figure 10: "An election meeting in Trafalgar Square, London, 1868."

The next morning, however, the government proclaimed a state of siege in London.[124] During the ensuing days the workers' meetings continued and tensions with the government mounted resulting in a confrontation between the workers and the military.[125] On the Sunday appointed for their next (and final) meeting, large crowds of mostly unarmed workers

122 Morris, *News from Nowhere*, 141.
123 Morris, *News from Nowhere*, 141.
124 Morris, *News from Nowhere*, 142.
125 Morris, *News from Nowhere*, 78, 143.

assembled in Trafalgar Square. As the peaceful meeting commenced there was no official response from the government.[126] But presently a column of soldiers emerged from the north-west and another from the south, "pushing the crowd into a denser and denser mass."[127] They were in a trap, old Hammond declares, and "it seemed as if the end of the world had come, and to-day seemed strangely different from yesterday."[128] Presently an officer on horseback read an order for the crowd to disperse, and a warning that the soldiers were authorized to fire on the crowd.[129] The crowd responded with a defiant roar. Machine guns were wheeled out in front of the ranks. At the officer's order, "deep lanes were mowed amidst the thick crowd; the dead and dying covered the ground, and the shrieks and wails and cries of horror filled all the air."[130] "It was as if the earth had opened," reports an eyewitness Hammond quotes, "and hell had come up bodily amidst us." The few armed workers fired back at the soldiers killing one or two. But instead of returning the fire the soldiers now maintained silence and the crowd of workers began to disperse. "I went, not feeling the ground under me," confides the same witness, "what with rage and terror and despair."[131]

The newspapers at first supported the government and the business owners—"the masters of labour ... the natural rulers of the people"[132]—in their efforts to dismantle the workers' movement. But after the army's murder of largely unarmed workers one "so-called 'liberal'" paper expressed support for the workers while the editor of a capitalist paper—"one of the most violent opponents of democracy"—asked "what a society was worth which had to be defended by the massacre of unarmed citizens."[133] Caught in the middle, the government became increasingly dysfunctional and, "after some vacillation," ended the state of siege. Since the army could no longer attack the unarmed workers, a portion of the upper and middle

126 Morris, *News from Nowhere*, 143.
127 Morris, *News from Nowhere*, 143.
128 Morris, *News from Nowhere*, 143.
129 Morris, *News from Nowhere*, 144.
130 Morris, *News from Nowhere*, 144.
131 Morris, *News from Nowhere*, 144.
132 Morris, *News from Nowhere*, 152.
133 Morris, *News from Nowhere*, 145–146.

classes organized their own militia, as they were "determined to set on foot a counterrevolution."[134] Bands of young men calling themselves "Friends of Order" armed, drilled, and began "on any opportunity or pretence to skirmish with the people in the streets."[135] During this time, according to Hammond's account, "A sort of irregular war was carried on with varied success all over the country."[136] Weighing its own interests, the government eventually sided with the moneyed resistance. They supplied what soldiers they could from the regular army (primarily officers) and made a "desperate effort to overwhelm 'the rebels,'"[137] though the majority of the regular soldiers fought on the side of the workers.[138] All ideas of peace "on a basis of compromise had disappeared on either side," concedes old Hammond, and the workers recognized that the outcome of their efforts "must be either absolute slavery for all but the privileged, or a system of life founded on equality and Communism."[139]

To bring the unrest to a head, the revolutionary Committee of Public Safety called for a general boycott of commerce. The railroads ceased running; meat, fish, and vegetables were left to rot in the marketplace.[140] The strike lasted for three days. As a sign of its weakened resolve, Hammond notes that the government sent a "duly accredited envoy"[141] to meet with the leaders of the Committee. The result of these negotiations was the official recognition of the Committee of Public Safety—though under a new name: The Board of Conciliation—as well as amnesty for the protesting workers.[142] "Carrying this new name, it became the leader of the people in the civil war which soon followed."[143]

134 Morris, *News from Nowhere*, 154.
135 Morris, *News from Nowhere*, 154.
136 Morris, *News from Nowhere*, 155.
137 Morris, *News from Nowhere*, 155.
138 Morris, *News from Nowhere*, 156.
139 Morris, *News from Nowhere*, 155.
140 Morris, *News from Nowhere*, 148–149.
141 Morris, *News from Nowhere*, 153.
142 Morris, *News from Nowhere*, 154.
143 Morris, *News from Nowhere*, 154.

Though the massacre at Trafalgar Square launched the civil war, "like all such events," old Hammond observes, "it gathered head slowly, and people scarcely knew what a crisis they were acting in."[144] And although the workers' movement had the entrenched forces of the upper and middle classes, government, and military officers opposing it, the renamed Board of Conciliation, "began to be a force in the country" and, says Hammond, "really represented the producing classes."[145] As the Board developed strength it became the "mouthpiece and intermediary of the whole of the working classes."[146] The business owners, realizing they had lost control over the workers, petitioned the government to respond again with violence. They feared that unless they could regain control they would have to accede to the demands of their workers for still "higher and higher wages" and for "shorter and shorter" work days.[147] In reaction to the successful demands of the workers and the growing government concessions, old Hammond reports, the upper and middle classes were determined to resist, "for the Communism which now loomed ahead seemed quite unendurable."[148]

Contrasting Morris's portrayal of a civil war with the peaceful transformation in *Looking Backward*, Goeghegan affirms Morris "obliterates the sense of continuity between capitalism and socialism which was a feature of Bellamy's work."[149] During the two-year civil war, Hammond tells Guest, the conditions of the poor had been "bettering, in spite of the struggle,"[150] and now they saw how little value there was in the "old world of slavery and inequality."[151] For the workers it was a time of hope as they felt they were equal to the task of rebuilding the world. In the end, Hammond declares, the opposing forces "destroyed commercialism!"[152]

144 Morris, *News from Nowhere*, 145.
145 Morris, *News from Nowhere*, 147.
146 Morris, *News from Nowhere*, 147.
147 Morris, *News from Nowhere*, 147.
148 Morris, *News from Nowhere*, 154–155.
149 Geoghegan, "The Utopian Past," 81.
150 Morris, *News from Nowhere*, 157.
151 Morris, *News from Nowhere*, 157.
152 Morris, *News from Nowhere*, 158.

When peace finally came the workers' progress was slow as "the once-poor had such a feeble conception of the real pleasure of life"[153] that they failed to demand their full measure of freedom and equality. As Morris laments in another work, "civilization [had] reduced the workman to such a skinny and pitiful existence, that he scarcely [knew] how to frame a desire for any life much better than that which he now endures perforce."[154]

Following the civil war, a "terrible period" of transition from "commercial slavery to freedom"[155] was necessary as the people realized that a classless society would no longer need many of the products they used to make: "slave-wares for the poor and mere wealth-wasting wares for the rich."[156] Frank and Fritzie Manuel report that Morris "analyzed the old economic system as loaded with fake, artificial 'necessaries' created by the capitalist market in a never-ending series."[157] Rob Breton estimates this excess production of "quantifiable waste" at about 75 percent.[158]

It was during this time at the close of the "machine period" and the dawn of the new "handicraft period" that people reevaluated the purpose of machines and their role in society.[159] While people widely believed before the civil war that time-saving machinery would increasingly perform the "ordinary daily work of the world,"[160] through the "half-century that followed the Great Change," explains character Henry Morsom ("an old, but very bright and intelligent man"), "machine after machine was quietly dropped under the excuse that the machines could not produce works of

153 Morris, *News from Nowhere*, 157.

154 William Morris, "How I Became a Socialist," in *Political Writings of William Morris*, ed. A. L. Morton (New York: International Publishers, 1973), 245. Analogously, respecting emancipated African American slaves, Sargent notes, "It is possible to so oppress people that the most they can imagine is improvement within the bounds of their oppression." Sargent, "African Americans and Utopia," 63.

155 Morris, *News from Nowhere*, 133.

156 Morris, *News from Nowhere*, 160.

157 Manuel and Manuel, *Utopian Thought in the Western World*, 768.

158 Rob Breton, "WorkPerfect: William Morris and the Gospel of Work," *Utopian Studies* 13, no. 1 (2002): 43–56, 54.

159 Morris, *News from Nowhere*, 199–200.

160 Morris, *News from Nowhere*, 200.

art."[161] During this period as well, Morsom continues, the old men "managed to teach the younger ones gradually a little artisanship, such as the use of the saw and the plane, the work of the smithy, and so forth."[162] These efforts, during the "exodus of the people from the town to the country," helped usher the rebirth of craftsmanship and manual labor as honorable occupations (blacksmiths, cobblers, stone masons, tailors) as many skills, including bread baking and carpentry, had all but disappeared.[163] Economic inequality was nearly at an end and a time lay in the future, Hammond proclaims, "when mastery has changed into fellowship" and a "new day" was shortly to emerge.[164] In what old Hammond calls its "second birth," the world displayed a peaceful and cooperative guise where, as Morris explains, the "true incentive to happy and useful labour is ... pleasure in the work itself."[165] This work involves only skills that produce personally satisfying products—those well designed to be functional and, when possible, beautiful—or necessary services pleasantly administered, with both products and services directed toward some obviously useful end.[166] As Morris's character Ellen observes, it is work "which is pleasure and pleasure which is work."[167]

In concluding his talk with William Guest, old Hammond recounts the success of their post-revolutionary society, noting that "We have been living for a hundred and fifty years ... in our present manner, and a tradition or habit of life has been growing on us; and that habit has become a habit of acting on the whole for the best."[168] "Thus," says Ernst Bloch, "the earth is freed of factories and urban monsters, capitalism and industrialism are

161 Morris, *News from Nowhere*, 201.
162 Morris, *News from Nowhere*, 199.
163 Morris, *News from Nowhere*, 198–199.
164 Morris, *News from Nowhere*, 228.
165 Morris, *News from Nowhere*, 158; William Morris, "Bellamy's Looking Backward," *Commonweal* 5, no. 180 (June 22, 1889).
166 Morris, "Useful Work Versus Useless Toil," 86–108.
167 Morris, *News from Nowhere*, 222.
168 Morris, *News from Nowhere*, 111.

abolished, complete human beings and old craftsmanship flourish again in place of mechanical horrors."[169]

Utopia: A Romance for Today

> "Who is more eager to change things than the man who is most discontented with his present position? Who is more reckless about creating disorder than the man who knows he has nothing to lose and thinks he may have something to gain?"[170]
>
> —Thomas More, *Utopia* (1516)

In *Utopia and Revolution*, Melvin Lasky distinguishes the utopia "from above" and the utopia "from below."[171] Frank Rosewater's *Utopia: A Romance for Today* (1897) is a utopia from below as the workers "take over the philosophical task of determining the perfect arrangements of men in society."[172] Of the two contrasting Lukkan societies the novel describes (see Chapter 2), Tsor, the eastern capital, was a "sickly patchwork of socialism, communism, individualism, democracy and despotism,"[173] as well as a capitalist plutocracy that the working poor ultimately destroy in a bloody uprising. Tsor's aristocracy, explains narrator Ross Allison, is "democratic and is not hereditary;"[174] it is an aristocracy "of cash and not of blood."[175] Wealthy citizens purchase power through their contributions to the operations of the state, a form of censitary suffrage.[176] "Instead

169 Ernst Bloch, *The Principle of Hope*, trans. Neville Plaice, Stephen Plaice and Paul Knight, vol. 1 (Cambridge: The MIT Press, 1986), 614.

170 More, *Utopia*, trans. Adams, bk. 1, 33.

171 Lasky, *Utopia and Revolution*, 351.

172 Lasky, *Utopia and Revolution*, 351.

173 Rosewater, *Utopia: A Romance of Today*, 197.

174 Rosewater, *Utopia: A Romance of Today*, 45–46.

175 Rosewater, *Utopia: A Romance of Today*, 106.

176 Under censitary suffrage, says Piketty, "the number of votes an elector had depended on how much tax he paid and how much property and income he had." Piketty, *A Brief History of Equality*, 103–105.

of tax evasion people overtax themselves voluntarily in order to enter a higher social circle."[177]

The capitalist system requires workers to accept any pay offered them, as the alternative is prison. Tsor's penal system and the brutal conditions of its prison are the catalysts for a prisoner revolt culminating in an insurrection. The Kar Tuki, the national prison, is a "combination of prison and poor house."[178] Since poverty is a crime,[179] the prison serves as "the final refuge of the unemployed."[180] The Kar Tuki is "an awful place, but it was a safety valve to Lukka and for this reason was regarded largely as a grand institution."[181] Within its walls are "mingled the unfortunate with the most hardened wretches."[182] The prisoners' labor is "farmed out" to contractors at "pitifully low prices"[183] permitting the contractors to undercut their competitors, imposing downward pressure on the workers' wages.

The prison's policy is that "however full were its dark cells there was always room for more,"[184] and so each day this "colossal theatre of misery"[185] attracts new inmates. As a result of its burgeoning population, observes the narrator, the prison now contains a "whole city within itself."[186] In accordance with Tsor's system of criminal justice, crimes punishable by imprisonment include business failures and bankruptcies. "Debt was the first step toward the violation of commercial integrity … and inability to pay a debt was a crime."[187] As Tsor's income and wealth inequality worsened, cracks appeared in its economy; business failures increased, and the "wheels of enterprise were clogged."[188] Tsor was "tottering on the verge of

177 Rosewater, *Utopia: A Romance of Today*, 45–46.
178 Rosewater, *Utopia: A Romance of Today*, 57.
179 Rosewater, *Utopia: A Romance of Today*, 161.
180 Rosewater, *Utopia: A Romance of Today*, 58.
181 Rosewater, *Utopia: A Romance of Today*, 57.
182 Rosewater, *Utopia: A Romance of Today*, 161.
183 Rosewater, *Utopia: A Romance of Today*, 58.
184 Rosewater, *Utopia: A Romance of Today*, 161.
185 Rosewater, *Utopia: A Romance of Today*, 161.
186 Rosewater, *Utopia: A Romance of Today*, 162.
187 Rosewater, *Utopia: A Romance of Today*, 58.
188 Rosewater, *Utopia: A Romance of Today*, 117.

ruin. Not a day but betrayed new evidence of impending revolution."[189] Society had become "too complicated and unwieldy through its division of rank between rich and poor."[190] While the wealthy were idolized, the poor "were trampled under the heels of the State."[191] To Rosewater, says Pfaelzer, "the abuses brought about by industrial capitalism would inevitably lead to violence."[192]

Tsor's crippling emphasis on paying one's debts meant assigning to a next of kin the balance for a prisoner unable to complete his term.[193] Two brothers, Zuzo and Ortro, who are central to the impending prison revolt and eventual insurrection, were serving out their father Orm's ten-year sentence for bankruptcy.[194] Zuzo communicates a scheme for an uprising to his fellow prisoners expressing their common predicament and his intended solution. Though they are all prisoners now, being held in the Kar Tuki, formerly, Zuzo explains, they were prisoners of the capitalist system in which they struggled to survive. Their imprisonment by that economic system resulted from the scarcity of jobs the wealthy capitalists afford them, a system the capitalists used to ensure a bottomless pool of unemployed workers competing for the few low-wage jobs available.[195] Effectively, as Zuzo relates to the other prisoners, their ability to work was only achievable by the capitalists loaning them the facilities and tools they needed to perform their work and for which the capitalists charged a levy they seized directly from their wages (described in Chapter 2).[196] In this system, notes Zuzo, the capitalist masters held their workers captive. The workers can never earn enough to escape their economic predicament because the capitalists control the supply of work and the flow of money.[197]

189 Rosewater, *Utopia: A Romance of Today*, 117.
190 Rosewater, *Utopia: A Romance of Today*, 122–123.
191 Rosewater, *Utopia: A Romance of Today*, 161.
192 Pfaelzer, *The Utopian Novel in America*, 118.
193 Rosewater, *Utopia: A Romance of Today*, 58.
194 Rosewater, *Utopia: A Romance of Today*, 83.
195 Ending unemployment, the theme of Rosewater's *The Making of a Millennium*, is described in Chapter 4.
196 Rosewater, *Utopia: A Romance of Today*, 178.
197 Rosewater, *Utopia: A Romance of Today*, 179.

Zuzo's entreaties to the other prisoners and his description of the conditions resulting in their imprisonment constitute the stimulus for their organizing a rebellion. During the following week "all sorts of schemes were concocted" and arrangements made to inform the prisoners in the other divisions of their plans.[198] As Zuzo's account of their plight spread throughout the cells, a plot emerged by which the prisoners could escape as a body and ultimately capture the city of Tsor.[199] As a signal, they devised a plan involving a feigned disturbance in the cell of the two brothers. This commotion attracted the guards, whom the prisoners attack and overcome, setting in motion a widespread disturbance. According to plan, this ruse and the subsequent attack on the guards were conducted simultaneously on each floor of the prison "to prevent the guards from reinforcing each other."[200] At the climax of the revolt the inmates secured possession of the prison—but were not yet free. Preliminary to releasing the rest of the 10,000 prisoners, a contingent of freed inmates managed to batter their way into the prison supervisor's office and there obtain the keys with which to unlock the manacles restraining the prisoners in pairs.[201]

Following their escape, the leaders of the prisoners' thirty-six divisions select Zuzo as commander-in-chief of the revolution. Their strategy was to apprehend the heads of the city's "civil, police and military authority ... under cover of darkness."[202] "Even the heads of the general government were proscribed and a large special squad was delegated to make the seizure."[203] A body of men left the prison shortly before midnight and captured a store of supplies, including "weapons of warfare."[204] This "little army of Tsoran ex-prisoners" then dispersed through the city seeking the capture of eight hundred targeted officials.[205] "Thus a great revolution was on the way while Tsor was peacefully sleeping."[206]

198 Rosewater, *Utopia: A Romance of Today*, 179.
199 Rosewater, *Utopia: A Romance of Today*, 180.
200 Rosewater, *Utopia: A Romance of Today*, 182.
201 Rosewater, *Utopia: A Romance of Today*, 194.
202 Rosewater, *Utopia: A Romance of Today*, 195.
203 Rosewater, *Utopia: A Romance of Today*, 195.
204 Rosewater, *Utopia: A Romance of Today*, 196.
205 Rosewater, *Utopia: A Romance of Today*, 196.
206 Rosewater, *Utopia: A Romance of Today*, 196.

Before the dawn of the following day squads of escaped prisoners were leading the captive officials into the "mouth of the now almost empty prison."[207] In the streets "great throngs were exultant over the success of the night's work."[208] In his rallying speech to the ex-prisoners Ortro, while carefully avoiding calls to "violence in any form,"[209] implores the crowd: "You must have your own property or you shall remain slaves today, tomorrow and through all eternity."[210] Furthermore, he exclaims: "Let no man in all Tsor hereafter prey upon the labor of others, and let no man depend upon others for the privilege to work!"[211] Ortro assures the listeners that the "dread word 'poverty' will in the days to come live but a memory!"[212] Under the new régime, no rich man was to "enter this little 'kingdom of heaven;' no poor man would be found there."[213] But when brother Zuzo's turn came to speak his "deep voice seemed charged with an almost unearthly intensity." Declaring that he had just found his wife murdered, "butchered by a hireling" paid for by "one of Tsor's proud nobles," he proclaims: "Justice for justice; aye, and blood for blood!"[214] "Down with the lords!" "We will be avenged!" "We've all been wronged!"[215] Abandoning his earlier revolutionary plans to announce the "industrial liberty of a true self-government"[216] (declared in the spirit of Arendt's prescription, noted earlier, that revolutions "are more than successful insurrections"[217]), Zuzo now urges the mob:

> in the name of all the persecutions; in the name of the long hours we have been kept degraded on our knees; in the name of the unmerciful lash; in the name of the soulless rack of killing anxiety on which our lives have been stretched; in the name of

207 Rosewater, *Utopia: A Romance of Today*, 209.
208 Rosewater, *Utopia: A Romance of Today*, 209.
209 Rosewater, *Utopia: A Romance of Today*, 210.
210 Rosewater, *Utopia: A Romance of Today*, 212.
211 Rosewater, *Utopia: A Romance of Today*, 212
212 Rosewater, *Utopia: A Romance of Today*, 214.
213 Rosewater, *Utopia: A Romance of Today*, 209.
214 Rosewater, *Utopia: A Romance of Today*, 214.
215 Rosewater, *Utopia: A Romance of Today*, 215.
216 Rosewater, *Utopia: A Romance of Today*, 195.
217 Arendt, *On Revolution*, 24.

> the foul air and cruel floggings of the Kar Tuki; O, friends, in the name of murder unavenged, we'll dip our hand this day in tyrant blood.[218]

With these words the peaceful plans of the previous night were swept aside.[219] Zuzo's singular goal of revenge now blinded his quest for freedom. The first victim of the enraged mob was the prison itself, the Kar Tuki. "Huge casks of pitch were rolled in front of the prison, and … the walls were rapidly being coated with the black liquid. … Torches were then applied and fierce flames began to shoot upward."[220] As the fire progressed the glass in the prison's towers began to melt, "running down along the walls in ruby streams."[221] News of the insurgence spread rapidly and soon a hundred thousand persons converged on the center of the city.[222]

The royal temple—half-pyramid, half-tower, the 300-year-old Kar Yuk—stood at the center of the city, and Zuzo realized it too must be destroyed. The building was the "heart of this democratic despotism of wealth … with its upper halls all filled with records upon whose entries rested all the titles to property in Tsor."[223] The fate that befell the national prison soon overtook the temple building as well. As night fell and the fires and melting glass diffused, a "crazed and rampant mob occupied the foreground and their deeds of lawlessness added to the horrors of the scene."[224] Vandalism quickly spread to the homes of the "stately lords." As in *Caesar's Column*, "Bands of lawless men and furious women ransacked and pillaged houses, killing and outraging with a brutality worse than that of beasts … and madness became truly epidemic."[225] "The terrible reign of inhumanity that darkened the city for many days thereafter," observes the narrator, "was but the extension of the rule that had preceded. It was the out-growth of a society cemented only by force and forced beliefs."[226]

218 Rosewater, *Utopia: A Romance of Today*, 216–217.
219 Rosewater, *Utopia: A Romance of Today*, 221.
220 Rosewater, *Utopia: A Romance of Today*, 217–218.
221 Rosewater, *Utopia: A Romance of Today*, 224.
222 Rosewater, *Utopia: A Romance of Today*, 225–226.
223 Rosewater, *Utopia: A Romance of Today*, 226.
224 Rosewater, *Utopia: A Romance of Today*, 229.
225 Rosewater, *Utopia: A Romance of Today*, 232.
226 Rosewater, *Utopia: A Romance of Today*, 234.

Other Brief Examples

> "The imaginative extension of political ideas and their embellishment by myth and metaphor induce an ideological atmosphere in which men ... come to think of their activities in terms of the life-and-death purposes of missions and destiny."[227]
>
> —Melvin J. Lasky, *Utopia and Revolution* (1976)

Kurt Vonnegut's statement in *Player Piano* that "The business of one set of values being replaced by force by another set of values has come up often enough in history"[228] extends to utopias as well. Edward House's 1912 *Philip Dru: Administrator* portrays an attempted coup and its successful quashing by Philip Dru. The most powerful US senator (Selwyn) conspires with the richest American businessman (John Thor) "the high priest of finance"[229] to install a new puppet president (Rockland) while gaining control over both the Senate and the Supreme Court.[230] When the conspiracy is discovered, Philip Dru, an egalitarian social reformer with a military background, leads a force of local militias against the standing army of the US in a civil war to prevent the oligarchic forces of the federal government from undermining democracy.

As the "Great Central Committee" meets in W. E. B. Du Bois's *Dark Princess* (1928) its "High Command" is split on an international strategy for the coming twenty-five years, after which—in 1952—"the Dark World goes free." One faction, says the Princess, "of whom I am one, believe in the path of Peace and Reason, of cooperation among the best and poorest, of ... [the] world-wide abolition of the color line, and of poverty and war." The opposing revolutionary faction sees the path of "Blood and Storm." They believe "only in Force," confirms the Princess. "Nothing but bloody defeat in a world-wide war of dark against white will, in their opinion, ever beat sense and decency into Europe and America and Australia."[231]

227 Lasky, *Utopia and Revolution*, 520.
228 Vonnegut, *Player Piano*, 290.
229 House. *Philip Dru Administrator*, 68–69.
230 House. *Philip Dru Administrator*, 42.
231 Du Bois, *Dark Princess*, 213.

Woman on the Edge of Time (Piercy, 1976), Tom Moylan remarks, "is a tendentious work, uncompromising in its political assessment and alternatives, its angry tone, its direct assault on a very undisguised phallocratic/bureaucratic capitalism, and its firm commitment to armed struggle."[232] The Mattapoisett community, 150 years in the future,[233] is the product of a "thirty-year war," explains Luciente a spokesperson, "that culminated in a revolution that set up what we have."[234] "It was part of women's long revolution," Luciente emphasizes, "When we were breaking all the old hierarchies."[235] The revolution's aim was "no more power for anyone" including the power to give birth—which the "brooders" now fulfill—because "as long as we were biologically enchained, we'd never be equal."[236]

232 Moylan, *Demand the Impossible*, 145.
233 Piercy, *Woman on the Edge of Time*, 150.
234 Piercy, *Woman on the Edge of Time*, 214.
235 Piercy, *Woman on the Edge of Time*, 110.
236 Piercy, *Woman on the Edge of Time*, 110. Reproduction is accomplished in "brooders" where "our genetic material is stored. Where the embryos grow" (106).

CHAPTER 6

Economic Leveling

"For instead of anarchy, idleness, poverty, and meanness, the natural consequences, as I narrowly thought, of a ridiculous leveling scheme, I saw nothing but order, industry, wealth, and magnificence."[1]

—Thomas Spence, "A Further Account of Spensonia" (1794)

"'Why,' asked one professor," in Samuel Butler's *Erewhon* (1872), "'should a man want to be better than his neighbors? Let him be thankful if he is no worse.'"[2] Barbara Goodwin explains that inequality is one of the social evils "which utopian writers condemn: their attempts to eradicate it lead them to propose dramatic innovations in the economic and social spheres."[3] For More, Campanella, Bellamy, and others, the dramatic innovation was leveling. For critics of leveling, however, the proposed changes produce an environment inimical to our natural inclinations for competition and hierarchical ordering. "The levellers," cautioned Edmund Burke (1729–1797)—a critic of economic equality—"only change and pervert the natural order of things."[4] Responding to Burke, however, Thomas Paine replies, "the only system to which the word levelling is truly applicable, is the hereditary monarchical system. It is a system of mental levelling. It indiscriminately admits every species of character to the same authority."[5]

1 Thomas Spence, "A Further Account of Spensonia," in *Pig's Meat: Selected Writings of Thomas Spence, Radical and Pioneer Land Reformer* (Nottingham: Spokesman, 1982), 81.

2 Butler, *Erewhon*, 113.

3 Goodwin, "Economic and Social Innovation in Utopia," 69.

4 Burke, *Reflections on the Revolution in France*, 49.

5 Paine, *Rights of Man*, 114.

Historically, the term *levellers* is associated with Gerrard Winstanley's (1609–1676) Diggers movement, which he called the "True Levellers." Winstanley proposed making the earth, once again, "a common treasury for all, both rich and poor."[6] Winstanley sets out the spirit of his utopia in *The Law of Freedom* (1652). "There shall be store-houses in all places ... to which all the fruits of the earth, and other works made by tradesmen, shall be brought, and from thence delivered out again to ... everyone as they want for their use."[7]

Sociologist Georg Simmel in *The Philosophy of Money* (1900) warns, however, that "the tragic consequence of any leveling process inescapably takes effect where the higher level is pulled down to a greater extent than the lower level can be raised."[8] Kenneth Guthrie's 1919 *A Romance of Two Centuries* (as noted in Chapter 2) recommends "leveling up" as preferable to "leveling down."[9] In this chapter I sketch leveling measures selected utopians designed to eliminate economic inequality.

Thomas More's *Utopia*

> "We yet looked forward to a time when society will no longer be divided into the idle and the industrious; when the rule that they who do not work shall not eat, will be applied not to paupers only, but impartially to all."[10]
>
> —John Stuart Mill, *Autobiography* (1873)

Utopia (1516), says William Grace, "was written by a prudent man and a prince's councilor as a means, not to escape from reality, but to throw the clear light of reality on the perplexing problems and crying social

6 Gerrard Winstanley, *The True Levellers' Standard Advanced* (1649) (N.p., 2014), 13.

7 Gerrard Winstanley, *The Law of Freedom in a Platform; or True Magistracy Restored* (Oxford: Benediction Classics, 2009), 87.

8 Simmel, *The Philosophy of Money*, 392.

9 Guthrie, *A Romance of Two Centuries*, 59.

10 John Stuart Mill, *Autobiography* (New York: Penguin Books, 1989), 175.

abuses."[11] *Utopia*, explains J. H. Hexter, bears the mark of More's ability "to grasp the interconnections of social phenomena, and shrewdness in devising remedies that attack the roots of social ills."[12] Among the practical economic problems he addressed in *Utopia*, observes Nell Eurich, are poverty and the apportionment of wealth.[13]

In *The English Utopia*, A. L. Morton describes the world in which More grew up as "a world of despair and hope, of conflict and contrast, of increasing wealth and increasing poverty."[14] It was a world that "lavishes rich rewards on so-called gentry, goldsmiths and the rest of the crew, who don't work at all or are mere parasites, purveyors of empty pleasures."[15] This outcome is what Hertzler terms "the alignment of men into hereditary, useless, protected groups."[16] At the same time, as More's narrator Raphael Hythloday reflects, there is no provision for the welfare of "farmers and colliers, labourers, carters and carpenters, without whom the commonwealth would simply cease to exist."[17] "What is worse," Hythloday continues, "the rich constantly try to grind out of the poor part of their daily wages, not only by private swindling but by public laws ... a conspiracy of the rich, who are advancing their own interest under the name and title of the commonwealth."[18] More's achievement, says Hexter, "lay not

11 William J. Grace, "The Conception of Society in More's 'Utopia,'" *Thought* 22, no. 2 (1947): 283–296, 296.

12 J. H. Hexter, *More's Utopia: The Biography of an Idea* (New York: Harper Torchbooks, 1965), 95.

13 Nell Eurich, *Science in Utopia: A Mighty Design* (Cambridge, MA: Harvard Univ. Press, 1967), 77–78.

14 Morton, *The English Utopia*, 49.

15 More, *Utopia*, trans. Adams, bk. 2, 104.

16 Hertzler, *The History of Utopian Thought*, 133.

17 More, *Utopia*, trans. Adams, bk. 2, 104–105.

18 More, *Utopia*, trans. Adams, bk. 2, 104–105. "Acknowledging humans' tendency toward greed is critical to a vision for what is possible," says Bapat. "A sanitized picture of utopia that erases the darker sides of human drive would be one in which we are never striving to be better." Sheila Bapat, "Imperfectly: A Feminist Utopian Economy that Embraces and Addresses Human Flaws," in *The Feminist Utopia Project*, ed. Alexandra Brodsky and Rachel Kauder Nalebuff (New York: Feminist Press, 2015), 188.

in discovering these evils in detail but in dealing with them as a related whole."[19]

Utopia imposes leveling measures across interconnected dimensions both economic and social. The primary leveling devices are the common ownership of property and the equal amount and dignity of work (cited in Chapters 3 and 4). In *Utopia* Hythloday declares, "wherever you have private property, and money is the measure of all things, it is hardly ever possible for a commonwealth to be just or prosperous."[20] Money, according to Keynes, is a "subtle device for linking the present to the future."[21] Accordingly, in More's moneyless Utopia the future is of no concern—it is simply an extension of the present. This is a feature it shares with certain later utopias including Bellamy's *Looking Backward* and Morris's *News from Nowhere*—what Sargent calls "the utopian rejection of time."[22]

In More's Utopia the common ownership of property, says Dominic Baker-Smith, "is not just one feature of the Utopian polity, it is the transforming principle which makes all the others possible."[23] More's Utopian economy "does not justify itself as modern economies do," explains Hexter, "by claiming to give men the fullest measure of the things they want."[24] At the core of More's *Utopia* is his moral insight that what appear to be shortages or excesses are really moral problems of distribution. After a "barren year of failed harvests," that cost thousands of lives, the barns of the rich, Hythloday observes, will still be filled with enough grain to have "kept all those who died of starvation and disease from even realizing that a shortage ever existed."[25] More foresees the importance of equitable allotment not

19 Hexter, *More's Utopia*, 66.

20 More, *Utopia*, trans. Adams, bk. 1, 37. Although the citizens do not own gold or silver as money, the government maintains a stockpile of riches to use in war and to lend to other nations at interest (51).

21 Keynes, *The General Theory of Employment, Interest, and Money*, 297–294.

22 Sargent, "Authority and Utopia: Utopianism in Political Thought," 583. Timeless utopias are freed from the concern for future generations expressed by utopias such as Kim Stanley Robinson's *The Ministry for the Future*.

23 Dominic Baker-Smith, *More's Utopia* (London: HarperCollins Academic, 1991), 178–179.

24 Hexter, *More's Utopia*, 70–71.

25 More, *Utopia*, trans. Adams, bk. 2, 105.

only for food but for other necessities and for work. Residents consume ample meals in each city's neighborhood dining halls. Everyone receives standardized uniforms—"unpretentious garments"—as well as public housing (noted in Chapter 3).[26]

The division of labor in Utopia includes its allocation across the island's fifty-four identical cities ("If you know one of their cities you know them all."[27]) and the universal requirement of physical labor. "Above all," says Hexter, "idleness, the great emblem of pride in the society of More's time, a sure mark to elevate the aristocrat above the vulgar, is utterly destroyed by the common obligation of common daily toil."[28] Accordingly, More's scheme includes putting the "crowd of languid idlers" to "productive tasks"[29] in a useful trade as well as conscripted farming (noted in Chapter 4).[30] In Utopia, once the workload is equally distributed, the required workday is six hours for both women and men.[31] With a mandatory workday no one will sit idle, we learn, and "no one has to be exhausted with endless toil from early morning to late at night."[32] While More's structure calls for six hours of daily physical labor, exceptions are permitted for roughly 500 citizens in each city including ambassadors, governors, magistrates (syphogrants), scholars, and priests, whose tasks are seen as benefiting the wider community.[33] The most demeaning tasks, including slaughtering and cleaning animals, are assigned to their slaves.[34]

By making these adjustments More hopes to put an end to "the crass avarice of a few," with the rich "buying up anything and everything,"[35] resulting always in unemployment, poverty, and famine. This system, aiming to uphold the general welfare, allows each person "to live joyfully and

26 More, *Utopia*, trans. Adams, bk. 2, 53.
27 More, *Utopia*, trans. Adams, bk. 2, 44.
28 Hexter, *More's Utopia*, 80.
29 More, *Utopia*, trans. Adams, bk. 2, 51.
30 More, *Utopia*, trans. Adams, bk. 2, 43–44.
31 More, *Utopia*, trans. Adams, bk. 2, 49–50.
32 More, *Utopia*, trans. Adams, bk. 2, 49–50.
33 More, *Utopia*, trans. Adams, bk. 2, 44, 52.
34 More, *Utopia*, trans. Adams, bk. 2, 55.
35 More, *Utopia*, trans. Adams, bk. 1, 20, 38.

peacefully, free from all anxieties, and without worries about making a living." In the end, "where everything belongs to everybody," Hythloday observes, "no one need fear that, so long as the public warehouses are filled, anyone will ever lack for anything for his own use."[36]

Tommaso Campanella's *City of the Sun*

> "'Am I to believe,' I asked … 'that in Upsidonia the chief things that are desired are, as you say, high character and knowledge and poverty?' … 'Those are the best things in life. … Well, of course, poverty in itself isn't one of the best things; it is only a means to an end.'"[37]
>
> —Archibald Marshall, *Upsidonia* (1919)

The economic leveling accomplished in Tommaso Campanella's *City of the Sun* (1602) takes the form of a Spartan community Ernst Bloch describes as functioning "like clockwork in a military monarchic fashion."[38] "Men and women perform the same tasks, whether of a mental or a mechanical nature."[39] Among their forms of work, both sexes are "trained in all pursuits,"[40] though tasks that are "the least fatiguing" are assigned to women.[41] The citizens' common education begins at age 3, where children "learn their alphabet and language," which are inscribed on the city walls.[42] At the age of 10, explains Genoese, the sea captain narrator "they all study mathematics, medicine, and other sciences."[43] Citizens "are selected for their tasks in infancy according to the constellation that was

36 More, *Utopia*, trans. Adams, bk. 2, 103–104.
37 Archibald Marshall, *Upsidonia* (New York: Dodd, Mead and Company, 1919), 57–58.
38 Bloch, *The Principle of Hope*, 524.
39 Campanella, *The City of the Sun*, trans. Donno, 49.
40 Campanella, *The City of the Sun*, trans. Donno, 41.
41 Campanella, *The City of the Sun*, trans. Donno, 81.
42 Campanella, *The City of the Sun*, trans. Donno, 41.
43 Campanella, *The City of the Sun*, trans. Donno, 43.

visible at their birth,"[44] though all join in military service and "work in the fields and pastures"[45] (noted in Chapter 4). In the division of labor "no one is assigned to things that are destructive to his individuality but rather to things that preserve it."[46] In this way, explains the narrator, "each citizen, working according to the inclination of his nature, does his work happily and well because it is natural to him."[47]

Robert Owen

> "Even the narrowest and most selfish have learned that the happiness and continued prosperity of the individual lies in, and is indissolubly interwoven with, the happiness and prosperity of the whole."[48]
>
> —Marie Howland, *Papa's Own Girl* (1874)

Rather than confronting society's problems at a national level, Robert Owen (1771–1858) argues, "the large accumulated masses of poverty, vice, crime, misery, and pernicious habits, must be gradually separated, divided into manageable portions, and distributed over the country."[49] Owen's views on poverty, explains A. L. Morton, "were directly contrary to the orthodox thinking of his time and class. It was for them an article of faith that the masses were poor because they were idle, vicious, intemperate and ignorant."[50] Owen's theories on social improvement, writes Taylor, were "based on gradualism and co-operation rather than upheaval and conflict."[51] Accordingly, Owen's

44 Campanella, *The City of the Sun*, trans. Donno, 79.
45 Campanella, *The City of the Sun*, trans. Donno, 81.
46 Campanella, *The City of the Sun*, trans. Donno, 81.
47 Campanella, *The City of the Sun*, trans. Donno, 79.
48 Howland, *Papa's Own Girl*, 507.
49 Owen, *A New View of Society and Other Writings*, 174. In this his views are similar to Fourier and in contrast with Cabet. Taylor, *The Political Ideas of the Utopian Socialists*, 182.
50 Morton, *The Life and Ideas of Robert Owen*, 20–21.
51 Taylor, *The Political Ideas of the Utopian Socialists*, 83.

primary weapon for implementing what Geoghegan calls his "environmental determinism"[52] was a uniform system of education (described in Chapter 3).

Owen's vision of leveling society requires dispersing the population into townships (nuclei or home colonies) of roughly 2,000–2,500 people comprising workers and their families living and working together as a self-sufficient community. It is critical, Owen contends, that each township "should be devised to be self-educating, self-employing, self-supporting, and self-governing."[53] Accordingly, he advises, each township must encompass sufficient land for farming and manufacture.[54] Though each community operates autonomously, Owen says, the same six laws[55] will govern them all "in a like manner."[56] These laws, Owen claims, are "deduced from, and in unison with, the ascertained *laws of nature*." As such, they "are plain and simple, and will be readily understood by everyone made rational from birth."[57]

To facilitate these leveling measures, Owen explains, "a rational government is required to gradually supersede those governments which experience has proved to be most irrational and injurious in practice."[58] The result, he predicted, would be a "change of the most extensive magnitude ... accomplished without violence or confusion, or any very apparent opposition."[59] Geoghegan notes that Owen was "mesmerized" by his "simplistic theory" and "underestimated the resistance to social change generated by capitalism."[60] Owen, observes Ernst Bloch, "expected dukes, ministers and manufacturers to renounce capitalism out of sheer insight and love of mankind."[61] Marx and

52 Vincent Geoghegan, *Utopianism and Marxism* (London: Methuen, 1987), 16.
53 Owen, *The Revolution in the Mind and Practice of the Human Race*, 43.
54 Robert Owen, *The Book of the New Moral World* (New York: Augustus M. Kelley Publishers, 1970), fifth part, chap. 6, 58; Owen, *The Revolution in the Mind*, 118.
55 Owen, *The Book of the New Moral World,* third part, chap. 14, 77.
56 Owen, *The Revolution in the Mind*, 125.
57 Owen, *The Book of the New Moral World,* sixth part, chap. 6, 82 (italics in original).
58 Owen, *The Revolution in the Mind*, 138.
59 Owen, *A New View of Society and Other Writings*, 225.
60 Geoghegan, *Utopianism and Marxism*, 16–17.
61 Bloch, *The Principle of Hope*, 556.

Engels chided Owen for appealing "to the feelings and purses of the bourgeois" for support in fulfilling his scheme.[62]

Private property, Owen believes, is "a never-failing source of deception and fraud" and the cause of endless evils.[63] "The land became permanent individual private property," Owen continues, "through oppression and gross injustice. It has, however, through succeeding events, become the private possession of individuals."[64] Under his proposed social order, land will return, gradually and peacefully, to the public domain. Owen recommends the government purchase property from landowners and make it "the public property of each succeeding generation."[65] As his scheme unfolds, Owen foresees a progression of uniform communities arising and spreading throughout England, then Europe, and eventually worldwide.[66] In this way, Claeys confirms, "Owen envisioned a world government built upon a federal structure, with communities as the basic units of organization."[67] Owen's son Dale "marveled" that his father, "a self-made and self-taught man, ... should have [so] miscalculated the immediate value of his social methods."[68]

Edward Bellamy's Looking Backward and Equality

> "The annual expenses of a national government ... [were] so equally and exactly distributed among them that the annual cost to the 100-millionaire and the annual cost to the sucking child of the day-laborer was precisely the same—each paid $6. Nothing could be equaler than that, I reckon."[69]
>
> —Mark Twain, *A Connecticut Yankee in King Arthur's Court* (1889)

62 Karl Marx and Friedrich Engels, "The Communist Manifesto," in *A Handbook of Marxism* (New York: International Publishers Co., 1935), 57.

63 Owen, *The Book of the New Moral World*, sixth part, chap. 4, 41.

64 Owen, *The Revolution in the Mind*, 121.

65 Owen, *The Revolution in the Mind*, 121; see also 42.

66 Owen, *The Revolution in the Mind*, 120.

67 Claeys, *Citizens and Saints*, 99.

68 Robert Dale Owen, *Threading My Way* (London: Turner and Co., 1874; Forgotten Books, 2012), 166.

69 Twain, *A Connecticut Yankee in King Arthur's Court*, 153.

The last two decades of the nineteenth century, observes Louis Kern, "witnessed the birth pangs of a new social and economic order in America." This order, he writes, occasioned "the most sever maldistribution of wealth in American history,"[70] rivaled, of course, by our current age. It was John Dewey's assessment that "No one has carried through the idea that equality is obtainable only by complete equality of income more fully than Bellamy."[71] "Like Dewey," reports Gutek, "Bellamy believed that a gulf between men was an impediment to the complete self-realization of the individual. Such bifurcation could be checked only by complete and total economic equality."[72]

Dr. Leete tells Julian West in *Equality* (1897), "the industrial system of the world before the great Revolution was wholly based upon the compulsory servitude of the mass of mankind to the possessing class, enforced by the coercion of economic need."[73] In the early years of the twentieth-century, Dr. Leete continues, "the evolution was completed by the final consolidation of the entire capital of the nation," now organized as "one great business corporation."[74] Under the citizens' common ownership, businesses operate in support of the general welfare and everyone shares equally in the results. In Bellamy's utopia, advises Gib Prettyman, "citizens could be materially equal stockholders while working within a meritocratic, professionalized, and highly centralized system."[75]

The scope of Bellamy's general welfare embraces protecting "every citizen against hunger, cold, and nakedness, and provid[ing] for all his physical and mental needs."[76] Kenneth Roemer reports that Bellamy's utopia "popularized a concept of government that strongly influenced important

70 Kern, "Evangelical Environmentalism and the New Commonwealth," 42.

71 John Dewey, "A Great American Prophet," *Common Sense* 3 (April, 1934): 6–7, in *John Dewey: The Later Works: 1925–1953*, vol. 9: 1933–1934 (Carbondale: Southern Illinois University Press, 1989), 103.

72 Gutek, "An Analysis of Formal Education in Edward Bellamy's *Looking Backward*," 254.

73 Bellamy, *Equality*, 80.

74 Bellamy, *Looking Backward*, 65–66.

75 Prettyman, "Gilded Age Utopias of Incorporation," 28.

76 Bellamy, *Looking Backward*, 67.

American leaders and articulated a type of socialism that has had national and international influence."[77] In Bellamy's vision, industrial army participation is mandatory for a career of twenty-four years (for men—potentially fewer for women).[78] While the twenty-four years of work is binding, the choice of occupation is left to each citizen "in accordance with his natural aptitude"—limited by the state's needs.[79] The principle on which the industrial army rests, Dr. Leete explains, is that "a man's natural endowments ... determine what he can work at most profitably to the nation and most satisfactorily to himself."[80] The daily hours of labor, however, differ according to the "arduousness" of the given trade.[81] To attract adequate candidates for the most distasteful jobs, Dr. Leete confirms, it might be necessary to reduce the time commitment to ten minutes a day.[82] This is an expression of the leveling principle that "no man's work ought to be, on the whole, harder for him than any other man's for him."[83]

Upon completion of his schooling and a three-year boot camp (noted in Chapter 4), Dr. Leete explains, "the young man is allowed to elect a special avocation."[84] Excluded from the menu of productive endeavors, however, are attorney, banker, or soldier as well as creative pursuits of "original genius"—artists, dancers, musicians, poets, and sculptors. Bellamy's economic leveling thus leads to a predictable narrowing of opportunity.[85]

Service in the industrial army, while limited to twenty-four years, entails a significant qualification: "Effort alone is pertinent to the question of desert."[86] As a result, applying less than one's full energy is a cause for discipline. "The way it strikes people nowadays," explains Dr. Leete, "a man who can produce twice as much as another with the same effort, instead of

77 Roemer, "Contexts and Texts: The Influence of Looking Backward," 209.
78 Bellamy, *Looking Backward*, 70.
79 Bellamy, *Looking Backward*, 71.
80 Bellamy, *Looking Backward*, 71.
81 Bellamy, *Looking Backward*, 72.
82 Bellamy, *Looking Backward*, 72.
83 Bellamy, *Looking Backward*, 72.
84 Bellamy, *Looking Backward*, 73.
85 Endeavors of "original genius" may be pursued as hobbies. Bellamy, *Looking Backward*, 128–129.
86 Bellamy, *Looking Backward*, 88.

being rewarded for doing so, ought to be punished if he does not do so."[87] To speak of service in the industrial army being "compulsory," Dr. Leete declares, "would be a weak way to state its absolute inevitableness. Our entire social order is so wholly based upon and deducted from it that if it were conceivable that a man could escape it, he would be left no possible way to provide for his existence."[88]

Digression: The Machines of Equality in the Coming Race

Dr. Leete in *Looking Backward* speaks of the industrial army as a machine "so logical in its principles and direct and simple in its workings, that it all but runs itself."[89] In Bellamy's *Equality* (1897), Edith Leete, clarifying the role of women in the labor force declares: "Almost no heavy work is done directly now; machines do all," and (as noted in Chapter 3), "we only need to guide them."[90]

These principles were earlier applied by the "Vril-ya" in Edward Bulwer-Lytton's *The Coming Race* (1871) where ubiquitous machines are central to society's economic structure. Among this advanced subterranean people a "distinct and separate working class" has been "dispensed with altogether."[91] All labor is performed either by machines (robots, automata[92]) or by its children, both male and female.[93] The children's labor consists in guiding the machines that are "employed to an inconceivable extent ... within and without doors."[94] The children "whose strength was never overtasked ...

87 Bellamy, Looking Backward, 88.
88 Bellamy, *Looking Backward*, 69–70. Prison awaits those who refuse to work or to apply their best efforts. The sentence of "solitary imprisonment on bread and water" stands until the prisoner submits (107).
89 Bellamy, *Looking Backward*, 140.
90 Bellamy, *Equality*, 44.
91 Bulwer-Lytton, *The Coming Race*, 115.
92 The narrator describes these robots as "mechanical contrivances which, with these people, answer the ordinary purposes of domestic service." Bulwer-Lytton, *The Coming Race*, 15, 60.
93 Bulwer-Lytton, *The Coming Race*, 82.
94 Bulwer-Lytton, *The Coming Race*, 29.

loved their employment as sport and pastime."[95] During this period of child labor, the well-remunerated children receive wages that are set aside for their future benefit such that when they reach the age of marriage their savings will be sufficient "for an independent competence during life."[96] In this way, as the narrator explains, "no matter what the disparity of fortune in the parents," all the children receive an equal endowment setting them up for a comfortable life.[97] "This practice," declares the narrator, serves "to render the notion of social equality familiar and agreeable."[98]

Bellamy's Uneven Leveling

The leveling in *Looking Backward* breaks down on three important dimensions, (1) the inequality of women and men, (2) the hierarchical governance structure, and (3) the use of eugenics for those not fully qualified to serve in the industrial army. The unequal treatment of women is discussed in Chapter 3 (gender equality in the workplace). Bellamy's nation was organized as "a monopoly in the profits and economies of which all citizens shared.[99] The governance of the single conglomerate—"the sole employer, the final monopoly"[100]—is carried out in the industrial army by the most experienced industrial leaders, its officers. Since each branch of industry has a guild to represent it, the honorary (retired, male) members elect a general and the top ten generals elect the president from among their ranks.[101] The structure of Bellamy's government, observes Krishan Kumar, "breathes the spirit of Saint-Simon throughout."[102] Bellamy,

95 Bulwer-Lytton, *The Coming Race*, 115.
96 Bulwer-Lytton, *The Coming Race*, 82. The age of marriage is 16 for the "Gy-ei" (females) and 20 for the "Ana" (males), (29).
97 Bulwer-Lytton, *The Coming Race*, 82.
98 Bulwer-Lytton, *The Coming Race*, 82.
99 Bellamy, *Looking Backward*, 65–66.
100 Bellamy, *Looking Backward*, 65–66.
101 Bellamy, *Looking Backward*, 144–145.
102 Kumar, *Utopia and Anti-Utopia in Modern Times*, 156.

notes Prettyman, combines hierarchy and "managerial oversight" with "political and economic inclusiveness."[103]

The economic leveling in *Looking Backward* is effected in part by the use of eugenic policies to weed out those who cannot contribute a meaningful share to the industrial army (discussed in Chapter 4). This includes people who are "too deficient in mental or bodily strength to be fairly graded with the main body of workers."[104] These less fortunate citizens, Dr. Leete clarifies, are still "conceded the full right to live on the produce of [the fully able]."[105] Thus, observes Bellamy, "economic equality, without regard to differences of industrial ability, is necessitated by precisely the same logic which justifies political equality."[106]

Reactions Against Leveling—Bellamy's Detractors

> "'Looking Backward' has been the bane of this nation. It breeds a notion in the minds of thousands that somehow the government will be compelled by agitation to do for them what God, nature, and society demand they shall do for themselves."[107]
>
> —John W. Roberts, *Looking Within: The Misleading Tendencies of "Looking Backward" Made Manifest* (1893)

The Gilded Age, writes Justin Nordstrom, "witnessed an avalanche of utopian texts, most of which reflect the immensely popular *Looking Backward*."[108] More than one hundred "continuations, refutations, re-affirmations, and parodies" followed *Looking Backward* according to

103 Prettyman, "Gilded Age Utopias of Incorporation," 32.
104 Bellamy, *Looking Backward*, 109.
105 Bellamy, *Looking Backward*, 111.
106 Edward Bellamy, "How and Why I Wrote Looking Backward," in *America as Utopia*, ed. Kenneth M. Roemer (New York: Burt Franklin and Company, 1981), 22–27, 26.
107 Roberts, *Looking Within*, 64.
108 Justin Nordstrom, "Looking Backward's Utopian Sequels: 'Fictional Dialogues' in Gilded-Age America," *Utopian Studies* 18, no. 2 (2007): 193–221, 198.

Figure 11: "A Socialist orator at 'Speakers' Corner' in London's Hyde Park, near the Marble Arch, attracts an audience of working men, while a gentleman in a top hat passes by." 1892

Everett Bleiler,[109] five of which I discuss here. Some specifically reject the concept of leveling. In contrast to Bellamy's utopia, for example, the New

109 Bleiler, *Science-Fiction: The Early Years*, 49–50.

Society in Theodor Herzl's *Altneuland: The Old-New-Land* (1902) promotes unequal pay. "There was no parity of wages! The diligent worker received more, the slacker less."[110] Some of the replies this section describes attack the methods or consequences of Bellamy's leveling and suggest alternatives that modify—rather than eliminate—certain institutions and conventions Bellamy had abandoned. To the extent they defend the pre-Bellamy status quo, they are anti-utopian.[111]

A frequent focus of these writers' criticism stresses the importance of competition. While competition is not altogether lacking in *Looking Backward*, it is not competition for financial incentives but for positions of authority and prestige ("the high places in the nation are open only to the highest-class men"[112]). It is one thing, however, to embrace competition in principle and another to support policies that encourage and develop the deepest field of competitors by promoting equality of opportunity (described in Chapter 4). For some of Bellamy's critics, the social Darwinian underpinnings of their understanding of competition precluded the imposition of societal remedies for equalizing the diverse educational, financial, and social starting points into which people are born—capriciously limiting, thereby, the potential spectrum of competitors.

Looking Backward and What I Saw

In W. W. Satterlee's reply to Bellamy, *Looking Backward and What I Saw* (1890), an observer/traveler, Mr. R. E. Former, looks back to Bellamy's year 2000 from the year 2101. He recognizes systemic problems with Bellamy's leveling scheme that have spawned unintended consequences leading to society's economic decline. During the intervening century Bellamy's reforms have received a thorough trial and their many weaknesses have

110 Theodor Herzl, *Altneuland: The Old-New-Land*, 118.

111 Sargent says of "anti-utopia" that it is "useful to have a term to describe those works that use the utopian form to attack either utopias in general or a specific utopia." He cites certain attacks on Bellamy's *Looking Backward* as "*anti-utopias* without being *dystopias*." Sargent, "The Three Faces of Utopianism Revisited," 8.

112 Bellamy, *Looking Backward*, 106.

been revealed. Mr. Pathfinder, the local host, tells his guest Mr. Former, "years of experimenting have now gone by."[113] Specifically, the lack of financial incentives and competition have demoralized the workers in the industrial army. Since eliminating the "incentive to labor because of the laborer's personal interest," Satterlee's spokesperson Moses Heartway asserts, production lags consumption.[114] In addition, political corruption and "systematic fraud" have resulted in a de facto oligarchy running the country—a reversion to the Bellamy era.[115] As a result of his experiences in touring the country, Mr. Former says, "Wherever we went, it was but a repetition of the same scenes of ruin and decay."[116] The highways were in a "sad condition" and the villages were "dilapidated."[117] "The nation was on the verge of utter bankruptcy."[118]

A critical problem, Satterlee insists, is the ratio of the citizens who are employed—those, as Bellamy had stipulated, between the ages of 21 and 45—and those either younger and in school or older and hence retired. These dependent citizens, Satterlee argues may, "in less than two generations" comprise "two-thirds or three-fourths of the whole"[119] and will be "consumers without producing."[120]

Contrary to a smooth transition to the social organization Bellamy pictured in *Looking Backward*, the clashes between organized labor and the forces of capital resulting from "the absorption of business by ever-larger monopolies"[121] led, in Satterlee's sequel, to a quarter of a century of "heated civil contests and social friction, followed by ten years of bloody revolution"[122]—a "war of classes and races" to open the twentieth century (noted in Chapter 3).[123] The revolution's conclusion led eventually to the

113 Satterlee, *Looking Backward and What I Saw*, 156.
114 Satterlee, *Looking Backward and What I Saw*, 140.
115 Satterlee, *Looking Backward and What I Saw*, 164–166.
116 Satterlee, *Looking Backward and What I Saw*, 164.
117 Satterlee, *Looking Backward and What I Saw*, 159.
118 Satterlee, *Looking Backward and What I Saw*, 160.
119 Satterlee, *Looking Backward and What I Saw*, 136.
120 Satterlee, *Looking Backward and What I Saw*, 139.
121 Bellamy, *Looking Backward*, 64.
122 Satterlee, *Looking Backward and What I Saw*, 119.
123 Satterlee, *Looking Backward and What I Saw*, 55.

formation of a new government. To provide historical context for his visitor, Pathfinder reads the transcripts of important speeches presented at the political convention assembled to choose the new form of government. General Dick Tator—a socialist patriot and "great military genius"[124] had called the convention and spoke there presenting Bellamy's plan for an industrial army. "He thoroughly believed in the possibility of a system of universal cooperation. ... From his brain was evolved the great system of a military republic."[125] In opposition to the General's speech and the principles of *Looking Backward*, the author's spokesperson Heartway explains that "the main fault of this as of all other forms of socialism, [is] that it ignores the fact of the natural depravity of the race."[126] As in any political arrangement, he stresses, "there will still be lust, pride, selfishness and love of power."[127] It should not be forgotten, Heartway observes, that the recent revolution "was born amid the throes of the lowest order of materialistic selfishness."[128] His speech provides suggestions for removing the causes of the problems that marred the otherwise "Golden Age" of the nineteenth century—solutions less dramatic than Bellamy's industrial army. In *Utopia and Revolution*, Lasky affirms that utopias may often achieve the revolutionary ends they seek through incremental reforms.[129] Satterlee agrees, prompting his spokesperson to propose measures for raising the earning power of the working poor while curtailing the swelling fortunes of the wealthy. To ensure the evils of the past will not repeat, Heartway's reforms include reducing the salaries of public officials and raising those of "professional and other laboring men."[130] He further embraces shortening the working day to eight hours and establishing minimum wage laws.[131] Other reforms comprise laws restricting land ownership[132] and "equality"

124 Satterlee, *Looking Backward and What I Saw*, 56.
125 Satterlee, *Looking Backward and What I Saw*, 57.
126 Satterlee, *Looking Backward and What I Saw*, 126.
127 Satterlee, *Looking Backward and What I Saw*, 128.
128 Satterlee, *Looking Backward and What I Saw*, 120.
129 Lasky, *Utopia and Revolution*, 79.
130 Satterlee, *Looking Backward and What I Saw*, 153.
131 Satterlee, *Looking Backward and What I Saw*, 153.
132 Satterlee, *Looking Backward and What I Saw*, 145.

for women including suffrage[133] (noted in Chapter 3). Election reforms ensure the president and executive officers are "chosen by ballot directly," and campaign finance laws prohibit wealthy individuals from contributing to their own campaigns so that "offices will not seek millionaire candidates only."[134] Other measures include government support for public education (to include instruction in the Bible)[135] and restrictions on "monopolies, trusts, combinations, options, and other forms of gambling" that "wrecked the civilization of the past century, and brought untold hardships to the people."[136] Rather than the twenty-four years of work in Bellamy's scheme, Satterlee's spokesperson implores, "let us provide for labor for all, from the age of manhood to decrepitude."[137]

Looking Further Forward

Richard Michaelis's parallel novel, *Looking Further Forward* (1890), features Julian West living in 1887. Impressed by the society Bellamy describes in *Looking Backward*, West is transported in a dream to the year 2000. At the recommendation of his host Dr. Leete, West is offered a teaching post in history at the Shawmut College of Boston. There he meets his predecessor, Mr. Forest, who has been demoted to a janitor as retribution for expressing his "radical" views on the alleged failures of Bellamy's system. Forest opposes Bellamy's communism and believes the previous system of competition, while executed poorly, could have been rehabilitated to salvage its beneficial features.

When West asks Mr. Forest, "Don't you think that the abolition of absolute poverty, the elevation of all men and women to a standard at least nearly equal, is a great and priceless gain to humanity?"[138] Forest replies that the abolition of "absolute poverty" could have been accomplished

133 Satterlee, *Looking Backward and What I Saw*, 147.
134 Satterlee, *Looking Backward and What I Saw*, 148.
135 Satterlee, *Looking Backward and What I Saw*, 149.
136 Satterlee, *Looking Backward and What I Saw*, 152–153.
137 Satterlee, *Looking Backward and What I Saw*, 153.
138 Michaelis, *Looking Further Forward*, 62.

without a "descent into communism and the terrible consequences of this worst system of production."[139] Mr. Forest is critical of Bellamy's approach to poverty remediation, which he says amounts to the "enrichment of the awkward, lazy and stupid people with the proceeds of the clever and industrious women and men."[140] As a result, he says, the clever and industrious workers are "no longer putting forth their best efforts and are becoming indifferent,"[141] and society suffers accordingly.

The society of your day, declares Mr. Forest, "suffered chiefly from unsystematized production, the monopolies that made possible the amassing of immense fortunes at the expense of the people, and the want of intelligence on the part of the workers who would either submit to these extortions or strike."[142] Michaelis has Mr. Forest make this claim against the background of his conviction that inequality "is the law of nature and the attempt to establish equality is therefore unnatural and absurd."[143] As his solution, Mr. Forest maintains that an ideal society should rest on two fundamental principles. The first of these is establishing a state where "everybody should be protected against undeserved poverty." The second is preserving competition, as it stimulates "everybody to use his best efforts to elevate himself and humanity."[144] The route to these goals, Michaelis believes, includes avoiding political structures that breed corruption and organizing workers into "mutual producing associations'"[145] (discussed in Chapter 2).

In his summary to West, Mr. Forest declares, "I suppose I have successfully demonstrated that our organization of society, with its pretended basis of human equality, has proved to be a failure." Since competition was abolished, he stresses, "the people are mentally degenerating for want of intellectual exercise, and ... not even a greater wealth is a consolidation for the loss of the greater liberty and independence the people enjoyed in

139 Michaelis, *Looking Further Forward*, 62.
140 Michaelis, *Looking Further Forward*, 36.
141 Michaelis, *Looking Further Forward*, 85.
142 Michaelis, *Looking Further Forward*, 96.
143 Michaelis, *Looking Further Forward*, 30.
144 Michaelis, *Looking Further Forward*, 114.
145 Michaelis, *Looking Further Forward*, 96.

your time."[146] As if these arguments were not sufficient to convince West of the system's breakdown, Mr. Forest claims that Bellamy's shortened years of productive labor and the increasing numbers of people the workers are supporting have combined to reduce the average daily income of the inhabitants of the United States to a "very frugal living."[147]

Forest's concluding argument proclaims, "there prevails to-day an inequality in many respects more oppressive than that of your time." It results from "favoritism and corruption," which are "as potent under our communistic rule as they were at the end of the nineteenth century."[148] When West asks for his solution to the question of corruption, Mr. Forest's suggestion involves a form of central planning where a "national bureau of statistics" ascertains both the demand and supply of the nation's "necessities of life," while leaving the "regulation of production to the members of each trade."[149] When West asks why this scheme might not itself give way to corruption, Mr. Forest can only suggest a national law to prevent that eventuality.[150]

Mr. East's Experiences in Mr. Bellamy's World

In Conrad Wilbrand's *Mr. East's Experiences in Mr. Bellamy's World* (1891), Friedrich East, having read Bellamy's *Looking Backward* in 1890, is enamored by its world and contrives a scheme to awake in the year 2001. Instead of Boston, however, Mr. East (Mr. Ost), who is German, will confront the conditions in Germany in 2001—though the same economic problems have spread worldwide. By way of introduction to his journey, Mr. East presents the issues he hopes to address through the vehicle of an internal dialogue: The present social system, "'where selfishness reigns

146 Michaelis, *Looking Further Forward*, 93.

147 Michaelis, *Looking Further Forward*, 94.

148 Michaelis, *Looking Further Forward*, 93. The corruption includes workers' bribery of superiors "with a part of their own credit cards" to "secure a desirable position" (92–93).

149 Michaelis, *Looking Further Forward*, 96–97.

150 Michaelis, *Looking Further Forward*, 97–98.

and constantly creates rich and poor, is a poisonous growth which must be eradicated,' said one voice. 'The present social system,' said another, 'is a work of Nature, and the human race will perish if it leaves the paths the universal mother has assigned.' 'Wealth must disappear,' urged one voice, 'for it ceaselessly draws poverty like a satellite in its circles.' 'Wealth is a blessing,' retorted another, 'for it will crowd out poverty as light dispels darkness.'"[151]

Upon his arrival in 2001 Mr. East is generally disillusioned by the situation he finds, though at first he attempts to defend Bellamy's predictions. "The world had certainly grown richer and fairer," reports Mr. East. "Everywhere I beheld the plainest signs that people had labored assiduously for reformation, refinement, beauty."[152] As he reads the mood on people's faces, however, he judges that human nature has not been altered and that people appear no happier than they were in their former world. The new world "possessed all the qualities needed for an imperfect world, nothing which suited a Utopia."[153]

Mr. East, through discussions with various figures, recognizes the difficulties confronting a socialist economy that Bellamy had not addressed. For one thing, a society based on equality, he says, "may sink into poverty, but can never rise to wealth."[154] During the course of the novel Wilbrandt, says Parrington, "produces all the conventional arguments against socialism: that the supply of labor would be inadequate, that the system of distribution and supply would break down, and that there were no adequate rewards for genius."[155]

In a discussion with Herr Büchner, the German Chancellor, Mr. East learns that "[w]ant of profitable employment had been the source of all the troubles of the lower classes in former days."[156] The motivation to work earlier connected to "the *secret spur* which urges them to constant toil" is

151 Wilbrandt, *Mr. East's Experiences in Mr. Bellamy's World*, 6.
152 Wilbrandt, *Mr. East's Experiences in Mr. Bellamy's World*, 184.
153 Wilbrandt, *Mr. East's Experiences in Mr. Bellamy's World*, 184.
154 Wilbrandt, *Mr. East's Experiences in Mr. Bellamy's World*, 128.
155 Parrington, *American Dreams*, 84. "All of these objections are pretty well answered in Bellamy's second book, Equality" (84).
156 Wilbrandt, *Mr. East's Experiences in Mr. Bellamy's World*, 172.

lacking under Bellamy's socialism.[157] A socialistic government, says the Chancellor, "will not go to destruction because it lacks human hands to labor, but because it lacks labor for the human hands."[158] "Wilbrandt's completely negative reply to Bellamy," says Franz Riederer, "is based on nineteenth-century economic assumptions."[159]

Mr. East's diagnoses of the problems Bellamy's world creates leads to his claim that it violates natural laws. Socialism, proclaims Wilbrandt (in the appendix) is a "contradiction to the changeless laws of nature" and "nothing save a stupendous folly of the utmost magnitude."[160] As Mr. East concludes, "They have thrust Mother Nature from her throne and put social democracy in her exalted seat."[161]

One of Mr. East's guides describes another difficulty, one Mandeville anticipated in his *Fable of the Bees* (1714). Without the demand for luxury goods in the bee hive, "rarities cannot be had" and "everything is cheap, tho' plain."[162] As Wildebrandt's guide explains, "with the socialization of society, certain changes in the manner of production must have taken place."[163] It was no longer possible to produce the luxurious wants of the rich as wealth itself had disappeared. As a result of the leveling process, the workers formerly making items of luxury currently had employment "creating such useful articles as would now be universally wanted by all whose incomes had formerly been *less* than the average one."[164] Accordingly, Mr. East remarks, the market is "everywhere closed against all costly products, and all manufacturing nations find themselves compelled to devote their attention to the articles which will supply simpler needs."[165] This problem

157 Wilbrandt, *Mr. East's Experiences in Mr. Bellamy's World*, 27–28 (italics in original).

158 Wilbrandt, *Mr. East's Experiences in Mr. Bellamy's World*, 172.

159 Franz X. Riederer, "The German Acceptance and Reaction," in *Edward Bellamy Abroad* (New York: Twayne Publishers, 1962), 178.

160 Wilbrandt, *Mr. East's Experiences in Mr. Bellamy's World*, 248.

161 Wilbrandt, *Mr. East's Experiences in Mr. Bellamy's World*, 192.

162 Mandeville, *The Fable of the Bees*, vol. 1, 34.

163 Wilbrandt, *Mr. East's Experiences in Mr. Bellamy's World*, 173.

164 Wilbrandt, *Mr. East's Experiences in Mr. Bellamy's World*, 173–174 (italics in original).

165 Wilbrandt, *Mr. East's Experiences in Mr. Bellamy's World*, 175.

was later addressed in Piercy's *Woman on the Edge of Time* (1976) where "circulating luxuries pass through the libraries of each village,"[166] to be loaned out for special occasions.

Looking Within: The Misleading Tendencies of "Looking Backward" Made Manifest

In his 1893 response to *Looking Backward*, John Roberts describes a number of problems with Bellamy's ideal society. Of the citizens the narrator interviews, one exclaims, "'Looking Backward' has been the bane of this nation." The "poison" of its paternalistic teachings "is more insidious than that of a rattle snake."[167] As Parrington, notes however, "Like most of Bellamy's critics [Roberts] over-emphasizes Bellamy's influence."[168] Roberts's principal complaint is that people require financial incentives for their work and that without them they will devolve into indolence. "There is no hurry anywhere," complains Roberts's character Mr. Hume. "A man gets the same pay for his work if he is deliberate as if he is in haste."[169] Bellamy, of course, provides incentives but they are not financial but personal, political, or punitive.

Protagonist James North and his fiancée Effie have access to a sleeping potion which they had first taken in 1892, sleeping for thirty-five years until 1927.[170] Finding the country embroiled in an unwinnable war between labor and capital, they plan to take another "protracted nap"[171] until the war is over. Their selected dosage allows them to sleep until the year 2000.[172] When their sleep concludes as planned, the society confronting them is one configured on Bellamy's outline but not the one Dr. Leete so favorably described. As first introduced Bellamy's plan afforded hope for a new social accord; they find instead a system that is widely abused and its

166 Piercy, *Woman on the Edge of Time*, 188–189.
167 Roberts, *Looking Within,* 64.
168 Parrington, *American Dreams,* 78.
169 Roberts, *Looking Within,* 168.
170 Roberts, *Looking Within,* 72–73.
171 Roberts, *Looking Within,* 134.
172 Roberts, *Looking Within,* 137.

institutions unraveling. As Satterlee had likewise warned, the workforce of those between 21 and 45 is not sufficiently productive to support the rest of the citizens—including those under 21 and those over 45.[173] While there is now equality of income, "there is great inequality in the distribution of the burdens of labor."[174] In Roberts's retelling, the majority of workers have flocked to the easiest jobs, primarily in the cities, leaving the farmers and miners the toughest physical labor but for no additional compensation.[175] The half of the farmers who continue to work in earnest are especially the victims of the city workers' sloth, as the latter's quality and quantity of work has continued to degrade.

Since Roberts pictures most workers as giving only minimal effort to their jobs, they are in violation of Bellamy's requirement that prison with solitary confinement awaits those who buck the system by slacking.[176] Regarding work of a poor quality, "or other overt remissness on the part of men," Bellamy's Dr. Leete had declared, "the discipline of the industrial army is far too strict to allow anything whatever of the sort."[177] In Roberts's response, however, he has the police chief of Boston, Mr. Hume, explain that the budgeting is insufficient to police the vast number of reprobates. "The whole plan of our government," Mr. Hume declares, "is based on the supposition that people who are properly fed, clothed, and housed will naturally be virtuous." As a result, the chief grumbles, "I have a very inadequate force at my disposal."[178]

The extensive leisure time, both for those in the work force and those who have retired, has led to excessive gambling and drinking and to the destruction of many families as workers in Roberts's sequel spend their fixed income on their vices (noted in Chapter 4). More troubling is the dwindling supply of food and other goods and the prospect of growing shortages. As one observer notes, "there is terrible want, suffering, and distress all over the country, and especially in the cities."[179]

173 Satterlee, *Looking Backward and What I Saw*, 136.
174 Roberts, *Looking Within*, 190.
175 Roberts, *Looking Within*, 191.
176 Bellamy, *Looking Backward*, 107.
177 Bellamy, *Looking Backward*, 107.
178 Roberts, *Looking Within*, 152–153.
179 Roberts, *Looking Within*, 220.

As the situation reaches a crisis point, the government is forced to admit the experiment with Bellamy's plan has failed after two generations. This leads to calls for a peaceful transition back to the system the nineteenth century employed, with certain modifications to ensure greater economic equality. Two modifications (described in Chapter 2) comprise the assessment of a 10 percent wealth tax as Mr. Acre (a farmer) suggested and the imposition of a graduated income tax Dr. Butler (a minister) recommended.[180]

News from Nowhere

William Morris scoffed at Bellamy's failure to improve the aesthetic dimensions of labor, focusing largely on its duration—twenty-four years. His only idea for "making labour tolerable," Morris argues, was to reduce its amount "by means of ... fresh developments of machinery."[181] To this Berneri adds, "Indeed, there is hardly a single point on which *News from Nowhere* is not the antithesis of *Looking Backward*."[182] In contrast to the complexities of Bellamy's industrial army, observes Robertson, *News from Nowhere* offers "a vision of non-ascetic simplicity."[183]

"A central issue for utopia," explains Sargent, "is whether a better social order allows people to become better or better people create a better social order" and whether or not a better social order "can be created with the people we now are."[184] Morris believes the answer to the latter question is yes. The extreme economic inequality Morris describes in *News from Nowhere* (1890) transpired 200 years before narrator William Guest wakes in an England he finds nearly unrecognizable. The England he knew proclaimed inequality and poverty "as the law of God and the bond which held the world together."[185] The leveling that occurred during the first fifty years of the transformation to their

180 Roberts, *Looking Within*, 181, 268–269.
181 *Morris, "Bellamy's Looking Backward."*
182 Berneri, *Journey Through Utopia*, 256.
183 Robertson, *The Last Utopians*, 127.
184 Lyman Tower Sargent, *Utopianism: A Very Short Introduction* (Oxford: Oxford University Press, 2010), 111.
185 Morris, *News from Nowhere*, 109.

present social configuration (described in Chapter 5) destroyed the capitalist economy and replaced it with decentralized communism.

As in More's *Utopia* and Bellamy's *Looking Backward*, the leveling in *News from Nowhere* means there are no rich or poor. But Morris's leveling extends beyond money eliminating even the shadow of a social hierarchy. Work is self-managed with neither magistrates (syphogrants) overseeing it as in More nor industrial army officers as in Bellamy. No supervision is necessary because each person performs pleasant work of their own choosing, though people are generally prepared to pitch in where workers are needed, such as the seasonal wheat harvest or hay making.[186] As Kumar remarks, "what matters most are not institutions but the habits of mind and body generated in the people by their whole way of life."[187]

News from Nowhere raises the further question of work itself as an agent of leveling. In a chapter on the lack of incentive to work in a communist society, Guest asks old Hammond how they get people to work "when there is no reward of labour?" The "reward of labour," replies Hammond, "is life."[188] When people are "freed from the daily terror of starvation," Morris argues, they will "find out what they really wanted, being no longer compelled by anything but their own needs."[189] In Morris's communist society, people perform only necessary work, and each person's work complements the others' (as noted in Chapter 3). Thus, Hammond advises Guest, it is each person's business "to make his own work pleasanter and pleasanter, which of course tends towards raising the standard of excellence, as no man enjoys turning out work which is not a credit to him."[190] And since "nothing can be made except for genuine use ... no inferior goods are made."[191]

Morris urges a penultimate leveling measure embracing contrasting abilities exercised in the performance of a variety of work. "To compel a man to

186 Morris's narrator describes a group of workers who decline to participate in the wheat harvest. This earns them the benign label "obstinate refusers" as they are gently scolded. Morris, *News from Nowhere*, 195.

187 Kumar, "A Pilgrimage of Hope, 97.

188 Morris, *News from Nowhere*, 122.

189 Morris, "Useful Work Versus Useless Toil," 106.

190 Morris, *News from Nowhere*, 128.

191 Morris, *News from Nowhere*, 127.

do day after day the same task, without any hope of escape or change, means nothing short of turning his life into a prison-torment."[192] This was the workers' predicament in the earlier time of William Guest. For this reason, each person is now encouraged to practice "at least three crafts, varying sedentary occupation with outdoor—occupation calling for the exercise of strong bodily energy for work in which the mind had more to do."[193] Thus, all the work that we do," explains Hammond, "is an exercise of the mind and body."[194]

To the leveling afforded by the equality and freedom of work, Morris's leveling is given a bodily presence in the people's physical beauty and youthful appearance that results from performing desirable work rather than drudgery. Narrator William Guest registers this fact, declaring, "I could hardly have believed that there could be so many good looking people in any civilized country."[195] To this Hammond replies that the increase of beauty is the direct result of "our freedom and good sense."[196] Since the conditions under which people perform their daily work transformed from the coercive "burden of unnecessary production" to "the freedom for every man to do what he can do best,"[197] people no longer prematurely age from arduous, artificial, and unrewarding labors.[198]

In his own age Morris believed members of the "privileged class" lived longer and were more beautiful as a result of their leisure.[199] In his reconfigured society, as everyone works shorter and more pleasant hours, leisure is abundant. Accordingly, "men and women ... are free, happy, and energetic ... and most commonly beautiful of body."[200] In this, at least, there is

192 Morris, "Useful Work Versus Useless Toil," 101.
193 Morris, "Useful Work Versus Useless Toil," 101.
194 Morris, *News from Nowhere*, 127.
195 Morris, *News from Nowhere*, 96.
196 Morris, *News from Nowhere*, 96.
197 Morris, *News from Nowhere*, 123.
198 In *News from Nowhere*, William Guest quotes an old saying, "one ages very quickly if one lives among unhappy people" in support of this belief. Morris, *News from Nowhere*, 57.
199 Morris, "Useful Work Versus Useless Toil," 94.
200 Morris, *News from Nowhere*, 159. Rather than the release from drudgery, Parrinder interprets the change in people's physical appearance to eugenic forces. Citing other writings (*The Roots of the Mountains* and *The Wood Beyond the World*), he

consonance with Bellamy, who links the "strong and beautiful" bodies of "young men and women" to the physical exercise and recreation economic equality affords.[201]

says Morris's writing, "was steeped in the discourse of eugenics." Patrick Parrinder, "Eugenics and Utopia: Sexual Selection from Galton to Morris," *Utopian Studies* 8, no. 2 (1997): 1–12, 6–7.

201 Bellamy, *Equality*, 144–145.

CHAPTER 7

The Future of Economic Inequality: (Mostly) Dystopian Visions

> "The only reason why we cannot see the future as plainly as the past, is because we know too little of the actual past and actual present."[1]
>
> —Samuel Butler, *Erewhon* (1872)

"Life in the future haunts the utopian's mind in many different ways" is Richard Gerber's assessment in *Utopian Fantasy*.[2] "The historical present has become opaqued and packaged by the reifying mechanisms of contemporary capitalism," Tom Moylan observes, "rendering the social situation even more resistant to being radically perceived and transformed."[3] The prospect that the future will see income and wealth inequality grow unchecked has spawned dystopias projecting the demise of society as a vehicle of mutual benefit and sacrifice. "For 40 years," says Cory Doctorow (in 2020), "the world's wealth has been gathered into fewer and fewer hands, as oligarchy's musical chairs game has run faster and more vicious."[4] This chapter tracks the future of increasing income and wealth inequality as H. G. Wells, Kurt Vonnegut, Jr. Kim Stanley Robinson, Octavia Butler, and Cory Doctorow envisioned it. Since the societies they describe are more economically fractured than our own, the term dystopia is fitting. A dystopia, notes Sargent, is a "non-existent society ... that the author intended a contemporaneous reader to view as considerably worse than the society in which

1 Butler, *Erewhon*, 131.
2 Gerber, *Utopian Fantasy*, 81.
3 Moylan, *Demand the Impossible*, 35.
4 Twitter, October 25, 2020 @doctorow.

that reader lived."[5] Goodwin and Taylor explain that dystopias present "warnings of future horrors, based on extrapolation and projection of current tendencies or ideas."[6] Claeys adds that dystopia is "a modern phenomenon, wedded to secular pessimism." The adjective *dystopian*, he continues, "implies fearful futures where chaos and ruin prevail."[7] "Most utopias appearing in the twentieth century," advises Sargent, "have been dystopias."[8]

Economist Branko Milanović concedes in *Global Inequality* (2016) that economic forecasts "tend to be very wrong."[9] For more accurate projections of times to come he examined "less formal" discussions of political and economic trends hoping they would prove more prescient. He mentions such works as John Kenneth Galbraith's *The New Industrial State* (1967) and Daniel Bell's *The Coming of Post-Industrial Society* (1973) as well as other future-oriented books through the 1990s.[10] Of these works, he reports, they "failed to predict or even imagine the most important future developments" and are largely "anchored in the popular beliefs of their age." Common mistakes of such predictions, Milanović continues, comprise "the belief that the trends that appear to be most relevant at a particular time will continue into the future."[11] Experience shows that utopian (and dystopian) authors have frequently suffered the same fate—often thankfully.

5 Lyman Tower Sargent, Utopian Literature in English, Definitions. <https://openpublishing.psu.edu/utopia/content/definitions>
6 Goodwin and Taylor, *The Politics of Utopia*, 17.
7 Gregory Claeys, *Dystopia: A Natural History* (Oxford: Oxford University Press, 2017), 4–5.
8 Sargent, "Authority and Utopia: Utopianism in Political Thought," 565.
9 Milanović, *Global Inequality*, 155.
10 Milanović, *Global Inequality*, 156.
11 Milanović, *Global Inequality*, 158.

H. G. Wells

> "But should we not regard it as our problem to recast our organization of labor so that each man can rejoice in his work as we do?"[12]
>
> —Bertrand De Jouvenel (1903–1987), "Utopia for Practical Purposes"

Inequality of wealth, according to Piketty, "is above all inequality of power in society, and in theory it has no limit."[13] H. G. Wells explores the future of limitless income and wealth inequality in *When the Sleeper Wakes* (1899). Wells's story, says John Partington, is of a "comatose socialist awakening under a ruthless oligarchy in the year 2100."[14] Wells's image of the future world, says Darko Suvin, was "an explicit polemic against Bellamy's complacent optimism."[15] Graham, Wells's central character, having endured the "flaccid phase"[16] of a cataleptic trance—a motionless sleep lasting just over two hundred years, awakes to the prospect of vast personal wealth and power. "You are the Master of the Earth," he is told, "You are owner of half the world."[17]

Graham's fortune had amassed through an auspicious inheritance from two benefactors and through twelve trustees' judicious investments over the two-century duration of his trance. Graham wakes to a London beset with the same extremes of social and economic inequality he recalls from his earlier life, but now manifest in a more intractable configuration of which he is the symbol. In his first days in this new world, Graham comes to recognize that "the ancient antithesis of luxury, waste and sensuality on the one hand and abject poverty on the other, still prevailed."[18] And yet,

12 Bertrand De Jouvenel, "Utopia for Practical Purposes," in *Utopias and Utopian Thought*, ed. Frank E. Manuel (Boston: Houghton Mifflin Company, 1966), 219–235, 234.

13 Piketty, *Capital and Ideology*, 265.

14 Partington, "H. G. Wells: A Political Life," 521.

15 Suvin, *Metamorphoses of Science Fiction*, 243.

16 H. G. Wells, "When the Sleeper Wakes," in *Three Prophetic Novels of H. G. Wells* (New York: Dover Publications, Inc., 1960), 12.

17 Wells, *When the Sleeper Wakes*, 57.

18 Wells, *When the Sleeper Wakes*, 40.

the narrator explains, "everyone had a sufficiency of food and clothing, was warmed in the city ways and sheltered from the weather.[19] But the hopes of Graham's day, as reflected in Morris's *News from Nowhere* and Hudson's *Crystal Age*, still go unfulfilled and Graham "knew, greater than ever, grown with the city to gigantic proportions, were poverty and helpless labour and all the sorrows of his time."[20] Jack Williamson suggests that "every feature of the future world reveals Wells's scientific certainty that progress is more likely to destroy the free individual than to create the utopia he longs for."[21]

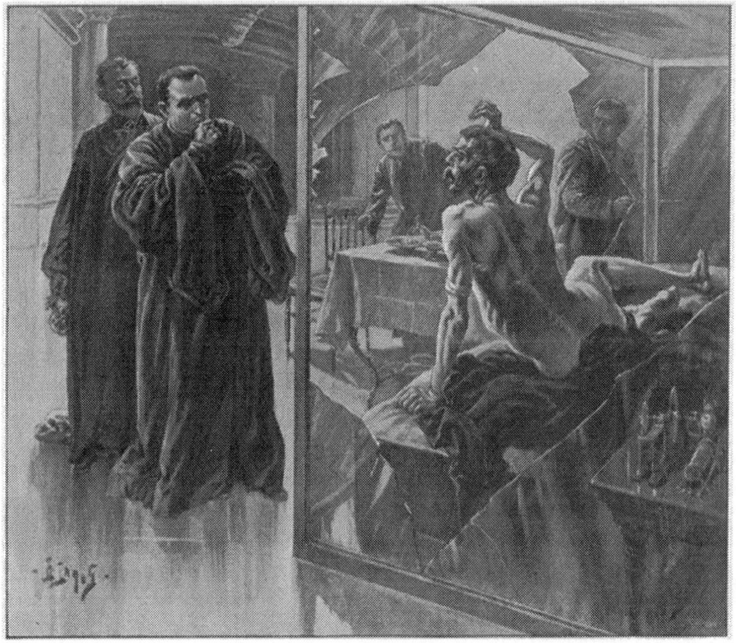

Figure 12: "Graham wakes after sleeping for two centuries."

19 Wells, *When the Sleeper Wakes*, 97.
20 Wells, *When the Sleeper Wakes*, 98.
21 Williamson, *H. G. Wells: Critic of Progress*, 109.

> "Looking over his shoulder Graham saw approaching a very short, fat, and thickset beardless man, with aquiline nose and heavy neck and chin. Very thick black and slightly sloping eyebrows that almost met over his nose and overhung deep grey eyes, gave his face an oddly formidable expression. He scowled momentarily at Graham."

One third of the population of London—which had grown to more than "thirty-three millions"[22]—lives in poverty, existing day-to-day. The poor are recognizable by their uniforms of light blue canvas, which the Labour Company—the employer of last resort—provides. These blue canvas-clad workers live "without pride or delight or hope. ... They are born, they are thwarted and they die."[23] "Millions of such men and women ... had never been out of the city, had never seen beyond the little round of unintelligent grudging participation in the world's business."[24] Graham realizes that after two hundred years, "the same hope, still unfulfilled, cried passionately through the city." The employer of the poor—the ubiquitous Labour Company—is the successor to the Salvation Army, reconstituted as a for-profit corporation and one of the earliest investments the twelve trustees of Graham's estate had acquired. The Labour Company offers "food, shelter and a blue uniform for all comers"[25] in exchange for a day's work. Its aim "was to give work to starving homeless people" as "nowadays there are no workhouses, no refuges and charities, nothing but that Company."[26]

Before his protracted sleep Graham was aware of the "moral decay that had followed the collapse of supernatural religion" and the fact that those who had lost their faith in God had retained their faith "in property, and wealth ruled a venial world."[27] In what one character describes as the "the new lordship of wealth,"[28] the state has privatized traditional tasks of government such as education and sanctioned profitable monopolies. The Public School Trust, for example, holds a monopoly on education for the working classes.[29] Its curriculum stresses "a few simple

22 Wells, *When the Sleeper Wakes*, 86.
23 Wells, *When the Sleeper Wakes*, 129–131.
24 Wells, *When the Sleeper Wakes*, 97–98.
25 Wells, *When the Sleeper Wakes*, 129–131.
26 Wells, *When the Sleeper Wakes*, 129–131.
27 Wells, *When the Sleeper Wakes*, 98.
28 Wells, *When the Sleeper Wakes*, 129.
29 Wells, *When the Sleeper Wakes*, 105–106.

principles—obedience—industry." Students' education consists largely of amusement for they are "taught very little"—as such learning "only leads to trouble and discontent."[30] As the Education Trust's Surveyor-General explains, "Where the labourers get their ideas, one cannot tell."[31] Other monopolies, run by wealthy businessmen, include the European Food Trust, the Medical Faculty Company, and the European Piggeries.

The factions fighting for power over Graham's vast estate are the White Council (the "Council of Trusts," successor to the twelve trustees) with its red police, and Ostrog with his vast force of squalid followers. Graham realized that these two great political factions were fighting to "possess him." On the one hand, the "White Council, with its red police," was "set resolutely ... on the usurpation of his property and perhaps his murder." On the other hand was "the rebellion that had liberated him, with this unseen 'Ostrog' as its leader."[32] Ostrog, Graham is told, "is the organizer ... of the revolt. Our Leader—in your name."[33]

Wells's "sketch of the future," observes Suvin, "was full of brilliant and detailed insights (as, for example, those about competing police forces and stultifying mass media) that turned out to be close to actual developments in the twentieth century."[34] Yet Orwell claims of Wells's story that "it suffers from vast contradictions because of the fact that Wells, as the arch-priest of 'progress,' cannot write with any conviction *against* 'progress.'" While Wells "draws a picture of a glittering, strangely sinister world in which the privileged classes live a life of shallow gutless hedonism," affirms Orwell, the workers are "reduced to state of utter slavery and sub-human ignorance."[35]

30 Wells, *When the Sleeper Wakes*, 106.
31 Wells, *When the Sleeper Wakes*, 106.
32 Wells, *When the Sleeper Wakes*, 66–67.
33 Wells, *When the Sleeper Wakes*, 57.
34 Suvin, *Metamorphoses of Science Fiction*, 243.
35 Orwell, *The Road to Wigan Pier*, 202 (italics in original). In his 1921 preface, Wells admits that Ostrog and the White Council represented his earlier overestimation of capitalist businessmen possessing the "character and the largeness of imagination necessary to combine and overcome the natural insubordination of the worker." H. G. Wells, "Preface to *When the Sleeper Wakes*," in *H. G. Wells's Literary Criticism*, ed. Patrick Parrinder and Robert M. Philmus (New Jersey: Barnes and Nobel Books, 1980), 239.

Kurt Vonnegut, Jr

"Accumulation of wealth at one pole is, therefore, at the same time accumulation of misery, agony of toil, slavery, ignorance, brutality, mental degradation, at the opposite pole."[36]

—Karl Marx, *Capital* (1867)

In *Player Piano* (1953) Kurt Vonnegut Jr. treats economic inequality as an inevitable structural outcome of commercial and technological progress. *Player Piano*, writes David Hughes, "is remarkable for assimilating institutions both past and present into the future."[37] While the first industrial revolution "devalued muscle work," explains Vonnegut's protagonist Dr. Paul Protius, "the second one devalued routine mental work.[38] Characteristic of the third industrial revolution, which has been underway "for some time," are computers that "devaluate human thinking"[39] by supplanting human judgment. As machines and then computers replace an expanding number of manual or menial jobs, society makes a place for the discarded workers either in the Reconstruction and Reclamation Corps or in the bloated and largely impotent military. The highly regimented society rewards a minority of intelligent and highly educated managers and engineers, including Dr. Paul Protius who garners the highest income in the town.[40] These individuals are segregated from the mass of society physically as well as intellectually and financially. Completion of college and graduate school is the dividing line controlling the type of life one is assigned. A national IQ exam—the National Standard General Classification Test—determines summarily who will or will not attend college. The IQ scores are a matter of public record.[41] The result, says

36 Marx, *Capital*, vol. 1, part 7, chap. 25, sec. 4, 452.

37 David Y. Hughes, "The Ghost in the Machine," in *America as Utopia*, ed. Kenneth M. Roemer (New York: Burt Franklin and Company, 1981), 110.

38 Vonnegut, *Player Piano*, 14.

39 Vonnegut, *Player Piano*, 15.

40 Vonnegut, *Player Piano*, 23.

41 Vonnegut, *Player Piano*, 89.

Finnerty, one of the highly educated engineers, is "about as rigid a hierarchy as you can get." "How's somebody going to up his IQ?" he asks rhetorically. To this observation, a fellow engineer replies, "Not only must a person be bright, he must be bright in certain approved, useful directions: basically, management or engineering."[42] The specter of a lost segment of the population—unable to compete in the economy with their higher IQ neighbors—was a concern Herrnstein and Murray expressed forty years later in *The Bell Curve* (discussed in Chapter 3). Membership in this "underclass," note Herrnstein and Murray, is "through no fault of their own but because of inherent shortcomings about which little can be done."[43]

As computers progressively usurp even the managers' judgment, a central computer (EPICAC XIV) decides "how many engineers and managers and research men and civil servants, and of what skills, would be needed in order to deliver the goods; and what IQ and aptitude levels would separate the useful men from the useless ones, and how many Reconstruction and Reclamation Corps men and how many soldiers could be supported at what pay level and where, and ..."[44] Regarding the now useless workers, Reverend Lasher (a social scientist by training) observes, "For generations they've been built up to worship competition and the market, productivity and economic usefulness, and the envy of their fellow men—and boom! it's all yanked out from under them. They can't participate, can't be useful any more. Their whole culture's been shot to hell."[45]

42 Vonnegut, *Player Piano*, 93.

43 Herrnstein and Murray, *The Bell Curve*, 523. For a discussion of the detrimental effects on the poor of stigmatizing terms like "underclass" and "culture of poverty" see, Herbert J. Gans, *The War Against the Poor: The Underclass and Antipoverty Policy* (New York: BasicBooks, 1995).

44 Vonnegut, *Player Piano*, 118 (ellipsis in original).

45 Vonnegut, *Player Piano*, 90–91. In 1919 Veblen wrote of the division between "business management and industrial management," which he saw as approaching a "critical pass." Management at some point must be wrested from businessmen and placed under the control of "production engineers without a commercial interest." Thorsten Veblen, *The Engineers and the Price System* (Mansfield Centre, CT: Martino Publishing, 2012), 58, 60.

Vonnegut's story takes place in Ilium, New York, where the Iroquois River separates the large homes and affluent lives of the managers and engineers from the workers in Homestead, where a "bank of gray porches"[46] and "gray façades, and lifeless neon tubes"[47] greets the rare traveler crossing the bridge from the prosperous north. Machines displaced the work of the majority of Homestead's residents, and the government now supports them in menial jobs. A cluster of workers, however—including bartenders, policemen, firemen, professional athletes, cab drivers, and "specially skilled artisans,"—while they lived among those who had been displaced, "were aloof and often rude and overbearing with the mass."[48] These workers, because of their independent professions, identify with the engineers and managers across the river, though the feeling was unrequited.

As the third industrial revolution took hold, workers' wages declined while the engineers and managers saw their salaries increase dramatically. As one worker explains, before the war "I could make better'n a hundred a week with overtime ($1,113 in 2023). Best week I ever had, I guess, was about a hundred and forty-five dollars. Now I get thirty a week," a drop of "about eighty per cent."[49] At the same time the average annual pay of the engineers and managers increased almost sevenfold from $8,449.27 to $57,896.41[50] (in 1953—equivalent to from $94,000 to $644,000 in 2023). Before the war the workers earned 60 percent of the wages of the engineers and managers ($8,449.27 × 60% = $5,070 ≈ $100 × 52). After the war, those on the north side of the Iroquois River earned thirty-seven times as much as those on the south side.[51] In defense of this striking income inequality, its champions provide a self-serving trickledown argument. As one character explains, because of the technological advancements the engineers had made possible—including thermostatically controlled windows, radar ranges, electrostatic dust precipitators, ultrasonic clothes washers, 40-inch

46 Vonnegut, *Player Piano*, 14.
47 Vonnegut, *Player Piano*, 257.
48 Vonnegut, *Player Piano*, 27.
49 Vonnegut, *Player Piano*, 214.
50 Vonnegut, *Player Piano*, 215.
51 $57,896.41/52 = $1,113 a week /$30 = 37.

television screens[52]—the workers have now "become far richer than the wildest dreams of Caesar or Napoleon or Henry VIII!" Though thirty dollars a week ($334 in 2023) is how much money the workers make, "not with all his gold and armies could Charlemagne have gotten one single electric lamp or vacuum tube!"[53]

Kim Stanley Robinson

> "Social structures, types and attitudes are coins that do not readily melt."[54]
>
> —Joseph A. Schumpeter, *Capitalism, Socialism and Democracy* (1942)

Kim Stanley Robinson's California triptych offers alternative histories of future Orange County, California—where "water flows uphill toward money."[55] *The Wild Shore* (1984) depicts the scene in 2047 after a nuclear attack. *The Gold Coast* (1988) explores the inter-corporate arms race in 2027 between Laguna Space Research and its Orange County defense-contractor rivals. A corrupt Air Force bidding system mediates the competition.[56] *Pacific Edge* (1990), says Robert Markley, "reimagines the road to utopia as a series of eco-managerial solutions to late-twentieth-century problems."[57] Robinson, observes Moylan, "provides a totalizing exploration of society and agency that concerns itself with economy and production, multiplex class struggles, and a collective engagement that opposes the new capitalist ideology and discipline of 'globalization.'"[58] *Pacific Edge* is a vision of the utopian community of El Modena, California in 2065.

52 Vonnegut, *Player Piano*, 149.
53 Vonnegut, *Player Piano*, 216.
54 Schumpeter, *Capitalism, Socialism and Democracy*, 12.
55 Robinson, *Pacific Edge*, 101.
56 Kim Stanley Robinson, *The Gold Coast* (New York: Tom Doherty Associates Book, 1988), 289.
57 Robert Markley, *Kim Stanley Robinson* (University of Illinois Press, 2019), 71.
58 Moylan, *Scraps of the Untainted Sky*, 204.

Prior to 2012 a cluster of giant multinational corporations had controlled the world's global economy. Tom Barnard, a character in all three California novels, is Robinson's history chronicler and a crusading attorney. At the outset of *Pacific Edge* Tom is engaged in writing a utopia—brief musings in a journal which appear at the beginning of chapters 2 to 11. Tom's 2012 experiences, including his confinement to a Virginia internment camp on trumped-up charges, sour his enthusiasm for a literary utopia and transform his goals toward practical action in remaking the world. As Moylan notes, Tom "begins to connect the present and the future social spaces by way of the political action of forging the new society."[59] Tom's concluding journal entry reflects his utopian resolve: "I have to do something. Not just write a utopia, but fight for it in the real world."[60] Subsequently, Tom participates in the twenty-first century equivalent of international "trust busting"—a "struggle to make the international agreements curtailing corporations"[61]—which work, he says, spanned two working generations.[62] "It was war," Tom elaborates. "They bought people, courts, newspapers—they killed people. And we really had to put the arm on the countries who decided that becoming a corporation haven would be a good source of revenue."[63] But unlike a traditional war, the political strategy did not aim at conquering the existing system of multinational capitalism. The reason the process took two generations to unfold was the quality of its utopian temperament—comprising, as Moylan describes, "economic as well as political democracy,"[64] and a mixed system of "ecological respect and restoration, human diversity and decency, and economic and political justice, within a democratically-regulated ethical balance of altruism and self-interest."[65]

As a result of these efforts, the global economic structure reverted to the smaller units that had constituted those large corporations. This change took a "revolution of all the people, using the power of government—laws,

59 Moylan, "Utopia is when our lives matter," 6.
60 Robinson, *Pacific Edge*, 299.
61 Robinson, *Pacific Edge*, 282.
62 Robinson, *Pacific Edge*, 282, 284.
63 Robinson, *Pacific Edge*, 282.
64 Moylan, "Utopia is when our lives matter," 11.
65 Moylan, "Utopia is when our lives matter," 9.

police, armies—against the very small executive class that owned and ran the multinationals.'"[66] It required slicing corporations up and distributing their assets "down through their systems to constituent businesses."[67] The result was a "massive downloading of capital, a redistribution of wealth,"[68] while setting limits on "the more extreme forms of greed."[69] "It took everyone to do it," reports Tom. "A consensus of world opinion, governments, the press."[70] "Governments hated multinationals because they were out of government control."[71] The key to the success of the project, explains Moylan, was "the alliance of government and popular movements and the curbing of the unlimited economic activity enjoyed by the forces of a highly mobile capital."[72] This "quiet revolution," says Lisa Garforth, "dismantled global capitalism and legislated the building of a decentralized, radically democratic, and environmentally careful society."[73] The result says Tom, is "nothing but small businesses scattered everywhere."[74] The process of reallocating power from the international conglomerates to local businesses and governmental units included nationalizing energy, water, and land (see Chapter 2).[75] Residents, as noted in Chapter 3, must perform ten hours a week of "town work"—work at town-owned businesses.[76] The relative economic equality of the resulting society relies on a graduated income tax (described in Chapter 2) and a regulated income ceiling and floor—the latter comprising a universal basic income (discussed in Chapter 2).

The solutions for economic inequality provided in Robinson's *Pacific Edge* contrast sharply with his dystopian vision in *New York 2140* (2017). The most graphic symbol of income and wealth inequality in *New York 2140* is the contrast between the wealthy owners of apartments near the

66 Robinson, *Pacific Edge*, 283–284.
67 Robinson, *Pacific Edge*, 283.
68 Robinson, *Pacific Edge*, 283.
69 Robinson, *Pacific Edge*, 284.
70 Robinson, *Pacific Edge*, 283.
71 Robinson, *Pacific Edge*, 283–284.
72 Moylan, "Utopia is when our lives matter," 10.
73 Lisa Garforth, "Green Utopias: Beyond Apocalypse, Progress, and Pastoral," *Utopian Studies* 16, no. 3 (2005): 393–427, 407.
74 Robinson, *Pacific Edge*, 284.
75 Robinson, *Pacific Edge*, 284.
76 Robinson, *Pacific Edge*, 91.

high ground of Central Park in New York City and the plight of a burgeoning mass of the city's population who have become homeless after a hurricane destroyed their more modest apartment buildings in the lower parts of the city. Upper Manhattan "remained above water and had become more crowded with buildings than ever, including many new superscrapers ... north of Central Park that thrust far higher into the sky than those in downtown and midtown ever had. This had the effect," observes the narrator, "of making lower Manhattan look more sunk than it really was."[77] For the wealthy, "the revolution in building materials had allowed the construction of skyscrapers three times taller than ever before. And it still pleased the rich to stash away a billion or three in a skypartment somewhere in New York, visit for a few days a year, enjoy the great city of the world."[78] Below these magnificent towers lay Central Park, now functioning as a refugee camp for residents displaced from lower regions of the city.[79] "It was a tent city now, punctuated by hundreds of downed trees. ... The whole city was a mess."[80]

Octavia Butler

> "'This is what you're to do,' God said. 'You will help humankind to survive its greedy, murderous, wasteful, adolescence.'"[81]
>
> —Octavia E. Butler, "The Book of Martha" (1996)

Octavia Butler's *Parable of the Sower* (1993), observes Peter Stillman, weaves together "contemporary tendencies such as increasing social divisions, economic inequality, [and] global warming" and their "imagined future

77 Robinson, *New York 2140*, 41.
78 Robinson, *New York 2140*, 282.
79 Robinson, *New York 2140*, 525–526.
80 Robinson, *New York 2140*, 523–524.
81 Octavia E. Butler, "The Book of Martha," in *Bloodchild and Other Stories*, 2nd ed. (New York: Seven Stories Press, 1996), 192.

development."[82] The *Parable of the Sower* projects the course of economic inequality in the United States by 2024; Butler's sequel, *Parable of the Talents*, extends the future into the 2030s. Characteristic of Butler's work, says Tarshira Stanley, is the idea that humanity is "unlikely to evolve into a caring and peaceful society, because … [its] social structures are too hierarchical and thereby negate pervasive equity and equality."[83] Butler's novels, notes Claire Curtis, are set in "states of nature where political authority is usually absent."[84] In Butler's *Parable of the Sower* an untenable gulf has emerged between the wealthier classes with their accommodating government and a shrinking working class—to which the narrator, Lauren Oya Olamina (age 15 at the outset), and her family belong—struggling to subsist. "The new American dystopia," explains Stillman reflecting on Butler's *Parable*, "stems from extremes of economic wealth and consequent inequalities of political power, so that the private power of the rich and of corporations dominates."[85] Threatening the remaining elements of civilized life is a growing army of homeless people living an often anarchic day-to-day warfare for survival and for whom unemployment, scavenging, and crime is a way of life. Early in the novel Lauren writes in her journal that a new president of the United States was elected the previous day, Christopher Charles Morpeth Donner, though what he can accomplish is in question. "Donner has a plan for putting people back to work. He hopes to get laws changed, suspend 'overly restrictive' minimum wage, environmental, and worker protection laws for those employers

82 Peter G. Stillman, "Dystopian Critiques, Utopian Possibilities, and Human Purposes in Octavia Butler's *Parables*," *Utopian Studies* 14, no. 1 (2003): 15–35, 15. The status of Butler's work as utopian is subject to dispute. For a brief summary of contrasting views see, David Morris, "Octavia Butler's (R)evolutionary Movement for the Twenty-First Century," *Utopian Studies* 26, no. 2 (2015): 270–288, 286n2. *Utopian Studies* dedicated an issue to Butler's work in 2008 (vol. 19, no. 3).

83 Stanley, "Re-Read and Recover: Afrofuturism as a Reading Practice," 249.

84 Claire P. Curtis, "Theorizing Fear: Octavia Butler and the Realist Utopia," *Utopian Studies* 19, no. 3 (2008): 411–431, 413.

85 Stillman, "Dystopian Critiques, Utopian Possibilities, and Human Purposes in Octavia Butler's *Parables*," 17.

willing to take on homeless employees and provide them with training and adequate room and board."[86]

Outside the pockets of civilization—walled communities like Lauren's—packs of dogs and drug-crazed arsonists threaten the unwary. "There are always a few groups of homeless people and packs of feral dogs living out beyond the last hillside shacks," Lauren reports in her journal. "People and dogs hunt rabbits, possums, squirrels, and each other. Both scavenge whatever dies."[87] As Lauren advises, "Dogs now are wild animals who will eat a baby if they can."[88] In their desperation some people resort to cannibalism, scavenging human remains.[89]

The teenage narrator Lauren and her family live in a walled-in cul-de-sac with eleven other families in Robledo twenty miles from Los Angeles. When they must go outside of the walls, bicycles are the preferred mode of transportation, as gasoline is out of reach for all but the wealthy. The families of the inter-racial community are reliant on what food they can grow or purchase with the wages of the few members who work in the outside, including Lauren's father, a minister who teaches at the local university. His wife Cory (Lauren's stepmother) operates a school out of their home for the neighbors' children. As Lauren records in her journal, "The neighbors pay a per-kid fee, but it isn't much. No one could support a household on it."[90] Illiteracy is widespread among the homeless and even working classes.

The constant threat of robbery and other crimes led Lauren's community to organize an armed self-protection team. Since the police are "no threat" to criminals,[91] her father explains, "there's nobody to help us but God and ourselves." Neighbors protect each other and their property. "We all look out for one another,"[92] he says. As another character notes, "Federal, state, and local governments still exist—in name at least—and sometimes they manage to do

86 Octavia E. Butler, *Parable of the Sower* (New York: Grand Central Publishing, 1993), 27.

87 Butler, *Parable of the Sower*, 40.

88 Butler, *Parable of the Sower*, 209.

89 Butler, *Parable of the Sower*, 289.

90 Butler, *Parable of the Sower*, 148.

91 Butler, *Parable of the Sower*, 143. The police have a fee-for-use arrangement with the public, and their reputation for looking out for themselves is well known.

92 Butler, *Parable of the Sower*, 75–76.

something more than collect taxes and send in the military."[93] Though Lauren's is a walled community—with walls "three meters high and topped off with pieces of broken glass as well as the usual barbed wire and the all but invisible Lazor wire"[94]—residents are under constant siege by thieves and other miscreants. For the working poor, jobs are hard to come by and the prospects for any better life are illusory. If a couple gets married, and if they're lucky, remarks Lauren, "they get a room or a garage to live in—with no hope of anything better and every reason to expect things to get worse." "The best they could hope for," she explains, "would be to move into some rich people's compound as domestic servants and work for room and board. There's no way to save any money or ever do any better."[95]

As climate change and the increasing costs of scarce resources—electricity and water—threaten communities in California, like Olivar on the coast, international corporations acquire the cities and transform them, providing armed security guards and restrictions on freedom.[96] "Olivar's flat, sandy beach is already just a memory," Lauren laments. "So are the houses and businesses that used to sit on that beach. Like coastal cities all over the world, Olivar needs special help."[97] To escape the chaos of Robledo some families consider taking refuge in Olivar, which as Lauren posts in her journal, was "one more beach/bedroom suburb of Los Angeles, small and well-to-do."[98] Recently, the city became the property of an international corporation, KSF.[99]

93 Butler, *Parable of the Sower*, 328.

94 Butler, *Parable of the Sower*, 74.

95 Butler, *Parable of the Sower*, 87.

96 Milanović reports, "The decline of the middle class and its diminished economic power trigger a number of social and political effects," including a reduction of social services, "principally education and health. … Rather than financing public education, the rich," he says, "might prefer to use public funds on increased policing … called guard labor." As an index of increasing economic inequality, Milanović cites research showing that by 2000 "more than 5 million workers in the United States [were] employed as guard labor." Milanović, *Global Inequality*, 197–198.

97 Butler, *Parable of the Sower*, 118.

98 Butler, *Parable of the Sower*, 118.

99 Kagimoto, Stamm, Frampton, and Company (KSF). Butler, *Parable of the Sower*, 118.

Olivar, observes Lauren, is a lot richer than Robledo. "It's an upper middle class, white, literate community ... getting an influx of salt water from one direction and desperate poor people from the other."[100] Though it has its own solar powered desalination plant, "it can't protect itself from the encroaching sea, the crumbling earth, the crumbling economy, or the desperate refugees."[101] For these reasons, the residents of Olivar "permitted their town to be taken over, bought out, privatized."[102] KSF, its corporate owner, "will expand the desalination plant to vast size. ... The company intends to dominate farming and the selling of water and solar and wind energy over much of the southwest."[103] In privatizing Olivar, KSF gets "an eager, educated work force" of people with limited options. The people of Olivar, Lauren notes, have decided "to accept smaller salaries than their socio-economic group is used to in exchange for security, a guaranteed food supply, jobs, and help in their battle with the Pacific."[104]

In some cities, like the factory or mining towns of the nineteenth century, the corporate owners are the sole employer. In her journal, Lauren describes a typical present-day example where wages are paid in company scrip. "Rent was charged for the workers' shacks. Workers had to pay for food, for clothing ... for everything they needed," and they could only spend their company money at the company store.[105] As wages "were never quite enough" to pay the bills, she notes, the result was a town of debt slaves who were precluded from leaving the employer.[106] If they refused to work, "they could be arrested, jailed, and in the end, handed over to their employers." Thus they were obligated to work off their debts "either as quasi-indentured people or as convicts."[107] In accordance with laws recently enacted, these debt slaves could be "forced to work longer hours for less pay" and "'disciplined' if they failed to meet their quotas." Furthermore,

100 Butler, *Parable of the Sower*, 118–119.
101 Butler, *Parable of the Sower*, 119.
102 Butler, *Parable of the Sower*, 119.
103 Butler, *Parable of the Sower*, 119.
104 Butler, *Parable of the Sower*, 119.
105 Butler, *Parable of the Sower*, 288.
106 Butler, *Parable of the Sower*, 288.
107 Butler, *Parable of the Sower*, 288.

as Lauren explains, the workers could be "traded and sold with or without their consent, with or without their families, to distant employers who had temporary or permanent need of them."[108] As in former times, "children could be forced to work off the debt of their parents if the parents died, became disabled, or escaped."[109]

By 2026 the fate of Lauren's community is described as inevitable. "I thought something would happen someday," she relates in her journal. "I didn't know how bad it would be or when it would come. But everything was getting worse: the climate, the economy, crime, drugs, you know. I didn't believe we would be allowed to sit behind our walls, looking clean and fat and rich to the hungry, thirsty, homeless, jobless, filthy people outside."[110] Though Lauren had planned to escape from her community when she turned 18, the disappearance of her father, the burning and sacking of Robledo, and the murder of her family by homeless invaders meant she must leave immediately. Her goal was to travel north, perhaps to Canada, disguised as a man. She had prepared for this eventuality as she had written earlier. "I've finally assembled a small survival pack for myself—a grab-and-run pack." "I've collected a hatchet, for instance, and two small, light, all-metal pots."[111] She had saved almost a thousand dollars, which, she believed, "*might* feed me for two weeks. ... Food prices are insane, always going up, never down."[112] Her pack also includes "a full change of clothing ... a couple of spoons and forks, a can opener, my pocket knife, ... [and] a lot of plantable raw seed, my journal, my Earthseed notebook, and lengths of clothesline."[113] Most importantly for her survival, she packed her handgun that her father had trained her to shoot. Lauren's journal, says Moylan, "gives

108 Butler, *Parable of the Sower*, 288.

109 Butler, *Parable of the Sower*, 288. This procedure was employed in Rosewater's 1897 *Utopia* discussed in Chapter 5.

110 Butler, *Parable of the Sower*, 187.

111 Butler, *Parable of the Sower*, 80.

112 Butler, *Parable of the Sower*, 80 (italics in original).

113 Butler, *Parable of the Sower*, 80. Earthseed is a theme running throughout the novel and its sequel. It is the name of a religion Lauren expounds to anyone who will listen. Its fundamental principle is that God is change.

shape to a counter-narrative" like D-503's in Zamyatin's *We*, "that exposes and opposes the social chaos of feudalized capitalism."[114]

As Lauren plans her journey north she locates two neighbors still alive, Zahra and Harry, and they consent to travel together. Initially they walk to the freeway which will lead to the coast highway, US 101 north. "The unused freeways," Lauren reports, were exploited by people "fleeing Los Angeles for Oregon, or Washington, or Canada."[115] As they travel, she records, "We became part of a broad river of people walking."[116] In her journal Lauren characterizes the "freeway crowd" as a "heterogenous mass—black and white, Asian and Latin, whole families ... on the move with babies on backs or perched atop loads in carts."[117] Continuing their treacherous journey her band grows larger as they incorporate people they believe they can trust, including an older male doctor, Bankole, who becomes Lauren's love interest. This larger group of travelers confers some measure of safety from the constant threat of thieves, scavengers, murderers, and rapists.

On the nearly empty highways leading north, water is available at commercial water stations to refill canteens and jugs. "You drink whatever the local householders are drinking. It might taste, smell, or look bad, but you can depend on it not to kill you."[118] But water stations, Lauren writes, "are dangerous places. People going in have money. People coming out have water, which is as good as money."[119] People travel during the day and take refuge where they can at night. In Lauren's group, members take shifts as armed guards while the others sleep.

On their journey further north, they alternate between interstate highways and smaller local roads. Lauren observes, "This was farm country. We'd passed through nothing for days except small, dying towns, withering roadside communities and farms, some working, some abandoned and growing weeds."[120] Reports of a Bay Area earthquake prompts their group

114 Tom Moylan, *Scraps of the Untainted Sky: Science Fiction, Utopia, Dystopia* (Boulder, CO: Westview Press, 2000), 230.

115 Butler, *Parable of the Sower*, 176.

116 Butler, *Parable of the Sower*, 176.

117 Butler, *Parable of the Sower*, 176–177.

118 Butler, *Parable of the Sower*, 201.

119 Butler, *Parable of the Sower*, 201.

120 Butler, *Parable of the Sower*, 227.

to head further east. "We had intended to follow U.S. 101 up through San Francisco and across the Golden Gate Bridge," she reflects, "But the radio warned us to stay away from the Bay Area. From San Jose up through San Francisco, Oakland, and Berkeley, there is chaos. The quake hit hard up there, and the scavengers, predators, cops, and private armies of security guards seem bent on destroying what's left."[121] As Bankole summarizes their situation, "You know, as bad as things are, we haven't even hit bottom yet. Starvation, disease, drug damage, and mob rule have only begun."[122]

The direction of Lauren's group is toward the relative safety they hope to find in Bankole's 300 acres of hilly farmland. His sister and her family have been living on the land and growing crops. With Bankole's permission, Lauren's group plans to form a farming community on the land. Upon their arrival, however, they find a fire has destroyed the sister's house and left her and all her family dead. The pilgrims hold a group funeral service honoring Bankole's sister and all the others they have lost. As the novel ends in 2027, they establish a small intentional community they name Acorn based on Lauren Olamina's Earthseed teachings.

In Butler's sequel, *Parable of the Talents* (1998), economic inequality is intensified when the United States elects a one-term fascist-misogynist president. President Andrew Steele Jarret, whose slogan is "Make America Great Again," encourages violence from his fanatical followers—who Zamalin terms the "totalitarian Christian Right"[123]—as he divides the country on racial and religious lines.[124] Jarret and his "rabid followers," observes Tom Moylan, scapegoat non-Christians, blaming them "for the ills that engulf society."[125] Jarret, says Philip Jos, "mobilizes support by

121 Butler, *Parable of the Sower*, 246.

122 Butler, *Parable of the Sower*, 328.

123 Zamalin, *Black Utopia*, 125.

124 Butler, *Parable of the Talents*, ("Make America Great Again,"15, 21); (fascist, 155); (misogynist, 218); ("Jarret was able to scare, divide, and bully people, first into electing him President, then into letting him fix the country for them. ... Jarret's fanatical followers were the greater danger," 241); (single term, 394).

125 Moylan, *Scraps of the Untainted Sky*, 240.

exploiting the fear engendered by economic collapse, environmental catastrophe, and public disorder."[126]

Cory Doctorow

> "It would be easier, where property was well secured, to live without money, than without poor; for who would do the work?"[127]
>
> —Bernard Mandeville, *Fable of the Bees* (1714)

Cory Doctorow's depictions of the future of income and wealth inequality include the blunt and unadorned version of *The Masque of the Red Death* and the ambiguous and evolving account of *Walkaway*. *The Masque of the Red Death* (2019) describes a society that has permitted the market's invisible hand to determine the fate of its citizens. "Little by little the world's cities filled up with powerful, self-governing people whose discipline, hard work and brilliance meant that they got richer and richer."[128] Under this social Darwinist régime, "people who didn't think ahead were self-correcting problems."[129] The markets "moved fallow, underutilized assets out of the hands of the incompetent and moved them into the hands of their betters, who put those assets to work."[130] The 99 percent "found themselves relieved of all their worldly goods and lacking the sums to rent anywhere to perch while they waited to die."[131] The market had "revealed" by "squeezing" people into "tinier, more uncomfortable places"[132] that most people were now expendable. Unnecessary people—"the

126 Philip H. Jos, "Fear and the Spiritual Realism of Octavia Butler's Earthseed," *Utopian Studies* 23, no. 2 (2012): 408–429, 411.
127 Mandeville, *The Fable of the Bees*, vol. 1, 193.
128 Doctorow, "The Masque of the Red Death," 250.
129 Doctorow, "The Masque of the Red Death," 267.
130 Doctorow, "The Masque of the Red Death," 250.
131 Doctorow, "The Masque of the Red Death," 251.
132 Doctorow, "The Masque of the Red Death," 248.

unnecessariate"[133]—were to be "eased out of existence."[134] Allowing the market meritocracy free rein meant that when the "best people were on top, things worked: they convinced the rational, cajoled the stubborn and … forced the rest."[135] The "greater good"[136] was restricted to the survival of the 1 percent. As smarter people bred only with smarter people[137] humanity would realign itself "around the strongest and brightest that evolution could select"[138]—"improving the species and its domination over the earth."[139]

"The defining feature of a market," observes Appelbaum in *The Economist's Hour*, "is the freedom to walk away."[140] Cory Doctorow's *Walkaway* (2017) describes a near-future, three-class post-society in Canada. The circumstances of the very rich (the "zottas") affect those of the other two classes in distinct ways. The "default" class comprises the powerless workers who survive by enabling the zottas; each default worker is no more than "an inconvenient surplus labor unit."[141] The walkaways, the third class, include those who have left either the default class or the zottas to survive as rootless, possessionless members of loosely structured volunteer communities. In default, people are selfish and want more than their neighbors. But in the condition of walkaway, where there are no formal rules, people coordinate their activities with others and find their place in the social mix. Limpopo, a central walkaway figure, expresses the spirit of walkaways, who live "like it's the first days of a better world, not like it's the first pages of an Ayn Rand novel."[142] "Out here," says Limpopo, "you want people to magically not take too much but also not earn the right to

133 Doctorow, "The Masque of the Red Death," 252.
134 Doctorow, "The Masque of the Red Death," 251.
135 Doctorow, "The Masque of the Red Death," 286.
136 Doctorow, "The Masque of the Red Death," 286.
137 Doctorow, "The Masque of the Red Death," 249.
138 Doctorow, "The Masque of the Red Death," 251.
139 Doctorow, "The Masque of the Red Death," 250.
140 Applebaum, *The Economist's Hour*, 332. Applebaum stresses that "markets are constructed by people for the purposes chosen by people—and they can be changed and rebuilt by people."
141 Doctorow, *Walkaway*, 98.
142 Doctorow, *Walkaway*, 116.

take more by working harder and also to work because it's a gift but not because they expect anything in return ... That's the walkaway dilemma. If you take without giving, you're a mooch. If you keep track of everyone else's taking and giving, you're a creep scorekeeper."[143]

Walkaways live in discarded buildings or other unused assets on a temporary basis; squatters without permission of the owner. They rely on the materials an earlier social order left behind. The form of entrepreneurship the walkaways practice is "post-scarcity"[144]—to make do with what they find. Iceweasel, a zotta character who walked away explains, "Being a walkaway was supposedly about refusing to kid yourself about your special snowflakeness, recognizing even though different people could do different things, that all people were worthy and no one was worth more than any other."[145]

In *The Philosophy of Money* (1900) sociologist Georg Simmel explains that "passionate and aggressive class hatred does not emerge where the classes are separated by an unbridgeable gulf."[146] The zottas are people who have amassed sufficient wealth that they are no longer accountable to any other class. The zottas, observes Limpopo, "are trying to secede from humanity. They don't see their destiny as tied to ours. They think that they can politically, economically, and epidemiologically isolate themselves."[147] Zottas embody a repressive force. Jacob Redwater is the archetypal zotta figure. His daughter Iceweasel is a walkaway whom Jacob has forcibly captured, returned home, and imprisoned. She says of her father, "Being a zotta means worrying you're not zottta *enough,* grafting away to make your pile of gold bigger than those other assholes' piles."[148] What we learn of the zottas comes through how the walkaway personae characterize them. For example, according to Tam, "The zottas weren't anyone's friend, but they had an interest in the continuation of the civilization whose apex they occupied."[149] From her observations of the zottas, Gretyl concludes, "There

143 Doctorow, *Walkaway*, 88.
144 Doctorow, *Walkaway*, 19.
145 Doctorow, *Walkaway*, 392.
146 Simmel, *The Philosophy of Money*, 408.
147 Doctorow, *Walkaway*, 67.
148 Doctorow, *Walkaway*, 401.
149 Doctorow, *Walkaway*, 159.

wasn't a hint of doubt that every privilege they enjoyed was deserved. The world was correctly stacked. The important people were at the top. The unimportant were at the bottom."[150] Zottas are "just as good at self-delusion as anyone," explains Limpopo. "Better—they're convinced they got to where they are because they're evolutionary sports who deserve to be exalted above baseline humans, so they're primed to believe anything they feel must be true."[151] The zottas Gretyl knew, she says, "were good at compartmentalizing, sociopath style, understanding other peoples' emotions well enough to manipulate them, without experiencing actual empathy."[152] The zottas, notes another walkaway, "want to control who gets to adopt which technologies, but they don't want to bear the expense of locking up all walkaways in giant prisons or figuring out how to feed us into wood chippers without making a spectacle, so here we are on the world's edge, finding our own uses for things."[153]

Limpopo explains that walking away is "not walking out on 'society,' but acknowledging that in zottaworld, we're problems to be solved, not citizens. That's why you never hear politicians talking about 'citizens,' it's all 'taxpayers,' as though the salient fact of your relationship to the state is how much you pay. Like the state was a business and citizenship was a loyalty program that rewarded you for your custom with roads and health care."[154] "Zottas cooked the process so they get all the money and own the political process. ... Talking about 'taxpayers' means that the state's debt is to rich dudes, and anything it gives to kids or old people or sick people or disabled people is charity we should be grateful for, since none of those people are paying tax that justifies their rewards from Government Inc."[155]

Nadie, Jacob Redwater's Russian private security guard—charged with watching his daughter Iceweasel, provides an overview of the changing role of the rich in terms of the poor. "There isn't going to be default world and walkaway world trading people forever. When you have big rich people,

150 Doctorow, *Walkaway*, 465.
151 Doctorow, *Walkaway*, 66.
152 Doctorow, *Walkaway*, 465.
153 Doctorow, *Walkaway*, 167.
154 Doctorow, *Walkaway*, 67.
155 Doctorow, *Walkaway*, 66–67.

and everyone else poor as poor, the result is ... *unstable*."[156] "If there are rich and poor," she says, "you need a story to explain why some have so much and so many have little. You need a story that explains this is fair."[157] In the last century, she continues, "the rich made things stable by giving some money back, tax and education and so on." But the rich of the previous century "only let their money be taxed because it was cheaper than paying for private security and official surveillance they needed to keep hold of wealth if the system grew unstable because of the gap between them and everyone."[158] Eventually the rich, now the zottas, "could hold onto more money, dispense with [the] pretense that being rich was from doing well, go back to [the] idea of divine right of kings, people born rich because fate favors them. It was more cost-effective to control people who didn't like this idea with technology than giving crumbs to support the fairy tale of rewards for virtue."[159]

One result of this increasing economic inequality is "diffused responsibility" for the fate of those who are not self-sufficient—the young, the sick, the old, the poor—the ones who can't walk away. "Those people can be most easily rounded up and institutionalized," observes Limpopo. "No one decides to imprison the poor in record numbers, it just happens as a consequence of tougher laws, less funding for legal aid, added expense in the appeals process. ... There's no person, decision, or political process you can blame. It's systemic."[160]

156 Doctorow, *Walkaway*, 402 (ellipses and italics in original).
157 Doctorow, *Walkaway*, 402.
158 Doctorow, *Walkaway*, 402.
159 Doctorow, *Walkaway*, 402.
160 Doctorow, *Walkaway*, 68 (ellipsis in original).

Afterword

When I immersed myself in this project, I had no idea what I would find. It was an exploration born of personal interest—a search for the Northwest Passage to economic equality. If there is enough to go around, how might things be organized so that after a famine (or pandemic), to paraphrase More's Hythloday, the barns of the rich might not be quite so full and fewer people will have died?[1] Economic inequality, as we have seen, resolves itself into innumerable discrete and apparently independent issues—the right to vote, inheritance laws, racism, gender equality, public transparency, marriage restrictions, and so on. Their common thread is one group's unequal treatment of another (class, race, gender) using laws like Anatole France (1844–1924) cites that prohibit "the wealthy as well as the poor from sleeping under the bridges, from begging in the streets, and from stealing bread."[2]

Even the most economically equalizing utopias, however, such as those of More and Bellamy, require laws that affect people in unequal ways; the "common" in their common good excludes those for whom the utopian system will not work. More's Utopia, for example, denies atheists citizenship and considers them—or anyone rejecting a belief in the afterlife—less-than-human.[3] Outcasts occur in Bellamy *Looking Backward*—those lacking "the power of leading a good life, however assisted"[4]—and in other egalitarian utopias, including those of Wells (*A Modern Utopia*) and Piercy (*Woman on the Edge of Time*).

Utopias that appear to elude this fate, including Morris's *News from Nowhere* and S. Byron Welcome's *From the Earth's Center*, for example, do so at great cost, having altered human nature—at least in some conventional sense—to make the utopian scheme work. In *From the Earth's Center*

1 More, *Utopia*, trans. Adams, bk. 2, 105.

2 Anatole France, *The Red Lily* (N.p.: Dodo Press, n.d. [1894]), 65.

3 More, *Utopia*, trans. Adams, bk. 2, 95.

4 Bellamy, *Equality*, chap. 37, 363.

everyone "without respect to condition" is equal and enjoys the "privileges and pleasures, that under a less perfect system of economic government would be restricted to a chosen few!"[5] Though a discussion of human nature in utopia is beyond the scope of this book, Immanuel Kant identified one critical problem. "Man," observes Kant, "has an inclination to *live in society* since he feels in this state more ... able to develop his natural capacities." On the other hand, he notes, each person has a "tendency to *live as an individual*, to isolate himself, since he also encounters in himself the unsocial characteristic of wanting to direct everything in accordance with his own ideas."[6] Designing a utopia to accommodate these conflicting tendencies without either excluding some people from the scheme or modifying humans to enable them to comply with its constraints, remains a utopian challenge and an obstacle to modeling economic equality.

While some of the equalizing measures described in this text, eugenics or conscription, for example, have largely fallen out of favor; others, like universal basic income or universal health care are still gestating in the political incubator. A few of the most effective tools for combatting economic inequality—minimum wage laws, labor unions, and progressive taxation—because of their relative success, have been beaten back or watered down as described. Finally, the encouraging trajectory of a few measures, like gender equality in the workplace or reimagining marriage—however slow in developing—appears irreversible.

5 Welcome, *From the Earth's Center*, 56.

6 Immanuel Kant, "Idea for a Universal History with a Cosmopolitan Purpose," in *Kant: Political Writings*, trans. H. B. Nisbet (Cambridge University Press, 1970), 44 (italics in original).

Bibliography

Albinski, Nan Bowman. *Women's Utopias in British and American Fiction.* London: Routledge Taylor and Francis Group, 1988.

Anderson, Elizabeth S. "What Is the Point of Equality?." *Ethics* 109, no. 2 (January, 1999): 287–337.

Applebaum, Binyamin. *The Economist's Hour*. New York: Back Bay Books, Little, Brown and Company, 2019.

Arendt, Hannah. *The Human Condition*, 2nd ed. Chicago: The University of Chicago Press, 1958.

———. *On Revolution*. New York: Penguin Books, 1963.

Aristotle. *Politics.* Translated by Ernest Barker. Oxford University Press, 1958.

———. *Politics.* Translated by Benjamin Jowett. New York: The Modern Library, 1943.

Atkinson, Anthony B. *Inequality*: *What Can Be Done*? Cambridge: Harvard University Press, 2015.

Axelrad, Allan M. "Ideology and Utopia in the Works of Ignatius Donnelly." *American Studies* 12, no. 2 (Fall 1971): 47–65.

Bach, Ulrich E. "Seeking Emptiness: Theodor Hertzka's Colonial Utopia Freiland (1890)." *Utopian Studies* 22, no. 1 (2011): 74–90.

Bacon, Francis. "Of Usury." In *The Essays or Counsels Civil and Moral*, edited by Brian Vickers. Oxford, UK: Oxford University Press, 1999.

Baker-Smith, Dominic. *More's Utopia.* London: HarperCollins Academic, 1991.

Bandura, Albert. *Self-Efficacy: The Exercise of Control.* New York: W. H. Freeman, 1997.

Banerjee, Abhijit V. and Esther Duflo. *Poor Economics*: *A Radical Rethinking of the Way to Fight Global Poverty*. New York: PublicAffairs, Hachette Book Group, 2011.

Bapat, Sheila. "Imperfectly: A Feminist Utopian Economy that Embraces and Addresses Human Flaws." In *The Feminist Utopia Project,* edited by Alexandra Brodsky and Rachel Kauder Nalebuff. New York: Feminist Press, 2015.

Barley, Tony. "Prediction, Programme and Fantasy in Jack London's *The Iron Heel*." In *Anticipations*: *Essays on Early Science Fiction and Its Precursors*, edited by David Seed. Syracuse, NY: Syracuse University Press, 1995.

Beauchamp, Gorman. "Jack London's Utopian Dystopia and Dystopian Utopia." In *America as Utopia*, edited by Kenneth M. Roemer, 91–107. New York: Burt Franklin and Company, 1981.

Becker, Howard. *Outsiders: Studies in the Sociology of Deviance*. New York: The Free Press, 1963.

Bellamy, Edward. *Equality*, 3rd ed. New York: D. Appleton and Company, 1897.

———. "How and Why I Wrote Looking Backward." In *America as Utopia*, edited by Kenneth M. Roemer, 22–27. New York: Burt Franklin and Company, 1981.

———. *Looking Backward: 2000–1887*. New York: Penguin Books, 1982.

Berneri, Marie Louise. *Journey Through Utopia*. Freeport, NY: Books for Libraries Press, 1969.

Bleiler, Everett F. "Introduction." In *Three Prophetic Novels of H. G. Wells*. New York: Dover Publications, 1960.

———. *Science Fiction: The Early Years*. Kent, Ohio: The Kent State University Press, 1990.

Bloch, Ernst. *The Principle of Hope*. Translated by Neville Plaice, Stephen Plaice and Paul Knight. Cambridge: The MIT Press, 1986.

Bloomfield, Paul. "The Eugenics of the Utopians: The Utopia of the Eugenists." *The Eugenics Review* 40 (21 new series) (April 1948–January 1949): 191–198.

Bobbio, Norberto. *Left and Right: The Significance of a Political Distinction*. Translated by Allan Cameron. Chicago: The University of Chicago Press, 1993.

Boyer, Pascal. *Minds Make Societies*. New Haven, CT: Yale University Press, 2018.

Breton, Rob. "WorkPerfect: William Morris and the Gospel of Work." *Utopian Studies* 13, no. 1 (2002): 43–56.

Bruce, Stewart E. *The World in 1931*. New York: F. L. Searl and Co., 1921.

Bruère, Martha Bensley. *Mildred Carver, USA*. New York: The MacMillan Company, 1919.

Bulwer-Lytton, Edward. *The Coming Race* (1871). N.p.: Loki's Publishing, n.d.

Burke, Edmund. *Reflections on the Revolution in France*. Oxford: Oxford University Press, 1993.

Burton, Robert. *The Anatomy of Melancholy*, edited by Holbrook Jackson. New York: New York Review of Books, 2001.

Butler, Octavia E. "The Book of Martha." In *Bloodchild and Other Stories*, 2nd ed. New York: Seven Stories Press, 1996).

———. *Parable of the Sower*. New York: Grand Central Publishing, 1993.

———. *Parable of the Talents*. New York: Grand Central Publishing, 1998.

Butler, Samuel. *Erewhon*. Mineola, NY: Dover Publications, 2002.

Cabet, Étienne. *Travels in Icaria*. Translated by Leslie J. Roberts. Syracuse, NY: Syracuse University Press, 2003.

Campanella, Tommaso. *The City of the Sun*. Translated by Daniel J. Donno. Berkeley: University of California Press, 1981.

———. *The City of the Sun*. Translated by Thomas W. Halliday in *Ideal Commonwealths*. London: The Colonial Press, 1901.

Cattell, J. McKeen. "A Program of Radical Democracy." *Popular Science Monthly* 80 (June 1912).

Chan, Edward K. *The Racial Horizon of Utopia: Unthinking the Future of Race in Late Twentieth-Century American Utopian Novels*. Bern, Switzerland: Peter Lang, 2016.

Chase, Malcolm. "Paine, Spence, Chartism and 'The Real Rights of Man.'" In *Thomas Spence: The Poor Man's Revolutionary*, edited by Alastair Bonnett and Keith Armstrong, 13–25. London: Breviary Stuff Publications, 2014.

Chavannes, Albert. *The Future Commonwealth or What Samuel Balcom Saw in Socioland*. New York: True Nationalist Publishing Company, 1892.

Cioran, E. M. *History and Utopia*. The University of Chicago Press, 1960.

Claeys, Gregory. *Citizens and Saints: Politics and Anti-politics in Early British Socialism*. Cambridge: Cambridge University Press, 1989.

———. *Dystopia: A Natural History*. Oxford: Oxford University Press, 2017.

———. "The Five Languages of Utopia: Their Respective Advantages and Deficiencies; with a Plea for Prioritising Social Realism." In *Spectres of Utopia: Theory, Practice, Conventions*, edited by Artur Blaim and Ludmila Gruszewska-Blaim, 28–31. Frankfurt am Main: Peter Lang, 2012.

———. Introduction to *A New View of Society and Other Writings*, by Robert Owen. New York: Penguin Classics, 1991.

———. *Machinery, Money and the Millennium: From Moral Economy to Socialism, 1815–1860*. Princeton, NJ: Princeton University Press, 1987.

———. *Mill and Paternalism*. Cambridge, UK: Cambridge University Press, 2013.

———. "Paine's *Agrarian Justice* (1796) and the Secularization of Natural Jurisprudence." *Bulletin of the Society for the Study of Labour History* 52, pt. 3 (November 1987): 21–31; reprinted in *Thomas Paine*, edited by Bruce Kuklick. London: Ashgate Publishing, 2006; reissue Oxfordshire, UK: Routledge, Taylor and Francis Group, 2018.

———. *Searching for Utopia: The History of an Idea*. London: Thames and Hudson, 2011.

———. *Thomas Paine: Social and Political Thought*. Boston: Unwin Hyman, 1989.

Clemit, Pamela. *The Godwinian Novel*. Oxford: Clarendon Press, 1993.

Cohen, G. A. *Self-Ownership, Freedom, and Equality*. New York: Cambridge University Press, 1995.

Cole, G. D. H. *Robert Owen*. Boston: Little, Brown, and Company, 1925.

Craig, Alexander. *Ionia: Land of Wise Men and Fair Women*. Chicago: E. A. Weeks Co., 1898.
Criado-Perez, Caroline. *Invisible Women: Data Bias in a World Designed for Men*. New York: Abrams Press, 2019.
Curtis, Claire P. "Theorizing Fear: Octavia Butler and the Realist Utopia." *Utopian Studies* 19, no. 3 (2008): 411–431.
Dahrendorf, Ralf. *Class and Class Conflict in Industrial Society*. California: Stanford University Press, 1959.
———. *Life Chances: Approaches to Social and Political Theory*. The University of Chicago Press, 1979.
———. "Out of Utopia: Toward a Reorientation of Sociological Analysis." *American Journal of Sociology* 64, no. 2 (September, 1958): 115–127.
Dalton, Test. *The Richest Man on Earth*. New York: Lowe Shearon, 1931.
Darwin, Charles. *The Origin of Species*, sixth London edition (1876). Los Angeles: Enhanced Media Publishing Co., 2017.
Davis, J. C. *Utopia and the Ideal Society: A Study of English Utopian Writing 1516–1700*. Cambridge University Press, 1981.
De Jouvenel, Bertrand. *The Ethics of Redistribution*. Cambridge: Cambridge University Press, 1951.
———. "Utopia for Practical Purposes." In *Utopias and Utopian Thought*, edited by Frank E. Manuel, 219–235. Boston: Houghton Mifflin Company, 1966.
DeLong, J. Bradford. *Slouching Towards Utopia*. London: Basic Books, 2022.
Devinne, Paul. *The Day of Prosperity: A Vision of the Century to Come*. New York: G. W. Dillingham Company, 1902.
Dewey, John. *Art as Experience*. New York: Minton, Balch and Company, 1934.
———. *A Common Faith*. New Haven, CT: Yale University Press, 1934.
———. "Does Human Nature Change?" In *John Dewey: The Later Works: 1925–1953*, vol. 13: 1938–1939. Carbondale: Southern Illinois University Press, 1991.
———. *Experience and Education*. In *John Dewey: The Later Works: 1925–1953*, vol. 13: 1938–1939. Carbondale: Southern Illinois University Press, 1991.
———. "A Great American Prophet." *Common Sense* 3 (April 1934): 6–7. In *John Dewey: The Later Works: 1925–1953*, vol. 9: 1933–1934. Carbondale: Southern Illinois University Press, 1989.
———. *The Influence of Darwin on Philosophy*. New York: Henry Holt and Co., 1910.
———. "The President and the Special Session." *People's Lobby Bulletin* 1 (June 1931): 1. In *John Dewey: The Later Works: 1925–1953*, vol. 6: 1931–1932. Carbondale: Southern Illinois University Press, 1989.
———. *The Public and Its Problems*. Chicago: The Swallow Press, 1927.

Dixie, Florence Caroline. *Gloriana; or, the Revolution of 1900* (1890). N.p.: Mint Editions, 2021.

Doctorow, Cory. "The Masque of the Red Death." In *Radicalized*. New York: Tom Doherty Associates, 2019.

———. *Walkaway*. New York: Tom Doherty Associates, 2017.

Donnelly, Ignatius. *Caesar's Column: A Story of the Twentieth Century* (1890). N.p.: n.d.

———. *Donnelliana: An Appendix to Caesar's Column*. Chicago: Francis J. Schulte and Company, 1892.

———. *The Golden Bottle: The Story of Ephraim Benezet of Kansas* (1892). India: Pranava Books, n.d.

Du Bois, W. E. B. *Black Reconstruction in America*. New York: The Free Press, 1998.

———. *Dark Princess*. Oxford, UK: Oxford University Press, 2007.

Durkheim, Émile. *The Division of Labor in Society* (1893). Translated by George Simpson. New York, NY: Digreads.com Publishing, 2019.

Eurich, Nell. *Science in Utopia: A Mighty Design*. Cambridge, MA: Harvard University Press, 1967.

Fellman, Michael. *The Unbounded Frame: Freedom and Community in Nineteenth Century American Utopianism*. Westport, CT: Greenwood Press, 1973.

Fischer, David Hackett. *The Great Wave: Price Revolutions and the Rhythm of History*. Oxford, UK: Oxford University Press, 1996.

Fisher, Richard. "Henry George: Antiprotectionist Giant of American Economics." *Economic Insights. Federal Reserve Bank of Dallas* 10, no. 2 (2005).

Fitting, Peter. "Utopias Beyond Our Ideals: The Dilemma of Right-Wing Utopia." *Utopian Studies* 2, no. 1/2 (1991): 95–109.

Forbes, Allyn B. "The Literary Quest for Utopia, 1880–1900." *Social Forces* 6, no. 2 (December 1927): 179–189.

Forsyth, Archibald. *Rapara or the Rights of the Individual in the State*. London: T. Fisher Unwin, 1897.

Foster, John Bellamy. "William Morris's Romantic Revolutionary Ideal: Nature, Labour and Gender in *News from Nowhere*." *The Journal of William Morris Studies* 22, no. 2 (2017): 17–35.

Fourier, Charles. *The Utopian Vision of Charles Fourier*. Translated by Jonathan Beecher and Richard Bienvenu. Boston: Beacon Press, 1971.

France, Anatole. *The Red Lily* (1894). Reprint, n.p.: Dodo Press, n.d.

Frank, Robert. *Social Integration: A Brief Fictional History of the United States During the Period, 1935–1945*. Boston, MA: The Christopher Publishing House, 1935.

Frank, Robert H. *The Darwin Economy*. Princeton, NJ: Princeton University Press, 2011.

Frankel, Charles. "Equality of Opportunity." In *Against Equality: Readings on Economic and Social Policy*, edited by William Letwin, 167–188. London: The Macmillan Press, 1983.

Frankfurt, Harry G. *Inequality*. Princeton, NJ: Princeton University Press, 2015.

Freeman-Moir, John. "Crafting Experience: William Morris, John Dewey, and Utopia." *Utopian Studies* 22, no. 2 (2011): 202–232.

Friedman, Milton. *Capitalism and Freedom*. Chicago: The University of Chicago Press, 2002.

Frye, Northrop. "Varieties of Literary Utopias." In *Utopias and Utopian Thought*, edited by Frank E. Manuel, 25–49. Boston: Houghton Mifflin Company, 1965.

Fuller, Alvarado M. *A. D. 2000*. Chicago: Laird and Lee Publishers, 1890.

Gabriel, Elum. "Utopia, Science, and the Nature of Civilization in Theodor Hertzka's *Fieiland*." *Seminar* 48, no. 1 (February 2012): 9–29.

Galton, Francis. "Eugenics: Its Definition, Scope, and Aims." *The American Journal of Sociology* 10, no. 1 (July, 1904): 1–25.

Gandhi, M. K. *An Autobiography or The Story of My Experiments with Truth*. Translated by Mahadev Desai. Ahmedabad: Navajivan Publishing House, 1927.

Gans, Herbert J. *People, Plans, and Policies: Essays on Poverty, Racism, and Other National Urban Problems*. New York: Columbia University Press, 1993.

Garforth, Lisa. "Green Utopias: Beyond Apocalypse, Progress, and Pastoral." *Utopian Studies* 16, no. 3 (2005): 393–427.

Geiger, George Raymond. *The Philosophy of Henry George*. New York: The Macmillan Company, 1933.

Geissler, Ludwig A. *Looking Beyond: A Sequel to "Looking Backward," by Edward Bellamy, and an Answer to "Looking Further Forward," by Richard Michaelis*. London: William Reeves, 1891.

Geoghegan, Vincent. "Ralahine: An Irish Owenite Community (1831–1833)." *International Review of Social History* 36, no. 3 (1991): 377–411.

———. *Utopianism and Marxism*. London: Methuen, 1987.

———. "The Utopian Past: Memory and History in Edward Bellamy's *Looking Backward* and William Morris's *News From Nowhere*." *Utopian Studies* 3, no. 2 (1992): 75–90.

George, Henry. *Progress and Poverty*. 1879. New York: Robert Schalkenbach Foundation, 1953.

Gerber, Richard. *Utopian Fantasy: A Study of English Utopian Fiction since the End of the Nineteenth Century*. London: Routledge and Kegan Paul, 1955.

Gibbon, Edward. *The Decline and Fall of the Roman Empire*. In *Great Books of the Western World*, edited by Robert Maynard Hutchins and Mortimer Adler, vol. 40. Chicago: Encyclopaedia Britannica, 1952.

Giles, Fayette Stratton. *Shadows Before or a Century Onward* (1893). India: Pranava Books, n.d.

Gilman, Charlotte Perkins. *Herland*. Mineola: New York: Dover Publications, 1998.

———. *Human Work*. Lanham, MD: AltaMira Press, 2005.

———. "Is America Too Hospitable?" In *Charlotte Perkins Gilman: A Nonfiction Reader*, edited by Larry Ceplair. New York: Columbia University Press, 1991.

———. *Moving the Mountain* (1911). N.p.: n.d.

———. *Women and Economics*. Mineola, NY: Dover Publications, 1988.

Godin, Jean Baptiste Andre. *Social Solutions* (1873). Translated by Marie Howland. New York: John W. Lovell Company, 1886.

Godwin, William. *An Enquiry Concerning Political Justice*, 1st ed., 1793. Oxford: Oxford University Press, 2013.

———. *Enquiry Concerning Political Justice and Its Influence on Modern Morals and Happiness*, 3rd ed., 1798. New York: Viking Penguin, 1985.

———. *Things as They Are or the Adventures of Caleb Williams* (1794). New York: Penguin Books, 1988.

Goodwin, Barbara. "Economic and Social Innovation in Utopia." In *Utopias*, edited by Peter Alexander and Roger Gill, 69–83. London: Duckworth, 1984.

———. "Taxation in Utopia." *Utopian Studies* 19, no. 2 (2008): 313–331.

Goodwin, Barbara and Keith Taylor. *The Politics of Utopia: A Study in Theory and Practice*, Oxford: Peter Lang, 2009.

Gorn, Elliott J. *Mother Jones: The Most Dangerous Woman in America*. New York: Hill and Wang, 2001.

Grabb, Edward G. *Social Inequality: Classical and Contemporary Theories*. Toronto: Holt, Rinehart and Winston of Canada, 1984.

Grace, William J. "The Conception of Society in More's 'Utopia,'" *Thought* 22, no. 2 (1947): 283–296.

Graeber, David. *Debt: The First 5,000 Years*. Brooklyn, NY: Melville House, 2011.

Greenblatt, Stephen. *Renaissance Self-Fashioning: From More to Shakespeare*. The University of Chicago Press, 1980.

Greene, John O. *The Ke Whonkus People: A Story of the North Pole Country*. Indianapolis, IN: Vincent Publishing Co., 1893.

Griffith, Mary. *Three Hundred Years Hence* (1836). N.p.: n.d.

Grigsby, A. O. and Mary P. Lowe (Jack Adams, pseud.). *Nequa or the Problem of Ages*. Newton, KS: Mennonite Press, 2015; original publication Topeka, KS: Equity Publishing Company, 1900.

Gutek, Gerald. "An Analysis of Formal Education in Edward Bellamy's *Looking Backward*." *History of Education Quarterly* 4, no. 4 (December, 1964): 251–263.

Guthrie, Kenneth Sylvan. *A Romance of Two Centuries: A Tale of the Year 2025* (1919). India: Pranava Books, n.d.

Hansot, Elisabeth. *Perfection and Progress: Two Modes of Utopian Thought*. Cambridge, MA: The MIT Press, 1974.
Harrison, John F. C. *Utopianism and Education*. New York: Teachers College Press, Columbia University, 1968.
Hartman, Matthew. "Utopian Evolution: The Sentimental Critique of Social Darwinism in Bellamy and Pierce." *Utopian Studies* 10, no. 1 (1999): 26–41.
Harvey, David. *A Brief History of Neoliberalism*. Oxford: Oxford University Press, 2005.
Hayek, Friedrich A. *Law, Legislation and Liberty*, 3 vols. Chicago: University of Chicago Press, 1979.
Hayes, Christopher. *Twilight of the Elites: America after Meritocracy*. New York: Crown Publishers, 2012.
Hazlitt, William. *The Spirit of the AGE: Or, Contemporary Portraits*. Paris: A. and W. Galignani, 1825.
Heinzelman, Kurt. *The Economics of the Imagination*. Amherst: The University of Massachusetts Press, 1980.
Herrnstein, Richard J. and Charles Murray. *The Bell Curve: Intelligence and Class Structure in American Life*. New York: Simon and Schuster, 1994.
Hertzka, Theodor. *Freeland: A Social Anticipation*. Translated by Arthur Ransom. University of California Libraries; London: Chatto and Windus, 1891.
Hertzler, Joyce Oramel. *The History of Utopian Thought*. New York: The Macmillan Company, 1926.
Herzl, Theodor. *Altneuland: The Old-New-Land* (1902). N.p.: n.d.
Hexter, J. H. *More's Utopia: The Biography of an Idea*. New York: Harper Torchbooks, 1965.
Hobbes, Thomas. *Leviathan: Or the Matter, Forme and Power of a Commonwealth Ecclesiasticall and Civil*, edited Michael Oakeshott. London: Collier-Macmillan, 1962.
Hofstadter, Richard. *Social Darwinism in American Thought*. Boston: Beacon Press, 1944.
Holland, Owen. "Spectatorship and Entanglement in Thoreau, Hawthorne, Morris, and Wells." *Utopian Studies* 27, no.1 (2016): 28–52.
Holtzman, Michael. "Anarchism and Utopia: William Morris's News from Nowhere." ELH 51, no. 3 (Autumn, 1984): 589–603.
House, Edward Mandell. *Philip Dru: Administrator: A Story of Tomorrow 1920 – 1935*. New York: B. W. Huebsch, 1912.
Howells, William Dean. *A Traveler from Altruria*. New York: Sagamore Press, 1957.
Howland, Marie. *Papa's Own Girl: A Novel*. New York: John P. Jewett, 1874.
Hudson, W. H. *A Crystal Age* (1887). New York: E. P. Dutton and Company, 1917.

Hughes, David Y. "The Ghost in the Machine." In *America as Utopia*, edited by Kenneth M. Roemer. New York: Burt Franklin and Company, 1981.

Hurst, Charles E. *Social Inequality: Forms, Causes, and Consequences*, 5th ed. Boston: Pearson, 2004.

Huxley, Aldous. *Brave New World.* New York: HarperCollins Publishers, 2004.

Jameson, Frederic. *Archaeologies of the Future: The Desire Called Utopia and Other Science Fictions*. London: VERSO, 2005.

Jendrysik, Mark. "Tom Paine: Utopian?." *Utopian Studies* 18, no. 2 (2007): 139–157.

Jones, Alice Ilgenfritz and Ella Merchant. *Unveiling a Parallel.* New York: Syracuse University Press, 1991.

Jos, Philip H. "Fear and the Spiritual Realism of Octavia Butler's Earthseed." *Utopian Studies* 23, no. 2 (2012): 408–429.

Kant, Immanuel. "Idea for a Universal History with a Cosmopolitan Purpose." In *Kant: Political Writings*. Translated by H. B. Nisbet. Cambridge University Press, 1970.

Kateb, George. *Human Dignity*. Cambridge, MA: The Belknap Press of Harvard University Press, 2011.

———. *Utopia and Its Enemies.* New York: The Free Press, 1963.

———. "Utopia and the Good Life." In *Utopias and Utopian Thought*, edited by Frank E. Manuel, 239–259. Boston: Houghton Mifflin Company, 1965.

Kaufmann, Moritz. *Utopias: Or, Schemes of Social Improvement from Sir Thomas More to Karl Marx.* London: C. Kegan Paul and Co., 1879.

Kern, Louis J. "Evangelical Environmentalism and the New Commonwealth: Visions of Labor, Urban Culture, and Technological Transformation in Futuristic Fiction, 1883–1903." *Utopian Studies* 4 (1991): 42–54.

Kessler, Carol Farley, "Women Daring to Speak: United States Women's Feminist Utopias." *Utopian Studies* 2 (1989): 118–123.

Keynes, John Maynard. *The End of Laissez-Faire* (1926). N.p.: BN Publishing, n.d.

———. *Essays in Persuasion*. N.p.: Classic House Books, 2009.

———. *The General Theory of Employment, Interest, and Money*. New York: A Harvest Book, Harcourt, 1964.

King, J. E. and John Marangos. "Two Arguments for Basic Income: Thomas Paine (1737–1809) and Thomas Spence (1750–1814)." *History of Economic Ideas* 14, no. 1 (2006): 55–71.

Knapp, Adeline. *One Thousand Dollars a Day* (1894). N.p.: n.d.

Kolmertan, Carol A. "Texts and Contexts: American Women Envision Utopia, 1890–1920." In *Utopian and Science Fiction by Women*, edited by Jane L. Donawerth and Carol A. Kolmerten, 107–125. New York: Syracuse University Press, 1994.

Kropotkin, Peter. *Mutual Aid: A Factor in Evolution.* McClure, Philips and Company, 1902.

Kumar, Krishnan. "A Pilgrimage of Hope: William Morris's Journey to Utopia." *Utopian Studies* 5, no. 1 (1994): 89–107.

———. *Utopia and Anti-Utopia in Modern Times.* Oxford: Basil Blackwell, 1987.

Lasky, Melvin J. *Utopia and Revolution: On the Origins of a Metaphor.* Chicago: University of Chicago Press, 1976; republished, New Brunswick, NJ: Transaction Publishers, 2004.

Lawson, John and Harold Silver. *A Social History of Education in England.* London: Methuen and Co., 1973.

Leopold, David. "Education and Utopia: Robert Owen and Charles Fourier." *Oxford Review of Education* 37, no. 5 (October 2011): 619–635.

Lerner, Steve. *Sacrifice Zones: The Front Lines of Toxic Chemical Exposure in the United States.* Cambridge, MA: The MIT Press, 2010.

Levitas, Ruth. *The Concept of Utopia.* Oxford: Peter Lang 2011.

———. *Utopia as Method: The Imaginary Reconstruction of Society.* New York: Palgrave Macmillan, 2013.

———. "'Who Holds the Hose?' Domestic Labour in the Work of Bellamy, Gilman and Morris." *Utopian Studies* 6, no. 1 (1995): 65–85.

Locke, John. *An Essay Concerning Human Understanding.* New York: Dover, 1959.

London, Jack. *The Iron Heel.* New York: The Macmillan Company, 1908.

Lovchik, John. *Racism: Reality Built on a Myth.* Eugene, Oregon: Resource Publications, 2018.

Lovejoy, Arthur O. *The Great Chain of Being.* New York: Harper and Row, 1936.

Lowrey, Annie. *Give People Money: How a Universal Basic Income Would End Poverty, Revolutionize Work, and Remake the World.* New York: Broadway Books, 2018.

Maas, Jolanda, Robert A. Verheij and others. "Green Space, Urbanity, and Health: How Strong Is the Relation?." *Journal of Epidemiology and Community Health* 60, no. 7 (July): 587–592, 2006.

Macnie, John. *The Diothas, or, a Far Look Ahead.* New York: G. P. Putnam's Sons, 1883.

Malthus, Thomas. *An Essay on the Principle of Population.* Oxford: Oxford University Press, 1993.

Mandeville, Bernard. *The Fable of the Bees*, vol. 1. Oxford: Clarendon Press, 1924; Reprint, Indianapolis: The Liberty Fund, 1988.

Manuel, Frank E. *The Prophets of Paris.* New York: Harper Torchbooks, 1962.

———. "Toward a Psychological History of Utopias." In *Utopias and Utopian Thought*, edited by Frank E. Manuel, 69–98. Boston: Houghton Mifflin Company, 1965.

Manuel, Frank E. and Fritzie P. Manuel. *Utopian Thought the Western World.* Cambridge, MA: The Belknap Press of Harvard University Press, 1979.

Markley, Robert. *Kim Stanley Robinson*. Urbana, IL: University of Illinois Press, 2019.

Marquis, Don. *The Almost Perfect State.* New York: Doubleday, Page and Company, 1927.

Marshall, Archibald. *Upsidonia.* New York: Dodd, Mead and Company, 1919.

Marx, Karl. *Capital: A Critical Analysis of Capitalist Production*, vol. 1. Translated by Samuel Moore and Edward Aveling. Ware, Hertfordshire: Wordsworth Editions Limited, 2013.

———. *Theories of Surplus Value*. London: Lawrence and Wishart, 1969.

Marx, Karl and Friedrich Engels. "The Communist Manifesto." In *A Handbook of Marxism.* New York: International Publishers Co., 1935.

McCowan, Archibald. *Philip Meyer's Scheme: A Story of Trades Unionism.* New York: J. S. Ogilvie, 1892.

McDonald, David A. "Environmental Racism and Neoliberal Disorder in South Africa." In *The Quest for Environmental Justice: Human Rights and the Politics of Pollution*, edited by Robert D. Bullard, 255–278. San Francisco: Sierra Club Books, 2005. Citing "Environmental Justice Networking Forum." *Environmental Justice Newsletter* (Autumn 1997): 1.

Merton, Robert K. *On Social Structure and Science.* Chicago: The University of Chicago Press, 1996.

Michaelis, Richard C. *Looking Further Forward.* Chicago: Rand, McNally and Company, 1890.

Michels, Robert. *Political Parties: A Sociological Study of the Oligarchical Tendencies of Modern Democracy.* Translated by Eden and Cedar Paul. New York: The Free Press, 1962.

Milanović, Branko. *Global Inequality: A New Approach for the Age of Globalization.* Cambridge, MA: The Belknap Press of Harvard University Press, 2016.

———. *The Haves and the Have-Nots: A Brief and Idiosyncratic History of Global Inequality.* New York: Basic Books, 2011.

———. "The Return of 'Patrimonial Capitalism': A Review of Thomas Piketty's *Capital in the Twenty-First Century.*" *Journal of Economic Literature* 52, no. 2 (2014): 519–534.

Mill, John Stuart. *Autobiography*. New York: Penguin Books, 1989.

———. "Essays on Economics and Society." In *Collected Work of John Stuart Mill*, vol. 5. Toronto: University of Toronto Press: Routledge and Kegan Paul, 1967.

———. *Principles of Political Economy.* Abridged by J. Laurence Laughlin. New York: Appleton and Company, 1884.

———. *Socialism* (1879). N.p.: S. M. B, Special Edition, n.d.

———. *The Subjection of Women*. Mineola, NY: Dover Publication, 1997.

Moore, David. *The Age of Progress; or a Panorama of Time*. New York: Sheldon, Blakeman and Co., 1856.

More, Thomas. *Utopia*. Translated by Robert M. Adams. Cambridge: Cambridge University Press, 1975.

———. *Utopia*, editor, Henry Morley (Project Gutenberg). <https://www.gutenberg.org/files/2130/2130-h/2130-h.htm>

Morris, Donald. "A Case for Company-Specific Public Disclosure of Corporate Tax Returns." *Accounting and the Public Interest 15*, no. 1 (2015): 1–21.

Morris, William. "Bellamy's Looking Backward." *Commonweal* 5, no. 8 (June 21, 1889).

———. "How I Became a Socialist." In *Political Writings of William Morris*, edited by A. L. Morton. New York: International Publishers, 1973.

———. "News from Nowhere." In *News from Nowhere and Other Writings*, edited by C. Wilmer. New York: Penguin Books, 1993.

———. "Useful Work Versus Useless Toil." In *Political Writings of William Morris*, edited by A. L. Morton. New York: International Publishers, 1973.

Morton, A. L. *The English Utopia*. London: Lawrence and Wishart, 1952; Reprint, Berlin: Seven Seas Books, 1968.

———. *The Life and Ideas of Robert Owen*. London: Lawrence and Wishart, 1962.

Mosley, Walter. *Folding the Red into the Black or Developing a Viable Utopia for Human Survival in the 21st Century*. New York: OR Books, 2016.

Moylan, Tom. *Demand the Impossible: Science Fiction and the Utopian Imagination*, edited by Raffaella Baccolini. Oxford: Peter Lang, 2014.

———. *Scraps of the Untainted Sky: Science Fiction, Utopia, Dystopia*. Boulder, CO: Westview Press, 2000.

———. "'Utopia is when our lives matter': Reading Kim Stanley Robinson's *Pacific Edge*." *Utopian Studies* 6, no. 2 (1995): 1–24.

Mullainathan, Sendhil and Eldar Shafir, *Scarcity*. New York: Picador, Henry Holt and Company, 2013.

Nagel, Thomas. "Equality." In *Mortal Questions*, 106–127. *Cambridge* University Press, 1979.

———. *Equality and Partiality*. New York: Oxford University Press, 1991.

———. "The Policy of Preference." In *Mortal Questions*, 91–105. Cambridge University Press, 1979.

Negley, Glen and J. Max Patrick. *The Quest for Utopia*. New York: Henry Schuman, 1952; Reprint, New York: Anchor Books, 1962.

Nordstrom, Justin. "Looking Backward's Utopian Sequels: 'Fictional Dialogues' in Gilded-Age America." *Utopian Studies* 18, no. 2 (2007): 193–221.

Norton, Seymour Francis and Robert H. Cowdrey. *Ten Men of Money Island*. New York, Columbia University, 1891.

Noto, Cosimo. *The Ideal City*. New York, 1903.
Nozick, Robert. *Anarchy, State, and Utopia*. New York: Basic Books, 1974.
Nussbaum, Martha C. *Frontiers of Justice: Disability, Nationality, Species Membership*. Cambridge, MA: The Belknap Press of Harvard University Press, 2006.
O'Donnell, Edward T. *Henry George and the Crisis of Inequality*. New York: Columbia University Press, 2015.
Olson, Mancur. *The Logic of Collective Action: Public Goods and the Theory of Groups*. Cambridge: Harvard University Press, 1965.
Orwell, George. *Down and Out in Paris and London*. New York: A Harvest Book, Harcourt, Inc., 1961.
———. "The Lion and the Unicorn: Socialism and the English Genius." In *Essays*. New York: Everyman's Library, 1998; Alfred A. Knopf, 1968.
———. *Nineteen Eighty-Four*. New York: PLUME/Penguin/Harcourt Brace, 2003.
———. *The Road to Wigan Pier*. New York: A Harvest Book–Harcourt, 1958.
Owen, Robert. *The Book of the New Moral World*. New York: Augustus M. Kelley Publishers, 1970.
———. *A Development of the Principles and Plans on Which to Establish Self-Supporting Home Colonies*. London: Published by the Home Colonization Society, 1841.
———. *Lectures on an Entire New State of Society*. London: J. Brooks, 1830.
———. *The Life of Robert Owen Written by Himself*. New York: Augustus M. Kelley Publishers, 1967.
———. *A New View of Society and Other Writings*. New York: Penguin Classics, 1991.
———. *The Revolution in the Mind and Practice of the Human Race*. London: Effingham Wilson, Publisher, 1849.
Owen, Robert Dale. *Threading My Way*. London: Turner and Co., 1874. Forgotten Books, 2012.
Paine, Thomas. "Agrarian Justice." In *The Thomas Paine Reader*. New York: Penguin Books, 1987.
———. *Rights of Man*. Mineola, NY: Dover Publications, 1999.
Pareto, Vilfredo. *Manual of Political Economy*, edited by Aldo Montesano and others. Oxford, UK: Oxford University Press, 2014.
Parrinder, Patrick. "Eugenics and Utopia: Sexual Selection from Galton to Morris." *Utopian Studies* 8, no. 2 (1997): 1–12.
Parrington, Jr, Vernon Louis. *American Dreams: A Study of American Utopias*. New York: Russell and Russell, 1964.
Partington, John S. "The Death of the Static: H. G. Wells and the Kinetic Utopia." *Utopian Studies* 11, no. 2 (2000): 96–111.
———. "H. G. Wells: A Political Life." *Utopian Studies* 19, no. 3 (2008): 517–576.

———. "The Time Machine and a Modern Utopia: The Static and Kinetic Utopias of the Early H. G. Wells." *Utopian Studies* 13, no. 1 (2002): 57–68.

Peck, Bradford. *The World a Department Store: A Story of Life Under a Cooperative System*. Boston: Bradford Peck, 1900.

Pfaelzer, Jean. "The Impact of Political Theory on Narrative Structures." In *America as Utopia*, edited by Kenneth M. Roemer. New York: Burt Franklin and Company, 1981.

———. *The Utopian Novel in America, 1886–1896: The Politics of Form*. University of Pittsburgh Press, 1984.

Pfohl, Stephen. "The 'Discovery' of Child Abuse." *Social Problems* 24, no. 3 (February 1997): 310–323.

Piercy, Marge. *Woman on the Edge of Time*. New York: Ballantine Books, 1976.

Piketty, Thomas. *A Brief History of Equality*. Translated by Steven Rendall. Cambridge, MA: The Belknap Press of Harvard University Press, 2022.

———. *Capital and Ideology*. Translated by Arthur Goldhammer. Cambridge, MA: The Belknap Press of Harvard University Press, 2020.

———. *Capital in the Twenty-First Century*. Translated by Arthur Goldhammer. Cambridge, MA: The Belknap Press of Harvard University Press, 2014.

———. *The Economics of Inequality*. Translated by Arthur Goldhammer. Cambridge, MA: The Belknap Press of Harvard University Press, 2015.

Plato. *Critias*. Translated by A. E. Taylor. In *Plato: The Collected Dialogues*, edited by Edith Hamilton and Huntington Cairns. New York: Pantheon Books, 1961.

———. *Laws*. Translated by A. E. Taylor. In *Plato: The Collected Dialogues*, edited by Edith Hamilton and Huntington Cairns. New York: Pantheon Books, 1961.

———. *Laws*. Translated by Benjamin Jowett. In *Great Books of the Western World*, vol. 7, edited Robert Maynard Hutchins and Mortimer J. Adler. Chicago: Encyclopaedia Britannica, 1952.

———. *Phaedrus*. Translated by R. Hackforth. In *Plato: The Collected Dialogues*, edited by Edith Hamilton and Huntington Cairns. New York: Pantheon Books, 1961.

———. *Republic*. Translated by Allan Bloom, 2nd ed. Basic Books, 1968.

———. *Republic*. Translated by Benjamin Jowett. New York: Vintage Classics, a division of Random House, 1991.

Plutarch. *Plutarch's Lives*, the Dryden translation. New York: The Modern Library, 1992.

Pohl, Frederik and C. M. Kornbluth. *The Space Merchants*. New York: Thomas Dunne Books imprint of St Martin's Griffin, [1953] 2011.

Polanyi, Karl. *The Great Transformation: The Political and Economic Origins of Our Time*. Boston: Beacon Press, 1944.

Prettyman, Gib. "Gilded Age Utopias of Incorporation." *Utopian Studies* 12, no. 1 (2001): 19–40.

Proudhon, Pierre-Joseph. *General Idea of the Revolution in the Nineteenth Century.* Translated by John Beverley Robinson. Mineola, NY: Dover Publications, 2003.

Proust, Marcel. *Remembrance of Things Past*, vol. 1 "Within a Budding Grove." Translated by C. K. Scott Moncrieff and Terrence Kilmartin. New York: Vintage Books, a division of Random House, 1981.

Quissell, Barbara C. "The New World That Eve Made: Feminist Utopias Written by Nineteenth-Century Women." In *America as Utopia*, edited by Kenneth M. Roemer, 148–174. New York: Burt Franklin and Company, 1981.

Rae, Douglas. *Equalities.* Cambridge, MA: Harvard University Press, 1981.

Rand, Ayn. *The Romantic Manifesto.* New York: Signet Books, 1971.

———. *The Virtue of Selfishness.* New York: Signet Books, 1964.

Randall Jr, John Herman. *The Making of the Modern Mind: A Survey of the Intellectual Background of the Present Age.* Boston: Houghton Mifflin, 1926.

Ransom, Arthur. "A Competitive Utopia." In *The Gentleman's Magazine* 271. London: Chatto and Windus, 1891.

Ricoeur, Paul. *Lectures on Ideology and Utopia.* New York: Columbia University Press, 1986.

Riederer, Franz X. "The German Acceptance and Reaction." In *Edward Bellamy Abroad.* New York: Twayne Publishers, 1962.

Roberts, John W. *Looking Within: The Misleading Tendencies of "Looking Backward" Made Manifest.* New York: A. S. Barnes and Company, 1893.

Robertson, Michael. *The Last Utopians: Four Late Nineteenth-Century Visionaries and Their Legacy.* Princeton, NJ: Princeton University Press, 2018.

Robinson, Cedric J. *Black Marxism.* Chapel Hill: The University of North Carolina Press, 1983.

Robinson, John Mark. "The Neoliberal Utopianism of Bitcoin and Modern Monetary Theory." *Utopian Studies* 33, no. 1 (2022): 127–143.

Robinson, Kim Stanley. *The Gold Coast.* New York: Tom Doherty Associates Book, 1988.

———. *The Ministry for the Future.* New York: Orbit, 2020.

———. *New York 2140.* New York: Orbit, 2018.

———. *Pacific Edge.* New York: A Tom Doherty Associates Book, 1988.

Robinson, Richard. *Definition.* London: Oxford University Press, 1954.

Roemer, Kenneth M. "Contexts and Texts: The Influence of Looking Backward." *The Centennial Review* 27, no. 3 (Summer, 1983): 204–223.

———. *The Obsolete Necessity: America in Utopian Writings, 1888–1900.* The Kent State University Press, 1976.

Rosewater, Frank. *The Making of a Millennium*. Omaha, NE: Centry Publishing, 1908.

———. *Utopia: A Romance of Today Presenting a Solution of the Labor Problem, a New God and a New Religion* (1897). London: F. Tennyson Neely Publisher, 1987.

Rousseau, Jean-Jacques. *Discourse on the Origin and Foundations of Inequality Among Men*. In *Rousseau's Political Writings*. Translated by Julia Conway Bondanella. New York: Norton, 1988.

Sabia, Dan. "Democratic/Utopian Education." *Utopian Studies* 23, no. 2 (2012): 374–405.

Saint-Simon, Henri. *The Political Thought of Saint-Simon*, edited by Ghita Ionescu. Oxford: Oxford University Press, 1976.

Sandel, Michael J. *Justice: What's the Right Thing to Do*? New York: Farrar, Straus and Giroux, 2009.

———. *The Tyranny of Merit: What's Become of the Common Good*?. New York: Farrar, Straus and Giroux, 2020.

Sargent, Lyman Tower. "African Americans and Utopia: Visions of a Better Life." *Utopian Studies* 33, no. 1 (2020): 27–96.

———. "Australian Utopian Literature: An Annotated, Chronological Bibliography 1667–1999." *Utopian Studies* 10, no. 2 (1999): 138–173.

———. "Authority and Utopia: Utopianism in Political Thought." *Polity* 14, no. 4 (Summer 1982): 565–584.

———. "Capitalist Eutopias in America." In *America as Utopia*, edited by Kenneth M. Roemer, 192–205. New York: Burt Franklin and Company, 1981.

———. "Edward Bellamy's Boston in 2000 from 1888 to 1897: The Evolution of Bellamy's Future Boston from *Looking Backward* Through *Equality*." *Utopian Studies* 27, no. 2 (2016): 152–181.

———. "Theorizing Utopia/Utopianism in the Twenty-First Century." In *Spectres of Utopia: Theory, Practice, Conventions*, edited by Artur Blaim and Ludmila Gruszewska-Blaim, 13–25. Frankfurt am Main: Peter Lang, 2012.

———. "The Three Faces of Utopianism Revisited." *Utopian Studies* 5, no. 1 (1994): 1–37.

———. *Utopianism: A Very Short Introduction*. Oxford: Oxford University Press, 2010.

———. "Women in Utopia." *Comparative Literature Studies* 10, no. 4 (December, 1973): 302–316.

Satterlee, W. W. *Looking Backward and What I Saw*. New York: Arno Press and the New York Times, 1971.

Satz, Debra and Stuart White. "What Is Wrong with Inequality?." *Inequality the IFS Deaton Review* 1–29: 4. <https://ifs.org.uk/inequality/what-is-wrong-with-inequality/>

Saxton, Alexander. "'Caesar's Column': The Dialogue of Utopia and Catastrophe." *American Quarterly* 16, no. 2, pt. 1 (Summer, 1967): 224–238.

Scheidel, Walter. *The Great Leveler: Violence and the History of Inequality*. Princeton, NJ: Princeton University Press, 2017.

Scheve, Kenneth and David Stasavage. *Taxing the Rich*. New York: Russell Sage Foundation and Princeton: Princeton University Press, 2016.

Schindler, Solomon. *Young West: A Sequel to Edward Bellamy's Celebrated Novel, Looking Backward.* Boston: Arena Publishing Company, 1894.

Schumpeter, Joseph A. *Capitalism, Socialism and Democracy*. New York: Harper and Row Publishers, 1976.

Schuyler, George S. *Black No More*. Victoria, BC, Canada: Must Have Books, 2021.

Schwartz, Madeline. "Less Work, More Time." In *The Feminist Utopia Project,* edited by Alexandra Brodsky and Rachel Kauder Nalebuff. New York: Feminist Press, 2015.

Seligman, Edward R. A. *Progressive Taxation in Theory and Practice*, 2nd ed., *American Economic Association Quarterly*, third series, 9, no. 4 (1908).

Sen, Amartya. *Inequality Reexamined.* Cambridge, MA: Harvard University Press, 1992.

———. *On Economic Inequality*. Oxford University Press, 1973.

Sensat, Julius. "Exploitation." *Noûs* 18, no. 1 (1984): 21–38.

Shapiro, Thomas M. *Toxic Inequality*. New York: Basic Books, 2017.

Simmel, Georg. *The Philosophy of Money*. (1900) Translated by Tom Bottomore and David Frisby. Boston: Routledge and Kegan Paul, 1978.

Skinner, B. F. *Cumulative Record*, 3rd ed. New York: Appleton-Century-Crofts, 1959.

———. *Walden Two.* New York: Macmillan Publishing Co., 1976.

Smith, Adam. *The Theory of Moral Sentiments*. Indianapolis: Liberty Fund, 1976.

———. *Wealth of Nations.* Amherst, NY: Prometheus Books, 1991.

Smith, John Maynard. "Eugenics and Utopia." In *Utopias and Utopian Thought*, edited by Frank E. Manuel, 150–168. Boston: Houghton Mifflin Company, 1965.

Spence, Thomas. "The Constitution of Spensonia." In *Pig's Meat: Selected Writings of Thomas Spence, Radical and Pioneer Land Reformer.* Nottingham: Spokesman, 1982.

———. "A Further Account of Spensonia." In *Pig's Meat: Selected Writings of Thomas Spence, Radical and Pioneer Land Reformer*. Nottingham: Spokesman, 1982.

Spencer, Herbert. *The Principles of Biology*, vol. 1. New York: D. Appleton and Company, 1888.

———. *Social Statics* (1850). New York: D. Appleton and Company, 1885.

———. *Synthetic Philosophy: First Principles.* New York: D. Appleton and Company, 1890.

Spotswood, Claire Myers. *The Unpredictable Adventure: A Comedy of Woman's Independence.* Garden City, NY: Doubleday, Doran and Company, 1935.

Stanley, Tarshia L. "Re-read and Recover: Afrofuturism as a Reading Practice in George S. Schuyler's *Black No More* and Octavia E. Butler's 'The Book of Martha.'" In *Race and Utopian Desire in American Literature and Society*, edited by Patricia Ventura and Edward K. Chan, 243–260. Gewerbestrasse: Palgrave MacMillan, 2019.

Steer, Philip. "National Pasts and Imperial Futures: Temporality, Economics, and Empire in William Morris's *News from Nowhere* (1890) and Julius Vogel's *Anno Domini 2000* (1889)." *Utopian Studies* 19, no. 1 (2008): 49–72.

Stern, Andy. *Raising the Floor.* New York: PublicAffairs, 2016.

Stiglitz, Joseph E. *The Price of Inequality.* New York: W. W. Norton and Company, 2012.

Stillman, Peter G. "Dystopian Critiques, Utopian Possibilities, and Human Purposes in Octavia Butler's *Parables.*" *Utopian Studies* 14, no. 1 (2003): 15–35.

———. "'Nothing is, but what is not': Utopias as Practical Political Philosophy." In *The Philosophy of Utopia*, edited by Barbara Goodwin, 9–24. London: Routledge, Taylor and Francis Group, 2001.

Stimpson, Catherine R. "Feminism and Utopia." *Utopian Studies* 3 (1991): 1–6.

Suvin, Darko. *Metamorphoses of Science Fiction: On the Poetics and History of a Literary Genre*, edited by Gerry Canavan. Bern, Switzerland: Peter Lang, 2016.

Tawney, R. H. *Equality.* London: Unwin Books, 1931.

Taylor, Keith. *The Political Ideas of the Utopian Socialists.* London: Rutledge, 1982.

Taylor, Walter Fuller. *The Economic Novel in America.* Chapel Hill: University of North Carolina Press, 1942.

Thomas, Chauncey. *The Crystal Button, or Adventures of Paul Prognosis in the Forty-Ninth Century.* Boston: Houghton, Mifflin and Company, 1891.

Tilman, Rick. "The Utopian Vision of Edward Bellamy and Thorstein Veblen." *Journal of Economic Issues* 19, no. 4 (December, 1985): 879–898.

Tolstoy, Count Lev. *What Shall We Do Then?*, edited and translated by Leo Wiener. Boston: Dana Estes and Company, 1904.

Twain, Mark. *A Connecticut Yankee in King Arthur's Court.* New York: Bantam Books, 1981.

van Creveld, Martin. *Equality: The Impossible Quest.* Kouvola, Finland: Castalia House, 2015.

Van Parijs, Philippe. "The Universal Basic Income: Why Utopian Thinking Matters, and How Sociologists Can Contribute to It." *Politics and Society* 41, no. 2 (2013): 171–182.

Van Parijs, Phillippe and Yannick Vanderborght. *Basic Income.* Cambridge, MA: Harvard University Press, 2017.

Van Petten, Albert Archer. *The Great Man's Life: 1925 to 2000 A. C.* New York: Utopian Publishers, 1959.

———. *The Prosperity Plan.* Utopian Publishers, 1972.

Vaninskaya, Anna. "Janus-Faced Fictions: Socialism as Utopia and Dystopia in William Morris and George Orwell." *Utopian Studies* 14, no. 2 (2003): 83–98.

Varoufakis, Yanis. *Another Now.* Brooklyn: Melville House, 2021.

Veblen, Thorstein. *The Engineers and the Price System.* Mansfield Centre, CT: Martino Publishing, 2012.

———. *The Theory of the Leisure Class.* Oxford, UK: Oxford University Press, 2007.

Ventura, Patricia. "Introduction: Race and Utopian Desire." In *Race and Utopian Desire in American Literature and Society*, edited by Patricia Ventura and Edward K. Chan, 1–19. Gewerbestrasse: Palgrave Macmillan, 2019.

Vernon, John. *Money and Fiction: Literary Realism in the Nineteenth and Early Twentieth Centuries.* Ithaca, NY: Cornell University Press, 1984.

Vonnegut, Kurt, Jr. "Harrison Bergeron." In *Welcome to the Monkey House.* New York: Dial Press, 1968.

———. *Player Piano.* New York: The Dial Press, 2006.

Wagner, Jack. *The Great Change.* Trinidad, CA: Trinidad Press, 1979.

Wasserman, Louis. "The Essential Henry George." In *Critics of Henry George*, edited by Robert V. Andelson. Malden, MA: Blackwell Publishing, 2003.

Wegner, Phillip E. *Imaginary Communities: Utopia, The Nation, and the Spatial Histories of Modernity.* Berkeley: University of California Press, 2002.

Welcome, S. Byron. *From the Earth's Centre: A Polar Gateway Message.* Chicago: Charles H. Kerr and Company, 1895.

Wells, H. G. *Anticipations* (1901). N.p.: n.d.

———. "Discussion." In Francis Galton, "Eugenics: Its Definition, Scope, and Aims." *The American Journal of Sociology* 10, no. 1 (July, 1904): 1–25.

———. *Mankind in the Making.* New York: Charles Scribner's Sons, 1904.

———. *A Modern Utopia.* New York: Digireads Publishing, 2011.

———. *The Outline of History* (1920). N.p.: n.d.

———. "Preface to *When the Sleeper Wakes.*" In *H. G. Wells's Literary Criticism*, edited by Patrick Parrinder and Robert M. Philmus. New Jersey: Barnes and Nobel Books, 1980.

———. "When the Sleeper Wakes." In *Three Prophetic Novels of H. G. Wells.* New York: Dover Publications, 1960.

Wheeler, David Hilton. *Our Industrial Utopia and Its Unhappy Citizens.* Chicago: A. C. McClurg and Company, 1895.

White, Richard. "George Orwell: Socialism and Utopia." *Utopian Studies* 19, no. 1 (2008): 73–95.

Wilbrandt, Conrad. *Mr. East's Experiences in Mr. Bellamy's World.* Translated by Mary J. Safford. New York: Harper and Brothers, 1891.

Williams, Raymond. *Culture and Society: 1780–1950*. New York: Columbia University Press, 1983.

Williamson, Jack. *H. G. Wells, Critic of Progress*. Baltimore, MD: The Mirage Press, 1973.

Winstanley, Gerrard. *The Law of Freedom in a Platform; or True Magistracy Restored.* Oxford: Benediction Classics, 2009.

———. *The True Levellers' Standard Advanced* (1649). N.p., 2014.

Wisman, Jon D. with James F. Smith. "Legitimating Inequality: Fooling Most of the People All of the Time." *American Journal of Economics and Society* 70, no. 4 (October, 2011): 974–1013.

Young, Michael. *The Rise of the Meritocracy*. London: Routledge Taylor and Francis Group, 2017.

Zadek, Simon. *An Economics of Utopia.* Brookfield, VT: Ashgate Publishing Company, 1993.

Zamalin, Alex. *Black Utopia: The History of an Idea from Black Nationalism to Afrofuturism*. New York: Columbia University Press, 2019.

Zamyatin, Yevgeny. *A Soviet Heretic: Essays by Yevgeny Zamaytin*, edited and translated by Mirra Ginsburg. Chicago: The University of Chicago Press, 1970.

———. *We*. Translated by Natasha Randall. New York: The Modern Library, 2006.

Zilbersheid, Uri. "The Utopia of Theodor Herzl." *Israel Studies* 9, no. 3 (Fall 2004): 80–114.

Index

Ralahine Utopian Studies

Ralahine Utopian Studies is the publishing project of the Ralahine Centre for Utopian Studies at the University of Limerick in association with the University of Bologna, the University of Cyprus, and the University of Florida.

The series publishes high-quality scholarship that addresses the theory and practice of utopianism (including Anglophone, continental European and indigenous and post-colonial traditions, and contemporary and historical periods). Publications (in English and other European languages) include original monographs and essay collections (including theoretical, textual and ethnographic/institutional research), English-language translations of utopian scholarship in other national languages, reissues of classic scholarly works that are out of print and annotated editions of original utopian literary and other texts (including translations).

While the series editors seek work that engages with the current scholarship and debates in the field of utopian studies, they will not privilege any particular critical or theoretical orientation. They welcome submissions by established or emerging scholars working within or outside the academy. Given the multilingual and interdisciplinary remit of the series, the editors especially welcome comparative studies in any disciplinary or transdisciplinary framework.

Those interested in contributing to the series are invited to submit a detailed project outline to one of the series editors listed below.

Email queries can also be sent to ireland@peterlang.com.

Series editors:
Raffaella Baccolini (University of Bologna)
Antonis Balasopoulos (University of Cyprus)
Joachim Fischer (University of Limerick)
Michael G. Kelly (University of Limerick)
Tom Moylan (University of Limerick)
Phillip E. Wegner (University of Florida)

Ralahine Centre for Utopian Studies, University of Limerick
http://www3.ul.ie/ralahinecentre/

Volume 1 Tom Moylan and Raffaella Baccolini (eds):
Utopia Method Vision. The Use Value of Social Dreaming.
343 pages. 2007. ISBN 978-3-03910-912-8

Volume 2 Michael J. Griffin and Tom Moylan (eds):
Exploring the Utopian Impulse. Essays on Utopian Thought and Practice.
434 pages. 2007. 408 pages. 2015. ISBN 978-3-03910-913-5

Volume 3 Ruth Levitas:
The Concept of Utopia. (Ralahine Classic)
280 pages. 2010. ISBN 978-3-03911-366-8

Volume 4 Vincent Geoghegan:
Utopianism and Marxism. (Ralahine Classic)
189 pages. 2008. ISBN 978-3-03910-137-5

Volume 5 Barbara Goodwin and Keith Taylor:
The Politics of Utopia. A Study in Theory and Practice. (Ralahine Classic)
341 pages. 2009. ISBN 978-3-03911-080-3

Volume 6 Darko Suvin:
Defined by a Hollow. Essays on Utopia, Science Fiction and Political Epistemology. (Ralahine Reader)
616 pages. 2010. ISBN 978-3-03911-403-0

Volume 7 Andrew Milner (ed.):
Tenses of Imagination. Raymond Williams on Science Fiction, Utopia and Dystopia. (Ralahine Reader)
253 pages. 2010. ISBN 978-3-03911-826-7

Volume 8 Nathaniel Coleman (ed.):
Imagining and Making the World. Reconsidering Architecture and Utopia.
393 pages. 2011. ISBN 978-3-0343-0120-6

Volume 9 Henry Near:
Where Community Happens. The Kibbutz and the Philosophy of Communalism.
256 pages. 2011. ISBN 978-3-0343-0133-6

Volume 10 Robert C. Elliott:
The Shape of Utopia. Studies in a Literary Genre.
Edited with an Introduction by Phillip E. Wegner. (Ralahine Classic)
170 pages. 2013. ISBN 978-3-0343-0772-7

Volume 11 Michael E. Gardiner:
Weak Messianism. Essays in Everyday Utopianism.
284 pages. 2013. ISBN 978-3-0343-0716-1

Volume 12 Matthew Beaumont:
The Spectre of Utopia. Utopian and Science Fictions at the Fin de Siècle.
319 pages. 2012. ISBN 978-3-0343–0725-3

Volume 13 Artur Blaim:
Gazing in Useless Wonder. English Utopian Fictions, 1516 –1800.
366 pages. 2013. ISBN 978-3-0343-0899-1

Volume 14 Tom Moylan:
Demand the Impossible. Science Fiction and the Utopian Imagination.
Edited by Raffaella Baccolini. (Ralahine Classic)
358 pages. 2014. ISBN 978-3-0343-0752-9

Volume 15 Phillip E. Wegner:
Shockwaves of Possibility. Essays on Science Fiction, Globalization, and Utopia.
328 pages. 2014. ISBN 978-3-0343-0741-3

Volume 16 Angelika Bammer:
Partial Visions. Feminism and Utopianism in the 1970s.
(Ralahine Classic)
408 pages. 2015. ISBN 978-3-0343-0897-7

Volume 17 Edward K. Chan:
The Racial Horizon of Utopia. Unthinking the Future of Race in Late Twentieth-Century American Utopian Novels.
226 pages. 2016. ISBN 978-3-0343-1916-4

Volume 18 Darko Suvin:
Metamorphoses of Science Fiction. On the Poetics and History of a Literary Genre.
Edited by Gerry Canavan. (Ralahine Classic)
515 pages. 2016. ISBN 978-3-0343-1948-5

Volume 19 Michael S. Cummings:
Children's Voices in Politics.
554 pages. 2020. ISBN 978-3-0343-1943-0

Volume 20 Maïté Maskens and Ruy Blanes (eds):
Utopian Encounters. Anthropologies of Empirical Utopias.
246 pages. 2018. ISBN 978-1-78707-247-3

Volume 21 Peter Fitting:
Utopian Effects, Dystopian Pleasures.
Edited by Brian Greenspan.
458 pages. 2020. ISBN 978-1-78874-353-2

Volume 22 Raffaella Baccolini and Lyman Tower Sargent (eds):
Transgressive Utopianism: Essays in Honor of Lucy Sargisson.
274 pages. 2021. ISBN 978-1-78997-880-3

Volume 23 and 24 — Darko Suvin:
Parables of Freedom and Narrative Logics: Positions and Presuppositions in Science Fiction and Utopianism.
Edited by Eric D. Smith (VOLS I & II)
706 pages. 2021. ISBN 978-1-80079-047-6 (set)

Volume 25 — Valentina Romanzi:
American Nightmares: Dystopia in Twenty-First-Century US Fiction.
304 pages. 2022. ISBN 978-1-80079-715-4

Volume 26 — Lyman Tower Sargent:
Rethinking Utopia and Utopianism: The Three Faces of Utopianism Revisited and Other Essays.
434 pages. 2022. ISBN 978-1-80079-489-4

Volume 27 — Mónica Martín:
The Rebirth of Utopia in 21st-Century Cinema: Cosmopolitan Hopes in the Films of Globalisation.
240 pages. 2023. ISBN 978-1-80079-442-9

Volume 28 — Alexander Popov:
Zone Theory: Science Fiction and Utopia in the Space of Possible Worlds
368 pages. 2023. ISBN 978-1-80079-438-2

Volume 29 — Pekka Kilpelainen:
Postcategorical Utopia: James Baldwin and the Political Unconscious of Imagined Futures.
326 pages. 2023. ISBN 978-1-80079-233-3

Volume 30 — A. L. Morton:
The English Utopia.
Edited with an Introduction by Antonis Balasopoulos.
(Ralahine Classic)
302 pages. 2023. ISBN 978-1-78997-418

Volume 31 — Pavla Veselá:
The Polyphony of Utopia: Critical Negativities Across Cultures from Bellamy and Bogdanov to Yefremov, Piercy and Butler.
322 pages. 2024. ISBN 978-1-80374-055-3

Volume 32 — Donald Morris:
Economic Inequality: Utopian Explorations.
368 pages. 2024. ISBN 978-1-80374-176-5

Volume 33 — Heather Alberro:
Terrestrial Ecotopias: Multispecies Flourishing in and Beyond the Capitalocene.
304 pages. 2024. ISBN 978-1-80079-576-1

Printed by
CPI books GmbH, Leck

FSC
www.fsc.org
MIX
Papier | Fördert
gute Waldnutzung
FSC® C083411